The State of Welfare

GILBERT Y. STEINER

The State of Welfare

THE BROOKINGS INSTITUTION
Washington, D.C.

Copyright © 1971 by
THE BROOKINGS INSTITUTION
1775 Massachusetts Avenue, N.W., Washington, D.C. 20036

Title-page drawing by Charles K. Steiner

ISBN 0-8157-8122-9 (cloth)
ISBN 0-8157-8121-0 (paper)

Library of Congress Catalog Card Number 70-150952

1 2 3 4 5 6 7 8 9

4/28/73 Berkers Tylor 7.80

THE BROOKINGS INSTITUTION is an independent organization devoted to nonpartisan research, education, and publication in economics, government, foreign policy, and the social sciences generally. Its principal purposes are to aid in the development of sound public policies and to promote public understanding of issues of national importance.

The Institution was founded on December 8, 1927, to merge the activities of the Institute for Government Research, founded in 1916, the Institute of Economics, founded in 1922, and the Robert Brookings Graduate School of Economics and Government, founded in 1924.

The general administration of the Institution is the responsibility of a Board of Trustees charged with maintaining the independence of the staff and fostering the most favorable conditions for creative research and education. The immediate direction of the policies, program, and staff of the Institution is vested in the President, assisted by an advisory committee of the officers and staff.

In publishing a study, the Institution presents it as a competent treatment of a subject worthy of public consideration. The interpretations and conclusions in such publications are those of the author or authors and do not necessarily reflect the views of the other staff members, officers, or trustees of the Brookings Institution.

Foreword

Few sentiments evoke more general assent in America today than President Nixon's characterization of welfare—now usually thought of as cash assistance to needy families with children—as "a failure that grows worse every day." The nation continues to struggle to find a better approach to public relief that will help those who truly cannot help themselves, while somehow causing those who can help themselves to do so. But judgments diverge sharply about who can help himself and who cannot, and they differ too about how help should be provided, and how much. The loss of the Family Assistance Plan in the Ninety-first Congress is only the most recent illustration of how difficult it is to find a public welfare policy that commands general support.

Each of the three most recent Presidents of the United States—John F. Kennedy, Lyndon B. Johnson, and Richard M. Nixon—gave the problem of the poor priority attention early in his administration. President Kennedy's first executive order dealt with improved distribution of surplus food; President Johnson, at his first meeting as President with the chairman of the Council of Economic Advisers, instructed the latter to move full speed ahead with work on an antipoverty program; President Nixon's first major domestic proposal was to overhaul the widely criticized program of aid to families with dependent children. Hunger, poverty, and family assistance promptly became major political issues. Yet proposed substantive solutions have foundered on the way to adoption or to implementation.

This book, by Gilbert Y. Steiner, Director of Governmental Studies at Brookings, is an inquiry into the politics of stability and of change in public relief policy. The author traces the emergence of policy proposals, and examines their interaction with the strengths, weaknesses, stakes, and strategies of proponents of various approaches to the welfare problem. In reviewing a decade of welfare reform efforts, Mr. Steiner identifies flaws in many solutions proposed by Democrats and Republicans alike, but he finds the present prospect for constructive change in the state of welfare to be improving.

The search for sound public policies in the welfare field, and the effort to promote wider public understanding of welfare issues, claimed the attention of staff members of the Brookings Institution many years ago; Lewis Meriam's *Relief and Social Security* was published by Brookings in 1946. It is a sign, perhaps, of how slowly new programs emerge and are accepted that this volume by Mr. Steiner, like that by Meriam, considers the fragmentation of relief into cash, food stamps, public housing, and veterans' pensions. Today's welfare problem has additional complexities: significant increases in the percentage of children receiving public assistance, newly organized groups of relief clients, a different kind of population in public housing, an enlarged dependence on the food stamp technique, and the non-service-connected pension claims of veterans of three new wars.

The author had the benefit of imaginative, intelligent, and industrious research help from Pauline H. Milius. The entire manuscript was read and commented upon in detail by James L. Sundquist of Brookings, Edward K. Hamilton, then vice-president of Brookings, and several anonymous readers; individual chapters profited from comments by Henry Aaron, Herbert Kaufman, Richard P. Nathan, Alice Rivlin, David T. Stanley, and Louise K. Steiner. Expert typing was provided by Imogene Anderson, editing by Alice M. Carroll, and indexing by Rachel M. Johnson.

The Brookings Institution is grateful to the Carnegie Corporation of New York for a grant in partial support of this work. The Corporation took no part in its direction, and has no responsibility for the views expressed. Nor do the author's views necessarily represent those of the trustees, the officers, or other staff members of the Brookings Institution.

KERMIT GORDON
President

January 1971
Washington, D.C.

Contents

Tables

The State of Welfare

1

Crude and Subtle Relief Systems

Welfare is a public business whose liquidation under honorable conditions has been a stated goal of political leaders from Franklin Roosevelt to Richard Nixon. "What I am seeking is the abolition of relief altogether," Roosevelt wrote in a November 1934 letter. "I cannot say so out loud yet but I hope to be able to substitute work for relief."[1] Thirty-five years later, explaining his family assistance proposal over nation-wide television, President Nixon concluded that "what America needs now is not more welfare but more 'workfare.'"[2] In those intervening thirty-five years, however, neither work for relief nor work instead of relief nor work-related social insurance displaced the dole. Instead, by 1970, at least 14 million people unable to support themselves, and willing to satisfy a means test to prove it, benefited from one or more than one cash, food, or housing assistance program.

About 11 million additional persons with incomes below the so-called poverty line—roughly $3,700 for a four-person family—were not assisted. Many were employed but could not earn enough to bring their families out of poverty. Some benefited from private charity, some had been and might again be public charges but were temporarily independent, some were only technically in poverty (for example, low-income graduate students). Most of the 11 million, however, probably did without basic needs because of pride, because they did not know they could get help, because they could not meet one or another noneconomic eligibility condition, or because an appropriate program was not operative where they lived.

1. To Col. E. M. House; quoted in William E. Leuchtenburg, *Franklin D. Roosevelt and the New Deal* (Harper & Row, 1963), p. 124.
2. August 8, 1969. The text is in *New York Times*, Aug. 9, 1969, p. 10, and *Congressional Quarterly Weekly Report*, Aug. 15, 1969, pp. 1517–20.

This book is primarily about stability, change, and proposed change in a variety of important relief programs: cash payments to families with dependent children, budgeted for 1971 at $4.67 billion; veterans' non-service-connected pensions, $2.27 billion; food stamps, $1.25 billion; public housing, $646 million.[3] Their combined budgets for 1971 add to nearly $9 billion. That figure will shock some as huge, appall others as puny. In either event, it should invite attention not only to the relief programs, but to policy makers and the relief policy making process as well.

Crude Relief

Public subsidies to the poor have two principal styles or techniques, one crude, one subtle. The crude technique limits benefits to those who can establish need through disclosure of their income and resources to an administrative official, and also explicitly pinpoints the beneficiaries. The subtle technique spreads benefits across a broad spectrum of the population, subsidizing many without need as well as those in need. Both crude and subtle techniques are compatible with payments either in cash or in kind.

In the subtle class the leading program is compulsory, contributory social insurance (social security) to provide income for old age, for survivors, for hospital care of the aged, and for disability. Social security provides more cash assistance to poor people than does public assistance; social security also provides cash assistance to a good many people who are not poor and would not be poor even without these benefits.[4] A different example of subtle relief is the federal college housing loan program, which has the effect of reducing room rent by $6 to $7 per month for students at publicly supported colleges. While some very poor students benefit from the program, at least 45 percent of the beneficiaries come from families with incomes above $10,000 per year.[5]

3. *The Budget of the United States Government for the Fiscal Year Ending June 30, 1971*, pp. 167, 174, 250, 336. In pensions, food stamps, and public housing, the amounts shown are all federal funds; in aid to families with dependent children, $2.54 billion is federal, $2.13 billion state and local.

4. Henry J. Aaron, "Income Transfer Programs," *Monthly Labor Review*, Vol. 92 (February 1969), p. 53.

5. Charles Schultze, *The Politics and Economics of Public Spending* (Brookings Institution, 1968), p. 120.

A shift from crude to subtle relief affecting hundreds of thousands of elderly Americans resulted from an amendment to the Excise Tax Act of 1966. It provided persons over seventy-two with benefits of $35 a month labeled social security rather than old age assistance although the beneficiary had never worked in covered employment. With benefit payments administered by the Social Security Administration, restrictive state administration is entirely eliminated; efforts at rehabilitation, self-help, and self-care required under the old age assistance titles are not tied to the social security benefits. Nothing about the recipients changed; the responsible administrators and the style of the support being provided recipients changed. Untold thousands of aged poor who needed help but who would not or could not adjust to old age assistance became beneficiaries under this new label. Still public relief cases, they became part of a larger and more readily acceptable class of beneficiaries of subtle rather than crude relief.

Crude relief programs—with which this book is concerned—include cash assistance for the needy aged, for families with dependent children, for the blind, and for the disabled; non-service-connected cash pensions for needy military service veterans and for their widows and children; medical services for the low income population; stamps that will buy food costing more than the cost of the stamps; public housing that can be rented for a cost below its economic rent and private housing on which rent supplements are paid. The most crude techniques of all are those that completely bypass money, eliminate recipient discretion, and meet need by making direct gifts of surplus food or of shelter in a municipal lodging house or of such items as new shoes or lunches to school children.

Along with separate constituencies, separate federal administrative units, and separate histories of success and failure, all the relief programs—crude and subtle—also have their separate mythologies. The most valuable mythology displaces relief and instead installs a program explanation that its sponsors believe will have readier political acceptance. Thus, despite major modification made as early as 1939 in the principle of individual equity in social security, three decades later the system continues to benefit politically from its insurance mythology. Among the crude programs, it has become an important part of the veterans' pension mythology to deny that a pension is relief and to insist that it represents deferred compensation for wartime service. In agriculture there is a myth that the food relief programs are really not welfare programs but are designed to benefit the farmer by removing surpluses from the free market. Public housers like to play down the idea of decent shelter for the poor and play up a social pacifier mythology, a vision of public housing providing low cost housing for nice old people who might otherwise be a burden to the young, and providing an educational experience for decent poor people who can be inspired by successful, well-adjusted neighbors.

The effort to disassociate at least some of the crude techniques from the idea of relief is also related to an assumption that because they put a stigma on the recipient, they produce the kind of real or imagined disgrace expressed by over half of New York City's publicly assisted mothers, who agreed that "getting money from welfare makes a person feel ashamed."[6] Although the public assistance cash benefit is versatile and confidentiality is preserved, recipients sometimes find other crude techniques less shameful. For example, in explaining to an interviewer how she managed to support herself and four children on an income of $216 monthly from a federally sponsored work training program, a District of Columbia mother discussed the rent on her public housing unit ($75) and provided extensive details on her use of food stamps ($100 worth for $68 cash) but proudly had the interviewer report that "Mrs. Colter is *not* on welfare."[7]

Crude programs tend to favor some target populations among the poor over others. None of the crude programs are universally available based solely on economic need; among the things that can trigger or block access to particular programs are family status, age, place of residence, and military service history. Generally, the poor veteran—without regard to overseas service—may have more and earn more without jeopardizing his relief status than can the poor nonveteran. The elderly poor tend to be better provided for than the young poor. These are deliberately planned cases of special advantage. Other cases, not deliberately planned, are, once established, resistant to change: for instance, the probabilities are better for a poor child outside the inner core of a central city to have a free school lunch than they are for an equally poor child inside that inner core.

Still in the category of special advantage related to accidents of residence, the probability of a poor family securing public housing relief

6. Lawrence Podell, *Families on Welfare in New York City* (City University of New York, Center for the Study of Urban Problems, n.d.), p. 31.

7. *Washington Post*, March 6, 1969, p. E-1.

is substantially greater in Ohio than in Michigan because there are nearly twice as many low rent units in the former as in the latter. But the cash relief benefit provided comparable poor families is likely to be 20 percent greater in Michigan than in Ohio. In some cases, the only accessible program may be useless because it pays off with a benefit in kind that the client cannot use. This would be the case, for example, for an adequately housed but inadequately fed needy family in Wichita Falls, Texas, where there was a relatively large public housing program in 1969 but neither a federal food relief program nor a cash relief program for the intact family whose head was unemployed.

Within all but a handful of counties (40 of 3,133), the poor supposedly have some chance of food relief through one or another kind of federal food program. Once again, depending on the accident of county of residence, some more advantaged residents will be able to buy food stamps and thus maximize their options in the selection of the food bounty while others must accept their counties' predetermined surplus commodity package. (It should be remembered, however, that the specially advantaged group may be the reverse when the need for "pump priming" money with which to buy stamps is taken into account. Surplus commodities require no cash outlay by the beneficiary.) And the hungry poor in the few holdout counties are the least advantaged of all.

Subtle relief programs that are not directly related to work or to work history are resisted as a deviation from the American way. The continued need for them is unwanted evidence of the inability of full employment and universal social insurance together to provide at least minimum incomes for all Americans. In the ideal free enterprise society, earnings-related income sufficient to afford a decent standard of living would be available to all family groups and unattached individuals. For some, this income would come from employment, for others from savings or from the proceeds of equity in insurance or retirement systems. Because the free market does not insure an adequate income from these sources, private charity and crude public relief take up part of the slack. On top of the traditional preoccupation with relating relief to the work ethic, however, a new concern is that income subsidies be adequate and that they be provided in a manner that preserves human dignity, avoids putting a stigma on the poor, and provides no special advantage to any public official. To adjust the older emphasis on employment to these newer goals requires a hard-to-achieve balancing of charity, suspicion, incentives, inequalities, and duress.

Calls for Reform

The call for reform that would emphasize subtle over crude relief is more intense now than at past periods in modern American history, but it is not a new call. Paul Douglas made it in 1925 when his studies of income distribution led him to rethink the principle of the living wage and to conclude that family allowances for dependents should be paid separate from and complementary to a worker's basic compensation.[8] The Townsend Plan of the early 1930s called for a $150 monthly pension, financed by a national sales tax, for everyone over sixty. At the same time, Huey Long was espousing a campaign to "share our wealth." In response to the political threat Long represented, a national program to forestall indigency and to provide support for the indigent was enacted by the New Deal. After a hundred and fifty years of only local or state and local public charity administered crudely and sparingly, development of a federal-state program to provide support for the needy was a landmark accomplishment: the old age assistance, aid to dependent children, and aid to the blind titles of the Social Security Act properly are regarded as the basic element in the country's welfare program. (Significantly, it was originally expected that subtle social insurance would ultimately drive out crude public assistance.) Other key measures also date to the New Deal period: public housing, both surplus commodity distribution and food stamps, public employment of the poor, special youth programs, and the insistence on need as a condition for veterans' pensions.

Proposals to use the tax system as a welfare device are found with increasing frequency after World War II. One of the first, from Lewis Meriam, suggested that an income tax return serve in lieu of a conventional means test in determining eligibility for welfare benefits.[9] A tax lawyer who was later to become assistant secretary of the treasury for tax policy, Stanley S. Surrey, in 1948 began writing articles noting that the income tax was already being used as a welfare device, although those whose welfare was being benefited from the existing law were

8. Paul H. Douglas, *Wages and the Family* (University of Chicago Press, 1925). The discussion in the next several pages of the development of the guaranteed income idea borrows from a paper by Judith Heimlich Parris of the Brookings Institution, "The Guaranteed Annual Income as a Political Issue" (August 1967).

9. *Relief and Social Security* (Brookings Institution, 1946), pp. 850–51.

generally the nonpoor.[10] In 1950 Senator Hugh Butler, a Republican stalwart from Nebraska, called for a basic federal pension of $50 a month to all citizens with less than $600 a year in income. He would have used the income tax return as the device for establishing eligibility.[11] Byron L. Johnson, a professional economist and later a Democratic congressman from Colorado, pointed out in 1955 that income tax deductions serve as a de facto family allowance. He urged that benefits be extended to those below the income tax line as well.[12]

Family allowances—subtle relief in the form of unrestricted cash payments for children—had their supporters during the same period. Noting that larger family size correlates with lower family income, not to mention per capita income, several Roman Catholic welfare specialists called for family allowances as an alternative to limiting family size.[13] The family allowance idea was raised also by some witnesses at two sets of hearings held by the congressional Joint Economic Committee prior to its important 1968 hearings on income maintenance programs. In 1949 the committee heard testimony on low income families. John L. Thurston, acting administrator of the Federal Security Agency, termed family allowances like the Canadian program "a sound idea" for the United States. At the same hearing, Maurice J. Tobin, secretary of labor, said it would be "desirable" for states to "pay minimum additional [unemployment insurance] allowances for dependents."[14] When the committee had more hearings on the same topic in 1955, a distinguished

10. "The Federal Income Tax Base for Individuals," *Columbia Law Review*, Vol. 58 (June 1958), pp. 815–30, and "Federal Taxation of the Family—The Revenue Act of 1948," *Harvard Law Review*, Vol. 61 (July 1948), pp. 1097–1164.

11. *Congressional Record*, Vol. 96, Pt. 7, 81 Cong. 2 sess. (1950), pp. 8768–71, and Vol. 96, Pt. 18, pp. A7284–86.

12. *Low-Income Families*, Hearings before the Subcommittee on Low-Income Families of the Joint Committee on the Economic Report, 84 Cong. 1 sess. (1955), p. 144.

13. Francis J. Corley, S.J., *Family Allowances* (St. Louis: Institute of Social Order, 1947); Robert and Helen Cissell, "The Case for Family Allowances," *America*, Oct. 16, 1954, pp. 65–67; R. A. Lassance, S.J., "Economic Justice for Families," *Eagle*, June 1955, pp. 9 ff. On Dec. 5, 1968, Msgr. Leo J. Coady, president of the National Conference of Catholic Charities, wrote the *Evening Star* (Washington), "The concept of guaranteeing a minimum of income is not new or revolutionary; it is completely consistent with programs already enacted, such as Social Security."

14. *Low-Income Families*, Hearings before the Subcommittee on Low-Income Families of the Joint Committee on the Economic Report, 81 Cong. 1 sess. (1949), pp. 62, 138.

economist, President Howard R. Bowen of Grinnell College, suggested that the applicability of foreign family allowance systems to the United States should be explored. Princeton economist Richard A. Lester and Professor Eveline Burns of the New York School of Social Work also endorsed such an investigation in their statements to the committee.[15] That same year, Democratic Senator Richard L. Neuberger of Oregon introduced a resolution to create a select Senate committee to undertake a study of the Canadian family allowance system and its possible application to the United States.[16] The resolution died in committee. By 1958 James C. Vadakin could publish a comprehensive analysis entitled simply *Family Allowances*.[17] It was clear that he believed on balance that some measure of this sort was desirable.

Taking a different approach to welfare policy, Milton Friedman, a professor of economics at the University of Chicago, called for what he termed a "negative income tax" in *Capitalism and Freedom*, published in 1962.[18] The book was a general exposition of laissez-faire liberalism, and discussion of the negative income tax occupied only part of one slim chapter. However, Friedman's proposal to eliminate all existing welfare programs and replace them with payments equal to unused income tax deductions and other credits generated particular interest when the author became an economic policy adviser to Barry Goldwater's presidential campaign in 1964.

The view from the Right was quickly followed by a view from the Left. In 1963 Robert Theobald, an Englishman who described himself as a "socioeconomist," produced *Free Men and Free Markets*, in which he urged a guaranteed annual income to sustain demand on the part of those who would be inevitably displaced from their jobs as a result of automation.[19] Theobald contended that the United States, and probably the Western world generally, was now in the dawn of an age of cybernetics. Machines, he said, would take over most of the common-

15. *Low-Income Families*, Hearings, 84 Cong. 1 sess. (1955), pp. 50, 138, 713.

16. S. Res. 109, *Congressional Record*, Vol. 101, Pt. 11, 84 Cong. 1 sess. (1955), p. 709; see also Richard L. Neuberger, "Family Allowances," *America*, May 11, 1957, pp. 189–91.

17. With the renewal of interest in income maintenance a decade later, Vadakin published a new version, *Children, Poverty, and Family Allowances* (Basic Books, 1968).

18. (University of Chicago Press, 1962), especially pp. 190–95.

19. "We need to adopt the concept of an absolute constitutional right to an income." *Free Men and Free Markets* (New York: Clarkson N. Potter, 1963), p. 184.

place work of man, and no program of job development could recon-struct the preexisting market. To meet this challenge, the link between jobs and income should be broken. The government must provide two sorts of payments to maintain demand. To the former working class would go "basic economic security" in lieu of gainful employment. To the former middle class would go something called "committed spend-ing," payments at a rate higher than to the erstwhile workers but less than their own former white collar salaries. Theobald kept the idea of income maintenance alive in a report made public in 1964 by a group in which he was a leading force, the Ad Hoc Committee on the Triple Revolution. Its membership, concerned with the implications for society of the threefold changes in race relations, cybernation, and weaponry, recommended a variety of new policies, including establishment of a federally guaranteed annual income.

But all of this was small stuff from which policy change is not fashioned. Intellectuals' musings do not surface as public policy ques-tions until political leaders find it necessary or desirable to take stands on them. By early 1964 some stands were being taken on income main-tenance and on poverty. In March, Labor Secretary Willard Wirtz told the United Auto Workers that a guaranteed annual income was the "wrong answer" to the unemployment problem. "I don't believe that the world owes me a living," Wirtz said, "and I don't believe it owes anybody else a living."[20] He added that he thought society owed an opportunity to work to all its members, in part by the provision of adequate educational facilities.

President Johnson's decision to support a war on poverty in 1964 first pushed income maintenance close to the forefront of policy issues. Those actively engaged in the poverty effort included some who had already endorsed subtle relief proposals and who now achieved a new respect-ability. Other poverty workers, forced to contend with a revolution of rising expectations as the widely publicized poverty program failed to bring quick change, became interested in new solutions to persistent problems. Supporters of the guaranteed income took advantage of the chance to gain a forum for discussion. Thus, reform of the relief system came to be discussed with increasing seriousness in policy-making circles at the same time as civil disorder in American cities accelerated the search for equality in American life.

20. *Congressional Quarterly Weekly Report*, March 27, 1964, p. 632.

Public policy decisions to make war on poverty by emphasizing community action and economic opportunity did not carry with them any immediate instructions about the categorical aids for the old, the young, the blind, or the underfed. The war on poverty engendered attacks on the deficiences in the older relief programs by many who realized that the old programs did not do enough, rather than only by those who thought public welfare did too much. It became routine to hear categorical assistance referred to as bankrupt because it cannot meet its obligation to relieve human need, to hear public housing characterized as a failure because it houses too few people and houses them cheerlessly, to hear food relief programs deplored as demeaning handouts and inadequate ones at that.

Relief compatible with minimum standards of health and decency and available without regard to prior work history or presumptions about current employability was elevated to national issue status by Johnson's belated appointment of an income maintenance commission in 1968. In calling for an examination of all alternatives, however unconventional, Johnson invited public attention to income maintenance techniques and to the idea of radical change in the public assistance mechanism.[21] Toward the end of the 1960s, a decade of tinkering could be shown to be without results. Concluding that the existing welfare policy was a failure and had to be changed, President Nixon proposed a family assistance plan that is a start at restructuring the whole crude relief apparatus, albeit less than comprehensively.

The family assistance system comes down for work relief over honorable dependency: "Under this proposal," said the President, "everyone who accepts benefits must also accept work or training provided suitable jobs are available either locally or at some distance if transportation is provided."[22] Family assistance would never pay a nonworking family more than the total income available to a working family of comparable size—"benefits would be scaled in such a way," explained the President, "that it would always pay to work"[23]—although the actual needs of the nonworking unit might be greater than those of the working family. In this respect the plan shies away from need as a determinant of benefit level and tends instead to keep even the involuntary nonworker (for example, a female heading a household of small children) in a less advantageous position than the worker.

21. *Economic Report of the President, January 1967*, p. 17.
22. *Congressional Quarterly Weekly Report*, Aug. 15, 1969, p. 1518.
23. *Ibid.*

President Nixon's proposal was designed both to provide additional help to some already assisted poor families and to add to the whole number of assisted poor by putting a federal floor under the income of all working as well as nonworking families with children. The Nixon plan introduces improved financing by providing federal funds to insure families in every state at least half a poverty level income. Since the basic federal benefit would presumably be paid automatically on receipt of a valid application, immediate relief would be provided, and it would be provided independently of social casework (if not of job counseling) services. Still, differences between states in total family assistance benefits will continue to be possible; some lucky families will continue to benefit from more than one program (for example, family assistance and public housing) while other similarly situated families will not; unattached individuals and childless couples who are neither aged, blind, nor disabled will be left no better protected than before. And if "more workfare and less welfare" became a program that coerced poorly educated blacks into menial service jobs in urban areas under threat of loss of benefits, the consequences could be socially unsettling.

In any event, as the cost, the inadequacies, and the inequalities of public poor relief have been exposed and publicized, it has become clear that these programs that started in the New Deal have become a poor deal. We have come to a period of great doubt about most of our crude relief programs. Self-help, community organization, and education and training of the poor are newly emphasized, but these and other brave new words and phrases of the sixties—rehabilitation, model cities, sweat equity, outreach—are not easily translated into sure shot programs that overcome the need for relief. While the effort continues to universalize economic opportunity, there is a widespread demand for massive changes in the old crude relief system, a demand sustained by President Nixon's conclusion that "our studies have demonstrated that tinkering with the present welfare system is not enough."[24]

Fragmentation and Coordination

The federal commitment to relieve human need, while antedating by thirty years the federal war on poverty's effort to overcome the causes of need, is not adequately met either with cash assistance, or with food, or

24. Message to the Congress, April 14, 1969.

with shelter, or with a careful combination of the three. For years the missing ingredient in public relief has been a combination of federal and state and local support adequate to provide clients with minimum standards of health and decency. That problem still exists. In January 1970 the Gallup Poll reported $120 per week the median amount the nonfarm public thought necessary to sustain a family of four at a minimum level. At that same time the more conservative Social Security Administration poverty line figure was $72. But the national average weekly payment to a family of four in the aid to families with dependent children (AFDC) program was $42 and the Nixon family assistance program proposed an assured federal benefit of $31, to be supplemented by mandatory state payments only sufficient to keep total benefits from falling below preexisting AFDC levels.

But even with a willingness to add to the public investment in relief of the poor, it is clear that how to do it is no less difficult a question than is how much to do. What is a desirable balance between crude and subtle programs? And among the several crude programs themselves? Although "welfare" is usually used to refer only to categorical assistance programs that make cash payments—old age assistance (OAA), aid to families with dependent children (AFDC), aid to the blind (AB), aid to the permanently and totally disabled (APTD), and the purely state and local programs of general assistance—there are growing interconnections and trade-offs at the local and state levels between those cash payment programs and the relief-in-kind programs that provide food or housing or medical services. For example, the New York City Housing Authority, badly squeezed for money in 1969, increased its rents by an average of 47 percent but exempted non-welfare-assisted tenants. The annual federal contribution to the authority to meet capital costs was fixed. Federal, state, and local funds to support public assistance were elastic. By increasing the take from tenants whose rents are fully welfare paid, the authority in effect increased the value of the relief it furnished low income tenants who might not qualify for categorical assistance. But categorical assistance was indirectly paying for that increase to nonclients. For clients it was an empty increase.

A comparable juggling of the sources of benefits without an increase in recipients' checks often occurs in the social security–public assistance relationship. A highly publicized increase in social security benefits ostensibly designed to improve the status of all those dependent on social security frequently will yield no net increase to those most in need—

persons poor enough to need both old age assistance and old age insurance or both AFDC and survivors insurance. For these especially indigent beneficiaries, the result of a higher social security check may be a lower public assistance check because Congress habitually makes it a matter of state option whether to disregard social security increases in computing relief benefits. There are more states that do not disregard the benefit increase than do. Almost surely, the real reason is that any state choosing not to disregard social security increases is able to substitute federal social security money for state public assistance money. But the rationalization is that equity must be maintained between persons dependent exclusively on public assistance and those who benefit both from assistance and from social security. To permit the latter group to retain the social security increase would put the former at a comparative disadvantage. This argument assumes the worst about very poor people, that the welfare beneficiary is comforted to have other dependent persons kept in an exactly comparable state of indigency.

The several older commitments to relieve need are the subject of belated attention as concerned groups in and out of the administration analyze reality: a variety of often competitive, categorical programs; a mixture of relief in cash and in kind, of waiting lists and of immediate access, of federally funded programs and of federal-state-local shared funding arrangements, of relief with casework services and of relief with money alone. Among the responsible departments and agencies, and various congressional committees, trade-offs are infrequent because communication between, say, the Senate Finance Committee and the Senate Agriculture Committee on the relationship between cash relief and food relief is infrequent, as is communication between the responsible administrative agencies, the Social and Rehabilitation Service of the Department of Health, Education, and Welfare (HEW) and the Food and Nutrition Service (or its predecessor, the Consumer and Marketing Service) of the Department of Agriculture. The outcome is high costs, low benefits, most favored and least favored beneficiary groups and individuals, and a degree of administrative complexity so profound that change in administrative organization or procedure is itself considered progress without regard to improved tangible benefits for the recipients.

The picture is said to have its redeeming features. For example, one recent assistant secretary of HEW sees at least two important advantages in multiple programs: "I suspect that the multiplicity of programs increases the total transfer to the poor, because it brings some political allies on board who would not otherwise be there . . . and because it hides from the average congressman the true magnitude of the transfer."[25] A multiplicity of programs also invites participation, however, from some unsympathetic groups that would consider it useless to fight a comprehensive program. And if a multiplicity of programs hides from the average congressman the true magnitude of the transfer—perhaps a somewhat doubtful virtue in a democratic society—it can also encourage the average congressman to believe erroneously that the inadequacies of one program are compensated for by other programs.

One concern of this book is to reach a judgment about the consequences of federal relief program fragmentation. Public assistance clients—whether in the adult programs or in family assistance—living in public housing and using food stamps are beneficiaries of programs that channel through three separate legislative committees and three separate appropriations subcommittees in each house of Congress. Veterans' pension eligibility would introduce additional legislative committees; free school lunch participation involves yet another House committee and could involve another Senate committee if Labor and Public Welfare were to exercise its legitimate claim under the Congressional Reorganization Act. Would the relief policy output be either "different" or "better" under committee jurisdiction arrangements other than those in effect?

Four separate departments—Health, Education, and Welfare (HEW), Housing and Urban Development (HUD), Agriculture (USDA), and the Veterans Administration (VA)—are responsible for administration. Should any agency's interest in acquiring responsibility for a program now in a different department be supported? What are the likely consequences of a shift? Are some agencies indifferent or even inherently hostile to relief programs and others sympathetic and interested?

The competitive public relief apparatus now in operation grew out of ad hoc decisions made at different times rather than as part of a concerted national drive against poverty. Poverty and welfare are now major public issues, however, and it is tempting to assert that an efficient, management-minded national administration would arrange for coordination of federal relief programs and thus have the best of both worlds, unity within diversity. But federal level coordination of relief programs

25. Confidential communication.

is the impossible dream because no cabinet department secretary can be expected to defer to an administrative coequal in the leadership of a major national program with which both departments are concerned. To do so is not only ego-shattering, it is to invite contempt from administrative inferiors in the department and to weaken the department in the view of the clientele groups with which it deals. No sure formula that will automatically effect coordination of programs at the federal level has yet been invented. An act of Congress mandating coordination is not the formula. The White House–based Urban Affairs Council, created by President Nixon at the beginning of his administration, was not the formula either. In less than a year any expectation that it might be a high-level coordinating unit had evaporated along with most of its staff and any regularity of meetings. And while a Domestic Council was created in the reorganization of the Executive Office of the President in 1970, its justification did not emphasize coordination.

When the first concerted drive against poverty was formalized by adoption of the Economic Opportunity Act (EOA) in 1964, it incorporated an explicit interest in coordination of programs in aid of the poor, and President Johnson, touching off the drive that year in his message to Congress, showed a sensitivity to the coordination problem: "I do not intend that the war against poverty become a series of uncoordinated and unrelated efforts." In the subsequently enacted legislation, the director of the Office of Economic Opportunity was assigned responsibility for coordinating the antipoverty efforts of all federal agencies. Ostensibly, not only the few new programs authorized by the EOA would be coordinated, preexisting efforts would be coordinated too. It did not happen that way. Writing in 1969, Sar Levitan, who has been OEO's academic chronicler, concluded, "OEO exerted little effort to fulfill its government-wide role, and other agencies, in turn, were not anxious to call attention to the deficiency. . . . If OEO is viewed as a coordinating agency . . . its record must be viewed with skepticism."[26]

Discussions of coordination are more likely to go on within than among the major departments with responsibilities for social programs. And within the departments, coordination is a euphemism for aggrandizement because Congress has distributed among them a collection of overlapping programs that, in the continuing view of some people in each of them, can best be handled by one of the departments. Judg-

26. *The Great Society's Poor Law* (Johns Hopkins Press, 1969), p. 57.

ments about which particular department should be repository of which particular programs depend on the location of the judge. Just before leaving office in January 1969, for example, HEW Secretary Wilbur Cohen told several congressional committees that HEW could and should handle food relief programs of the Department of Agriculture. Agriculture's Orville Freeman did not agree. Cohen's proposal was "coordinated" with the Agriculture Department to the extent of a memorandum saying "Orv, you will be interested in this," which arrived at Agriculture with a copy of the Cohen prepared statement the morning it was made. Expertise is not always the rationalization. As early as the second month of the Nixon administration, an unpublicized HEW policy task force report to Secretary Robert Finch recommended that "HEW should assume responsibility for the school lunch program," although that same report asserted that "HEW has little knowledge of the workings of this program whose potential as an educational medium is unmatched."

Congressional committees and federal bureaucracies are only part of the story. Interest groups ranging from over two thousand part-time, unpaid, local housing authorities to tens of thousands of banks and retail stores participating in food stamp projects, to the American Legion and a dozen other veterans' service organizations, to name only some of the most obvious, are committed to and involved in public housing, food stamps, and veterans' pensions, respectively. In public assistance the clients themselves are being organized into a National Welfare Rights Organization. Whether the benefits are tangible or psychic, each of these groups is likely to know its program and to have a stake in the program's visible, independent existence.

The point is that for all of its commonsense appeal, coordination "is not neutral."[27] Coordination means that there is agreement on a course of action; agreement means that some agency or some program will step aside in favor of some other agency or some other program. In turn, this means that while there may be a focusing of responsibility, there is also an exclusive dependence. If the job does not get done, it is easier to decide who should be fired but this does not much help the potential beneficiary of the nonperformed service.

Whatever the case to be made for or against either competition, coordination, or complementarity of relief policies, inconsistency is a

27. The perceptive phrase is that of Harold Seidman, formerly assistant director of the Bureau of the Budget.

consequence of the competitive way things are presently managed. Inconsistency sometimes occurs to facilitate controlled experimentation; more commonly it occurs out of ignorance of other programs. What appears to be settled public policy turns out to be settled policy only in one agency. In another agency, dealing with the same clientele, that policy may be unknown, inapplicable, ignored, or deliberately rejected. One result is that clients sometimes find themselves in the relief equivalent of a higher tax bracket. For example, the most carefully developed efforts to improve cash relief standards and benefits can be washed away by resulting higher purchase costs for food stamps or a resulting public housing rental increase. Decisions about people in need taken in a public assistance office pursuant to policy established by the Social Security Act's public assistance titles are good for that place and for that program only; there is no certainty that the decisions even about the existence of need will have validity in another relief program where a different federal statute controls, where a different department interprets, where a different orientation is provided to the workers who retail the service. And when a needy client looks for prompt and adequate help, he faces the problem posed in the fable about the lady and the tiger: which is the right door to open?

Policy Options

The style of a public relief program is determined by implicit or explicit answers to half a dozen policy questions. How these questions are answered—or avoided—produces a negative income tax, family allowances, marginal changes in the present system, or nothing.

Benefits: In Cash or in Kind?

No state plan in any of the federally aided public assistance categories—old age assistance, aid to the blind, aid to families with dependent children, or aid to the disabled—could legally be approved by the Department of Health, Education, and Welfare if that plan provided for meeting the need of eligible clients with cash to cover clothing, shelter, and incidentals, and with stamps in lieu of cash to cover food needs. Yet the same worker who may not dispense stamps in lieu of cash is expected to call his client's attention to and to urge the "voluntary" use of food stamps, which the client can often purchase in the same bank that cashes his welfare check. The cash payment that is supposed to maximize self-respect and self-determination and minimize stigmatization is settled policy in categorical assistance and in veterans' pensions, but it is denied in food relief and in the various federal housing assistance programs that pay subsidies directly to public or private landlords, subsidies that are actually relief in kind rather than in cash for the tenants.

Growing interconnections between the cash payment programs and the relief-in-kind programs that provide food or housing or medical services are increasingly apparent. For example, while the New York State–New York City budget frenzy was at its peak early in 1969, Mayor Lindsay and his social services administrator quite properly warned that the inevitable consequence of tightening eligibility for medicaid would be increases in the categorical aid cases. Similarly, after Governor Nelson Rockefeller accepted some deep cuts in most welfare grants as the cost of legislative approval of his 1969–70 state budget, he announced plans to expand the state's use of food stamps and surplus foods programs in order to ease the impact of the cuts in categorical aid. The same day, independent of Rockefeller's plan, Mayor Lindsay moved toward switching New York City from the surplus food program to food stamps, again in order to compensate for some of the cash losses. But these food relief activities promptly ran into two barriers: the absence of enough federal money to bring New York City into the food stamp program, and opposition from New York City's Social Service Employees Union of caseworkers and from the New York Citywide Coordinating Committee of Welfare Groups, the recipients' organization, both of which prefer cash relief.

The sole exception allowed to the money payment principle in public assistance—vendor payments for medical service—is rationalized in terms of the utter unpredictability of costs:

A person cannot foresee when he will be ill, for how long, or how much the cost will be. He cannot plan for medical care as he can for other necessities. Even if assistance payments were much larger, the recipient could not be sure of having enough to meet medical costs, just as wage-earning families and even well-to-do families cannot always be sure.[28]

28. Arthur Altmeyer, "Medical Care for Persons in Need," *Social Security Bulletin*, Vol. 8 (May 1945), p. 4. On cash relief during the Great Depression, see Joanna Colcord, *Cash Relief* (Russell Sage Foundation, 1936). A case for benefits

But the decision to provide direct payments to medical vendors rather than to make payments to clients for transmittal to the vendor inevitably results in disaffected doctors who complain about the paper work and in disaffected clients who are embarrassed by the grumblings of their doctors. It is not unknown for welfare clients to forestall that embarrassment by making cash payments for medical services. The combination of medical vendor payments and the money payment for all other needs means that public policy since 1950 has provided that the dependency status of a categorical assistance client will be made known automatically to a medical vendor but not to a clothing vendor. Significantly, the 1967 Social Security Amendments quietly put the not-quite-so-poor, the so-called medically indigent, in a more favored category than the OAA and AFDC cases. Direct reimbursement to the client for medical services costs is now possible if the client is a beneficiary only of medicaid and not of any cash relief program.[29]

If it is possible to rationalize medical vendor payments as a question of administrative convenience based on the uncertainty of costs, the same rationalization will not cover surplus commodity distribution or food stamps. Food is a recurring, predictable cost item for which an allowance is regularly made in all welfare budgets. A client may not know if he is going to be sick but he knows that he is going to have to eat. The original case for the money payment principle grew out of distress with commissaries and grocery orders. Admitting that commissaries were one of the cheapest forms of relief, the founding fathers of public assistance also found it to be the most degrading, a view that is implicit in the assistance titles of the Social Security Act. Categorical assistance clients, however, today collect sacks of surplus commodities by virtue of an agriculture policy that gives no attention to the alleged merits of cash relief, not because those alleged merits have been debated and rejected but because neither the Department of Agriculture nor congressional agriculture committees consider themselves to be in the relief business at all.

---

in kind as an addition to adequate cash income is made in Gerald Holden, "A Consideration of Benefits-in-Kind for Children," in Eveline M. Burns (ed.), *Children's Allowances and the Economic Welfare of Children: Report of a Conference* (Citizens' Committee for Children of New York, 1968), pp. 150–62. A variation of relief in kind—"special credits" valid for medical service, housing, and food, respectively—is proposed in Edwin Kuh, "A Basis for Welfare Reform," *Public Interest*, Vol. 4 (Spring 1969), p. 112.

29. Social Security Amendments of 1967, Sec. 230.

When food stamps were reborn in 1964, no consideration was given to the merits of paying the food stamp bonus in cash as a direct federal supplement to public assistance. Neither has cash been considered as an alternative to surplus commodity distribution, a highly unsatisfactory relief technique. Nevertheless, the effect of the stamp program is to increase annual federal relief costs by an amount that escalated from $250 million to $1.25 billion between 1969 and 1971. Unlike the fiscal arrangements for relief in kind through public housing, there are no outstanding bonds in the food programs, no commitments to local authorities in the form of annual contributions contracts. The decision to provide relief in kind through food stamps and through commodity distribution is instantly reversible, a fact originally taken into account in the Nixon family assistance plan.

Whether these in-kind techniques are the best way to spend billions of dollars annually for food and housing aid to the poor has never been explicitly considered. One reason is that the very existence of separate programs of cash relief and of relief in kind enables those responsible for the cash effort to console themselves with the thought that inadequate benefits may be supplemented by food or housing or medical assistance. And dispensers of relief in kind can assure themselves that it is not meant to be a primary source of aid. If each group feels that it is running an unsatisfactory program, they are both right.

Financing: Federal or State and Local?

Public relief ceased to be exclusively a state and local responsibility when the states and localities were unable to meet need during the depression. The federal-state system then created meant state administration or state supervision of categorical assistance with divided financing—the bulk of the costs were to be federally assumed but the principle of state sharing was established and has been maintained since then. One adverse consequence of cost sharing by the states is loss of benefits to needy clients in poor or indifferent states. State control over who gets access to the assistance rolls has declined as federal regulations have increased. Recently, complete federalization of categorical assistance costs has been urged by former HEW Secretary Wilbur Cohen, and on the Republican side by Governor Nelson Rockefeller of New York and by Vice President Spiro Agnew. Federalization of costs, however, must also mean federal control of administration unless the states are to be in the enviable political position of giving away money that they do not have to raise.

Mandatory cost sharing has had the effect of keeping authorized and available federal money from reaching public assistance cases. If eighteen states had been able and willing to spend $58 million more during fiscal 1968, almost $110 million more in federal money would automatically have been available for aid to families with dependent children in those states. Any state with an average AFDC recipient payment below $32 forfeited some federal money under the formula calling for federal payment of $15 of the first $18 of monthly benefit plus at least half of the remainder up to $32. Cost sharing in the eighteen states that made average payments below $32 meant an absolute loss to the poorest people in America. Rather than the federal and state governments sharing the cost burden, each, in an Alphonse and Gaston situation, failed to make all the payments in which the other would share.

Cost sharing is not a sacred federal relief principle. Many states provide special benefits for veterans; the means test program of non-service-connected disability and death pensions is, however, entirely federal in financing and in administration and has never had a cost sharing component. In commodity distribution, in food stamps, and in housing relief, all but administrative costs are entirely assumed at the federal level, and under certain circumstances even administrative costs in food stamps have been federally assumed. A requirement for state sharing in food stamp costs was considered and explicitly rejected in recent years by a Congress that heard predictions that it would mean state rejection of the program. Cost sharing is played both ways in medical care: medicaid is federal-state on the categorical assistance model, medicare is fully federally financed through the social security mechanism.

A quid pro quo for cost sharing in categorical assistance has been the maintenance of state control not only over benefit amounts but over conditions of eligibility—particularly including residence—within limits established by federal law. Frontal attacks on those limits have been resisted, but there are increasing signs of successful side door attacks through judicial challenge. So, where cost sharing in relief benefits could have been considered the price a state had to pay to hold a five-year OAA residency requirement or to insist on a rule forbidding a man in the house of any female AFDC recipient, the Supreme Court has now struck down residency, has struck down the man in the house rule, and is clearly impatient with other barriers imposed by individual states that seem to result in denial of equal protection of the Social Security Act.[30] The case for cost sharing is harder and harder to sustain as state discretionary authority becomes more and more limited. Thus the Court, vigorous in its determination to improve the condition of the poor, appears unmoved by the argument that Congress deliberately allowed the states the right to buy some policy-making authority. The result is that states pay the same for less authority than heretofore.

After years of timidity, the Department of Health, Education, and Welfare took courage in lame duck status between November 1968 and January 1969. A series of HEW administrative orders having to do with establishing claim to relief benefits by client declaration and with continuation of benefits during a fair hearing, when they are finally and fully implemented, will be significant additional erosions of state authority over program. Whatever one's views on the merits of the administrative rulings, like the court actions, they leave the states with less freedom without reducing the price charged them for participation.

A decent burial for the cost sharing principle in public relief will not overcome all of the inadequacies of the welfare system or even automatically overcome welfare inequities. It is a necessary first step, however. Most states do not, cannot, or will not put up the amount of supplementary money necessary to elevate benefits to a subsistence level in all categories. Moreover, as states have less and less control over the program within their borders, it is less and less reasonable that they should be asked to pay an important fraction of the costs. Federal judicial and administrative rulings that have the effect of increasing costs and increasing the numbers of beneficiaries should reasonably be followed by legislative action to pay the freight. It is an old maxim in grant-in-aid programs that "who pays the piper shall call the tune." When the piper calls his own tune, he should pay his own bill.

Access: Wait Listing or Immediate Relief?

It is settled policy that federal money will expand to fit the number of veterans and their survivors eligible for pension payments in fixed benefit amounts spelled out by federal law. There are no waiting lists, nor are claims prorated to stay within a fixed appropriation. It is also settled policy that federal money expands to fit the claims of the several

30. As to a man in the house rule, *King* v. *Smith*, 392 U.S. 309 (1968); as to residency, *Shapiro* v. *Thompson*, 394 U.S. 618 (1969).

states under the categorical assistance programs. Federal money will be available to cover the federal share of payments to an unlimited number of relief clients. Together with the statutory requirement that a program be available in every jurisdiction of a state and with the prohibition on waiting lists, the result is to insure that no potential client be turned away for lack of public money. But this does not assure payment to the client of a fixed amount because state funds may be finite and states may therefore pay clients less than fully budgeted need. In April 1968 only twenty-four states were paying four-person AFDC families 100 percent of costs of basic needs established by state-determined standards.[31] States may not establish waiting lists in public assistance, but they may divide their money into smaller shares for more people.

To put it another way, states may either stretch a fixed state appropriation to cover whatever number of categorical assistance applicants are found eligible or fix benefit amounts and meet those amounts by making supplementary appropriations if necessary. On the federal level there is no option. A fixed appropriation for categorical assistance will not be stretched and prorated among states. Practically if not legally, the open-end authorization and the statutory matching formula mean that money must be appropriated to meet whatever the federal share of the total cost turns out to be. Similarly, in the veterans' program there is an unquestioned de facto obligation on Congress to appropriate necessary amounts to meet the valid pension claims of veterans and their survivors.

In housing relief and in food relief, however, the policy is different. Across the country, almost half a million eligible families are wait listed for public housing and an unknown number of persons eligible for rent supplement assistance are not receiving it because federal funds for the housing relief program do not automatically expand to meet the need of all eligible applicants. Relief in kind is provided only within the limits of funds previously appropriated. This same limitation obtains in food relief; on June 30, 1968, for example, there were 239 counties or independent cities certified for the food stamp program that had been wait listed for six months pending availability of funds.[32] On the specific issue of funding the food stamp program in a way that would permit

31. U.S. Department of Health, Education, and Welfare, Social and Rehabilitation Service, National Center for Social Statistics, Report D-2 (April 1968), Table 4.
32. *Congressional Record*, daily ed., July 30, 1968, p. H7808.

expansion to meet need, Congress rejected an opportunity to bring food stamps into conformity with the elastic funding provisions of categorical assistance. Wait listing for relief through food stamps again was highlighted in 1969 when John Lindsay found that there simply was not $100 million available then to take New York City into the stamp program although there was no denying the need of the city and its welfare poor whose cash benefits were about to be cut.

Obvious problems present themselves in any effort to expand housing units instantly to meet the number of eligibles. But if public housing is defined as one way of meeting the basic needs of families and individuals who can satisfy a means test, it becomes reasonable to ask why a direct cash payment is not made when it is not practical to provide relief in kind through a housing unit. Present housing relief policy either provides a publicly subsidized unit or wait lists eligibles who cannot be accommodated. But since the economic value of the housing subsidy can be computed, housing indigents could equitably be provided cash supplements in lieu of unavailable public units.

While some housing indigents who are wait listed may receive cash relief through public assistance, eligibility requirements for the two programs differ in several important respects. Thus, for example, the underemployed family that could have public housing if there were a unit available may not receive public assistance, even though there is money available, because it is a family unit that does not fit any of the program categories. It is not enough under present arrangements for the welfare-level poor to qualify for any authorized program, it must be a program that has been funded and is operative in their geographic area. The lucky poor family may have its income effectively doubled by food stamps and public housing while the otherwise comparable but unlucky poor family will be wait listed for both programs. Reappraisal and redirection should attend to that anomaly.

Casework: Mandatory Help or Elective Service?

Before 1962, welfare professionals had taken it as a matter of faith that they could help overcome problems of economic dependency by the application of social casework techniques. Small caseloads for the workers and large bundles of services for the clients were the ideals. After a reasonable test of this idea was made possible by the 1962 Public Welfare Amendments, it began to be evident that whatever merits there may be to casework services, they could not reduce the size of the relief rolls. Services were no substitute for support nor were observable numbers of relief clients rehabilitated by virtue of personal attention from a worker.

In 1967, as part of an important reorganization in Health, Education, and Welfare, services and assistance payments were administratively divorced. When the 1967 Social Security Amendments made their way through Congress, the old slogans—services instead of support, rehabilitation instead of relief—were abandoned and work incentives became the new thing in the continuing search for relief from relief costs.

Doubts about services as a poverty reduction mechanism continue to be confirmed. One more negative note was sounded late in 1968 in a report on "the multi-problem dilemma" from the New York Communities Aid Association.[33] After two and a half years of special, intensive service by highly trained welfare workers to fifty multiple problem families and of routine caseworker service to an equal number of families with comparable problems, the two groups showed almost identical progress. The "unsettling" findings, HEW reported a few months later, "resulted in a research conference at which specialists in social work education, social casework, social policy, and research met to examine the research and its meaning."[34] The meaning seemed clear enough to Gordon Brown, the study director, who said, "You cannot casework poor people out of poverty."[35] But the arguments for eliminating eligibility investigations in the categorical programs continue to include the importance of freeing workers' time for casework with their clients.

There is no casework component in any of the relief programs other than categorical assistance. Veterans' pension cases can be opened and go on indefinitely without threat or promise of such services as an inseparable part of the benefit. And during much of the time that casework services were being emphasized in public assistance, they could not be acquired at all with public housing money. In the same year, 1968, Congress authorized $10 million for services to public housing tenants, then declined to appropriate any of the $10 million, but did

33. Gordon E. Brown (ed.), *The Multi-Problem Dilemma: A Social Research Demonstration with Multi-Problem Families* (Metuchen, N.J.: Scarecrow Press, 1968); Henry J. Meyer and others, *Girls at Vocational High: An Experiment in Social Work Intervention* (Russell Sage Foundation, 1965), reported comparable empirical findings.

34. *Welfare in Review*, Vol. 7 (January–February 1969), p. 25.

35. *New York Times*, Sept. 19, 1968, p. 55.

appropriate $442 million for social services under public assistance. The Johnson budget for fiscal 1970 proposed $15 million for tenant services; the Nixon revisions eliminated the item for 1970. A year later the administration asked for $5 million—$2 per tenant—for services. Congress rejected the request.

Any services provided in public housing have been furnished by some outside public or private group. HEW itself undertook a services project in public housing for a few years but the effort fell apart for want of any real local enthusiasm. Private social agencies may sustain some service work in a development from time to time if an enterprising worker invents a program. There is neither certainty of continuity nor assurance of tenant interest.

The newest service thrust is in food stamps and in surplus commodity programs. It is not casework, but it is based on a faith that specialists can help poor people adjust to inadequate relief. If the poor were as wise or as inventive as the rest of us, they would be able to make tasty and nutritious meals out of inadequate amounts of food or limited varieties of food. As part of a pilot project in four Department of Health centers in New York City, health guides have received special instruction on how to take such surplus commodities as peanut butter, prunes, canned luncheon meats, canned chicken, and scrambled egg mix and turn them into tasty dishes. Providing skilled nutritionist service overcomes the need to acknowledge that $20 worth of peanut butter and scrambled egg mix has its limits.

Employment: Honorable Dependency or Work Incentives?

Federal policy used to be predicated on the belief that relief recipients were all outside the labor force, that as children or as aged, blind, or disabled persons, they need not be apologetic about it, and that incentives to economic self-improvement were hence irrelevant. As recently as April 1967, Joseph Califano, President Johnson's principal assistant for domestic affairs, using data furnished by the assistant secretary of HEW for program planning, William Gorham, reported on the work potential of the welfare population:

We have recently completed a preliminary study of the welfare programs supported by the federal government to answer a very simple question: How many persons capable of working are on welfare?

Some would say many millions. But analysis disclosed that, over the next few years, out of the 7.3 million Americans on welfare, only 50,000 males may be capable of getting off—even if every program, public and private, were adequately staffed and efficiently run.[36]

The "analysis" to which Califano referred was applied common sense. It subtracted from the total welfare population 2.1 million aged, 700,000 blind or severely handicapped, 3.5 million dependent children, 900,000 mothers of dependent children, and 100,000 incapacitated fathers of the total of 150,000 fathers on public assistance. Within a few months, however, the Congress was to enact, with technical help and encouragement from HEW, a program of work incentives and of earnings exemptions based on the belief that a great many mothers, as well as virtually all unemployed fathers, of AFDC children can be trained for and placed in productive employment.[37] The affirmative view from Capitol Hill as to whether significant numbers of AFDC parents were employable was clear, but the administration seemed to want to have it both ways in describing the welfare population as unemployable and as suited for work and training.

Of course, either view could be sustained, depending on the underlying assumptions. The most critical disputed assumption was that dealing with coercion. The old settled policy was that relief recipients should not be pushed into work training or jobs against their will, that mothers should be at home to care for their children, and that any casual earnings should be charged against the relief grant lest some persons be better off with a combination of relief and part-time or casual employment than others are with full-time employment alone.

It is not clear whether that policy has or has not been reappraised. The 1967 Social Security Amendments do not require AFDC mothers to take work or work training but they set up the mechanics, and the hottest new gimmick in public relief—reaffirmed by the Nixon family assistance plan—is day care to free AFDC mothers for work or work training. Most other poor relief programs involve no work or training conditions. No policy maker has been intrepid enough to suggest work or work training for the non-service-connected veteran's widow or day

36. Joseph A. Califano, Jr., "The Politics of Innovation and the Revolution in Government Management" (remarks before the Washington chapter of Sigma Delta Chi, April 19, 1967; processed), p. 6.

37. See remarks of Chairman Wilbur Mills of the House Ways and Means Committee, *Congressional Record*, daily ed., Aug. 17, 1967, pp. H10668–70, and remarks of Chairman Russell Long of the Senate Finance Committee, *Congressional Record*, daily ed., Nov. 15, 1967, pp. S16503–04.

care for his child to permit the widow to take work or work training. Neither the 1968 report of the Veterans Advisory Commission nor the reports of the congressional committees concerned mention self-support, work, or day care for this favored group.[38] Public housing provides its relief subsidy without regard to work status but food stamps now do not. Our analytical tools are up to making some judgment about work programs for all relief recipients as a way of decreasing public costs. Indeed, HEW's cost effectiveness team proposed government-subsidized training for young widows on social security. The plan was vetoed by the Social Security Administration, an agency both efficient and influential. If there is a case to be made for work and training, should not redirection be proposed across the board? If there is no case for them, surely it is important to know that in reappraising and redirecting.

Amounts: Least Eligibility or Full Need?

The hard question of whether any public relief program does enough if it does less than provide total unmet food, clothing, shelter, and health needs of its beneficiaries remains unresolved both within and among programs. The general rule has been that of least eligibility, that public relief shall not be provided in excess of what a comparably situated working family can secure. The working poor thus define the relief ceiling for the welfare poor even if both groups are inadequately sustained.

On the one extreme, the veterans' pension program is supposed to be "not a complete income-support program, but [one] designed to supplement other sources of income. . . ." At the same time the VA seeks "to insure that pensioners are afforded the basic necessities of life and are not reduced to indigence. . . ."[39] It is beyond the power of that administrative agency to provide benefits in excess of the dollar amounts spelled out in the statute for particular income levels, no matter what the unmet need of the recipient. For some pensioners, VA benefits do

38. U.S. Veterans Advisory Commission, *Report to the Administrator of Veterans Affairs*, March 18, 1968.

39. *Survey of Government Operations, Pt. 12—Veterans Administration*, Hearings before the Subcommittee of the House Committee on Government Operations, 90 Cong. 2 sess. (1968), p. 34.

not begin to meet need; for others, the pension is a kind of bonus on top of other, exempt income.

At the other extreme, in those states where no maximum is fixed by state statute, it is possible for a client's public assistance budget to be fixed at whatever amount is computed to be full need. In New York State, where the function of public assistance used to be understood to be the meeting of full if minimum need, the average payment per AFDC recipient family of four persons as long ago as June 1968 exceeded by $10 ($287 against $277) the total cash earnings of an employed head of a family of four who worked full time at the minimum wage of $1.60 per hour. In New York City, where high rents made budget allowances higher than in the rest of the state, a four-person AFDC allowance of $333 per month was common. An assistance payment of that amount raises the cash advantage of dependence over independence to $56 per month.

This is not an outcome that can be expected to be accepted with equanimity. Using medical assistance as a particular point of departure, Governor Ronald Reagan of California has spoken of what he considers an indefensible discrepancy between goods and services that many wage earners can afford to buy and goods and services provided the non-working poor by public relief:

> There are those among us today who have established the idea that welfare is an inalienable right of the recipient. But what of the right of those who work and earn, and share the fruit of their toil to make welfare possible, and those who earn their own way, pay their own doctors and provide for public welfare with their earnings? These people are restrained in the amount of care they can afford for themselves.
>
> The minor illness, the cold, the cut finger, is treated at home and then they call in a doctor when their reason tells them the trip is justified.
>
> The key to the problem we are here to discuss is that these same people are now providing medical care for their fellow citizens, more comprehensive than they can afford for themselves.[40]

Governor Reagan's base line for relief is set somewhere below what the most miserable of the working poor can afford for themselves. Another California Republican—President Nixon—would abandon least eligibility in favor of meeting minimum need—defined as not less than a poverty line income—for the working poor as well as for non-working poor families through an income guarantee mechanism accom-

40. "Excerpts from Speech by Governor Ronald Reagan" (speech delivered at Governors Conference on Medicaid, Sept. 20, 1967; processed), p. 3.

panied by a high (50 percent) tax rate on earnings above the guarantee.

Even among the most enthusiastic proponents of the Nixon plan, however, there is little expectation that any new income maintenance system—including family assistance—will entirely wipe out the existing programs. One reason for this is cost. Introduction of an adequate minimum income policy with appropriate incentives to work is estimated by James Tobin and his associates to cost between $25 billion and $40 billion annually.[41] Other reasons suggest themselves to students of politics and of bureaucracy: for example, opposition to change from organized constituencies composed of recipients of possible benefits of one or another program as well as opposition from those engaged in disbursing the benefits; congressional committee and subcommittee ties to and consequent interest in maintaining particular existing programs; fiscal and political advantages that produce state and local government preferences; reluctance of a national administration to innovate on a massive scale before all possibilities for marginal change are exhausted.

The rest of this book considers the merits and the politics of four crude relief programs against the pressures for stability and for change. In the cash payment categories of public assistance, these pressures center on aid to families with dependent children. The latter is widely regarded as the public assistance problem because its costs are well over twice the costs of old age assistance, nearly five times those of aid to the totally and permanently disabled, and about forty-five times those of aid to the blind. In 1970 there were more families receiving AFDC than there were individuals receiving old age assistance. If a great miracle could take place and all actual and potential AFDC recipients were to disappear from the ranks of the needy, the remaining three categories would not constitute a public policy problem of major magnitude. Accordingly, the discussion turns first to efforts to tinker with AFDC (Chapter 2), and then to a consideration of why and how family assistance came to be offered as a substitute for AFDC (Chapter 3).

41. James Tobin, Joseph A. Pechman, and Peter M. Mieszkowski, "Is a Negative Income Tax Practical?" Yale Law Journal, Vol. 77 (November 1967), p. 26.

2

Tireless Tinkering with Dependent Families

Rehabilitation of clients and their consequent transformation into self-supporting persons is a commonly stated goal of legislators and administrators who deal with public assistance. An analysis of a decade of legislative, administrative, and organizational changes suggests, however, that the changes are better explained as attempts to rehabilitate an obsolete policy than as attempts to rehabilitate welfare clients.

The coming demise of the federal-state public assistance system created in 1935 by the Social Security Act will have been preceded by serious efforts to restore it to good repute. These efforts, directed especially at the most costly and most politically troublesome component, aid to families with dependent children (AFDC), have included adding social services to cash relief, pushing the states toward more active roles, adopting a new approach to work for AFDC mothers, reorganizing the welfare administrative apparatus at the federal level, and changing application and appeals procedures in response to demands from the client population. Little of this rehabilitation activity makes much difference, however, because too many AFDC mothers are not readily employable; because the Department of Health, Education, and Welfare (HEW), no matter what its organizational arrangements, is less in control of the public assistance program than are the states; because the states tend to be indifferent to most aspects of AFDC except its cost; and because procedural changes, while desirable for the sake of client dignity, are not a substitute for more relief money. But the activity is still important because tireless tinkering with the status quo is a probable prerequisite to innovation.

By the end of the 1960s it was evident that under the most prosperous of conditions, public assistance was not about to "wither away." A considerable fraction of the population was still outside the sweep of social security's old age pensions, survivors' benefits, or disability insurance, and also outside the sweep of the country's prosperity. "It becomes increasingly clear," the New York Times editorialized after the overall level of unemployment in New York City declined to 3.2 percent of the civilian labor force and the number of welfare clients in the city climbed to one million, "that the welfare rolls have a life of their own detached from the metropolitan job market."[1]

It is a separate life outside of the national job market as well. In 1961, when there were 3.5 million AFDC recipients, unemployment as a percent of the civilian labor force nationally was a high 6.7 percent. By 1968 the national unemployment figure was hovering around a record low 3.4 percent, and there was serious talk among economists about the possible need for a higher rate of unemployment to counteract inflation. But, as Table 1 shows, the average monthly number of

Table 1. AFDC Recipients and Payments, 1964 through June 1970

Year	Average monthly number of recipients	Child participation rate per 1,000[a]	Average monthly payment	Total expenditure
1964	4,118,000	45	$30.30	$1,496,525,000
1965	4,329,000	47	31.65	1,644,096,000
1966	4,513,000	49	34.15	1,849,886,000
1967	5,014,000	55	37.40	2,249,673,000
1968	5,705,000	63	41.25	2,823,841,000
1969	6,706,000	75	44.10	3,546,668,000
1970, January–June	7,912,000	—	46.35	—

Source: U.S. Department of Health, Education, and Welfare, National Center for Social Statistics, Report A-2 (3/70), and monthly statistical reports.

a. Number of children participating per 1,000 children in total population under 18.

AFDC recipients in 1968 was up to 5.7 million, almost 4.4 million of whom were children. In 1969 the monthly recipient total averaged 6.7 million, and for the first six months of 1970 it was 7.9 million. Public assistance also has a separate life outside the growth of the economy. The gross national product was $520 billion in 1961; in 1969 it was $932 billion. One of the things not expected to rise under those prosperous conditions was payments to relief recipients. Yet total payments in AFDC alone in 1961 were $1,149 million; in 1969 total payments

1. New York Times, Jan. 3, 1969.

were \$3,546 million and rising rapidly. To put it another way, it is roughly accurate to say that during the 1960s the unemployment rate was halved, AFDC recipients increased by almost two-thirds, and AFDC money payments doubled. Whatever the relationship between workfare and welfare, it is not the simple one of reduced unemployment producing reduced dependency.

Special efforts have been made to prepare the welfare population emotionally and vocationally to become labor market participants, and thus to partake both of the economic security provided by employment itself and of the access employment provides to unemployment insurance and to survivors' insurance, if needed. The first such effort—the professional social service approach characterized by a stated plan to emphasize services over support and rehabilitation over relief—showed no progress after running its full five-year trial period from 1962 to 1967. Then, a series of programs were invented in order to push relief clients to work. Work experience, work training, work incentives—whatever the titles and whatever the marginal differences in program content—were all designed, in the catch phrase often used, to move people off the relief rolls and onto the tax rolls. Each program assumed that the gulf between labor force participation with accompanying economic security benefits, on the one side, and relief status, on the other side, was bridgeable. At best, however, the gulf is bridgeable only for those who are not old or disabled or children or parents of small children.

It has become disturbingly evident that work training and its successor programs of work experience and work relief make only a tiny dent in the relief rolls, a dent too small even to keep up with the pace of new cases coming on the rolls. As the inability of the basic assistance system to meet need also becomes evident, many social insurance rationalists have given up on the possibility of social insurance obviating the need for large-scale public relief. By nationalizing public assistance, this group now would overcome inadequacies and inequities in benefits without, however, junking the social service or the work incentive features of the system. Complete nationalization of public assistance to assure benefit equity and hopefully to insure improvement in the benefit levels paid by most states is urged, for example, by an activist like former Health, Education, and Welfare Secretary Wilbur Cohen and by Douglas Brown, the Princeton University economist, both of whom were planners of the Social Security Act and subsequent revisions. "The time has come," wrote Brown in November 1968, "for a truly national system of public assistance, nationally financed and administered, with national standards adjusted to local conditions and requirements. Such a national system of public assistance, while distinct in purpose and administration, would serve to undergird our national system of contributory social insurance ('social security'). To distort social insurance to alleviate residual poverty would be a serious error."[2]

Nationalization of some assistance categories—which is the direction in which President Nixon's family assistance plan moves—may have much to commend it if public assistance is to continue to be the basis of income maintenance policy. For one thing, any nationalization would be a boon to financially hard-pressed state governments, a factor that accounts for Vice President Agnew's support for nationalization while he was still governor of Maryland and for the resolution favoring nationalization adopted by the Governors Conference in September 1969. Tinkering with public assistance by improving all benefit levels with federal funding can have advantages for many governors and for many relief beneficiaries, but such tinkering should be evaluated on its merits as a way of relieving need, which is the prime purpose of relief, rather than as a way of protecting the sanctity of the social security trust fund against wholesale blanketing-in of noncontributors.

New public relief policy should be based on frank recognition that neither full employment nor minimum wage legislation nor universal coverage under social insurance protects all persons against an absence of resources adequate to sustain life. It should be a relief policy most likely to meet the needs of a fraction of the population that may be dependent for as long as the first two decades of life and for whom neither social services nor work orientation is as important a consideration as is money. This is one strength of the negative income tax plan: it wipes away the rationalization for public relief as a temporary measure pending the full flowering of social insurance, frankly accepts the likelihood of a continuing dependent segment of the population, and meets immediate need with the instrument best designed to overcome immediate need, money.

Once it is understood and accepted—however grudgingly—that many children in recent years have been born into many low income households headed by women who are too little skilled or too little motivated or too child oriented to be fitted into the labor force, then the

2. Letter to the Editor, *New York Times*, Dec. 2, 1968.

choice is evident: the status quo with its frustrations of insufficient support and recipients who refuse to disappear; nationalization of public assistance with some improvement in benefit levels and retention of a link, in fact if not on the organization chart, with required special services for welfare clients; an alternative relief system that accepts public dependency as a fact but denies that it is shameful.

The present crisis in welfare is partly a consequence of the indecision of policy makers, of influential outsiders, and of recipients about what course to follow. The status quo will not do, yet the idea of a negative income tax that accepts honorable, indefinite dependency comes hard to dependent and to benefactor alike. Nationalization of public welfare runs afoul of the current kick for decentralization and for state and local involvement in social programs. The halfway house of children's allowances—a subtle relief program that reasonably enough defines all children as dependent—thus has an appeal despite its complexities for the tax structure. Guaranteed public service employment—another halfway house that assumes everyone can do something—has its proponents, too, for all of its nightmarish administrative characteristics. Change is widely demanded, but the unsolved problem is to find a relief system that is efficient, that is acceptable to its beneficiaries, and that does not leave one taxpaying segment of the population believing that it is sustaining another, parasitic segment. The path to that new relief system is full of parts and tools—counseling and social services to clients, fiscal pressures on the states, day care and work incentives—used in the process of tinkering with the old system in hopes that it could be made to work a while longer and thus forestall the high cost of a new system that could very well have defects of its own.

1962: Services without Servants

Following twenty-five years without high-level attention to public assistance, a decade of tinkering began in 1961. That year the Kennedy administration secured approval of federal financial assistance to states choosing to extend their aid to dependent children program to cover families whose heads are unemployed. Federal support was previously restricted to families with an absent, disabled, or dead parent. There was no rush by the states to adopt the unemployed parent option (AFDC-U); even by the end of the sixties only half the states had done so.

In 1962, faithful to a pledge made a year earlier by Abraham Ribicoff at his confirmation hearing as HEW secretary, the administration proposed extensive public assistance revisions in the first message from a President to Congress ever devoted exclusively to public assistance. Its family services approach was foreshadowed by an earlier internal memorandum by Ribicoff instructing the commissioner of social security, then responsible for welfare administration, that "too much emphasis has been placed on just getting an assistance check into the hands of an individual. If we are ever going to move constructively in this field, we must come to recognize that our efforts must involve a variety of helpful services, of which giving a money payment is only one, and also that the object of our efforts must be the entire family."[3] Not until seven years later did a high-ranking administration official, in this case Daniel P. Moynihan, President Nixon's iconoclast-in-residence, start talking about "cold cash" as a missing element in assistance. Welfare without a money emphasis was the dominant theme in the interim period.

Delighted with President Kennedy's interest and that of his HEW secretary, welfare specialists left the impression that the so-called services amendments enacted in 1962 with their enthusiastic support would have a restraining effect on the growth of public assistance. Hearings records were filled with accounts of success stories in demonstration programs attributable to intensive services by skilled workers; the legislation itself was termed "momentous" and "a landmark." Secretary Ribicoff summed it up:

We have here a realistic program which will pay dividends on each dollar invested. It can move some persons off the assistance rolls entirely, enable others to attain a higher degree of self-confidence and independence, encourage children to grow strong in mind and body, train welfare workers in the skills which will help make these achievements possible, and simplify and improve welfare administration.[4]

State response was good to the invitation in the 1962 amendments that "services" designed to prevent or reduce dependency be provided. For one thing, the financial incentive to respond was substantial. While the states' costs of services had previously been matched by federal

3. Office memorandum on "Administrative actions necessary to improve our welfare programs," in Public Welfare Amendments of 1962, Hearings before the House Committee on Ways and Means, 87 Cong. 2 sess. (1962), p. 161.
4. Public Welfare Amendments of 1962, Hearings, p. 166.

money on a dollar-for-dollar basis, the 1962 legislation offered three federal dollars for every state dollar spent. The secretary of HEW was to "prescribe" services essential to meeting the dual objectives of prevention and reduction of dependency and to "specify" desirable additional services, with both categories reimbursable at the three-for-one rate. As a presumed protection against low-quality services, states were also required to meet caseload and supervisory standards, the most significant of which limited caseworkers providing "prescribed" services to no more than sixty cases.

Proponents of the services amendments viewed them as a way of overcoming the tendency of the cash relief function to dominate in any welfare situation where cash is part of the agency's armamentarium. For a good many states, however, the services amendment simply provided a way of getting more federal money for doing pretty much the same thing they had been doing in the way of services. Services is a fuzzy concept, not an exact one. For example, in the roster of prescribed services in AFDC, states could choose one or more of the following in a category titled "Unmarried parents and their children with specified problems":

arranging for prenatal, confinement, and post-natal medical care for the mother and child; planning with mother for her future and that of her child; help to mother in child care and training if child remains with mother or planning for placement elsewhere; help to mother with respect to legal problems affecting the rights of mother and child; work to change environmental conditions seriously contributing to illegitimacy; use of available specialized agency and community resources for serious problems or needs.[5]

Since the question of whether its workers are actually providing such services as "planning with mother for her future and that of her child" is highly subjective and impossible to monitor, a state's qualification for the three-to-one aid came to depend on an objective, measurable test, that of the maximum sixty caseload. But recruitment of sufficient staff to fill the many new positions created was difficult; training workers with no background in family therapy to provide, for example, "help to parents with respect to problems and stresses of recent desertion" was a formidable job; and keeping up with the continuing problem of staff

5. U.S. Department of Health, Education, and Welfare, Welfare Administration, Bureau of Family Services, *Characteristics of State Public Assistance Plans Under the Social Security Act—Provisions for Social Services*, Public Assistance Report No. 53 (1965), p. 7.

turnover, especially in the cities, made recruitment and training difficulties unending.

While some states could turn the new three-for-one inducement into a net gain for the state, other states found that meeting the caseload maximum would be expensive. Consider a hypothetical situation where 4 workers provided at least casual kinds of social services to 600 cases, for which the state had been reimbursed at a 50-50 rate. In effect, the state had been paying for 2 workers, the federal government for the other 2. Under the new formula, if loads were to be cut to 60 cases, 6 more workers would be required. Of the new total of 10 workers, however, while the federal share would pay for 7.5, the new state share of 2.5 would still exceed in cost the state's old share. One state caught in this squeeze, Mississippi, dropped its prescribed services in AFDC after 1965 because the legislature set a ceiling on administrative costs of 10 percent of total assistance costs. States that found it possible at least to break even financially or to come out ahead—the situation in those states that had had a relatively low average caseload per worker before the new standard—complied with the new standard in a technical sense, but staff turnover and recruitment difficulties actually vitiated whatever value the service idea might have had.

Services cannot be provided without servants. When HEW's administrative review of all state social services programs was completed in the summer of 1967, it was clear that finding the bodies to hold the new positions remained an apparently insoluble problem. Trained social workers are predisposed to work in private agencies where the salaries are usually more attractive and where the absence of the cash relief element seems to make the work more professional. Untrained workers tend to be casual participants in the social work labor market. With a need to recruit large numbers of workers, states were less able than ever to be selective and were forced to hire persons not apt to remain at the job very long. The staff situation was so bad that when the 1967 administrative review of services was conducted, good intentions could be substituted for actual delivery. Active recruitment for and funding of the required positions became the standard for compliance with the caseload maximum which, in turn, was the principal test of whether services were being provided.[6] Active recruitment and funding of positions may be indicative of a state's good faith, but nonexistent workers can provide no services.

6. Bureau of Family Services, State Letter No. 966, April 12, 1967, enclosure.

The situation, then, in 1967 was that five years of prescribed and specified services could not be shown even to have started to prevent or to reduce dependency. In some ways the services emphasis did not have a real test, but the disturbing factor is that it was always obvious that personnel to do the job were not available. Ideally, every one of the workers carrying one of those caseloads of sixty dependent families would have been possessed of a Master of Social Work degree, a professional commitment, and a consequent stake in staying with his job. In fact, perhaps 4 percent of the workers in public assistance are so trained. While trained workers might have made some difference—although the evidence that social work intervention has little effect on poverty is growing—the program was carried out by a constantly shifting group of untrained workers. No one had ever claimed that just anybody could provide services. That is the way it worked out, however, and what the House Ways and Means Committee saw in 1967 was the big picture: five years of services, no results. Of course, there was no point in offering as an explanation the absence of trained personnel because there was no more likelihood that trained persons could be provided in subsequent years than had been the case in previous years.

Why were these seemingly self-evident impediments to success of the services philosophy not apparent before a five-year program that could not succeed was enacted? First, it should be remembered that 1962 preceded the great antipoverty thrust, preceded the time when poverty commanded widespread attention. Programs in aid of the poor were simply not scrutinized and critically analyzed in many quarters. Second, skeptics found it difficult to challenge investment in a program based on an hypothesis that highly trained workers carrying relatively small caseloads could "rehabilitate" dependent persons and move them to self-support because that hypothesis had supposedly been confirmed in various demonstration projects. For example, Winifred Bell's leading report on ten experimental efforts in which everything came up roses was emphasized.[7]

Whether the application of skilled services ever independently reduced dependency anywhere is doubtful. A shadow has been cast over welfare demonstration projects by Miss Bell herself, a recognized expert on aid to families with dependent children and until the fall of 1966

7. Winifred Bell, "The Practical Value of Social Work Service: Preliminary Report on 10 Demonstration Projects in Public Assistance" (New York School of Social Work, April 20, 1961); included twice in *Public Welfare Amendments of 1962*, Hearings, pp. 371–76, 410–15.

chief of the Demonstration Projects Group in the Welfare Administration's Bureau of Family Services. Miss Bell, who now regrets her role in helping to oversell the services amendments, told an inquiring congressional subcommittee some sad truths about the quality of demonstration projects in the welfare area:

One of the more sobering experiences of my professional life occurred when I had occasion several years back to review every progress report so far submitted in response to grants made under the Cooperative Research and Demonstration Grants program authorized by section 1110 of the Social Security Act. The search was for methods of intervention that worked to cure poverty or to mitigate its consequences, a subject I presumed to be one of the priorities in decision-making in this program. In my judgment, my review revealed that unpromising projects continued to be funded year after year, most studies were inconsequential, hard facts were difficult to locate and when located were rarely useful due to poor original conceptualization, inadequate methodology, failure to include or control sufficient variables, or inability to write clearly and concisely.

In the intervening years, attempts have been made to improve the quality of projects and to encourage projects of greater significance, but in my judgment the effort has met with indifferent success, so far as the area of welfare assistance is concerned.[8]

1967: Pressure on the States

By 1967, welfare spokesmen in and out of the administration were embarrassed by references to the rhetoric of 1962. They had cause to be. Principal emphases of the 1962 amendments had been on small caseloads, the better to allow public assistance workers to dispense the therapy that might turn relief clients from broken families into self-supporting (even taxpaying) citizens, and on community work and training programs for the unemployed parent—invariably male—component of the AFDC program. But the services emphasis made no difference. In 1967 the critical category—AFDC—was in more trouble than ever.

At the beginning of 1962 there had been about 3.5 million recipients of AFDC. That number rose steadily so that in June 1963 it stood at

8. Written communication from Winifred Bell, in *The Use of Social Research in Federal Domestic Programs, Pt. 2: The Adequacy and Usefulness of Federally Financed Research on Major National Social Problems,* Hearings before the Subcommittee on Research and Technical Programs of the House Committee on Government Operations, 90 Cong. 1 sess. (1967), p. 442.

3.9 million; in June 1964 at 4.2 million; in June 1965 at 4.4 million; in June 1966 at 4.5 million; and in June 1967, during House Ways and Means Committee executive sessions on the welfare amendments, the AFDC total reached 5 million persons and was growing. Federal costs in AFDC were then predicted to increase from $1.46 billion in 1967 to $1.84 billion by 1972.

A comparison of characteristics of the AFDC populations of 1961 and 1967 shows a constancy about the size of families, about the age distribution of children in the families, about the status of the mother, including her employment status, and, to the probable surprise of many observers, about the race of AFDC payees. There was some evident change for the worse in the status of the father, and considerable change in distribution of the welfare population between metropolitan and rural areas.[9]

The later survey shows family size distribution almost identical all along the line to that of 1961. About one-fourth of AFDC families have only one child recipient, 22 percent have only two child recipients, 18 percent have three child recipients; only one-fifth have five or more child recipients. Similarly, there are no important changes in age distribution. One in three AFDC children was under six in 1961; one in three was under six in 1967. Forty-four percent were between six and twelve in 1961; 41 percent fell in that group in 1967. Children between thirteen and seventeen were a constant 22 percent. The 3 percent of the total between eighteen and twenty on the rolls in 1967 represented a new category that first appeared in 1964 when persons in that age bracket regularly attending school became eligible.

The reported racial composition of AFDC cases changed little. In 1967 a majority (51.3 percent) of AFDC payees continued to be white. There had been only a 3 percent shift between white and nonwhite payees in the six-year period (1961–67) of intense civil rights activity, antipoverty outreach efforts, and poor black migration to the supposedly receptive northern central city welfare programs.

Only marginal changes occurred in the status of the AFDC mother. Nine out of ten were in the home in 1961, including the 13 percent who worked part or full time. In the 1967 sample 91.5 percent were in the home, including 13.7 percent who worked.

9. U.S. Department of Health, Education, and Welfare, Social and Rehabilitation Service, National Center for Social Statistics, *Preliminary Report of Findings— 1967 AFDC Study*, NCSS Report AFDC-1 (67), (1968).

Paradoxically, the biggest change in recipient characteristics was one over which the services approach had no influence. The AFDC population had metropolitanized along with the rest of America. Fifty-eight percent of AFDC families lived in metropolitan areas in 1961 when the total population in the category was 3.5 million. By 1967, with the population up to 5 million, the percentage of families in metropolitan areas was up to 70.7. Translated into rough numerical totals, 1.5 million AFDC recipients lived outside of metropolitan areas in 1961, a figure that had not changed after six years. But where there were 2 million metropolitan area AFDC beneficiaries in 1961, there were 3.5 million in 1967. It was as if the number of recipients outside the metropolitan areas was frozen between 1961 and 1967 while every one of the 1.5 million new AFDC beneficiaries was added to the welfare population of those areas.

The increases in absolute numbers of recipients and the increased visibility of welfare recipients clustered in metropolitan areas were trouble enough. In addition, the percentage of AFDC dependency attributable to absence of the father was up from two-thirds of the total in 1961 to three-fourths of the total in 1967; within the absent father category, illegitimacy—the cause of dependency least likely to be readily accepted outside limited professional circles—was up from 21.3 percent to 26.8 percent (Table 2). As the 1962 amendments came to the verge of expiration in 1967, neither a spontaneous tapering off of relief costs

Table 2. Status of Fathers of AFDC Families, 1961 and 1967

Status	Percent of total	
	1961	1967
Dead	7.7	5.5
Incapacitated	18.1	12.0
Unemployed	5.2	5.1
Absent from the home, total	66.7	74.4
Divorced }	13.7	12.6
Legally separated }		2.6
Separated without court decree	8.2	9.6
Deserted	18.6	18.2
Not married to mother	21.3	26.8
In prison	4.2	3.0
Other reason for absence	0.6	1.4
Other status	2.2	3.0

Source: U.S. Department of Health, Education, and Welfare, National Center for Social Statistics, Report AFDC-1 (67), p. 9.

nor a systematic effort at the state level to foster family life was in the offing.

With the understated conclusion that "those [1962] amendments have not had the results which those in the administration who sponsored the amendments predicted," the House Ways and Means Committee thereupon picked up, extended, and emphasized HEW's 1967 proposal that "there be work and training projects [for AFDC clients] in every State."[10] While Ways and Means has not hesitated to take responsibility for the work and training features of the 1967 legislation, the committee's principal contribution was to make it explicit that mothers in female-headed families would be included. HEW's explanation of the work and training provision had read simply:

Plans for aid to families with dependent children would have to include provisions for referral for all appropriate individuals who have attained age 16 to programs existing in the areas in which such individuals live.[11]

The Ways and Means Committee report gave clear indication that "appropriate individuals" could be mothers:

Your committee intends that a proper evaluation be made of the situation of all mothers to ascertain the extent to which appropriate child care arrangements should be made available so the mother can go to work. . . . The committee recognizes that in some instances—where there are several small children, for example—the best plan for a family may be for the mother to stay at home. But even these cases would be reviewed regularly to see if the situation had changed to the point where training or work is appropriate for the mother.[12]

In the House committee, cost effectiveness thus triumphed over social work. In the department there had been a standoff. Work and training was part of its package, but HEW thought in terms of non-coercive incentives—voluntary day care and retention of earnings to get mothers into the program. But a harder line from Congress could not have been entirely unexpected in view of earlier warning signs that some important congressmen felt cheated. For example, in 1965 while considering appropriations for public assistance, Appropriations Subcommittee Chairman John Fogarty reminded HEW witnesses that the 1962

10. *President's Proposals for Revision in the Social Security System*, Hearings before the House Committee on Ways and Means, 90 Cong. 1 sess. (1967), Pt. 1, p. 187.
11. *Ibid.*, p. 90.
12. *Social Security Amendments of 1967*, H. Rept. 544, 90 Cong. 1 sess. (1967), pp. 103–04.

amendments had been sold as a way of reducing dependency and costs; and in 1966 the Appropriations Committee had threatened an investigation of public assistance costs.[13]

Unlike state responses regarding services to prevent or reduce dependency, state responses to the optional unemployed parent segment of AFDC (AFDC-U), first authorized in 1961, and to the community work and training (CW&T) program, authorized in 1962, had been lackadaisical. Federal officials were discouraged when only twenty-two states had picked up the unemployed parent segment of AFDC by 1967. Even more discouraging was the total of only twelve states with community work and training programs. A primary reason for the lack of development of CW&T programs was that a more attractive federal offer became available almost immediately after 1962 in the form of Title V of the Economic Opportunity Act. CW&T authorized federal matching funds to pay adult AFDC recipients in work training, as well as to pay administrative costs, and for some social services; Title V, foreshadowed by a message from President Kennedy in June 1963 requesting federal funding of supervision and equipment costs of training projects, provided for 100 percent federal funding of all costs necessary for a comprehensive program. Delegated to the Welfare Administration of HEW as a parallel program to CW&T when states were not responding to the latter, fully funded Title V not unexpectedly drove out its partly funded counterpart.

HEW pronounced itself delighted with Title V superimposed on the CW&T effort. But by the time Ways and Means was holding hearings in 1967 on public assistance legislation, the facts were that 133,000 welfare recipients had enrolled in the programs since 1964, 22,000 had found jobs, and 70,000 were in training, but the total number of recipients of AFDC had increased by 800,000 during the three years. In an Alice in Wonderland kind of situation, the more work training successes reported, the larger the population dependent on public relief became.

The Welfare Freeze

President Johnson urged the Congress to extend and make permanent the AFDC-U program and urged the states "to avail themselves fully

13. *Departments of Labor, and Health, Education, and Welfare Appropriations for 1966*, Hearings before a Subcommittee of the House Committee on Appropriations, 89 Cong. 1 sess. (1965), Pt. 1, pp. 976–77; and *Departments of Labor, and Health, Education, and Welfare, and Related Agencies Appropriation Bill, 1967*, H. Rept. 1464, 89 Cong. 2 sess. (1966), p. 54.

of the promise which these programs hold."[14] Representative Wilbur Mills and his Ways and Means colleagues, however, could not accede to a simple extension of programs that from their point of view gave little promise of keeping up with—let alone reversing—the growth in the AFDC population.

The Mills–Ways and Means approach was a dual attack on AFDC. One phase dealt with incentives and penalties for clients: incentives for all adults—not just unemployed fathers—to work or to be trained for work and a penalty for refusal to work or to participate in work training. Specific incentives were a mandatory reduction of the preexisting 100 percent tax on earnings of welfare clients and an extended child day care program. The penalty was permission for states to drop from the rolls parents and out of school children declining to participate in work and training "without good cause." A second phase was directed at states, heretofore slow about mounting work programs and slow about combating illegitimacy and desertion, the largest causes of dependency in AFDC. Under a complex formula, federal matching funds would continue for an unlimited number of AFDC cases attributable to death of the father and for an unlimited number of cases of AFDC-U, but a freeze would be imposed on the extent of federal matching for AFDC cases attributable to desertion or illegitimacy. Using January 1967 as a base period in each state, for purposes of federal matching, no increase in the proportion of children under age twenty-one receiving AFDC because of absence of the parent from the home would be allowed. Although rejected by the Senate Finance Committee, in conference the limitation was retained virtually as it had been written in the House.

No congressional welfare action since adoption of the Social Security Act has been attacked more vigorously than this so-called welfare freeze. Two Presidents agreed to delay its imposition, three HEW secretaries opposed it, one social welfare spokesman termed its likely consequences "Draconian," others merely described it as punitive. The effort to impose the freeze was widely interpreted in Congress as a last, desperate attempt to sustain a federal-state public assistance program in the face of apparent state unwillingness to take a hand in efforts to reduce welfare dependency attributable to desertion and illegitimacy. Client groups, however, viewed it as punishment of helpless deserted and illegitimate children, and state officials perceived it as an effort to push

14. *Message from the President of the United States Relative to Community Work and Training Program Authorized by the Public Welfare Amendments of 1962*, H. Doc. 76, 90 Cong. 1 sess. (1967), p. III.

back on them welfare costs that they simply could not bear. All three interpretations are tenable.

More active state participation in relief programs surely was one goal of the freeze. The optional, unemployed parent segment of AFDC had been enacted in 1961 to meet the criticism that the original program both discouraged marriage and encouraged desertion because complete families could not gain entry to the relief rolls. Since the freeze would not apply to dependency caused by unemployment, its authors logically could believe that it might encourage the twenty-eight states that had not done so to create an AFDC-U component. States successful in cutting away in this fashion at the dependency total attributable to desertion and to illegitimacy would preserve federal fiscal participation. Pointedly noting that the freeze "should also give the States an incentive to make effective use of the constructive programs which the bill would establish," the Ways and Means report signified that the committee hoped to reduce foot-dragging at the state level by penalizing it.[15]

Representative Mills stated explicitly that the idea was to put pressure on the states:

We have done some things here, not in a negative way—with no thought of being negative—but with the thought in mind that it takes requirements on the States to reverse these trends. In 1962 we gave them options. For 5 years this load has gone up and up and up, with no end in sight. . . .

Are you satisfied with the fact that illegitimacy in this country is rising and rising and rising? I am not. We have tried to encourage the States to develop programs to do something about it. Now we are requiring them to do something about it. . . .

. . . If there are any jobs available for them [recipients], we want them to have them. This is what we wanted to do in 1962. We left it to the option of the States, and they did not do it. Five years later, today, we are on the floor with a bill which requires that it be done.[16]

But the threatened penalty was a clumsy and unrealistic way to do that job of prodding the states. Dependency resulting from desertion and illegitimacy was growing at a more rapid rate than was the total child population of most urban states, and it was naïve to believe HEW's prediction to the Senate-House conference committee that work incentive programs could be developed rapidly enough to make a consequential dent in the old and the new cases of AFDC dependency attributable to those causes. Accordingly, the likely result of the pro-

15. *Social Security Amendments of 1967*, H. Rept. 544, p. 110.
16. *Congressional Record*, Vol. 113, Pt. 17, 90 Cong. 1 sess. (1967), p. 23053.

posed freeze would be to force states to pay, without federal help, the relief costs attributable to any increased percentage of broken home dependents.

A substantial cost item was involved. Just three months after enactment of the legislation, HEW changed its prediction and was estimating that payments to about 475,000 AFDC recipients in fiscal 1969 would be ineligible for federal sharing—at a loss to the states of $125 million.[17] By April 1969, when President Nixon recommended a second delay in the freeze, the loss estimate was up to $322 million.[18] A majority of the state governors long before then had let it be known to their congressional delegations that failure to delay or eliminate the limitation would put an intolerable burden on state budgets. Led by California's delegation, which reflected the concern of that state's administration about the $40 million of federal funds involved, the House concurred at the end of 1969 in Senate action repealing the freeze. So much for that circuitous way of compelling states somehow to attend to AFDC costs.

Recipient groups and their supporters viewed the proposed freeze as a plot to reduce already inadequate benefits. Since a prohibition on waiting lists in AFDC was quickly affirmed by HEW, the sole alternatives for states affected by the limitation were to appropriate more state money or reduce benefit payments for all AFDC recipients in order to make money go further.[19] For many states, especially those with already low benefit amounts, there was no possibility of adding state money; consequently, reduced benefits would be the only way out. From the vantage point of a recipient, that result of course did appear to be punitive.

A Senate member of the conference committee on the 1967 legislation, George Smathers of Florida, implies that there was some bluff involved in the congressional action. Referring to the HEW estimates of state loss, Smathers says that during the conference HEW predicted that with quick implementation of work incentives, the states could trim their relief rolls so as to suffer no loss. The conference committee would

17. *Departments of Labor, and Health, Education, and Welfare Appropriations for 1969*, Hearings before a Subcommittee of the House Committee on Appropriations, 90 Cong. 2 sess. (1968), Pt. 3, p. 800.

18. *Congressional Quarterly Weekly Report*, April 18, 1969, p. 532.

19. U.S. Department of Health, Education, and Welfare, Social and Rehabilitation Service, "Limitation on Federal Sharing in AFDC—Public Law 90-248" (Jan. 22, 1965; processed).

have acted differently, Smathers believes, if the department had originally presented estimates of state losses of hundreds of millions of dollars. "None of the members of the conference committee suspected or intended that the AFDC limitation would have an impact of the magnitude [subsequently indicated]," Smathers says.[20] Representative James Utt, a Ways and Means Committee member who had supported the freeze, also acknowledged later that the potential consequences were more than he had bargained for. "I favored the freeze in the first place," said Utt, "but we did not have sufficient information before us to know what effect it would have."[21] It appears that to the extent there was a plan, it was to frighten the states into doing something—creating work and training programs, tracking down deserting fathers, reducing illegitimacy rates by birth control services—but it was nowhere contemplated that federal funds would actually be withheld.

HEW was in an awkward position when the Ways and Means Committee unveiled its bill. The department had quietly committed itself to a revolutionary concept in AFDC—individual plans of counseling, testing, and training of recipients, including women in female headed households. A Task Force on Services for Self-Support of AFDC Recipients, created in May 1967, by August of that year was in the process of developing a report that paralleled the work and training features of the Mills bill.[22] When the Ways and Means report referred to the help and advice of the Department of Health, Education, and Welfare, the reference was to more than technical assistance; insofar as the work and training features of the bill were concerned, there was philosophical agreement between administrative agency and legislative committee.

That agreement resulted from the confluence of two separate concerns. One concern was with costs and criticisms. Representative Mills' defense of the 1967 committee bill viewed with alarm the costs of an unchecked public assistance program:

I am sure it is not generally known that about 4 or 5 years hence when we get to the fiscal year 1972, the figure will have risen by $2.2 billion to an amount of $6,731,000,000.

. . . If I detect anything in the minds of the American people, it is this. They want us to be certain that when we spend the amounts of money that

20. *Congressional Record*, daily ed., March 25, 1968, p. S3273.
21. *Ibid.*, June 27, 1969, p. H5343.
22. U.S. Department of Health, Education, and Welfare, Social and Rehabilitation Service, "Report of the Task Force on Services for Self-Support of AFDC Recipients" (September 1967; processed).

we do, and of necessity in many cases have to spend, that we spend it in such a way as to promote the public interest, and the public well-being of our people.

Is it . . . in the public interest for welfare to become a way of life?[23]

A different concern motivated the HEW task force, department officials, and some of Mills' legislative colleagues. The task force nowhere concerned itself with how many billions of dollars public relief was costing, but did concern itself with the turmoil and deprivation that beset recipients in depressed rural areas and in urban ghettos. Thus, to the Mills conclusion that the costs are prohibitive, there was joined a related HEW conclusion, shared by some members of Congress, that the quality of life on welfare was intolerable.

One congressman with such a view is the only lady member of the Ways and Means Committee, Martha Griffiths. Mrs. Griffiths is especially indignant over the conditions imposed on AFDC mothers.

I find the hypocrisy of those who are now demanding freedom of choice to work or not to work for welfare mothers beyond belief. The truth is these women never have had freedom of choice. They have never been free to work. Their education has been inadequate and the market has been unable to absorb their talents. . . .

Can you imagine any conditions more demoralizing than those welfare mothers live under? Imagine being confined all day every day in a room with falling plaster, inadequately heated in the winter and sweltering in the summer, without enough beds for the family, and with no sheets, the furniture falling apart, a bare bulb in the center of the room as the only light, with no hot water most of the time, plumbing that often does not work, with only the companionship of small children who are often hungry and always inadequately clothed—and, of course, the ever-present rats. To keep one's sanity under such circumstances is a major achievement, and to give children the love and discipline they need for healthy development is superhuman. If one were designing a system to produce alcoholism, crime, and illegitimacy, he could not do better.[24]

Whatever the differing motivation, HEW's task force, Mills, and Mrs. Griffiths all pointed in the direction of change from the status quo. And the change agreed upon was abandonment of the heretofore accepted idea that the only employable AFDC recipients were unemployed fathers.

HEW had not counted on the freeze as part of the package, but when both the freeze and the requirement that all adult recipients be given

---

23. *Congressional Record*, Vol. 113, Pt. 17, 90 Cong. 1 sess. (1967), p. 23052.
24. *Congressional Record*, daily ed., July 17, 1968, p. H6858.

counseling, testing, and job training survived in the Senate and in conference, department leaders declined to join the ranks of liberal and labor spokesmen who urged the President to veto the bill despite the social security benefit increases it carried. Not only did HEW leaders support the work and training provision, they persuaded themselves and, as Senator Smathers has reported, informed the conference committee that the freeze would not be a problem because promptly implemented work incentive and day care services would make it unnecessary to restrict federal payments.

There are two explanations for this rosy view that resulted in outrageously inflated predictions of what HEW would accomplish in work incentives and day care: one is that little careful attention had been paid to the realities of day care; a second is that big changes were supposedly taking place in HEW where there was no more Welfare Administration, nor was there a welfare administrator. One week after the Ways and Means Committee had unveiled its bill on the House floor, HEW Secretary John Gardner unveiled his reorganization of the welfare agencies of the department.[25] That reorganization merged the Welfare Administration, the Administration on Aging, and the Vocational Rehabilitation Service into a new agency called the Social and Rehabilitation Service (SRS). To run it, Gardner named Mary Switzer, veteran commissioner of vocational rehabilitation, aptly described as "a diligent disciple of work."[26] This bit of tinkering was designed to send the message through the federal welfare bureaucracy that the secretary was receptive to policy change, apparently including a new work emphasis. The great drive to employ dependent mothers and provide day care for their children thus began both in the administration and in Congress two years before President Nixon discovered it anew.

Day Care

Despite an announcement by Miss Switzer in April 1969 that a reduction in the number of people on the welfare rolls is "a top priority of the Social and Rehabilitation Service" which she asked state welfare

25. Press release, U.S. Department of Health, Education, and Welfare, Office of the Secretary, Aug. 15, 1967.

26. The phrase is that of Jonathan Spivak, Wall Street Journal, June 13, 1968. Miss Switzer, 67 years old at the time of her appointment, served until 1970.

administrators "to make yours as well," it was really beyond the power of either Miss Switzer or the state administrators to effect a big breakthrough in the AFDC problem. The key to moving some people off the rolls is employment for the AFDC employable parent; but even training for employment, a first step, requires an expensive new industry—day care—which now lacks organization, leadership, personnel, and money for construction of facilities. Moreover, once the realities of work training and day care programs are examined, it becomes evident that the financial incentive for a poorly educated AFDC mother to accept training for herself and day care service of uncertain quality for her children is not attractive.

Training AFDC mothers for employment, actually finding jobs for them, and providing day care facilities for their children present formidable problems. As for work training, a recent survey of the AFDC population found that 43 percent of the mothers had gone no further than the eighth grade, including 10.6 percent with less than a fifth grade education. Work training leading to employment at wages adequate to support a family is likely to be prolonged, at best, for this undereducated group.

The realities of the coming crunch in day care are even more troublesome. If every place in every licensed day care facility in the United States were to be reserved for an AFDC child under the age of six, there would be in excess of one million AFDC children in that age group left over. There would also be consternation among the thousands of non-AFDC mothers with children of that age level who occupy places in the 46,300 licensed facilities caring for 638,000 children (Table 3). Day care provisions accompanying the 1967 work incentive (WIN) legislation did not extend to creation of a federal program authorizing funds for major renovation or for construction of new facilities. There are not enough facilities—good, bad, or indifferent—to accomplish the day care job envisioned by those congressional and those administration planners who still talk of moving parents from welfare rolls to payrolls, and Representative Fernand St. Germain is undoubtedly right in stating that "costs of new facilities are too much for the States to bear alone; centers will only be built in numbers that have any relation to the critical need if Federal assistance is forthcoming."[27] That point never got into the 1967 HEW program memorandum that

27. *Congressional Record*, daily ed., June 12, 1969, p. E4866.

Table 3. Number and Capacity of Licensed Day Care Facilities in the United States, 1960, 1965, 1967, 1968, 1969

Type	Total		Public		Voluntary[a]		Independent[b]		Auspices not reported	
	Number	Capacity	Number	Capacity	Number	Capacity	Number	Capacity	Number	Capacity
1960										
Day care centers	4,426	141,138	276	15,501	1,109	49,160	2,497	66,714	544	9,703
Family day care homes	13,577	42,194	618	1,724	147	490	11,611	36,716	1,201	3,264
1965										
Day care centers	7,334	252,000	347	20,000	2,234	92,000	4,753	140,000	...	...
Family day care homes	16,373	58,400	845	2,423	251	700	13,567	49,901	1,710	5,376
1967										
Day care centers	10,400	393,300	400	22,600	2,600	113,900	6,900	239,300	500	17,500
Family day care homes	24,300	81,900	800	2,500	400	1,300	18,400	63,900	4,700	14,200
1968										
Day care centers	11,700	438,000	580	27,700	3,100	139,000	6,800	231,000	1,200	40,100
Family day care homes	27,400	97,200	1,300	3,600	570	2,200	23,900	84,600	1,600	6,800
1969										
Day care centers	13,600	518,000	730	34,700	4,100	178,000	7,600	266,000	1,200	39,700
Family day care homes	32,700	120,000	2,500	8,000	550	2,100	27,600	102,000	2,000	8,400

Source: U.S. Department of Health, Education, and Welfare. According to HEW, a substantial part of the increases reported between 1960 and 1968 is attributable to the licensing of existing facilities as state licensing services developed. That catch-up activity is now largely completed.
a. Facilities operated by private social service agencies.
b. Facilities without private or public welfare agency sponsorship.

influenced the employable mother discussions and proposals from the House Ways and Means Committee.

The day care problem goes beyond space to an important philosophical and political question regarding the appropriate clientele for the service. There is no political conflict over the proposition that a young mother suddenly widowed and left dependent on social security survivors' benefits should be supported with public funds so that she can stay home and take care of her children. Nor is there congressional discussion or any HEW proposal for day care for those children. If 94.5 percent of AFDC dependency were attributable to death of the father, there would be no congressional interest to speak of in day care. But, in fact, 94.5 percent of AFDC dependency is not attributable to death of the father; only 5.5 percent of AFDC dependency is so attributable. Most of the political conflict and a good deal of the interest in day care is over whether the public should subsidize those women whom Senator Russell Long once called "brood mares"[28] to stay home, produce more children—some of them born out of wedlock—and raise those children in an atmosphere of dependency. While medical authorities and professional social workers are still divided philosophically over how accessible day care should be and to whom, Congress in 1967 and President Nixon in 1969 simply embraced the possibility of putting day care to work in the cause of reducing public assistance costs. Political attention has focused less on the practical limits of day care and more on its apparent similarities to baby sitting. The latter focus produces a positive answer to whether day care can be used to reduce spending in AFDC. The result is day care legislation for which there is inadequate preparation and that is likely to have disappointing results.

Day care was simply not ready to assume the responsibilities thrust on it by welfare legislation adopted in 1967, and it was not ready for President Nixon's proposal to expand it in 1969. Whether day care is a socially desirable or even an economical way of freeing low income mothers with limited skills and limited education for work or work training still has not been widely considered. In the few circles where it has been considered, there is no agreement. Both the 1967 legislation and the Nixon proposal for escalation should have been preceded by development of model publicly supported day care arrangements that could be copied widely; by attention to questions of recruitment and

28. *Washington Post*, Sept. 21, 1967.

appropriate educational training for day care personnel; by an inventory of available and needed physical facilities; by the existence of a high-spirited and innovative group of specialists in government or in a private association or both; and by enough experience to expose whatever practical defects may exist in day care as a program to facilitate employment of low income mothers. Instead of meeting these reasonable conditions for escalation, public involvement in day care programs for children, a phenomenon especially of the last ten years, remains unsystematic, haphazard, patchworky.

Conflict of Philosophies

At least eight different federal agencies from the Office of Economic Opportunity to the Department of Labor to the Department of Housing and Urban Development to several units within HEW subsidize day care in one way or another. But only in HEW's old Children's Bureau and its new Office of Child Development and in a few small, private organizations has prolonged professional attention been given to the subject. Many of the influential thinkers in the Children's Bureau and a good number in the private groups long maintained a purist approach that rejects day care when it is developed primarily as an instrument for freeing low income mothers of small children for work. Congress, however, has been appropriating money for day care on and off since 1963, and while neither legislative nor appropriations committees of Congress have formally ranked their ideas of the purposes of day care, it is a good bet that freeing low income mothers for work would be at the top. If congressional and administrative interpretations and priorities in this field do not neatly coincide, neither does the degree of interest of the national government and most state governments. State interest and activity have lagged far behind even the disjointed national effort. The federal system has not produced a model state or local day care program ready to be copied widely.

The AFDC program is evidence of the national commitment to the idea that a mother's place is in the home caring for her children—or at least AFDC was such evidence when created in 1935. World War II forced a departure from this mother-in-the-home idea because of the emergency need for women workers in wartime industries. With federal financing under the so-called Lanham Act, some 1,600,000 children of working mothers were cared for in vacant stores, private homes, churches, and a strange assortment of dwellings. At the end of the war the federal government apparently expected working mothers to resume their traditional role in the home. Federal aid ended and the day care centers and nurseries shut up shop, California and New York City alone continuing to provide public day care funds. Elsewhere public centers collapsed, leaving only voluntary and commercial ones, and also leaving widespread unmet needs.

Two postwar trends posed new challenges to the mother-in-the-home tradition. Some women call one of those trends female emancipation—more mothers as well as more women are choosing to go to work. The total number of working women has doubled since 1940, but the number of mothers in the labor force—to the delight of both feminists and punsters—has sextupled. The second and perhaps more important development is the rise of a large urban Negro lower class that includes many female-headed families where mothers cannot offer children much in the home and mother substitutes sometimes seem preferable, at least to many white observers. There has been some shift in attitudes as a result of these factors, both among medical and social work professionals and among nonprofessional people, including some members of Congress. But differences remain sharp. "The very people and institutions whose dogmas and self-interest have combined in the past to keep them [welfare mothers] in their homes and off the labor market are now castigating Congress for requiring training for them and day care services for their children," said Representative Martha Griffiths in defense of the proposition that many AFDC mothers would, could, and should work.[29] Professionals, laymen, and politicians have abandoned the dogmatic idea that all mothers belong at home. What they are still groping for is an alternative philosophy and alternative arrangements—the ground rules that determine when working mothers should be tolerated, when encouraged, and when insisted upon.

Psychological studies published in the 1940s and 1950s tended to agree on the harmful mental health effects for the child of separation from his mother.[30] An often cited example is John Bowlby's *Maternal Care and Mental Health*, published in 1951, which maintained that "a

29. *Congressional Record*, daily ed., July 17, 1968, p. H6858.
30. This discussion has been drawn from two articles in *Child Welfare*, Vol. 44: Milton Willner, "Day Care: A Reassessment" (March 1965), pp. 124–33, and Patricia Crowther, M.D., "Psychological Aspects of Motherhood" (July 1965), pp. 365–76.

warm, intimate, and continuous relationship with his mother" was believed to be "essential for [a child's] mental health."[31] One effect of the work of Bowlby and others was to discourage the development of day care by tending to equate maternal separation with deprivation.

Later reassessments question the validity of so sweeping a conclusion. Milton Willner, for example, writing in an important 1965 day care symposium in Child Welfare, points out that these early studies were made in impersonal institutions where no mother substitute was provided. Had these children been stimulated and provided with substitute attention and mothering, Willner suggests, separation from their mothers need not have had such deleterious effects. Willner's conclusion is that day care offering education for the child and relief for the mother "justif[ies] accepting any and all young children into day care programs."[32] Willner's is not a lone professional voice. Anna Mayer and Alfred Kahn in considering day care as a social instrument have called for the extension of day care and a modification of its content to offer compensatory educational and child development experiences for the very young. They suggest it should be available in deprived areas as a public utility or service and point out that in New York City at least, where the working mother is the main consumer of the service (77.3 percent), an elaborate social means test to determine a family's need for day care is misplaced.[33]

The Children's Bureau Approach

For many years before 1969, when a young (forty-four) secretary of HEW decided against the aging child welfare bureaucrats in the Children's Bureau, the latter ran the bulk of the federal day care program. It did not encourage an approach that would make day care readily available on demand. Stressing that day care can be harmful unless it is part of a broader program overseen by a trained social worker, the bureau defines day care as a child welfare service offering "care and protection." This definition and the accompanying emphasis on a social

31. John Bowlby, Maternal Care and Mental Health (Geneva: World Health Organization, 1951), p. 11.
32. Willner, "Day Care: A Reassessment," p. 129.
33. Anna Mayer with the collaboration of Alfred Kahn, "Day Care as a Social Instrument: A Policy Paper" (Ph.D. thesis, Columbia University School of Social Work, 1965), p. 76.

work context implied that the Children's Bureau was uniquely equipped among federal agencies to administer a proper day care program; other agencies, with primary interests in education or freeing mothers for jobs, were presumed to lack understanding of the special needs of a child separated from his mother a good part of the day.

But reservations about wholesale separation of mothers and children lead to a limited view of day care. This view is clearly expressed in the "Guides to State Welfare Agencies for the Development of Day Care Services," a bureau product first issued to clarify the 1962 amendments but still a preferred if not exclusive philosophy of bureau specialists. The child in need of day care is identified as one who "has a family problem which makes it impossible for his parents to fulfill their parental responsibilities without supplementary help." A proper day care program for such a child would have four basic components: social services, educational opportunities, health supervision, and "daily care which meets the physical and emotional needs of the child and promotes healthy growth and development. . . ."[34] The social worker is seen as necessary to help determine whether the family needs day care and if so to develop an appropriate plan for the child, to place the child in a day care program, to determine the fee to be paid by the parents, and to provide continuing supervision. Apparently the bureau view is not atypical of social welfare professionals. In most social welfare discussions of day care, Florence Ruderman has written, "the day care center is not something chosen, or preferred, by independent, responsible parents; it is something prescribed by a social worker, as a remedy for parental failure or inadequacy."[35]

If the Children's Bureau did not accept day care as a public utility, bureau day care experts at least have given some indication in the last couple of years of an awareness that other attitudes toward day care are possible. Speaking at an important May 1965 conference on day care, Katherine Oettinger, then bureau chief, first hinted at a new outlook. As if in instant response to publication that same month of a sharp

34. U.S. Department of Health, Education, and Welfare, Welfare Administration, Children's Bureau, "Guides to State Welfare Agencies for the Development of Day Care Services" (June 1963; processed), p. 6.

35. "Conceptualizing Needs for Day Care: Some Conclusions Drawn from the Child Welfare League Day Care Project," Day Care: An Expanding Resource for Children (Child Welfare League of America, 1965), p. 24. Child Care and Working Mothers (Child Welfare League of America, 1968) is the final report by Florence Ruderman of her study of child care arrangements of working mothers.

criticism of the bureau and of social work generally for stunting day care's growth by insisting on an unreasonably narrow view, Mrs. Oettinger said that research and experience involving the effects of separation of mother and child and the fact that mothers were working in increasing numbers were forcing the Children's Bureau to reconsider its position.[36]

Research and demonstration support thereupon became available to explore family day care and even to experiment with group care for children under three. One such experiment—a project at the Upstate Medical Center of the State University of New York—tested the hypothesis that an appropriate environment can be created that can both offset any detriment to development associated with maternal separation and add a degree of enrichment frequently not available in families of limited social, economic, and cultural resources. Preliminary findings filed at HEW in mid-1968, after two years of operation, held that children did gain in cognitive skills in the experimental environment.[37]

Change comes slowly to child welfare—as to other—specialists. Those in the Children's Bureau have found it difficult to adjust to the idea of day care available to all comers and especially to low income working mothers. On the one hand, the talk from the top of the bureau has been about the need to face reality in the day care picture. "The Children's Bureau must share part of the blame for the failure to look at reality in today's day care picture," said Mrs. Oettinger as early as June 1967, "when thousands of infants and young children are being placed in haphazard situations because their mothers are working."[38]

On the other hand, down the line at the bureau the experts continue to emphasize the importance of the intake procedure to insure that

36. U.S. Department of Health, Education, and Welfare, Welfare Administration, Children's Bureau, Spotlight on Day Care: Proceedings of the National Conference on Day Care Services, May 13–15, 1965, CB Publication No. 438-1966 (1966), p. 127.

37. State University of New York at Syracuse, Upstate Medical College, "Development of a Demonstration Day Care Center for Young Children" (D-156) (n.d.; processed). For a discussion of the center, see Maya Pines, Revolution in Learning: The Years from Birth to Six (Harper & Row, 1967), pp. 160–66.

38. U.S. Department of Labor, Women's Bureau, Preliminary Report of a Consultation on Working Women and Day Care Needs Held June 1, 1967, Washington, D.C., Labor D.C. (WB 68-18), (August 1967), p. 8.

children placed in day care "need" the service. Bureau day care specialists profess a belief that day care should be widely available much as is public education—but simultaneously qualify that position by arguing that some selection is necessary because a mother's desire for the service for her child is not sufficient justification. Observing that parents readily follow the advice of their pediatrician, they insist that parents should be equally willing to accept the intake services (screening) of the caseworker.

With this approach it might be expected that while the day care expansion movement has ground along slowly, it has ground exceedingly fine. Day care undoubtedly is a risky enterprise. Every center should be a genuinely high-quality, sympathetic environment; no center should be countenanced without clear evidence that such an environment is being created, and all centers that do not give such evidence should be discouraged. The payoff, therefore, for what might seem to be excessive caution by the Children's Bureau could be a jewel of a limited program and no second or third rate imitations. Then, when money and will were at hand, the jewel could be reproduced.

In fact, no day care activity was discouraged, whether of low quality or not. Caution on the subject of quantity did not work to guarantee quality. Whether or not there would be any day care activity depended on state interest. The federal agency was accommodating, both because it was hard to interest the states in day care at all, and because Congress provided money in fits and starts, rather than in a steady flow. When the money did come, there was an urgent need to spend it.

Funding

Selling the states on day care started—or would have started save for congressional failure to appropriate money—in 1962. The Public Welfare Amendments of that year authorized up to $5 million of child welfare funds for distribution to the states for day care services for fiscal 1963 and up to $10 million in succeeding years. The authorization was small even by 1962 standards. Presumably, states would match the earmarked federal day care funds with state general expenditures for child welfare services. Federal funding of the earmarked day care provision, before it was dropped entirely in 1965, was disappointing. While the total authorization for the first three years was $25 million, only

$8.8 million was actually appropriated. Funds for fiscal 1963 were included as a part of the first supplemental appropriation bill but then lost when Congress adjourned in the fall of 1962 without enacting the measure. In a second supplemental appropriation in the spring of 1963, the House committee recommended $3 million for day care but the Senate committee cut out these funds, saying day care money could wait until fiscal 1964.[39]

In fiscal 1964 and in 1965 the administration requested $8 million for day care. In 1964 the House Committee approved the full amount; in 1965 it cut the amount to $6 million. Each year the Senate Appropriations Committee would approve only $4 million, and each year its cuts were sustained in conference. Perhaps more important, support was growing in Senate Appropriations to require earmarked state matching of the earmarked federal day care funds. HEW, certain that states would be unable to match without being given notice and guessing that states would be unwilling to match even after notice, opposed matching amendments. Working through Senator Abraham Ribicoff, who maintained a proprietary interest in the 1962 Public Welfare Amendments that he had supported as secretary of HEW, the department succeeded first in delaying an earmarked matching requirement until January 1, 1966. And before that date ever arrived, Ribicoff successfully moved to strike the earmarking of federal funds for day care from the law. With nonearmarked federal money available for day care out of the general child welfare appropriation, earmarked state matching money became a moot question.

Between 1962 and 1965, then, HEW had only $8.8 million to parcel out to the states for day care. Moreover, it was never able to count on having anything from year to year, so that it is understandable that the federal agency was in no position to threaten the states about the quality of service. The 1962 amendments required that federal day care money go only to facilities approved or licensed in accordance with state standards. The law said nothing about minimum federal standards. In 1962 a number of states had no day care licensing programs at all; among the states that did, the extent of licensing and the standards used varied considerably. The Children's Bureau's "Guides" were little more than advisory. To raise the quality of day care nationally, the bureau had to

39. *Supplemental Appropriation Bill, 1963*, S. Rept. 155, 88 Cong. 1 sess. (1963), p. 14.

fall back on persuasion and consultation, weak tools compared to money.

Licensing

One certain effect of the 1962 requirement that the available federal money go only to licensed facilities was to divert a substantial part of the funds into licensing activity itself and away from actual day care services. For fiscal 1965, for example, 43 percent of the $4 million appropriated for day care was spent on personnel engaged in licensing and only 36 percent was used to provide day care services in homes or centers. This increased licensing activity has the effect of distorting the picture of growth in day care spaces. In 1960, licensed day care facilities had a reported total capacity of 183,332; in 1965 this had increased to 310,400; in 1967 the figure was up to 473,700; in 1968 to 535,200; and in 1969 to 638,000 (Table 3). There is universal agreement, however, that the growth figure is illusory; in reality, the growth is less in total capacity and facilities and more in preexisting facilities formerly unlicensed, now licensed.

Given the nature of the licensing process, there is more form than substance to licensing decisions. Every state now has some kind and some degree of state regulation of day care, usually licensing and usually administered by the Welfare Department. Often, however, it is neither comprehensive nor fully carried out. State licensing laws are general. Many require that day care centers be adequate; the definition of adequacy is left to state administrators. But state administrators are in much the same position as are federal administrators. The demand or need for day care facilities is greater than the supply, and, therefore, it is self-defeating to crack down on substandard operations. The Children's Bureau has reduced the dilemma to writing without resolving it:

It is necessary to keep in mind that the prevailing standard in a State may be somewhat higher than the licensing requirement, since any licensing system must and should set its requirements low enough that most facilities can meet them, while the licensing authority and other forces work together to effect a statewide level of care which will support revision of the licensing standards upward at intervals of a few years. On the other hand, it is necessary to keep in mind that even in the best staffed and administered licensing service, there may be a section of the State, or a slum ghetto area, or an occasional "hard core" resistant facility where the licensing standards are not enforceable, at least temporarily: for lack of other resources which parents can use, for lack of community understanding, for lack of access to the courts on the part of the licensing worker.[40]

Thus, the fact that a day care facility is licensed cannot yet be taken to mean that its physical plant and personnel necessarily satisfy some explicitly defined and universally accepted standards. Like "premium grade" automobile tires, licensed day care facilities can differ sharply in quality—and for the same reason, the absence of industrywide standards. Licensing studies by public welfare agencies are invariably assigned to new and untrained caseworkers. The results are unpredictable and there is no monitoring body able and authorized to keep a watchful eye on who is being licensed.

The grand plan of the 1967 work incentive amendments to the welfare titles of the Social Security Act was to provide the necessary training, employment, and day care services and opportunities to AFDC recipients so that they could "become wage-earning members of society and restore their families to independence and useful roles in their communities." Essentially the same idea was incorporated in the Nixon family assistance proposal. This simplistic formulation implied that only the absence of child care services and of job or training opportunities precluded AFDC recipients from becoming wage earners, that AFDC and independence are incompatible, and that AFDC status and a useful role in the community are incompatible. Even from those who accept these assumptions as valid, however, there is no suggestion that just any kind of child care will do. Yet the state of the art in day care is not sufficiently advanced to make it reasonable to expect that states can meet the requirement to provide day care services other than in makeshift, low quality programs. There is clear validity in the complaint of the National Committee for the Day Care of Children that the 1967 legislation was not designed to help children develop mentally and physically, but was "a hastily put together outline for a compulsory, custodial service which is not required to maintain even minimal standards of adequacy."[41]

40. "State Day Care Licensing: Prepared by the Children's Bureau, Social and Rehabilitation Service, U.S. Department of Health, Education, and Welfare for the Fourth National Conference of Commissions on the Status of Women" (June 7, 1968; processed), p. 3.

41. *Social Security Amendments of 1967*, Hearings before the Senate Committee on Finance, 90 Cong. 1 sess. (1967), p. A178.

Challenge from Head Start

While the Children's Bureau was struggling with new concepts in mother-child relationships and while the states were doing virtually nothing to supply day care leadership, the Office of Economic Opportunity (OEO) was pouring resources into its preschool Head Start program. This immensely popular component of the antipoverty agency's community action program brushed aside the philosophical web that tied up the Children's Bureau and accepted the idea that providing a combination of health, nutrition, and educational benefits to the poor, preschool child would be to his advantage. Although the benefits may subsequently fade, there is no evidence to suggest that the experience is disadvantageous. Since almost 60 percent of full-year Head Start children were less than five years old, concern about maternal deprivation vanished as early-childhood development centers established themselves.

Only a month after taking office, in a message to Congress on his plans for reorganizing the war on poverty, President Nixon called for a "national commitment to providing all American children an opportunity for healthful and stimulating development during the first five years of life." A few weeks later Secretary of HEW Robert Finch welcomed the delegation of the Head Start Program to HEW as the occasion for a new and overdue national commitment to child and parent development. Finch indicated publicly that he was not inclined to put Head Start in the Children's Bureau where, he complained, the average age was fifty-eight. Nor did he award Head Start to the Children's Bureau's bureaucratic competitor, the Office of Education. Instead, Finch created an Office of Child Development (OCD), to be located within the Office of the Secretary. Head Start was placed in OCD, and the Children's Bureau was transferred there too.

Finch appointed Jule M. Sugarman, acting chief of the Children's Bureau, to be acting director of the Office of Child Development. Sugarman, a political scientist who for four years had been associate director of Head Start in OEO, had moved to HEW in 1968 in anticipation of the program's shift. His appointment in March 1969 as acting chief of the Children's Bureau to succeed P. F. DelliQuadri, a social worker of the old school who was eased out after only nine months in office, first suggested that the new Head Start look was about to displace the old social work look. When Sugarman was also given responsibility for OCD, it seemed like additional evidence in support of that proposition. Social planners in HEW, the Bureau of the Budget, and the White House envisioned a new era: day care programs for low income children would be modeled on Head Start; simple custodial arrangements would not be tolerated; parents would be involved. The way for this happy outcome had already been paved by issuance of the Federal Interagency Day Care Requirements, a joint product of HEW and OEO, approved in the summer of 1968. Sugarman had been their principal architect. When the requirements became fully effective, Head Start–type child-adult ratios would be mandatory for all federally supported day care, and so would parent advisory committees.

Things have not worked out. First, whatever Finch's initial intention, the day care programs operated by the Children's Bureau never made it to the OCD. In September 1969 a new Community Services Administration (CSA) was created within the Social and Rehabilitation Service to house all service programs provided public assistance recipients under the Social Security Act. The Head Start Bureau of the OCD, according to the terms of the reorganization, was given some responsibility in Social Security Act day care programs—to participate in policy making and to approve state welfare plans on day care. But effective control of the money and policy in the day care programs remains with the SRS. Interestingly enough, the person put in charge of day care under the CSA was not one of the new breed of early childhood development specialists à la Head Start, but the veteran day-care specialist under the old Children's Bureau.

Second, President Nixon's "commitment to providing all American children an opportunity for healthful and stimulating development during the first five years of life" has so far produced more talk than money. The widely heralded OCD, which requested about $27 million in fiscal 1971, was allocated $11.5 million in the Nixon budget: $8.5 million for research and demonstrations, $2.555 million for technical assistance and administration (including twenty new positions), and $400,000 for the White House Conference on Children and Youth.

Third, Jule Sugarman left HEW early in the summer of 1970 to become New York City human resources administrator.

Fourth, most if not all the states are having trouble meeting the adult-child ratio provisions of the interagency requirements, and sympathetic attention is being given by HEW day care specialists to relaxing the ratio and parent advisory committee requirements.

A High Cost Service

There has simply not been enough thinking about the benefits and costs of a good day care program to merit the faith political leaders now express in day care as a dependency-reducing mechanism. Federal day care program requirements are oriented to the idea of day care as a learning experience. They are, therefore, on a collision course with supporters of mass day care as an aspect of the struggle to reduce welfare costs. The high-quality program requirements reject any sentiment favoring simple warehousing of children, but the prospects for meeting those announced standards are not good. It seems inevitable that there will be disappointment for both those who perceive of day care as a welfare economy and those who perceive of public support of day care for AFDC children as an important social and educational advance.

Consider the situation in the District of Columbia, reasonably typical of the day care problem in large urban places. The District Public Welfare Department (DPW) in May 1969 was purchasing child care for 1,056 children, of whom about 400 were children of WIN trainees. Of the 1,056 provided care, 865 were in day care centers, 163—primarily infants too young to be placed in centers—were in family day care homes, and 28 were in in-home care arrangements, a service considered practical only for large families. The total anticipated day care load for the end of fiscal 1969 was 1,262. District day care personnel estimated that the 660 AFDC mothers to be referred to WIN during fiscal 1970 (on the basis of 55 per month) would need, on the average, day care for 2 children. These additional 1,320 children would bring the likely number for whom the District would be paying for care to 2,582 by July 1, 1970. Budget requests for day care for fiscal 1970 totaled $3,254,300 in local and federal funds ($1,148,000 of local funds brings $2,106,300 in federal money). Of this amount, about $3 million is for purchase of care, the remainder for administrative expenses. If budget requests were met, the purchase cost of day care in the District would thus be expected to average almost $1,200 per child. Costly as that may seem to be, it represents only a little more than half the actual cost.

It is the beginning of day care wisdom to understand that it is an expensive mechanism and to understand that there are qualitative differences in the care provided. The elegantly stated effort of the DPW is to secure "in addition to good physical care, the kind of exceptionally enriched day care experience that is specifically designed and programmed to stimulate and promote the maximum in emotional, physical, and educational growth and development of the child."[42] Alas, one-third of the centers with which the DPW contracts only "offer primarily custodial and protective care," a code phrase for warehousing. Fees paid day care centers by the District Welfare Department are supposed to be a function of the quality of services offered. Grade A centers are paid $4.00 a day, B centers $3.00 a day, and C centers $2.50 a day. The department's Standards for Day Care Centers say that it uses a fee schedule for two reasons: "to assure that proper value is received for each dollar spent and, secondly, to provide a monetary stimulus to contract day care facilities to up-grade the quality of their services to meet the Department's maximum expectations." Each center's "rating," known only to it and to the Welfare Department, is for "internal use" and is not revealed to the welfare mother because, according to department officials, it would not be fair to the center to do so. Since 25 of the 55 centers from which day care is purchased are graded B or C, and since half of all placements are in B or C centers, whether it is fair to the mother not to be told the relative quality of the center in which her child is placed is a pertinent question.

While all centers—whether A, B, or C—must meet the Health Department's licensing requirements and additional specific standards set down by the Welfare Department in the areas of educational qualifications of personnel, program content, and equipment and furnishings, two problems intrude on what might seem to be a tidy picture. The first is the insistence of close observers that while the Welfare Department's standards for centers look satisfactory on paper, they have not been put into practice very consistently. The second is that even the paper standards will not do when the federal interagency standards become effective July 1, 1971. Spokesmen for the National Capital Area Child Day Care Association (NCACDCA) and District Health Department licensing personnel are critical of the Welfare Department's day care operation. Both suggest lack of awareness in the Welfare Day Care Unit of what constitutes good day care. That high ranking is reserved, in

42. District of Columbia Department of Public Welfare, "Standards for Day Care Centers" (n.d.; processed), p. 1.

the judgment of these people, for the centers operated by NCACDCA. The critics complain that only the NCACDCA centers can legitimately meet the Welfare Department's own A standards and maintain that the other A centers simply do not meet them. They claim, for example, that one way these latter centers "meet" the educational qualifications for personnel is to list as a director an "absentee"—perhaps a kindergarten teacher in the District of Columbia school system or that of a neighboring county.

No one disputes that most centers in the District cannot meet the Federal Interagency Day Care Requirements—particularly the child-adult ratios and the educational qualifications for staff. Even a good number of the A centers do not meet the child-adult ratio requirements: 5 to 1 for 3-to-4-year-olds in a center with 15 to a group, and 7 to 1 for 4-to-6-year-olds with 20 to a group.[43] The Welfare Department's standards for day care centers do not specify staffing patterns but require only that the centers—whether A, B, or C—meet the Health Department's ratios which are 1 adult (exclusive of maintenance help) to every 10 children. The B and C centers meet neither the staff educational qualifications nor the child-adult ratios of the federal requirements. If the day care centers have not met the federal standards by July 1, 1971, DPW cannot continue making payments on behalf of children for whom it receives federal matching funds. Even before the Nixon plan for day care expansion, there was no possibility that the standards could be met by the deadline. But in the District Welfare Department the view is that the requirements are unrealistic and that widespread complaints from private users who cannot afford the costs involved may result in a lowering of standards.

All the evidence suggests that day care is expensive whether the auspices are public, private, or mixed. The District Welfare Department's internal studies conclude that the per child cost to the department to operate its own centers would be $2,100 per year, a figure almost twice the amount ($1,170) the department pays its A centers, most of which are subsidized by the Office of Economic Opportunity. The Day Care and Child Development Council of America, successor to the

43. *Federal Interagency Day Care Requirements Pursuant to Sec. 522(d) of the Economic Opportunity Act*, as approved by U.S. Department of Health, Education, and Welfare, U.S. Office of Economic Opportunity, and U.S. Department of Labor, Sept. 23, 1968.

National Committee for the Day Care of Children, also puts the annual per child rate for adequate day care at $2,100.

In a curiously chosen experiment, the Department of Labor decided in 1969 to fund an experimental day care program for its own employees at a time when emphasis was presumably being placed on supporting day care for the welfare poor. Its estimated budget for the first full year of care for thirty children was $100,000, one-third of which was for nonrecurring development costs, including renovation for code compliance, equipment, and evaluation.[44] The fee income to be derived from the group of working mothers involved amounted to only $7,300, leaving $59,600 of public funds necessary to provide care for thirty children—or almost $2,000 per child subsidy without considering nonrecurring cost items. Doubling the number of children served the second year would require a budget of $100,000, resulting in an average annual per child cost over the two years of $1,850, or of $2,225 if the renovation and equipment items are not dismissed as readily as the department sought to dismiss them in its official explanation.

The National Capital Area Child Day Care Association estimates costs at almost $2,400 per child per fifty-week year. Its standard budget for a thirty-child center exceeds $71,000 (Table 4). Tight-fisted budget examiners might effect reductions, but they cannot be consequential unless the pupil-teacher ratio is drastically revised. Moreover, NCAC-DCA salary figures are unrealistically low. Head teachers for a thirty-child center are hard to come by at $7,300.

If these per child costs of desirable day care are projected nationally, the annual bill for all preschool AFDC children must be figured conservatively at $3 billion.

Client Arithmetic

Most females in the District of Columbia WIN program are being trained in clerical skills in anticipation that they will take jobs with the federal government as GS-2s, an optimistic view since most trainees

44. For a speech by Representative William Scherle (Republican of Iowa) critical of the program, see *Congressional Record*, daily ed., March 4, 1969, p. H1430; Department of Labor reply in *Departments of Labor, and Health, Education, and Welfare Appropriations for 1970*, Hearings before a Subcommittee of the House Committee on Appropriations, 91 Cong. 1 sess. (1969), Pt. 1, pp. 765–66 See also *Washington Post*, Jan. 16, 1969.

Table 4. Standard Day Care Center Budget for Thirty Children

Item	Annual cost
A. Personnel	
3 Full-time teachers (head teacher, $7,300; teacher, $7,000; teacher assistant, $4,700)	$19,000
2 Full-time aides ($4,140 each)	8,280
1 Half-time clerk	2,400
Part-time maintenance help (cook, $2,610; janitor, $2,024)	4,634
Substitute (teacher aide, $4,300) and part-time student aide ($1,214)	5,514
Subtotal	$39,828
Fringe benefits (11 percent)	4,381
Total	$44,209
B. Consultant and Contract Services	
Part-time social worker ($2,500), psychiatric consultant ($5,000), and educational consultant ($1,000)	$ 8,500
Dietitian	500
Dental and emergency medical service	450
Total	$ 9,450
C. Space	
Rent ($1,800); custodial supplies and minor repairs ($1,800)[a]	$ 3,600
D. Consumable Supplies	
Office, postage, and miscellaneous (blankets, towels, etc.)	$ 450
Educational ($400) and health supplies ($30)	430
Food and utensils	4,674
Total	$ 5,554
E. Rental, Lease, or Purchase of Equipment	
Children's furniture ($3,000) and office equipment ($200)	$ 3,200
Equipment: basic (easels, blocks, etc., $1,500); expendable (dolls, puzzles, books, etc., $700); outdoor, with storage ($1,000)	3,200
Total	$ 6,400
F. Travel	
Staff ($240) and children's trips ($720)	$ 960
G. Other	
Telephone ($36 a month; installation $50)	$ 482
Insurance (liability, property, and transportation liability)	700
Total	$ 1,182
Total project cost	$71,355
Per child cost	$ 2,378

Source: Derived from budget of National Capital Area Day Care Association, Inc., Washington, D.C., August 1968.

a. Renovations estimated at 15 percent of building cost may be necessary for buildings over 15 years old.

have ninth to eleventh grade educations while a GS-2 needs a high school diploma or equivalency or six months' experience and the ability to pass a typing test. That problem aside, the District AFDC mother who completes work incentive training and is placed in a GS-2 job will be better off financially than the mother who stays on welfare. Her gain will be greater the smaller the size of her family. She will have fewer children to support on her fixed earnings, whereas the larger the family on AFDC, the larger the grant. For many a female head of a family of four in the spring of 1970, however, the work and day care arithmetic was not encouraging, as the following illustration shows. If the GS-2 mother has three children and claims four exemptions, about $39 of her monthly salary of $385 is deducted for retirement ($18.50) and for federal ($17) and local ($3.50) taxes, leaving take home pay of about $346 a month. If two of the three children are in Welfare Department child care arrangements, placed there when the mother entered the WIN program, the mother would pay the department about $6.00 a week toward their care; if the mother had only one child in care, she would pay $5.50. Assuming two children in care, the mother's monthly cost would be about $26, lowering her net earnings to $320.

Suppose, on the other hand, the woman stayed on AFDC. The average benefit for a four-person family on AFDC in the District would bring her $217 monthly. Both the welfare mother and the working mother would be eligible for Medicaid, but only the welfare mother would be eligible for food stamps. For $60 a month she could receive $106 in food stamps, a gain of $46. The welfare mother's child could also receive free lunches at school while the working mother's could not. (The working mother is considerably above the income scale used to determine eligibility for free lunches, although in cases where it is felt children are going hungry, exceptions to the income scale can be made.) A school lunch costs 25 cents in the District's elementary schools. If the welfare child took advantage of the free lunch the mother would save about $5 a month. Thus, the welfare mother would end up with a total of about $268 in welfare, food stamps, and school lunches while the working mother would have about $320 a month. In addition, the 1967 welfare amendments allow a welfare mother to earn $30 per month without loss of benefits. The net gain for working full time compared to working only nineteen hours a month at the minimum wage is thus reduced to $22. From this, the working mother would have expenses to cover such items as transportation and extra clothes for herself and might have to make some after school care arrangement for her third (school-aged) child.

City Arithmetic

How much work training and day care can save the District of Columbia will depend on how many trainees complete training successfully, get a job, and keep it, and how many children of trainees need child care. The Welfare Department will benefit financially by the AFDC mother's entering a training program and becoming employed as a GS-2 unless the mother has four or more children in day care—which would be most unusual. While it might give the AFDC mother of three $217 each month, the department would pay only part of her day care cost once she begins working (the department pays all costs for the first three months). With an average cost to the department for day care of $17.50 per child per week, using our hypothetical GS-2 mother with two children in day care and one in elementary school, the mother would pay $6 a week and the Welfare Department $29 a week for day care. This working mother thus represents a monthly saving to the department of about $56. If, however, the AFDC mother had four children in day care centers and one in elementary school, the mother would pay $6.50 a week toward their care (this figure is the same for three or more children) and the department $63.50. The department would thus spend $273 a month for child care—and save nothing compared to what it would have given her on AFDC to care for her own children at home.

Prospects

What are the prospects for success in turning day care into a program that will reduce the costs of AFDC? They hinge, first, on large numbers of AFDC mothers actually turning out to be trainable and able to be placed in jobs under any conditions and, second, on finding some cheaper substitute for traditional day care centers. The difficulty in securing physical facilities and staff needed to develop the traditional centers looked overwhelming to state welfare administrators examining the day care problem in 1967. They did, however, see some hopes for neighborhood day care, a kind of glorified, low income equivalent of the middle class baby-sitting pool. Stimulated by OEO's success in involving poor people in poverty programs, HEW early in 1967 started pushing neighborhood day care demonstration projects using welfare mothers to help care for other welfare mothers' children. This seemingly ideal solution has its own problems. One of them is sanitary and health requirements that, if enforced, disqualify the substandard housing used by many recipients. The unknown emotional condition of the AFDC mother is an equally important problem in this use of the neighborhood care idea. A spokesman for the Welfare Rights Organization puts the emotional uncertainty issue forward in warning:

. . . Do not force mothers to take care of other children. You do not know what kind of problem that parent might have. You do not know whether she gets tired of her own children or not but you are trying to force her to take care of other people's children and forcing the parents to go out in the field and work when you know there is no job.

This is why we have had the disturbance in New York City and across the country. We, the welfare recipients, have tried to keep down that disturbance among our people but the unrest is steadily growing. The welfare recipients are tired. They are tired of people dictating to them telling them how they must live.[45]

Not surprisingly, day care and work training through WIN are lagging as the hoped-for saving graces of public assistance. New York City's experience is instructive. In 1967 the City Council's finance committee concluded that an additional expenditure of $5 million for 50 additional day care centers to accommodate 3,000 additional children was warranted. "The Committee on Finance is informed," said its report, "that many [welfare] mothers would seek employment if they could be assured of proper care for their children while at work. We feel that expansion . . . on a massive scale is called for."[46] The mayor's executive expense budget for day care was thereupon increased by about 60 percent and appropriations in subsequent years have continued at the higher level. But the New York City Department of Social Services—like the U.S. Department of Health, Education, and Welfare—lacks a program for such a rapid expansion of day care. Actual expenditures have lagged. In contrast to the anticipated 50 new centers caring for 3,000 additional children, it was reported in June 1969 that 19 new centers accommodating 790 children had been established.

The national figures resulting from the 1967 amendments are no

45. *Social Security Amendments of 1967*, Hearings, p. 1465.
46. As quoted in Citizens Budget Commission, Inc. (New York City), "Day Care Centers: The Case for Prompt Expansion" (June 1969; processed), p. 2.

more encouraging. Like New York City, the federal government has not been able to shovel out the available money. Consider the situation around the time of the Nixon family assistance message. Of a projected June 1969 goal of 102,000 WIN enrollees, only 61,847 were in fact enrolled by the end of that month. Of a projected 100,000 child care arrangements, only about 49,000 children were receiving care at the end of June 1969, and 50 percent of them were receiving care in their own homes. Thus, when President Nixon proposed 150,000 new training slots and 450,000 new day care places in his August 1969 welfare message, Labor and HEW had already found that eighteen months after enactment of the 1967 legislation they were unable to meet more than 60 percent of their modest work and training goals or more than 50 percent of their even more modest day care goals.

That gap between original projections and depressing realities held constant into 1970. Labor first estimated a WIN enrollment level of 150,000 at the close of fiscal 1970, later scaled the figure down to 100,000. And as of February 1970 the cumulative WIN data took the shape of a funnel:

Welfare recipients screened by local agencies for possible referral	1,478,000
Found appropriate for referral to WIN	301,000
Actually referred to WIN	225,000
Enrolled in WIN program	129,000
Employed	22,000[47]

As for day care, 188,000 children were initially expected to be receiving "child care"—which includes care in their own homes by grandmothers or other relatives—on June 30, 1970. The target later was dropped to a more modest 78,000. In May 1970 there were just 61,000 reported in child care, and only about one-fifth of these children were really cared for in a day care facility. Approximately one-half were cared for in their own homes, one-tenth in a relative's home, and the last one-fifth were reported to have "other" arrangements—a category that actually includes "child looks after self."[48]

47. *Appropriations for 1970*, Hearings, Pt. 2, pp. 15–16, and *Departments of Labor, and Health, Education and Welfare Appropriations for 1971*, Hearings before a Subcommittee of the House Committee on Appropriations, 91 Cong. 2 sess. (1970), Pt. 4, pp. 15, 96, 111, 216.

48. *Appropriations for 1971*, Pt. 4, p. 111. National Center for Social Statistics, Monthly Report E-4, "Child Care Arrangements of AFDC Recipients Under the Work Incentive Program"; and Monthly Report Form SRS-NCSS-102.1.

By July 1970 the House Labor-HEW appropriations subcommittee was discouraged about the progress of work training–day care activity. "It doesn't sound too good," said Chairman Dan Flood (Democrat of Pennsylvania) after hearing the WIN program statistics.[49] The committee proposed a reduction of $50 million from the administration's request for $170 million in 1971 work incentive funds. There was no confusion about either the purpose of the program or its lack of accomplishment:

The objective of the work incentives program is to help people get off the welfare rolls and to place them in productive jobs. While the committee supports the program, it has just not been getting off the ground for several reasons, such as poor day care standards for children.[50]

Unfortunately, the sorry history and the limitations of day care and work training as "solutions" to the welfare problem could not be faced by the administration's welfare specialists in 1970 because all of their energies were directed toward support for the Nixon family assistance plan. But after a few years it will inevitably be discovered that work training and day care have had little effect on the number of welfare dependents and no depressing effect on public relief costs. Some new solution will then be proposed, but the more realistic approach would be to accept the need for more welfare and to reject continued fantasizing about day care and "workfare" as miracle cures.

49. *Appropriations for 1971*, Pt. 4, p. 217.
50. *Congressional Record*, daily ed., July 21, 1970, p. H6998.

3

Old Data, New Men

The federal-state system of aid to families with dependent children (AFDC) produced a situation where some poor states like Mississippi cannot pay clients even minimally adequate benefits, some not-so-poor states like Delaware choose not to, and other states like New Jersey do pay poverty level benefits but starve other social programs to do so. As a consequence, strengthening the federal role in welfare policy is a major public issue for the 1970s. Political leaders take stands on it, large numbers of legislative proposals are introduced in Congress, editorial comment appears not only in the *New York Times* and the *Washington Post* but also in papers like the Hutchinson (Kansas) *News*, the Seattle (Washington) *Times*, and the Marlborough (Massachusetts) *Enterprise*. Unlike earlier occasions when welfare issues aroused attention, indignation at "cheating" and outrage about costs do not eclipse concern over inadequate benefits and concern over socially undesirable effects of restrictions on eligibility.

In what is properly regarded as a message of historic importance, delivered in August 1969, President Nixon told Congress that "America's welfare system is a failure that grows worse every day."[1] The President asserted that the welfare system failed the recipient: "In many areas, benefits are so low that we have hardly begun to take care of the dependent." To overcome this failing, the administration proposed a basic income payment from the federal government "made upon certification of income, with demeaning and costly investigations replaced by simplified reviews and spot checks." At the time a payment of $1,600 annually for a family of four was recommended, it would have resulted in some

1. *Message from the President of the United States Relative to Welfare Reform*, H. Doc. 91-146, 91 Cong. 1 sess. (1969), p. 2. Text in *Congressional Record*, daily ed., Aug. 11, 1969, p. S59582.

benefit increases in as many as ten states, although even with a possible food stamp supplement, the payment would come to less than two-thirds of poverty level needs. The National Welfare Rights Organization found the benefit inadequate.[2] Mayors and governors in the better paying states tended to agree with the comment of Mayor John Lindsay of New York City who called the proposal "the most important step forward by the Federal Government in this field in a generation," but also complained that it did not relieve "the unfair burden of welfare on local taxpayers."[3]

Mr. Nixon stated that the welfare system failed the taxpayer: "Since 1960, welfare costs have doubled and the number on the rolls has risen from 5.8 million to over 9 million, all in a time when unemployment was low." Ironically, between benefit increases and extension of eligibility to the working poor, the administration proposed to increase welfare costs by at least $4.4 billion annually in the first year of family assistance.

Finally, the President concluded that the welfare system failed American society: "By breaking up homes, the present welfare system has added to social unrest and robbed millions of the joy of childhood; by widely varying payments, among regions, it has helped to draw millions into the slums of our cities." Under the Nixon plan, migration to the urban slums encouraged by variations in payments among regions would presumably become less attractive because the imposition of the basic federal payment would shrink the average benefit gap between the highest and the lowest paying states from almost $2,700 to about $1,600 per year for a four-person family. To stop the welfare system from breaking up homes and adding to social unrest, the federal family assistance payment would not include a requirement that the family be without a father. This plan to eliminate absence of the father as an eligibility condition in effect universalized the unemployed parent component of the AFDC program that had been optional with the states since 1961.

The Nixon proposal for welfare reform, characterized by the London Economist—to the delight of the President's staff—as a message that "may rank in importance with President Roosevelt's first proposal for a

2. "NWRO Raps on Nixon Plan," *Welfare Fighter* (monthly publication of the National Welfare Rights Organization, Washington, D.C.), September 1969, p. 6.
3. *New York Times*, Aug. 10, 1969.

social security system in the mid-1930's . . ."[4] was favored, according to an October 1969 Harris survey, by 47 percent of the American people, with only 17 percent opposed.[5] By the President's own explanation, the proposal was predicated on dissatisfaction with payments levels in many areas, on a belief that existing welfare policy contributed to family instability, especially desertion of the father, and on an accompanying belief that the prospect of higher payments helped lure millions of southern blacks into northern industrial slums. That benefits were often appallingly inadequate is indisputable if not startlingly new information. It is much less certain, however, that public assistance had the effect on family stability or on southern black migration that is assigned to it by the conventional wisdom on which the President depended. Nor was the evidence on the benefits and costs of eligibility by income certification available when Mr. Nixon adopted the certification method as part of his program. The development and justification of the family assistance plan provide an instructive political lesson in how a combination of well-placed, determined new people armed only with old and even uncertain data can significantly advance the prospects for policy innovation.

The Official Indictment

Benefits

Low benefit amounts, great variations among the states in assistance payments, and increasing costs and increasing numbers of recipients (especially deserted and unmarried mothers) despite both high employment and extensions of social security coverage could have been offi-

4. *Economist*, Vol. 232 (Aug. 16, 1969). The passage is quoted approvingly by Richard P. Nathan, assistant director of the Bureau of the Budget, in his Wherrett Lecture at the University of Pittsburgh, Oct. 22, 1969, and again in his remarks to the American Public Welfare Association in Dallas, Dec. 10, 1969. Domestic editorial reaction is found in *Congressional Record*, daily ed., Sept. 3, 1969, pp. E7081–82; Sept. 4, 1969, pp. H7535–38; Sept. 18, 1969, pp. E7599–7605.

5. Harris's specific question asked of a national cross section of people was, "All in all, do you tend to favor or oppose President Nixon's new welfare program?" *Washington Post*, Oct. 13, 1969. In June 1968 a Gallup poll reported that 58 percent of Americans opposed a guaranteed annual income while 78 percent supported a guaranteed jobs plan. *New York Times*, June 16, 1968.

cially labeled "crises" at least as early as 1965. By that year, child recipients of AFDC per 1,000 children in the population had doubled over the 1946 rate. Federal grants to the states for public assistance rose from $439 million in 1946 to over $1 billion in 1950 and $3 billion by 1965. State public aid costs increased over that same period from $0.5 billion to $1.5 billion; local costs grew from $127 million to $0.5 billion. The number of recipients rose from 3.5 million—of whom 2.2 million were old age assistance clients and only 900,000 of whom were AFDC clients— in 1946, to 6.6 million—3.6 million of whom were AFDC clients—in 1961, to 8 million—4.4 million of whom were AFDC clients—in 1965. And the numbers continued to grow.

Interstate variations in benefits were also extensive for at least twenty years before the Nixon family assistance proposal. In 1951, for example, after payment to an adult caretaker had been authorized, the average monthly dependent child benefit ranged from $5.25 in Mississippi to $37 in California. A decade thereafter, in the year of John Kennedy's inauguration, the range was from $9.20 in Mississippi and $10.20 in Alabama to $48 in Connecticut and Massachusetts. This is not to suggest that Mr. Nixon should not have been appalled by the 1969 spread—$10 in Mississippi to $65 in New Jersey—but that other presidents had plenty of cause to be appalled sooner.

During the Eisenhower years the concentration was on incremental shifts in the federal-state distribution of costs and on incremental changes in benefit amounts. While a few Democrats in Congress urged increases in the federal share of relief payments, the President's preoccupation was to avoid shifting public assistance costs to the federal level. As early as January 1954, in a special message to Congress on social security, Eisenhower suggested basic revision in the public assistance matching provisions to establish its financing on a "sounder" basis. Two years later the President's budget message asked that the existing formula, originally adopted in 1952, be temporarily extended to "allow time to reappraise the need for the present high level of the Federal contribution to public assistance."[6] Administration-sponsored draft bills would have extended the formula to June 30, 1959, but Congress instead adopted small increases in the maximum federal contribution. By 1958 the administration was unwilling just to hold the line. The budget message that year stated that "proposals will be sent to the Congress

6. *Congressional Record*, Vol. 102, Pt. 1, 84 Cong. 2 sess. (1956), p. 561.

for modernizing the formulas for public assistance with a view to gradually reducing Federal participation in its financing."[7]

Marion Folsom, secretary of health, education, and welfare, opposed a proposed 1958 public assistance benefit increase because "a further general expansion of the Federal Government's financial share . . . is undesirable."[8] So did his successor, Arthur Flemming, who said, "We assume it is possible for the States to participate to a greater extent in the public assistance program than is now the case."[9] So did Maurice Stans, then budget director, who denied that "a further increase in the already disproportionate overall Federal share in this program can be justified."[10] Eisenhower himself made his position explicit: "I believe deeply . . . that the State and local financial responsibility in these programs should be strengthened, not weakened."[11]

Neither John F. Kennedy nor Lyndon Johnson actively sought increases in the federal share of public assistance benefits, but their reluctance (as distinguished from opposition) was based on fiscal constraints rather than on principle. Throughout most of the Kennedy-Johnson years, public assistance policy had few partisan overtones. Kennedy's 1962 message to Congress on public assistance passed over benefit inadequacy and bought the great rehabilitation thrust, that attractive gloss that the welfare professionals were selling as a cheap way of covering up an ugly and starving system.[12] Republicans and Democrats in Congress accepted it with equal enthusiasm.

Who got what in AFDC was not constantly scrutinized because the structure of the public assistance titles of the Social Security Act did not encourage high-level attention to payments to recipients or to the characteristics of recipients. Financing relief through a continuing open-end authorization and a quasi-contractual obligation to pay state claims according to a predetermined formula created an automated system that

7. *Congressional Record*, Vol. 104, Pt. 1, 85 Cong. 2 sess. (1958), p. 397.

8. *Social Security Legislation*, Hearings before the House Committee on Ways and Means, 85 Cong. 2 sess. (1958), p. 6.

9. *Social Security*, Hearings before the Senate Committee on Finance, 85 Cong. 2 sess. (1958), p. 130.

10. *Ibid.*, p. 110.

11. Quoted in Wilbur J. Cohen and Fedele F. Fauri, "The Social Security Amendments of 1958: Another Significant Step Forward," *Public Welfare*, Vol. 17 (January 1959), p. 5.

12. The evolution of the Public Welfare Amendments of 1962 is detailed in Gilbert Y. Steiner, *Social Insecurity: The Politics of Welfare* (Rand McNally, 1966), pp. 34 ff.

minimized the opportunities and the need for full-scale policy review. Accordingly, years could and did elapse without presidential or congressional attention to any aspect of public assistance policy other than its apparently uncontrollable costs. And on that subject the routine way of handling benefit policy through the fifties and much of the sixties was occasionally to tack onto social security legislation a minor change in the federal-state cost sharing relationship.

Beginning in 1967 the partisan stands became very blurred. The public welfare provisions of the Social Security Amendments of that year, labeled the slave labor amendments by bitter welfare-oriented groups, were enacted by a Democratic Congress despite opposition from liberal Senate Democrats. It will be recalled that the Department of Health, Education, and Welfare came somewhat late to the opposition table, that the President had nothing to say until he signed the legislation, and that he then appointed a Commission on Income Maintenance, first promised a full year earlier. Before the 1968 election, HEW prevailed on President Johnson—who did not make up his mind quickly— to support a one year delay of the imposition of the bill's freeze on federal payments for additional AFDC cases where the father is absent from the home. After the 1968 election, given the color composition of the AFDC rolls and the color composition of the Nixon vote, the way was paved for the new Republican administration to take a hard line on welfare, blaming the Democrats for gross blunders in policy and administration and blaming the recipients for existing. Instead, the Nixon administration approved outright repeal of the freeze and moved to overcome intolerably low benefits by making its first order of domestic business a federally financed cash floor under income of the working as well as of the nonworking poor.

The conditions under which that approach developed will be considered after a review of the background of other counts in the President's indictment of the welfare system as a failure.

Desertion

The absent father syndrome in AFDC had manifested itself clearly by 1961 when 67 percent of the fathers in AFDC families were absent from the home, the majority of them having either deserted or never married the mother.[13] As we have seen, the Kennedy administration did recognize that problem and accomplished an important new program— only to reduce its value by leaving its adoption optional with the states —of AFDC payments where the family is complete and dependency attributable to parental unemployment (AFDC-U). In the majority of states it never became an allowable eligibility condition.

Even in the states that adopted the unemployed parent program, however, it had no clear effect on desertion as a cause of AFDC dependency. Nevertheless, the absence of a universal AFDC-U program came to be considered an explanation of the high rates of desertion among families on welfare. The low income AFDC father, according to this commonsense analysis, discouraged by his inability to sustain his wife and children, reasoned that he could not provide adequately for them when unemployed and underemployed, but that by deserting he could insure that his family would be supported by public funds. Since he would then only have to provide for himself, the pressures on him would be eased and the entire family would be benefited. This is the process to which President Nixon referred when he asserted that the welfare system broke up homes by denying relief to a family with an employable father.

The President's goal of providing public support to a family unit impoverished by involuntary unemployment is readily accepted in connection with the unemployment compensation features of the social security system. Extension of unemployment compensation under federal auspices to cover situations in which insurance benefits previously fixed by state statutes were exhausted has also been readily accepted. Humanitarianism and rationality could be justifications enough for proposing a further extension of the use of public funds to cover situations where conditions for insurance eligibility have not been met.

To suggest, however, that the welfare system needed reform because it caused desertions implied more than can likely be delivered. No one knows whether any or how many fathers desert in order to make their families eligible for AFDC because fathers who desert are not readily available for questioning. Nor is the deserted mother able to assign the cause of desertion. While the hypothesis that AFDC rules cause deser-

13. U.S. Department of Health, Education, and Welfare, Social and Rehabilitation Service, National Center for Social Statistics, *Preliminary Report of Findings— 1967 AFDC Study*, NCSS Report AFDC-1 (67), (1968), p. 9.

tion is reasonable on its face, an equally reasonable hypothesis is that AFDC is a consequence rather than a cause of desertion, that abandoned families fall back on AFDC rather than being forced to fractionalize further by parceling out children among relatives. Public assistance carries enough documented faults (like benefit inadequacy) to be spared President Nixon's sweeping undocumented indictment that it "robbed millions of the joy of childhood" by causing desertion.

If AFDC was encouraging low income fathers to desert, making unemployed parents eligible for AFDC should have reduced desertion rates in states with the AFDC-U component compared to states without it. On the other hand, if desertion is related more closely to causes other than making a family eligible for AFDC, an unemployed parent component would have no clear effect on the desertion–total caseload ratio. The state-by-state data (Table 5) on AFDC dependency caused by desertion will not support the proposition that AFDC breaks up homes.

Table 5. AFDC Cases Based on Desertion

State	Desertion cases as percent of total			AFDC-U cases as percent of total, 1967[b]
	1961[a]	1967[a]	Change	
New England				
Maine	9.9	5.8	− 4.1	c
New Hampshire	14.2	13.0	− 1.2	c
Vermont	15.3	11.9	− 3.4	c
Rhode Island	14.7	9.3	− 5.4	4.4
Connecticut	15.5	19.0	+ 3.5	3.4
Massachusetts	n.a.	10.8		1.6
Middle Atlantic				
New York	19.1	31.6	+12.5	8.0
New Jersey	35.7	32.6	− 3.1	c
Pennsylvania	15.4	17.5	+ 2.1	5.0
East North Central				
Ohio	12.4	14.1	+ 1.7	6.5
Indiana	12.6	12.0	− 0.6	c
Illinois	25.6	23.9	− 1.7	5.2
Michigan	10.7	10.4	− 0.3	4.1
Wisconsin	15.0	8.1	− 6.9	4.4
West North Central				
Minnesota	6.7	5.0	− 1.7	c
Iowa	8.6	10.2	+ 1.6	c
Missouri	18.4	15.5	− 2.9	c
North Dakota	12.6	9.7	− 2.9	c
South Dakota	11.9	9.3	− 2.6	c

Table 5. AFDC Cases Based on Desertion (continued)

State	Desertion cases as percent of total			AFDC-U cases as percent of total, 1967[b]
	1961[a]	1967[a]	Change	
West North Central (continued)				
Nebraska	12.8	10.6	− 2.2	0.9
Kansas	12.0	9.1	− 2.9	2.7
South Atlantic				
Delaware	15.9	24.4	+ 8.5	5.9
Maryland	15.2	20.4	+ 5.2	1.9
District of Columbia	26.8	23.3	− 3.5	c
Virginia	25.3	22.0	− 3.3	c
West Virginia	11.6	13.8	+ 2.2	32.9
North Carolina	26.9	20.9	− 6.0	c
South Carolina	19.2	28.3	+ 9.1	c
Georgia	20.5	24.8	+ 4.3	c
Florida	27.9	26.3	− 1.6	c
East South Central				
Kentucky	9.8	15.4	+ 5.6	c
Tennessee	13.5	15.9	+ 2.4	c
Alabama	18.4	17.5	− 0.9	c
Mississippi	24.3	21.2	− 3.1	c
West South Central				
Arkansas	14.8	14.8	Same	c
Louisiana	15.1	12.9	− 2.2	c
Oklahoma	8.3	6.9	− 1.4	3.0
Texas	16.0	19.6	+ 3.6	c
Mountain				
Montana	13.7	9.3	− 4.4	c
Idaho	13.5	13.7	+ 0.2	c
Wyoming	14.9	9.8	− 5.1	c
Colorado	19.3	15.0	− 4.3	7.0
New Mexico	14.4	12.9	− 1.5	c
Arizona	26.6	21.2	− 5.4	c
Utah	7.8	7.3	− 0.5	21.4
Nevada	20.4	14.3	− 6.1	c
Pacific				
Washington	8.3	9.7	+ 1.4	11.0
California	17.2	7.6	− 9.6	10.8
Alaska	10.5	4.8	− 5.7	
Hawaii	3.9	4.6	+ 0.7	8.9
Oregon	n.a.	8.8	. . .	14.2

Source: U.S. Department of Health, Education, and Welfare, National Center for Social Statistics, data for 1961 and 1967 studies of characteristics of AFDC recipients.

n.a. = not available.

a. Based on fourth quarter figures.

b. Based on December figures.

c. No AFDC-U program.

In nine of nineteen states with AFDC-U there was a higher percentage of AFDC cases caused by desertion in December 1967 than there had been six years earlier. In ten such states there was a decrease. Reducing or removing the economic advantage of deserting effected no consistent change in patterns of family stability. While desertion as a cause for AFDC did decline in California by 9.6 percent between 1961 and 1967, it increased in New York by 12.5 percent. Rhode Island's 5.4 percent decline is matched by Connecticut's 3.5 percent increase, and Wisconsin's 6.9 percent decline by Delaware's 8.5 percent increase. Nor do patterns in the twenty-nine states without AFDC-U support the "breaking up homes" hypothesis. Desertion as a cause of dependency still declined in twenty-two of those states between 1961 and 1967, and increased in only seven states, including five in the South. There is no ready explanation for the increases in the South although the "intuitive judgment" of an HEW regional official is that less repressive relief administration in Georgia, for example, would have given deserted mothers easier access to AFDC in the later year and helps account for the 4.3 percent increase in that state compared, say, to the 6 percent decrease in North Carolina where, in the judgment of a state political expert, administration became comparatively more repressive.

Nationally there were no grounds to be more concerned with desertion as a cause of AFDC status at the end of the sixties than at the beginning. Changes in dependency rates caused by desertion in states with an AFDC-U component did not differ significantly from changes in other states. For whatever reason, however, while the absolute number of deserted families increased, they actually represented a slightly smaller percentage of the national regular AFDC caseload in 1967 than 1961: 19.2 percent against 19.6 percent. Fully 42.6 percent of the national net increase in AFDC between 1961 and 1967 could be attributed to never-married women, but only 18 percent to deserted wives.[14]

It is possible to localize a major fraction of that 18.2 percent, and doing so further weakens the claim that men desert in order to qualify their needy families for relief. New York City alone accounted for 62.6 percent of the national net increase in deserted AFDC wives. In 1967

14. Report of Findings of Special Review of Aid to Families with Dependent Children in New York City, transmitted to the House Committee on Ways and Means by the U.S. Department of Health, Education, and Welfare and the New York State Department of Social Services, Sept. 24, 1969, 91 Cong. 1 sess. (1969), p. 29.

in the United States there were 65,000 more deserted AFDC wives than in 1961; in New York City, 40,717 more. The city accounted for 10.8 percent of the total 1967 national AFDC load—and for 22.4 percent of the national total of deserted wives.[15] New York, however, was one of the first states to adopt an AFDC-U program. Public assistance in New York City also includes a general assistance program that provides home relief for unemployed or underemployed family heads. There is probably less incentive for an otherwise stable family unit to be deserted by its unemployed or underemployed father in New York City than anywhere else in the United States. Yet the desertion figures show this appreciably steeper growth rate in New York than nationally.

Adding the New York City story to the desertion statistics in the AFDC-U states gives no grounds to conclude that there is any close tie between making a public relief program available to families with a father in the home and reducing the incidence of broken homes. In fact, Lawrence Podell's studies of families on welfare in New York City found that most separated families on the rolls were there before the time they reportedly separated.[16] Even New York's relatively high welfare benefits did not keep them together. Homes did not break up in order to qualify for welfare. Families could qualify in New York City without breaking up, but some other factors subsequently produced a high desertion rate. Presidential program proposals here seem to run well ahead of scientific knowledge. The case for universalizing relief benefits for intact families rests on equity, not on overcoming desertion and thereby giving millions "the joys of childhood," which cannot be very joyous—whether or not a father is present—on an average AFDC benefit of only $43 a month per recipient.

Migration

A month after President Nixon stated that widely varying payments among regions helped to draw millions into city slums, an HEW report

15. *Ibid.*

16. *Families on Welfare in New York City* (City University of New York, Center for Study of Urban Problems, n.d.), p. 4. Daniel P. Moynihan himself noted in 1967 that "there are not 5 cents worth of research findings" to sustain the argument that the availability of AFDC leads to family breakup. "The Crises in Welfare," *Position Papers for the Governor's Conference Commemorating the 100th Anniversary of the New York State Board of Social Welfare* [1967], p. 76.

to the House Ways and Means Committee seemed to make the same point:

These data indicate that AFDC migrants do move from States having low welfare payments to States having high welfare payments in larger numbers than would be expected from studying the national migration pattern. The AFDC migration percentages are disproportionate to the State's migration percentages in accordance with the amount of the State's welfare payment— the higher the payment, the higher the percent of welfare migrants exceeds the percent of State migrants.

The welfare migrant's destination tends to be a city that generally attracts more American migrants than other cities. In addition to whatever reasons are behind the move of all migrants, the welfare migrant has another—the amount of the welfare payment. For the poor the accessibility and size of public welfare assistance would seem to be too important for them to discount in case they need a "cushion" after moving from one State to another. These results do not prove that poor migrants move "just" for welfare benefits but that the amount of the payment may be one of the considerations in the decision to move.[17]

Examining the details of the state-by-state data on which the HEW findings were based suggests that "helped" is a key word in the Nixon statement. AFDC benefit levels explain more of the migration pattern of poor whites than of poor nonwhites. In the case of neither group, however, can AFDC benefits be shown to be the cause of migration. When the percent of white AFDC mothers born out of state is divided by the percent of persons in a relevant population group born out of state and the resulting ratios rank ordered, many industrial states containing America's large cities do cluster at the top of the rank order. For example, New York, Illinois, New Jersey, and Connecticut—all urbanized and high benefit states—rank first, second, third, and fourth among the ten states with a higher percentage of white persons on welfare who are migrants than the percentage of all white women between twenty-five and twenty-nine in the state who are migrants.[18] When the entire rank order of ratios is correlated with the rank order of state welfare payments, the correlation for white recipients is 0.549. There are some striking exceptions—both Rhode Island and Massachusetts, for example, are high benefit states that show surprisingly lower percentages of white welfare migrants than of all comparable white migrants in the respective states; again the low benefit state of Indiana ranks fifth, ten

17. *Report of Findings . . . in New York City*, pp. 36–37.
18. *Ibid.*, p. 76.

places above Michigan which is in the same geographical region and pays high benefits. But the data do not readily invite doubts that poor white migrants are more likely to move to high AFDC benefit industrial states than are comparable nonpoor white migrants. To say this is not to say that poor whites move to high benefit states in order to avail themselves of those benefits.

It is a good bet, though, that the President meant to refer especially to movement of southern blacks into northern big city slums. AFDC benefit standards explain less about the migration of poor nonwhites than of poor whites. Rank ordering the ratios of migrant nonwhite AFDC mothers to migrant nonwhite women age twenty-five to twenty-nine and correlating the ratios with the rank order of AFDC benefit standards yields only a 0.34 correlation.[19] The ten states with the highest ratios of migrant nonwhite AFDC mothers to migrant relevant nonwhite women do not include the urbanized industrial states of New York, Illinois, New Jersey, Pennsylvania, and Ohio, all of which are in the comparable top ten in the white group. The point is that there is not a more pronounced tendency for AFDC nonwhites to migrate to industrial states than for other nonwhites to do so. To the extent that the poor migrate to high benefit industrial states in greater proportions than do the nonpoor, the higher ratios are more likely to be produced by poor whites than by poor nonwhites. Thus there seems reason to doubt that benefit differences between low paying southern states and high paying northern states are themselves pulling millions of southern blacks into the slums of New York, Newark, Chicago, Philadelphia, or Detroit.

In the particular case of New York City, the HEW study sustains this doubt. Three-fourths of the city's AFDC mothers were born out of state, but only about 14 percent obtained assistance in New York City within twenty-three months of moving there. This 14 percent, as the report notes, represents the maximum number who could be said to have migrated with the calculated intent to seek higher welfare payments. "In spite of the coping problems facing the newly arrived migrant family, they appeared to be less likely to use public assistance than long-term migrant families."[20]

Urban places do have high in-migration both in general and by poten-

19. *Ibid.*, p. 36.
20. *Ibid.*, p. 39.

tial AFDC cases. A reasonable expectation is that the nonpoor who migrate to urban places and fail to accomplish their purpose will migrate out again. For the unsuccessful poor, however, whose families increase in size and who have neither jobs nor relatives to sustain them, a decent AFDC payment may be more attractive than migrating out. Under these circumstances, raising benefit levels in southern states—admirable as it may be from a humanitarian viewpoint—is not likely to keep poor blacks out of northern slums because the difference between benefit levels is less important than the benefit level in the state to which the poor migrate. Even equal benefits in Mississippi and Illinois are unlikely to make Mississippi as attractive as Illinois to blacks who have left Mississippi in search of greater freedom and opportunity.

Whatever the primary cause of southern black migration to the urban slums, the Census Bureau suggested in 1969 that it had slackened appreciably and that natural population increases rather than in-migration now account for most of the growth in big city black population. Had variations in AFDC payments been responsible for the migration, it was too late in 1969 to discourage it by narrowing those variations. But we are in no position to say that the variations were responsible in the first place.

Certification without Investigation

The Nixon proposal that assistance benefits be paid upon certification of income suggested an uncommon faith in the welfare client. Absence of an entirely persuasive explanation for persistently growing numbers of public assistance cases long sustained a popular suspicion that the fault is in the client—his motivation, his lack of ties to relatives, his ethics, his morals. Eligibility investigations with opportunities for subjective decisions regarding entry to the assistance rolls stem from that suspicion. Did the client migrate for the purpose of gaining welfare benefits in New York? If so, New York law for a time made that cause for temporary disqualification. Is there a relative who can be held responsible? That, too, would be cause for disqualification in numerous states. If the hurdles could be overcome, if the supplicant could satisfy conditions designed to show that he was not simply a ne'er-do-well, then acceptance became possible. In the meantime the client frequently dangled like a job applicant awaiting reference checks.

Some clients may have considered field investigations of eligibility to be reasonable, but no client or potential client could consider the eligibility investigation an effort to encourage applications. One of the troubles with the system was that it could make every applicant believe that he was being viewed with suspicion, that, until the contrary could be established, the applicant was presumed to be a cheat or a parasite. Yet how much that bothered applicants is unclear; data on client attitudes is not extensive. Joel Handler's studies in six Wisconsin counties found that clients, for the most part, report little feeling of bother or privacy invasion for questions about their own finances or about employment possibilities, but indicate more concern for queries about marriage plans and resources of relatives.[21] HEW's mail questionnaire sent to a national sample of AFDC mothers reported seven out of eight respondents of the opinion that the rules for getting welfare were either "very fair" (43.6 percent) or "somewhat fair" (40 percent), but the questionnaire did not cover attitudes to eligibility investigations pursuant to the rules.[22]

While a change in eligibility-determination procedures from field investigation to client self-certification has been discussed for a long time, it has been extremely difficult to get a reading on the benefits and costs of self-certification. Reform directed to that purpose was a major component of the administrative reorganization effected in HEW in 1967 by John Gardner.[23] Creation of the Assistance Payments Administration (APA) to handle money payments only, as distinct from services, was regarded as a necessary first step to a system whereby cash relief could be paid on the basis of a client's declaration of need. Stephen Simonds, appointed first chief of APA, had administered a system of eligibility by declaration as Maine's public welfare director; his appointment symbolized high-level HEW interest in achieving a declaration system universally. Moving ahead required the right combination of political conditions: an administrative leader concerned about the rehabilitation of public assistance policy and who believed in the declaration as a way of accomplishing that rehabilitation, sufficient strength to carry the decla-

---

21. Joel F. Handler and Ellen Jane Hollingsworth, "How Obnoxious is the 'Obnoxious Means Test'? The Views of AFDC Recipients," *Discussion Papers of the University of Wisconsin Institute for Research on Poverty* (January 1969), p. 19.

22. U.S. Department of Health, Education, and Welfare, Social and Rehabilitation Service, National Center for Social Statistics, *1967 AFDC Study, Preliminary Report of Findings from Mail Questionnaire*, NCSS Report AFDC-2 (67), (1968), p. 14.

23. The reorganization is discussed at pages 106–10, below.

ration idea with the President, a President indifferent to the political consequences of seeming to be "soft on welfare," and some way of immunizing the change against adverse congressional reaction.

This happy union of circumstances first occurred between the election of November 5, 1968, and President Nixon's inauguration on January 20, 1969, and Wilbur Cohen, then secretary of health, education, and welfare, made use of it. In those last several months in office, Cohen gave out lots of advice to his successors, including recommendations for an overhaul of the welfare system and specific proposals and regulations to improve it. Mandatory use of a declaration system was one of the most important of Cohen's lame duck regulations designed to implement his conviction that, "Today there is a growing recognition of the legal right to the receipt of public assistance, a legal right to insist that it be fairly designed and fairly administered—and a legal right to invoke the Constitution to assure the fairness of the system. What lies ahead is the task of applying these rights, point by point, so that the poor may come to stand truly equal before the law."[24]

Cohen's view of the timing of the declaration regulation was that it was not a politically easy change to make and that incoming Secretary Robert Finch would welcome having it already on the books. Actually, Finch chose to share responsibility. When the declaration method was announced in November, Finch concurred. In addition to doing Finch a favor, Cohen was also belatedly fulfilling a promise made six months earlier to the Poor People's Campaign that HEW would require states to develop a declaration system. In a letter to the Reverend Ralph Abernathy on May 25, 1968, Cohen wrote:

We will require that, effective July 1, 1968, every State must begin to develop a simple declaration of facts for the establishment of eligibility for assistance. This will include the necessary review and simplification of policies and procedures, drafting and testing of forms and instructions, developing a system for validation of a small sample of declarations, and appropriate reassignment of staff, toward the end that the system will be in operation by July 1, 1969. There may be difficulty in using a declaration system where complicated eligibility conditions are not eliminated. To the extent that these difficulties relate to Federal requirements we will move toward simplification of these requirements. To the extent that they relate to State requirements other means will have to be found.[25]

24. *Annual Report of the Department of Health, Education, and Welfare, Fiscal Year 1968: Secretary's Introduction,* p. 66.

25. The Cohen letter incorporated detailed responses to demands made on the Department of Health, Education, and Welfare by the Poor People's Campaign. The quoted section is an attachment labeled "Welfare," p. 3.

Later, however, the Assistance Payments Administration explained that the declaration method was not designed just to "appease" the Poor People's Campaign. In its analysis of responses to the proposed declaration, APA recorded the history of tireless tinkering in this area:

Departments' [sic] efforts toward accepting the applicant as the chief source of information (which is the principle expressed in the method) started with a policy issuance in 1940. Change is very slow and over the years this has involved some six or seven such issuances. The formal experiments date back to 1962 with redeterminations of eligibility that must be completed yearly. Later other experiments took place and we were sure of our directions for change when the Poor People marched on Washington. We were able by that time to substantiate this method as providing improvements in the system and as adding a "humane" process to the system. The Poor People sought the latter.[26]

The political situation did not permit the culmination of this asserted twenty-eight years of effort to occur by the September 1, 1968, date demanded in lieu of July 1, 1969, by Dr. Abernathy's reply to Cohen. "Dignity and justice require no less," wrote Abernathy in insisting on the earlier implementation date.[27] Whatever dignity and justice may require, political conventions and campaigns discouraged the issuance of controversial policy decisions thought to have appeal only to voters already safely in the Democratic camp. Once the election was lost, however, Cohen felt liberated. The White House had to be consulted only in a perfunctory way, the candidate could not be embarrassed, the cause of progress could be served. Exactly two weeks after the election, regulations—in the form of proposals—were first issued in the *Federal Register*. They required use of the declaration method in determining eligibility for financial and medical assistance programs beginning July 1, 1969.[28]

Political and popular reaction to the proposed declaration was not extensive but what there was was almost unanimously opposed. One hundred ninety of the 192 "man-of-the-street letters" received by HEW were against it. While state welfare agencies were more favorably inclined, with opposition to the principle coming from only 5 of the 38 state agencies commenting, unreserved endorsement came from only 8

26. "Questions (and Answers) Reflected from Respondents," in "Analysis of Letters in Response to the Notice of Proposed Rule Making Entitled 'Determination of Eligibility—Public Assistance Program'" (n.d.; processed), pp. 1 ff.

27. "Poor People's Campaign Answer to Response of the Department of Health, Education, and Welfare" (June 12, 1968; processed), p. 6.

28. *Federal Register*, Nov. 20, 1968, p. 17189.

states, all then using a declaration system in at least part of their programs. An additional 14 responses stated or implied support for the principle, although registering other objections, including objections from 12 states to the starting date and from 7 states to the mandatory rather than optional nature of the regulation. As it developed, just before July 1, 1969—the date on which the system "will be in operation" according to Cohen's assurances to Abernathy—33 states were trying the simplified method in some fashion, but in the great majority, only on a very limited basis. Just a handful of states used the simplified method in all categories statewide.

Final regulations, issued a few days after President Nixon's inauguration, included changes reflecting both the concern of the general public that a declaration would encourage cheating and the states' expressed desire for more time. Most of the sections added were precautions to insure that the simplified declaration method would not facilitate that continuing bugaboo of the middle class—welfare cheating. The simplified form must specify conspicuously the penalty for fraud; where fraud is suspected or found, notice must be made to the proper law enforcement official; recipients are required to make "timely and accurate reports of any change in circumstances." If a state makes more than 3 percent incorrect decisions on eligibility, the state agency must make a 100 percent, independent verification of those specific factors of eligibility identified as causing the errors.[29] Even the name was changed from declaration to "simplified method" because, one APA official said, "of all the flak we got from our dear public." Progress reports to HEW and state evaluation panels were mandated; an HEW national evaluation committee would review the whole system and make recommendations to the secretary. Before all these elaborate evaluation procedures could be implemented, the President's welfare reform message embraced certification as if well tested and found to have a positive benefit-cost ratio.

The history of the time schedule is of particular interest. States were at first to be required to use a "simplified method" of determining eligibility only in selected test areas beginning July 1, 1969. A schedule of dates (October 1, 1969, for old age assistance [OAA]; January 1, 1970, for aid to the blind [AB] and to the permanently and totally disabled [APTD]; and April 1, 1970, for AFDC) was specified when the simplified method could become mandatory in the various categories if the

29. *Federal Register*, Jan. 24, 1969, p. 1146.

secretary found the results of testing warranted implementation. That schedule was later abandoned: the earliest effective date for implementation in OAA was delayed to January 1, 1970, and for AFDC to July 1, 1970. On May 15, 1970, just twenty states were using the simplified method in their adult programs on a statewide basis; on that same date an HEW news release was vague about the status of the simplified method in AFDC: "Testing of the method in the AFDC program continues in a number of States; reports are in the process of being collected and analyzed by the Federal agency." Yet in August 1969 President Nixon committed himself to a certification system when actual field experimentation with the method in the AFDC category was barely under way.

The idea of accepting applicants on their own declaration with subsequent spot checks in the style of income tax administration is worth careful attention—and so are its consequences. If there is no difference in the net effect on the Treasury of losing tax money that legally should be paid in and losing public money that legally should not be paid out, there appears to be a difference in popular attitudes toward the petty tax cheat whose peccadillo is smiled away and toward the small-scale individual welfare cheat whose act is regarded as thievery. To institute a procedure that would appear to increase the possibilities for such thievery could invite complaints from congressional critics and from legitimate clients themselves. A declaration system can also open the door to unknown cost consequences since it would certainly remove no one from relief rolls and would equally certainly add some indeterminate number of eligible persons previously unwilling to subject themselves to investigation. Preliminary field experimentation before making a national commitment was the appropriate way to tie down answers to these unknowns.

In hurrying up the introduction of the system, political factors also encouraged sidestepping the question of whether there had been sufficient demonstrations or experience with the simplified method to know the answers to another kind of question: What problems develop when the welfare client is confronted with a form for self-completion? Are some clients intimidated by the form itself? Where do they go for help? Should help be offered through the public welfare agency itself or does that wash out the separation idea? Can intercessor groups of organized clients be helpful? Evidence cited to buttress the case for the declaration is based on the reported experience of the states using it, but when the regulation was issued in January 1969 only Maine, Utah, and Iowa were using the declaration in AFDC. Those three states account for less than 2 percent of the national AFDC family caseload. In-depth studies or demonstrations with careful evaluation procedures were simply not at hand. Evaluation of the system and consideration of possible, unanticipated consequences were almost nonexistent. The secretary of HEW did not get around to appointing a National Evaluation Committee on the Simplified Method of Determining Eligibility in Public Assistance until May 1970. The declaration system may be foolproof, humane, economical, and trouble free, but it is hard to see how the President and his advisers could have known that in August 1969.

Movers, Doers, and Footdraggers

Why some policy issues rise to top level attention and others remain submerged evades a precise answer. Among some post hoc explanations in the field of social policy, the timing of social security is thought to be related to President Roosevelt's anxiety about the demagogic potential of Huey Long. John Kennedy's campaign trips through West Virginia and Michael Harrington's book, *The Other America*, are often said to be the critical determinants of the war on poverty. Civil rights issues surfaced because a considerable number of Negroes were willing to sacrifice their technical freedom and jeopardize their lives for the purpose.

Unable to command much interest from the public or from political leaders for three decades, radical welfare reform rose in 1969 to become the first major domestic proposal by a new Republican President. There was no sudden new crisis in welfare. The welfare recipients' National Welfare Rights Organization was still without power and influence sufficient to constitute an important political bloc. The Poor People's Campaign of 1968 had collapsed. No Democratic leader had taken up the cause of welfare reform. The narrower question of food relief seemed a more likely subject for action.

A reasonable if imprecise explanation of the importance of welfare reform beginning in 1969 is that from a problem that earlier chiefly concerned social work professionals, growth of the welfare system and public assistance policy came to attract the attention of previously uninvolved influential groups: academic experts, particularly economists, who assembled data and offered plausible alternatives to the status quo; business leaders who, once content to let chamber of commerce secretaries automatically adopt a hard line about "welfare cheats," for the first time personally studied welfare policy and belatedly discovered its inadequacies; most important, men close to the new President who took up the welfare issue, urged its importance, and themselves had enough expertise to answer challenges to their proposals. Two other new elements influenced the details but not the direction of proposed change: judicial interpretation of equal protection was expanded by important Supreme Court rulings in 1968 and early 1969 to limit some previous exclusions from assistance coverage;[30] finally, an old welfare hand served as secretary of HEW during President Johnson's lame duck period and ordered some procedural changes that his successor had to confirm, modify, or vacate.[31]

In sum, welfare change had a higher place on the Nixon policy agenda than on that of previous presidents because the President chose important supporters and staff aides who were interested in it, because both the Supreme Court and the Department of Health, Education, and Welfare were staking out new approaches as the administration changed, and because there had been enough theoretical work done in the income maintenance field to make it possible to formulate specific proposals. All of this activity, however, did not add up to a single, agreed program. Proponents of change were uncertain or in disagreement about the most desirable specific alternative to the federal-state system. They did agree on diminished state and increased federal financing, power, and responsibility to accomplish greater uniformity, improved benefits, and wider coverage.

The Intramural Dispute

In May 1968, shortly before the Poor People's March, 5 eminent American economists circulated to 275 universities and research organi-

30. The decision in Shapiro v. Thompson, 394 U.S. 618 (1969), striking down the provisions of the Social Security Act that authorized limited residency requirements for public assistance eligibility, did not come until April 21, 1969, when planning for welfare change was well under way.

31. In the 75 days after the 1968 election and before President Nixon's inauguration, Cohen issued regulations on the simplified method of determining eligibility; issued other new regulations requiring states to continue assistance to a recipient seeking a fair hearing and to provide him with legal services for the process if he wants them; authorized federal matching funds of 75 percent of costs to states that would provide welfare clients with legal help in such matters as divorce, landlord-tenant disputes, and debt garnishment; and (on his last full day in office) approved final day care requirements, pending since Sept. 23, 1968.

zations a statement urging the Congress "to adopt this year a national system of income guarantees and supplements." The statement was ultimately subscribed to by about 1,200 economists, who offered it as a "professional opinion that income guarantees and supplements are feasible and compatible with our economic system."[32] It was a statement drafted with deliberate built-in ambiguities to accommodate the evident divisions between those intellectuals who believe the proper way to guaranteed income is one that makes the income tax symmetrical by providing a cash benefit to persons whose net incomes fall short of a minimum appropriate to their family size (the negative income tax), those who argue the superior merits of making payments of federal money to all children but recouping from the nonpoor by adjusting income tax rates (children's or family allowances), and those who are content to reshape the public assistance system to meet the income guarantee objective. With the circulation and publication of this statement, economists and tax experts replaced social work professionals as the principal theoreticians of public relief policy. And it is worth noting that even if the statement had narrowed in on the negative income tax alone, few signers would have been lost because that is surely the income guarantee technique that has had the greatest appeal to those professional economists who sensibly enough believe in money as a specific for need.

By the time of the 1968 election campaign, America's academics had established income assistance through some hitherto unconventional means as a realistic alternative to the existing public assistance system. The University of Wisconsin's Institute for Research on Poverty was embarked on a negative income tax experiment, the most ambitious socioeconomic experiment ever undertaken in America without a base in legislation or executive order. With funds provided by the Office of Economic Opportunity, the institute undertook to administer a carefully designed system of payments to a sample group of low income families in New Jersey and to observe their behavior. The experiment was expected to furnish evidence on the effects of large amounts of income redistribution on decisions regarding work versus leisure, spend-

32. "A Statement by Economists on Income Guarantees and Supplements" (n.d.; processed). The originators were Professors J. K. Galbraith (Harvard); Paul Samuelson (MIT); Robert Lampman and Harold Watts (Wisconsin); and James Tobin (Yale). The activity was managed by Professor Matthew Edel (MIT).

ing versus saving, and personal development versus social withdrawal.[33] The experiment had an additional importance: undertaking it extended the income maintenance issue beyond the "shall we change the status quo?" question to that of "what would happen if we guaranteed income according to a specific plan?" To the astonishment of OEO officials, there was scarcely a murmur of protest in or out of Congress when the negative tax experiment became public information.

Long before the welfare reform debate reached the stage of presidential or of Ways and Means Committee consideration, the sometimes genteel, sometimes not-so-genteel academic consideration produced virtually unanimous academic support for change. By June 1968, when Congress's Joint Economic Committee held hearings on income maintenance programs, a succession of prominent economists and other students of welfare endorsed a national system that would relate assistance to family size, composition, and income; make payments to all the poor with incomes below a specified break-even level; and permit the assisted poor to retain a portion at least of any earnings. Adoption of these fundamental attributes of a negative income tax was urged, for example, by James Tobin, a member of the Kennedy Council of Economic Advisers and Sterling Professor of Economics at Yale; by Harold Watts, director of Wisconsin's Poverty Research Institute; and by Joseph Pechman, director of Economic Studies at the Brookings Institution.[34]

A children's allowance was a principal alternative offered to the negative tax plan. Its supporters thought of themselves as political realists playing upon a supposed American affection for children and upon successful experiences with children's allowances in other countries. Either at the Joint Economic Committee hearings or through other outlets, the strengths of children's allowances were detailed by, for example, Eveline Burns, the economist turned social work professor; Lisle

33. Harold Watts, "Graduated Work Incentives: Progress Toward an Experiment in Negative Taxation" (n.d.; processed). Watts, director of the Institute for Research on Poverty, acknowledges that the experiment "was given a large push from possible toward practical implementation by a proposal prepared by Miss Heather Ross for United Planning Organization of Washington." Miss Ross, at the time, was a doctoral candidate at MIT. See also David Elesh and others, "The New Jersey-Pennsylvania Experiment: A Field Study in Negative Taxation," *Discussion Papers of the University of Wisconsin Institute for Research on Poverty* (February 1970).

34. *Income Maintenance Programs*, Hearings before the Subcommittee on Fiscal Policy of the Joint Economic Committee, 90 Cong. 2 sess. (1968), Vol. 1, pp. 244, 108, 93.

Carter, who had served as John Gardner's assistant secretary in HEW and moved with Gardner to the Urban Coalition; Mitchell Ginsberg, New York City's highly regarded human resources administrator; and Daniel P. Moynihan, director of the Harvard-MIT Joint Center for Urban Studies.[35] A third road to reform was espoused by Wilbur Cohen, then secretary of HEW, who supported shoring up the basic public assistance apparatus through federalization as a more practical and more satisfactory alternative than either negative taxes or children's allowances.

It may be that one of the reasons that the negative tax idea took hold so well with economists and less well with sociologists, social workers, and others—even others who are concerned professionally with the problem of income maintenance—is that the concept of negative income taxation is not easily understood, and not easily communicated to non-professionals. This point was emphasized at a small private conference on income maintenance at the Brookings Institution in October 1968 attended by some leading American economists, welfare administrators, tax experts, and journalists.[36] An economist made the point:

One of the problems of the negative income tax which is perhaps surmountable but not easily so is that it is so complicated. If you say to somebody, "Why don't we have a negative income tax," the first thing he says is, "What is that." It is not a self-explanatory thing that is easy to explain after half an hour, as compared to, say, a children's allowance. That is pretty simple. You are going to pay something to people who have children because it helps them support the children.

In any event, enough activity was generated in the various reform camps—negative tax, children's allowance, federalization of public assistance—to give concern that the area of agreement among the experts would be obscured by their disagreement about alternatives. Stalemate could be the result. No reform proposal was a live White House or legislative issue in the last part of 1968, but one product of the debate already was a Tobin characterization of children's allowances as a pro-

35. *Ibid.*, pp. 2, 8, 347. See also pertinent articles by Burns, Carter, Harvey Brazer, and Mollie Orshansky in Eveline Burns (ed.), *Children's Allowances and the Economic Welfare of Children: The Report of a Conference* (Citizens' Committee for Children of New York, 1968); Alvin Schorr, "Against a Negative Income Tax," *Public Interest*, Vol. 2 (Fall 1966); and Moynihan's introduction to James Vadakin's *Children, Poverty, and Family Allowances* (Basic Books, 1968).

36. A 217-page verbatim record of the conference was kept for use of the participants, but the ground rules forbid quoting participants by name.

gram most of whose benefits "would go to families that do not need them." There is no justification, Tobin went on, "for waste of this magnitude. . . . Though the label is appealing, 'children's allowances' are not a promising way of providing the new system of income supplementation that America urgently needs."[37] Moynihan, on the other hand, found allowances "an ideal solution" while complaining that "the Negative Income Tax, and similar arrangements, would divide the nation between those who receive the benefit and those who pay for it," thus emphasizing racial and political divisiveness rather than national unity.[38]

Moynihan was not the only one to worry about divisiveness. As economists and tax lawyers realized that they filled a goodly portion of the negative income tax tent, they took special pains to point out that there was no war among the good guys. At the Brookings conference, one of them referred to the sharply different approaches as "not undercurrents" but "an intramural debate. It is an intramural debate. If they say we have got to agree on one horse . . . we will get together." In the public prints a comparable theme was played by Tobin. He played down the debate among reformers by arguing that agreement on the desirability of reform oriented to more complete coverage of need, more uniformity across the nation, and more desirable incentive effects is "more important right now than the details of different schemes, and certainly much more important than the names of different schemes. I hope no one will think that there are deep conflicts among 'income guarantees,' 'negative income taxes,' and 'family allowances.' "[39]

Renewed conflict among the experts was unexpectedly invited and promptly shut off a few months after the Nixon family assistance plan had been offered as the one horse on which to get together. Some of the most prominent children's allowance proponents did climb on the one horse. For example, Moynihan had been an important leader of the children's allowance school, but as part author of family assistance, he had a new posture. New York City's Mitchell Ginsberg, who had been named a member of the Nixon preinaugural Task Force on Public Welfare, tacitly agreed to the one-horse strategy even though he preferred children's allowances. In October 1969, however, Eveline Burns and

---

37. "Do We Want Children's Allowances?" *New Republic*, Vol. 157 (Nov. 25, 1967), p. 18.
38. "The Crises in Welfare," p. 75.
39. "A Rejoinder," *Public Interest*, Vol. 2 (Fall 1966), p. 118.

twelve others—including such prominent economists as Harvey Brazer of Michigan, Richard Lester of Princeton, and Kenneth Boulding of the University of Colorado—circulated a proposed statement urging consideration of "a system of children's allowances as a feasible income maintenance program for the United States."[40] It did not catch fire. Indeed, Tobin, who regarded it as exactly the wrong time to start up such a movement in view of the Nixon proposal, wrote Mrs. Burns to that effect, and so did others. Unlike disputes over fiscal and monetary policy, the ranks of the theoreticians in the income maintenance field held surprisingly firm. If welfare reform could not be accomplished, its loss could not be attributed to overt division and disagreement among expert social and economic advisers. While the reform-minded politicians broke ranks—Senator George McGovern proposed family allowances in January 1970—the dispute among the experts remained intramural.

A Blank Check from Business

The role of the business community in the evolution of the relief reform package proposed in 1969 was unplanned and unique: organized business spokesmen helped to spark the question but pussyfooted too long before moving from generalities to specifics; as a result, they provided the political people working on reform a blank check.

Involving business leaders in public assistance policy, like many other efforts to achieve domestic progress, was initiated by Governor Nelson Rockefeller. He agreed to use the centennial anniversary of the New York Board of Social Welfare in 1967 as an opportunity to assemble one hundred executives (principally industrial, but including a handful of labor, foundation, and mass media representatives) at Arden House—at the expense of twenty private philanthropies. A small group of public officials met for one day and one evening of discussion of national and state public welfare problems with this heretofore uninvolved group, officially described as persons "who have no responsibility for past programs and, therefore, no sentimental attachments to them." When the

40. Other signers of the "Dear Colleague" letter were Harold Barger, Peter B. Kenen, and Carl S. Shoup (Columbia); Joseph M. Becker, S.J., and Gerald F. Cavanagh, S.J. (Cambridge Center for Social Studies); Seymour E. Harris (University of California, San Diego); William E. Haber (University of Michigan); George F. Rohrlich (Temple); James C. Vadakin (Florida). Five months later, a list of 158 signers was released.

discussion of background papers (including Daniel P. Moynihan's "The Crises in Welfare," which proposed a children's allowance) and data was finished, Rockefeller further agreed to appoint a steering committee —composed of participants who were considered best informed—to synthesize and consider ways of implementing proposals churned up at the Arden House session. (Invitations to serve on the steering committee went to those businessmen who had provided the "best" written responses to the material distributed before the conference assembled. In some cases, they had assigned as many as nine of their staff members to work out the response.) The steering committee's charge was to produce specific recommendations; the timing and the disposition of any such recommendations were left open.

The committee's product was a unanimous report, published in April 1968, characterizing the public assistance system as demeaning, inefficient, inadequate, and with so many disincentives built in that it encouraged continued dependency:

It should be replaced with an income maintenance system, possibly a negative income tax, which would bring all 30-million Americans up to at least the official Federal poverty line. Such a system should contain strong incentives to work, try to contain regional cost of living differentials, and be administered by the Internal Revenue Service to provide greater administrative efficiency and effectiveness than now exists.[41]

The twelve authors of the statement—only one of whom offered any reservation or resistance to the statement before it was issued—could have been spokesmen for a random sample chosen from *Fortune's* list of America's five hundred biggest businesses. The group included the chairmen of the boards of Xerox, Metropolitan Life Insurance Company, Marine Midland Corporation, Mobil Oil Corporation, and Consolidated Cigar Corporation; the chairman of the executive committee of Inland Steel; the chairman of Urban Investment and Development Company of Chicago; the vice chairman of Ford Motor Company; the vice president for community affairs of Pepsico, Inc.; the chairman of the board of governors of the New York Stock Exchange, and a senior partner of the member firm of Adler, Coleman and Company; and the president of the Committee for Economic Development.

Despite their prestige, power, and undoubted influence, and despite the sense of urgency accompanying the findings, when the steering com-

41. *Report from the Steering Committee of the Arden House Conference on Public Welfare* (n.d.), p. 12.

mittee members reassembled almost a year after their report was issued, they found that the organized business community had done nothing more about reform of public assistance. While the committee's concerns with jobs, job training, and education got continuing attention from a successor group, the public assistance reform idea was neither explicitly abandoned nor further developed. In part this was inevitable because the steering committee had decided to deliver its burden to a new Commission on Income Maintenance (Heineman Commission) appointed by President Johnson in January 1968. That commission, which had not asked to become heir to the Arden House effort, projected two years of work and a report around the beginning of 1970.

More prompt follow-up seemed likely, however, from the Committee for Economic Development (CED), the nonpolitical, nonprofit, educational, and research group made up of the heads of American business institutions who—with academic and professional help—consider, develop, and publish public policy recommendations.[42] CED invited itself in by proposing to devote a May 1968 public policy forum to public welfare and asked the Arden House steering committee to allow its report to serve as the agenda. When the steering committee accepted the CED proposal, it also concluded that its responsibility might officially end with the submission of its report to the CED policy forum. Responsibility thereupon became uncertain as CED failed to find a ready niche for review of public assistance reform, which fell between the cracks of its several subcommittees working on urban poverty, education, and metropolitan government.

Analyses, studies, public awareness, experimentation, and demonstration are to be expected, the Arden House steering committee acknowledged in April 1968. It urged that these not be used as excuses for inaction, that steps be taken as quickly as possible to implement reform suggestions. Surprisingly, the subsequent period saw considerable inaction from the business community itself. What happened is that organized business leaders asserted an interest and thereby an intention to participate but did not make a concerted intellectual or political effort to do so. The steering committee—an ad hoc group—turned the subject over to CED, which then failed to follow through as had been ex-

42. Karl Schriftgiesser, *Business Comes of Age: The Story of the Committee for Economic Development and Its Impact upon the Economic Policies of the U.S. 1942–1960* (Harper, 1960), and *Business and Public Policy: The Role of the Committee for Economic Development: 1942–1967* (Prentice-Hall, 1967).

pected. The CED policy forum convened in May 1968 with some two hundred businessmen, educators, and community leaders from across the country in attendance. Opening presentations were made by Xerox's Joseph C. Wilson, who had been chairman of the Arden House steering committee; Harvard's Moynihan; New York City's Mitchell Ginsberg; Marion Folsom, former HEW secretary and former treasurer of Eastman Kodak; and Ralph Lazarus, chairman of Federated Department Stores and chairman of the CED forum. Participants were thereafter assigned to ten workshops, each chaired by a leader of the business community and CED trustee. According to the CED *Bulletin*:

> Agreement among the participants was unanimous that the present welfare system needs a major overhaul, but opinion was divided on the issue of income maintenance, especially on what form such a system should take. Most felt that substantially more research and experimentation would be needed before a reasonable judgment of the problem could be made.[43]

Despite the presence of no less than thirty-seven CED trustees at the policy forum, despite the sense of urgency suggested by the Arden House report, despite its plea that studies and experimentation not be used as further justification for inaction, and despite the fusing of Arden House–CED activity, nothing moved. More than a full year after the Arden House report concluded that "public assistance does not work well . . . is demeaning, inefficient, inadequate . . . should be replaced with an income maintenance system," business leaders had no specific reform proposals. CED seems to have evaded the issue. Although Joseph C. Wilson had talked at the policy forum of the desirability of uniform national standards for assistance and of establishing welfare as a matter of right and need unaccompanied by "the degrading means test," CED had not been heard from on these basic questions by August 1969. It had not been heard from on the lesser questions either.

Depending on which CED functionary is discussing the question, one may learn that CED had "exercised its remarkable capacity for diffusion" or that "it would be a misreading of the situation to conclude that the sense of urgency imparted by the Arden House group [was] no longer felt. . . . It would be safer to say that it ha[d] become institutionalized!" Both comments can be translated to mean that CED leaders were troubled but that they foresaw resistance among some of the two hundred CED trustees to radical policy change.

43. *Bulletin*, Vol. 3, No. 1 (May 1968), p. 3.

It is nowhere discussed in the formal histories of the CED, but its leaders and its staff are alert to the importance of gradualism and of extensive discussion based on acceptable factual data in the education of CED members. A guaranteed income for the nonworking poor may have been too stiff a dose to contemplate in CED's introduction to the field. The probability was that there would be both dissent and agreement. If, however, the issue came through the back door trailing along after work-related questions like training the unemployed (a safe area), and upgrading the condition of the employed poor (another safe area), CED's members might then be more ready for the shock of guaranteed income as a possible public policy direction.

Accordingly, a CED subcommittee on problems of urban poverty, organized around the time of the Arden House meeting, became the apparent chosen instrument for development of a policy position in the welfare field. That subcommittee then decided first to undertake a study of how to identify, train, and employ the unemployed poor and how to improve the productivity and earnings of the employed poor. Recognizing what is now widely known—that neither the employable nor the employed poor constitute the basic welfare problem—the subcommittee indicated that it proposed in a later study to look at the problem of the unemployable poor—dependent children, their caretakers, and the aged, blind, and disabled. That second study would be several years off.

By early 1969, CED's own leaders realized that it was about to be left at the gate in a major race. The Arden House steering committee had reassembled to consider a continuing role; the National Industrial Conference Board held a welfare forum where Ben Heineman foreshadowed the report of the Commission on Income Maintenance with a speech favoring "cash income to all the poor," including wage supplements; New York City's Citizens' Budget Committee, largely a business group, announced for national standards in welfare. Belatedly, CED's program committee, in April 1969, proposed that CED's research and policy committee consider creation of a special subcommittee on public welfare problems.

The shilly-shallying (or "diffusion" or "institutionalization") by CED is important because its welfare studies did start with the advantage of the prior Arden House meeting, and because CED is recognized as representing responsible and enlightened business participation in public policy making. CED's conduct of its policy forum, and the constructive contributions of its trustees in attendance, created an impression of purpose to pursue the issues with all vigor. Both the policy pronounce-ments and programs of study of CED are decided formally by its re-search and policy committee, however, and active measures were very slow in taking shape, to put the matter mildly. CED did make a quasi commitment, when it seemed willing to volunteer in taking over for an ad hoc group that had emphasized the urgency of the problem involved. Having done so, it should have taken some continuing activity leading to specific and detailed policy proposals as the appropriate next step, but it did not.

Yet it would be a mistake to conclude that the Arden House–CED concern evaporated or that the resulting nonpolicy did not serve a posi-tive function. CED did come down squarely in support of the proposi-tion that welfare is a serious problem, and the Arden House group did assert business's support for change. The public and private statements of concern and of interest in reform, coupled with failure to offer a specific policy proposal, made it possible for the President's men to pursue welfare reform with some confidence that there would be busi-ness support for the product and that no particular business-sponsored proposal had to be taken into account in the planning process. When what became the family assistance plan was in the drafting stage, the White House politely invited comment from CED leaders. They bought family assistance. The same week the House of Representatives passed the family assistance bill, a CED crash program at last produced a welfare policy statement.

A Presidential Issue

The Kennedy-Johnson public assistance legacy to the new Repub-lican President was a services approach that had failed, a work and train-ing approach that could not get off the ground, an asserted interest in day care but no viable day care program, a reorganization of the welfare apparatus in HEW, some procedural changes mandated in the lame duck period, and a steadily increasing number of AFDC recipients.

In the last analysis, welfare reform became a presidential issue in the first months of the Nixon administration because the President kept his mind open on the subject while presidential appointees in critical loca-tions who were determined on welfare reform brought enough back-ground knowledge and interest with them and found enough prior activity within the bureaucracy to make the objective manageable. Pub-

lic relief was first accorded formal recognition as a major issue by the
new administration when it created a preinaugural task force on the
subject. Subsequently, officials at very high levels in and out of the
newly created Urban Affairs Council devoted substantial amounts of
time to it during their first months in office. What seemed at first to be
a manageable subject turned out to be a complicated one, but a necessary critical mass of strategically placed, high-level administration figures—the President's men—stayed interested in the welfare planning
process: the secretary of health, education, and welfare, who had become
aware of welfare issues as lieutenant-governor of California; the secretary
of agriculture, who inherited troubles over hunger and malnutrition; the
assistant to the President for urban affairs; the vice president, who had
worried over welfare issues as governor of Maryland; and the assistant
director for human resources of the Bureau of the Budget, who had been
chairman of the President-elect's Task Force on Public Welfare.

PRE-NIXON ACTIVITY AT HEW

Within the federal administrative apparatus, the groundwork for
separating income maintenance from social services had been laid by
John Gardner's 1967 reorganization of the welfare side of the department. Every new secretary of health, education, and welfare faces a
choice at the outset: he can concentrate on gaining control of his
sprawling department through administrative and organizational changes
or he can delay or forsake such changes while concentrating on high
policy for presidential consideration. Secretary Robert Finch made the
latter choice in the welfare field, but he would have met more resistance
in the department had John Gardner not shaken things up during his
tenure as secretary and prepared the way for an emphasis on money in
relief.

After Robert McNamara took hold of the affairs of the Department
of Defense and imposed a theretofore unknown control over that department's constituent units, the Department of Health, Education, and
Welfare quickly came to be known as the most ungovernable, unman-
ageable federal department. There was cause for the characterization.
Each of the three components of HEW had its own constituency outside the federal administrative structure, and each of the external constituencies was potent. Lavish funding and other kinds of sympathetic
support for the National Institutes of Health, for example, appeared to
be beyond the control of the HEW leadership; in education, state and

local educational groups were too well entrenched to yield gracefully to innovative proposals from the top. In welfare, no organized client groups were significant before 1967; in the absence of competition from any other source, organized groups of social workers dominated policy proposals offered to the President and Congress.[44] Although the HEW budget was large, formula grants and payments beyond the control of the secretary accounted for the great bulk of it. Free money to support innovative programs and creative people to develop them had been problems for the five secretaries who preceded Gardner between the time the department was created in 1953 and 1965. Two of them at least—Marion Folsom (1955–58) and Arthur Flemming (1958–60)—knew it, and their advice to Gardner turned to the importance of control over budget, legislation, and personnel occupying key positions.

When Gardner became HEW secretary, he was close to being a universally admired man. Nominally a Republican, his appointment by a Democratic President was well received in both parties. It was also well received by professionals, perhaps because, unlike all of his predecessors save Flemming who had been a college president, Gardner came from a post—president of the Carnegie Corporation—related professionally to part of the HEW job. As secretary, one of his major efforts was to effect a series of departmental reorganizations designed to improve the control of the secretary over HEW affairs.

It took almost two years for the reorganization of the welfare side to be accomplished. Its principal feature was the fusing of the Welfare Administration, the Vocational Rehabilitation Administration, and the Administration on Aging into the new Social and Rehabilitation Service (SRS) headed by Mary Switzer, theretofore vocational rehabilitation commissioner. The particular timing of the reorganization—August 1967—is primarily attributable to Commissioner of Welfare Ellen Winston's retirement earlier that year. Mrs. Winston had headed the Welfare Administration since 1963, a year after it was created specifically to emphasize the psychosocial services approach adopted by the Kennedy administration and its HEW secretary, Abraham Ribicoff. Gardner's plan was for creation of SRS to shake up the welfare apparatus, permit new administrative leadership, and lead to innovative policy proposals. But reorganization before Mrs. Winston's retirement would

44. Steiner, Social Insecurity, pp. 142–47, 169–75; Eveline Burns, "The Future Course of Public Welfare," Position Papers for the Governor's Conference, p. 31; Moynihan, "The Crises in Welfare," p. 66.

have implied dissatisfaction with her firm support of a sympathetic attitude to welfare, an implication that Gardner wished to avoid. "Secretary Gardner concentrated on different things at different periods," one of his assistant secretaries explained, "and the timing of SRS resulted from interaction of concentration on reorganization and the end of Ellen Winston's service. But it was more a result of the Winston retirement than it was the result of any earlier conclusion that the plan was not ready. The Secretary did not want to disavow Ellen, but he did want innovation."

Like previous secretaries, Gardner was held at a distance by the welfare bureaucracy and, rather than fighting his way through, turned away, not giving welfare issues the amounts of time and attention given to health and education. This barrier between the secretary and his immediate staff, on the one side, and the social work–oriented Welfare Administration leadership, on the other side, meant that the Social and Rehabilitation Service, which swallowed up the Welfare Administration, was born in confusion and resentment. Some of the confusion was probably beyond the secretary's control. For example, in the early stages of the SRS plan, provision was made for a Community Services Administration (CSA) to parallel organizationally the Assistance Payments Administration. Welfare people down the line believed that the CSA was to be the repository of the social service activities to which they had been giving so much emphasis. But the CSA was actually planned as a home for poverty program spin-offs then being contemplated in the White House. President Johnson decided not to proceed with transfers from OEO at that time and the CSA was erased by reorganization planners. For Welfare Administration officials, however, the tentative inclusion and then exclusion of the CSA seemed to be a deliberate decision to deemphasize services. And while welfare personnel then let themselves be thrown into confusion and disorder, no effort was made by the new leadership of SRS, which came from the vocational rehabilitation side rather than from the social work side, to define the role of old welfare hands.

Just how the reorganization really was meant to affect the relationship between money payments and services was a subject on which there did not seem to be total agreement even within the office of the secretary. Reorganization did create an Assistance Payments Administration to oversee the cash payments side of public assistance, and it parceled out responsibility for services in OAA, AFDC, AB, and APTD among the

Administration on Aging, the Children's Bureau, and the Rehabilitation Services Administration. All of them were folded under the SRS tent. Gardner, in explaining the reorganization to the field staffs, talked of separating cash and service programs and cited the "growing consensus that these quite different functions should be performed by different people."[45] But at almost the same time, Under Secretary Wilbur Cohen seemed to be explaining things differently: "The new reorganization reflects the recognition of the necessity of a unified approach to the problems of needy Americans by combining income support and social service and rehabilitation programs that many families need."[46]

The differences between the Gardner separation explanation and the Cohen unity explanation mirror the differences between two sets of recommendations that had been under consideration for a year before the SRS was created. One came from the Advisory Council on Public Welfare, last hurrah of the social welfare professionals who had long dominated public assistance policy development. The advisory council— appointed by the secretary pursuant to statute—urged in its June 1966 report that public welfare programs be structured to provide ever more effective social services, medical assistance, and income maintenance under one roof.[47] Around the same time an unpublicized internal HEW task force report, never made public, made a strong case for separation of income maintenance and service functions, the latter to be run by a new social services administration free of the taint of income maintenance. That task force, chaired by James Dumpson, formerly New York City welfare commissioner, also registered strong opposition to special, separate mechanisms for delivering essentially similar family services, citing as illustrations of agencies that "can no longer be permitted to pursue their independent paths" the Children's Bureau, the Administration on Aging, and the Vocational Rehabilitation Administration.[48]

What came out in the reorganization, of course, was some of every-

45. Speech of John Gardner to HEW field staffs, *Congressional Record*, Vol. 113, Pt. 17, 90 Cong. 1 sess. (1967), p. 23069.
46. Speech of Wilbur Cohen to Sesquicentennial Conference of the University of Michigan School of Social Work, *Congressional Record*, Aug. 31, 1967, p. A4451.
47. U.S. Department of Health, Education, and Welfare, Welfare Administration, *Having the Power, We have the Duty*, Report of the Advisory Council on Public Welfare to the Secretary of Health, Education, and Welfare (June 29, 1966), p. 48.
48. U.S. Department of Health, Education, and Welfare, "Report of the Task Force on Social Services," Submitted to Assistant Secretary Lisle Carter (Sept. 1, 1966; processed), p. 19.

thing, so that there was plenty of room for differing explanations of just what was being done. Income maintenance and services were separated as the Dumpson group urged, but they were left under the same roof, the advisory council's preference; special, separate mechanisms for delivering services were retained, contrary to the Dumpson proposal, but they were made part of a single service, responsible to a common administrator. The message was muddy. Was it sharp separation of money and services? Was it an end to "independent paths" for the several service bureaus? Was it a unified approach to the problems of the needy?

Probably the most accurate way of interpreting the creation of the SRS is to set aside the business of separating or unifying things, and, instead, to view the reorganization as a message from the secretary that change was demanded. Then, the nature of change could be expected to be reflected in the style of the new leadership. Nothing happens, in short, because boxes are shifted around on an organization chart, but something may happen because a decision to shift them was made and because the shifts may produce a new boss. Creating SRS was a signal to the welfare bureaucracy that the old order that made relief conditional on accepting services would not do. Shortly after the reorganization, Gardner left. Then there was a foreign war being fought and policy innovation in public assistance was not on President Johnson's list of things to accomplish before leaving office. When a careful Nixon task force report with which Secretary Finch agreed put it on President Nixon's list, however, the psychosocial services emphasis had already been downgraded at HEW in favor of program planning that emphasized money and jobs, where possible.

THE NIXON WELFARE TASK FORCE

The report of the preinaugural Task Force on Public Welfare was the early point of departure for the Nixon concern with welfare policy. That report was especially attractive because in an administration that, in its early months at least, had little in the way of specific program to offer, it was specific; moreover, it emphasized how the new administration could quickly make its mark in an important field, and it seemed to offer a lot for a little money. The focus of the report was on quick pay-off and on further tinkering to make public assistance work: "We have focused," the opening paragraph stated, "upon the most critical near-

term issues and opportunities facing the new Administration."[49] The
near term issues turned out to be a combination of procedural changes
dealing with the eligibility declaration and with retention of client benefit rights during an appeals process that Wilbur Cohen had already
initiated after the election; repeal of the so-called freeze on federal
sharing of AFDC costs; and proposals for increasing federal fiscal responsibility and establishing minimum national standards.

In most major respects the Republican task force simply fleshed out
recommendations made to Secretary Gardner in June 1966 by the Advisory Council on Public Welfare.[50] The latter group, last in a line of
such councils dominated by the inventors of the public assistance system, had a clear view of its job: to tinker with the system, but to preserve it. The point is made squarely by Guy Justis, director of the
American Public Welfare Association (APWA), and a member of the
advisory council: "There was never any thought that public welfare
should be scrapped and that a new system of providing its essential services should be established." Nor were the council's recommendations
"new and revolutionary concepts, but rather . . . the last step in freeing
public welfare from the shackles of the English Poor Laws. . . ."[51] Two
years after the report had been filed, Ellen Winston, HEW's last welfare commissioner, told the congressional Joint Economic Committee
that the advisory council work was a "blueprint for immediate reform."[52] But little of the blueprint had found its way into the Johnson
administration's welfare proposals in 1967, and the eventual legislation
of that year was widely regarded as a welfare disaster.

An accurate assessment of the reception of the advisory council report has been made by Leonard Lesser, the council's "labor" representative: "Nobody except a few scholars paid any attention to it after its
announcement." Council members believed this neglect to be due not

49. The task force produced a wide-ranging, 48-page report. It covered immediate
issues involving public assistance and related income support programs "as well as
the opportunity facing the Nixon Administration to initiate basic reforms of these
programs." It has not been made public, but at one point a copy was on the
"reserve" list of the Yale Law Library. The copy on which this discussion is based
was not provided by any member of the task force.

50. *Having the Power, We have the Duty.*

51. "A Message from the Director," *Public Welfare*, Vol. 24 (October 1966),
p. 266.

52. *Income Maintenance Programs*, Hearings, Vol. 1, p. 280.

to any deficiencies or fuzziness in the report itself, but to other considerations, especially the cost of proposed program changes. Actually, the council report never dealt with how much money its program would require. While it is true that by early 1967, nonmilitary money was hard to come by, the failure to project dollar costs and to resolve such ambiguities as how to enforce a mandatory minimum state fiscal effort discouraged administration planners from using the report as a basis for legislative proposals. In addition, the council was silent on the failure of the 1962 amendments to reduce or restrain the growth of the public assistance rolls, and that silence was construed as endorsement of a policy that was unrealistic and could not be allowed to continue unamended.

The Nixon task force was only tenuously linked to the 1966 and earlier advisory councils that had been dominated by social welfare professionals, but its problem was defined in the same way as the 1966 council's: to rehabilitate the existing system, not to challenge its continuing validity. The signal contribution of the task force was to inject its idea of political reality and to estimate the costs of its major proposals in a manner that made them seem attainable. In approaches to the policy questions, however, there is striking overlap between the neglected public recommendations of the advisory council and the well-leaked, confidential task force recommendations, as the following comparison illustrates. Indeed, it was as if the task force decided to limit itself to public assistance proposals that had previous, respectable origins and had not been shot down as too radical:

1. Eligibility by Declaration

Advisory Council: "Applicants for aid would establish their initial eligibility by personal statements or simple inquiry relating to their financial situation and family composition, subject only to subsequent sample review conducted in such manner as to protect their dignity, privacy, and constitutional rights."

Nixon Task Force: "HEW has proposed the mandatory use of a declaratory (or simplified form) application with spot checks for Public Assistance in all states. . . . The use of a declaration yields substantial administrative savings through reduction of paperwork and use of lower-level staff for eligibility determination. It promises even greater savings through more effective use of professional staff to concentrate on providing services, including referrals for employment. The Task Force recommends implementation of the HEW regulation. . . ."

2. AFDC for the Unemployed (AFDC-U)

Advisory Council: "[AFDC-U] Should Be Made Permanent and Mandatory Upon the States, and Provision Made for Covering More of the Unemployed Than Many of the States Now Include."

Nixon Task Force: "The Task Force recommends legislation restoring broader eligibility for [AFDC-U] and mandating state participation."

3. Minimum Benefits in Public Assistance

Advisory Council: "The Advisory Council . . . Recommends a Minimum Standard for Public Assistance Payments Below Which No State May Fall."

Nixon Task Force: "The Task Force recommends . . . programs for increased federal responsibility for Public Assistance and the establishment of national minimum standards."

4. Financing Minimum Benefits

Advisory Council: "Under the Council's proposal, the Federal Government would: Specify national standards. . . . Specify each State's share of the costs of the comprehensive program under the national standards. . . . Assume full financial responsibility for the difference in cost between the State share and the total cost of the comprehensive program in each State."

Nixon Task Force: "Under alternative one, we propose increasing the minimum benefit for all beneficiaries of OASDI (including the over-72 group) to $70 a month; blanketing into Social Security all persons now receiving OAA, AB, and APTD, as well as all aged, blind, and disabled persons now not receiving other public benefits. . . . We recommend a federal requirement that no state could have a state-wide AFDC average budget lower than $40 per month per person . . . the Federal Government would pay 100% of the first $30 in payments and 50% of the next $40. . . .

"Alternative Two: Establishing Minimum Standards for All Public Assistance Recipients. . . . For OAA, assuming a minimum average budget of $65 and 100% federal reimbursement of the first $50 in payments plus 50% of the next $40. . . . For AB, assuming a minimum average budget of $90 and 100% federal reimbursement of the first $65 in payments, plus 50% of the next $40. . . . For APTD, same basis. . . . Adding in the AFDC [$40 per month minimum, 100% federal reimbursement of first $30, plus 50% of the next $40]. . . ."

These and other important similarities between the proposals of the 1966 advisory council, pending HEW procedural reforms, and recommendations of the Nixon task force are not simply coincidental nor are they the proposals that would inevitably issue from any group of right-minded people. While there was no overlapping membership, both advisory council and task force had the cooperation—and felt the influence—of Wilbur Cohen, who also issued the HEW procedural reforms. Two task force members—Wilbur Schmidt, Wisconsin's welfare director, and Mitchell Ginsberg, New York City's human resources administrator—predictably reflected informed professional judgments similar to those reflected in the advisory council by Fedele Fauri, its chairman, and Elizabeth Wickenden, a well-informed social policy specialist who, together with Wilbur Cohen, had long constituted a kind of inner club of public assistance specialists. The Nixon task force's young chairman, Richard P. Nathan, owed much of his basic public assistance education to discussions of the Fauri report in 1967 and 1968 with his colleagues of the Brookings Institution and in a Washington discussion group known as the Conference on the Public Service, and to service with the National Commission on Civil Disorders (the Kerner Commission).[53] Cohen cooperated in a kind of postgraduate cram course. In two months the task force distilled the essence of the advisory council's two years of activity and added consideration of the role of the Office of Economic Opportunity, the future of the community action program, of model cities, of the Job Corps, hunger, health, Indian poverty, black capitalism, rural poverty, and use of Vietnam veterans in programs of assistance for the poor. There was little time to strike out in new directions.

Determined to be realistic and to submit a report likely to be acceptable to what it guessed would be an unsympathetic audience, the task force estimated the costs of the minimum benefits proposal. In worrying about satisfying its sponsors, however, and in its anxiety to achieve a "realistic" and "near term" proposal, the task force went further in redistributing welfare money than in meeting clients' needs. Appointed for technical and professional expertise, the task force limited itself to what it perceived to be politically possible. As is often the case, it underestimated the politicians, a fact that became evident when the new secretary of HEW, Robert Finch, was briefed on the report and said, in effect, "Is that all?"

If guesses about what could be sustained politically were not to be

53. See *Report of the National Advisory Commission on Civil Disorders* (March 1, 1968). Nathan served as associate director for research.

allowed to control recommendations for change, Finch's was a reasonable question. Consider the proposal for a $40 floor under AFDC, the most important single recommendation in the task force report. While the task force posited the principle that "no individual would receive less than at present and no state would receive less federal support," it decided against a requirement for maintenance of existing state effort "in order to provide financial relief for the states and localities which are presently bearing the heaviest burdens." Thus federal money would have been added to existing state payments in the low paying states in order to get the minimum benefit up to $40—still below the then national average payment of $41.55—but in the states already paying at or above the national average, federal money would only have been substituted for state and local money. The task force could report that the "estimated increased federal cost of this proposal would be $903 million, offset by state and local savings of $361 million, for a net increase of $542 million." When it applied the same factors to the proposed $65 floor under old age assistance (existing average payment: $68.65), and the proposed $90 floor under AB and APTD (existing average payments: $90.90 and $81.55, respectively), and added the AFDC estimate, it arrived at "a net increase in federal expenditure for establishing a minimum public assistance standard and increasing federal reimbursement of $1,373 million, offset by $547 million in reduced state and local costs, for a net increase in costs of $826 million."

The task force's satisfaction with this seemingly big benefit for a small cost was clearly stated. "Heretofore," the report said, "consideration of basic reforms of the nation's troubled Public Assistance system has concentrated on broad and very costly proposals. We believe that a highly significant start can be made on Public Assistance reform at a cost which should permit some action in this area in the relatively near-term future, assuming continued economic growth and somewhat reduced defense spending." But it would not be a very significant start, and it was not much reform.

What the report did not say was that its proposed net increased public expenditures in AFDC of $542 million represented an increased public expenditure of less than $100 per year per recipient, or an average increased public expenditure of only $8 per month per recipient. Nor did the report say that none of that increase was mandated for people already being assisted at the level of $40 per month or $1,920 annually for a family of four.

The task force package was as much a relief package for the states, including some of the wealthier states, as it was a relief package for the welfare poor. Among the states paying well under a $40 average and therefore standing to benefit significantly by the proposed federal funding were Delaware, Indiana, Missouri, and Nevada, all among the twenty states with highest average per capita incomes. In the case of Delaware, for example, the average per recipient AFDC benefit was $32.50. Under the existing formula the federal share was $22 (five-sixths of the first $18, plus 50 percent of the balance to $32), the state share $10.50. The task force proposal would have increased the average benefit to the new $40 minimum, $35 of which would be federally assumed (all of the first $30 plus 50 percent of the balance to $70), leaving a $5 state share in lieu of the existing $10.50 state share.

While recipients in states paying less than $40 would have benefited, the absence of a provision for maintenance of state effort meant that there would be no necessary benefit increase for AFDC recipients in such states as New York, California, Illinois, Massachusetts, and Michigan. But the relief afforded the states themselves would have been substantial. For example, Illinois—a state then levying no income tax—paid an average benefit of $46.50; of the total, $24.50 was state money, $22 federal money. The proposed $40 average minimum would not have affected the benefit level, but the proposed new sharing formula would have resulted in an $8.25 state share to match a $38.25 federal share—or a 66 percent drop in state costs.

A superficial attraction of the minimum benefit recommendation was that 31 of 51 jurisdictions were paying below the $40 figure. Presumably, therefore, the benefit would be widespread. But those 31 jurisdictions accounted for less than half—2.6 million—of the then 5.7 million AFDC beneficiaries in the 50 states and the District of Columbia. Moreover, of those 2.6 million clients in states where the average payment was below $40, more than 800,000 were in states where the average benefit was within $2 of the proposed minimum so that the improvement for them would not be substantial. The net effect, then, would have been to assure a measurable level of benefit improvement for approximately 30 percent of the AFDC population, but to do nothing for either the remaining 70 percent or for the 12 to 13 million working poor.

"A CLASSIC CONFRONTATION"

It is not surprising that there was no sharp break with incrementalism reflected in the task force report. Neither welfare professionals nor journalists specializing in domestic social affairs nor many members of Congress believed in the likelihood of an early move to a guaranteed income. Fedele Fauri, dean of the University of Michigan School of Social Work, chairman of the 1966 Public Welfare Advisory Council, and an influence in public assistance policy making since 1950, wrote almost two years after the 1966 report that he believed it unlikely that any radical plan would soon be adopted and that the job to be done, therefore, was to improve the existing welfare system.[54] Just before the 1968 election, after six hours of discussion of the income maintenance issue at the Brookings conference of economists, other welfare specialists, and journalists, three of the latter accepted the role of political realist and individually assessed the prospects for achieving the income maintenance system espoused by the experts:

I agree that people familiar with it come back to negative income tax, but . . . as a Communicator, in all candor, and you can all scream at me about it, I have stayed away from this problem because it is so impossible to write about.

You stick me with formulas and variables and it is awful. The general reader cannot hang in there. He just cannot. Now something happened about Medicare that said it is to help everybody get grandma off their back when she gets too sick and to keep me from getting strapped by that. It needs that. So I suppose I am saying it is almost a back-to-the-drawing-boards feeling I come out with.

* * *

I see a sort of generalized negative income tax as a rational wave of the future, but I do not see that it has at the moment any immediate political relevance . . . I see so many other issues that will impose a barrier to [any] sort of a rational approach to the whole problem of income maintenance.

* * *

I think there is pressure to do something, because of an open-ended system, and money is going up, and the question then becomes who gets caught with the tab shifting it from the counties to the states to the federal government, but I do not think that that kind of shift implies any expansion of the program or any real public interest in doing anything different and new.

Only the most utopian of congressmen saw much chance for comprehensive income maintenance before a most nonutopian President proposed it. William F. Ryan (Democrat of New York) both introduced the first guaranteed income bill ever offered in Congress, in May 1968,

54. "Public Welfare Copes with Society's Needs," *Public Welfare*, Vol. 26 (January 1968), p. 12.

and a few months thereafter predicted that the next President would be likely to support it:

If the nation can find an early respite from war, so that the new administration has the time and the budget to give income maintenance fuller consideration, the next president, Democratic or Republican, will undoubtedly recommend some form of the plan to Congress.[55]

Ryan's bill was drafted in the Office of Economic Opportunity where James Lyday had been working on it for several years. It provided a uniform basic benefit of approximately $2,000 yearly for a family of four—$50 per month for the family head plus $39 for each dependent—to be reduced by 50 percent of earnings to a break-even point of $4,000, after which any benefits would cease. Benefits would be claimed from a new bureau of income maintenance in the Treasury Department under a simplified method based on the filing of monthly declarations of income, while enforcement would be based on spot checks like those made by the Internal Revenue Service. Where AFDC benefits already exceeded the federal income guarantee, states would be expected to supplement the basic federal benefit so that no recipient would be worse off under guaranteed income than he had been under AFDC. The cost of the Ryan-Lyday program was put at $4.1 billion over existing welfare costs, and Ryan explained that the base benefit was fixed at around $2,000 rather than $3,000 because the latter would cost an additional $20 billion.

Most members of Congress were too politically realistic to get involved with the Ryan bill, which turned out to be strikingly similar to President Nixon's proposal introduced seventeen months later by the Republican leaders of the House and Senate. A position taken in 1967 by Senator William Proxmire, a liberal, was more typical of legislators' attitudes than was Ryan's bill. Proxmire said, "Frankly, there is almost no support for the guaranteed annual income in Congress. I don't support it. I don't know anyone else in the Congress who does."[56]

The latter conclusion was given further confirmation by a summer 1967 survey of opinion of the Senate Labor and Public Welfare Committee and the House Education and Labor Committee, the committees assumed to be most alert to the income maintenance issue because of their jurisdiction over the poverty program. Responses from forty-five of the forty-eight congressional offices provided no sign that guaranteed

55. "A 'Guaranteed Income' vs. Welfare," *Christian Science Monitor*, Oct. 15, 1968.

56. *Congressional Record*, Vol. 113, Pt. 6, 90 Cong. 1 sess. (1967), p. 7179.

income was a live issue. None felt that the concept would be legislatively relevant within five years, many put it twenty-five years off.[57]

A comparable kind of inquiry made by two University of California political scientists in the early months of the Ninety-first Congress brought the same kind of answers. Based on interviews with some fifty legislators, these scholars wrote in the draft paper they circulated for comment only a month before the Nixon speech, that "income by right is not politically feasible in the near future." Describing the difficulty of even getting congressmen to understand "what was meant by guaranteed income, negative income tax, income supplements, income maintenance, or any of the terms commonly used to describe income by right," they found that "as soon as the idea became clear enough the opposition was evident . . . the question of political feasibility was uniformly regarded as hopeless for the present." Further, although one of the authors was a frequent consultant to the Urban Affairs Council staff to whom he had ready access, "Calls at the Executive Office produced a consensus that President Nixon was not about to bring up a guaranteed income."

There is no reason to doubt the validity of either of these inquiries into legislative beliefs and attitudes. We do know that in July 1969 the President had not yet made up his mind on the scope of a welfare reform proposal. Yet incrementalism takes some of its strength from the assumption that everyone believes it to be the only "realistic" approach to policy change. To borrow an expression from Townsend Hoopes, the outcome of "the battle for the President's mind" determined the political feasibility of income by right. Once the President was persuaded to propose guaranteed income, there was no assurance that it could pass Congress, of course, but it instantly became feasible, and incrementalism ceased to be the only politically viable approach.

Like the Johnson Vietnam decision, President Nixon's welfare decision was made possible because of the concentration of well-placed men close to the top who dedicated themselves to bringing it about. Robert Finch refers to the process as "probably one of the most thorough examinations of a problem and one of the leakiest episodes in the history of the Federal Government."[58] Significantly, one of the people Finch borrowed to help in the thorough examination was OEO's James Lyday

57. Data collected by Daniel Segal, a Yale University political science student, "Guaranteed Annual Income as a Political Issue" (Nov. 15, 1967).

58. Press conference at the National Press Building, Washington, D.C., Jan. 13, 1970 (transcript prepared by Ace-Federal Reporters, Inc. [Jones re CR# 10183]).

whose work on guaranteed income was no secret. The new administration struggled for eight months, missing a series of self-imposed deadlines for a decision as the differences between presidential advisers were leaked to the press by one or another participant. Finch considered the internal administration debate "a classic confrontation" between innovators and incrementalists, between, he told an interviewer, "those who recognize that the present system is just a disaster and that we had to break out of the old mold, and those who wanted to rewrite the old system."[59]

Starting point for the confrontation was the preinaugural welfare task force report with its emphasis on "near-term" possibilities. This task force did not fit the archetype described by Nathan Glazer as a group from which "no one stays behind to fight for anything; it is pure input with no liability."[60] Its chairman, Richard Nathan, resigned from the Brookings Institution to stay behind as the Budget Bureau's assistant director for human resources. Nathan, an acknowledged Republican partisan who had twice managed the domestic research side of Nelson Rockefeller's noncandidacy for the presidency and who had close ties to Republican congressmen, was the only person to chair two preinaugural task forces, that on intergovernmental fiscal relations as well as that on welfare. He stayed behind, well located in the Bureau of the Budget, to fight for both welfare reform and revenue sharing. Once it became apparent—as it did when the welfare report was leaked to the New York Times and the Washington Post—that leaders of the new administration were not horrified by welfare reform, Nathan worked toward a more radical proposal than he had earlier told his task force colleagues he thought possible.

The remaining thrust came from Moynihan and his Urban Affairs Council, which must count the family assistance program its sole accomplishment. When the council was created at the outset of the administration, it appeared to be President Nixon's response to the frequently heard hope that he would give the so-called urban crisis as much high-level attention as national security. Whether there are distinct urban issues separable from national issues of race, crime, poverty, housing, and pollution is far from clear, however, and by the fall of 1969 there was hardly a report of council meetings. The small council staff was dismantled as Moynihan became counselor to the President

59. News and Observer (Raleigh), Aug. 14, 1969.
60. "On Task Forcing," Public Interest, Vol. 4 (Spring 1969), p. 43.

and Stephen Hess, his deputy, was appointed to plan the decennial White House Conference on Children.

The welfare reform issue was made to order for Moynihan in 1969's first months. A coauthor of the Economic Opportunity Act in 1964, he had become disenchanted with a substantial part of that effort, especially the community action emphasis. In March 1965, in what became a celebrated paper, Moynihan, then assistant secretary of labor, had argued the case for national action to deal with what he found to be a critical breakdown in the stability of Negro family life, a breakdown which, according to the paper, "has led to a startling increase in welfare dependency."[61] In preparing his background paper for Governor Rockefeller's November 1967 Arden House conference on public welfare, Moynihan discovered the defects in the public relief system and related them to his earlier concern about family stability.[62] The family assistance package—legislation and official explanation—ultimately proposed by the President then turned out to be a composite of Ryan's guaranteed income bill of May 1968 and Moynihan's November 1967 explanation of the crises in welfare. The package, once accepted by the President, meant that the incremental approach to consideration of welfare policy change was ended. President Nixon later explained the underlying philosophy:

Our basic policies for improvement of the living conditions of the poor are based on this proposition: That the best judge of each family's priorities is that family itself, and that the best way to ameliorate the hardships of poverty is to provide the family with additional income—to be spent as that family itself sees fit.[63]

The President's men were of two minds about what that basic policy meant for the future of other public relief programs. They shilly-shallied about food stamps, said nothing about veterans' pensions, and, until prodded by the Senate Finance Committee, said nothing about public housing. All three merit attention.

61. The complete text of the report, "The Negro Family: The Case for National Action," is in Lee Rainwater and William L. Yancey, *The Moynihan Report and the Politics of Controversy* (MIT Press, 1967).

62. "The Crises in Welfare."

63. Address to the White House Conference on Food, Nutrition, and Health, Dec. 2, 1969. Text in *Congressional Quarterly Weekly Report*, Dec. 5, 1969, pp. 2515–16.

4

Thirty Years of Public Housing

A comprehensive national income maintenance strategy should take into account both the economic value of the relief benefit paid through public housing and the conditions under which that benefit is made available. Public housing is a means test relief program assisting about 2.5 million poor people by increasing the availability to them of a necessary commodity—low rent housing—inadequately supplied by private enterprise. There is no disputing the need of public housing tenants: median annual income of all families housed is $2,800; among elderly residents, who occupy more than one-third of all dwelling units, it is $1,700. Nor can it be doubted that the program provides substantial relief. Because of the public subsidy the median gross rent nationally for all families is $51 per month; for the elderly it is $37. Rents are 40 to 50 percent of those in unsubsidized private housing of comparable quality. Whether or not public housing is folded into a comprehensive public relief strategy, however, there are policy decisions to be made regarding the allocation of a limited number of housing units between the well-adjusted, hard-luck poor and those poor people who are also maladjusted or unconventional in their social patterns. The universe of people poor enough to qualify for public housing includes both groups, but the number of available dwelling units is far smaller than is the universe of eligible poor.

Providing decent, safe, and sanitary low cost housing for those who cannot afford to acquire it on the free market can be accomplished through an unrestricted cash payment to the poor adequate to meet the costs of standard housing as well as other necessities, or through some form of subsidy paid to private enterprise or to poor people that is, in either case, earmarked exclusively for low income housing. The earmarked subsidy can take the form of publicly financed and publicly owned new or rehabilitated dwellings, of publicly leased dwellings made available to low income persons at reduced rents, of guaranteed rent supplements to encourage nonprofit groups to enter the low income housing field as a public service, or of tax and other incentives that will make it attractive for private enterprise to produce low rent housing.

The earmarked subsidy, and particularly the publicly financed and publicly owned dwelling, has been and continues to be the most common way of providing decent housing for low income persons and families. One reason is that cash grants in lieu of standard housing units would not assure as large a number of families living in standard housing as does the public housing program because all of the cash subsidy would not necessarily be diverted to housing. Public policy assumes that it can more surely improve housing conditions through publicly produced housing than through unrestricted cash subsidies equivalent to the costs of the public program.

An additional reason for providing housing relief in kind rather than in cash is that many public housing tenants are multiproblem families considered undesirable tenants who would likely face a demand for premium rents from private landlords. Nonprofit private housing sponsored by church, fraternal, and charitable groups with government subsidies of interest costs or of rents has become an alternative attractive to many who dislike publicly owned housing but recognize both the special difficulties of housing the multiproblem family and the reluctance of builders to construct very low income housing. Nonprofit housing is a latecomer to the business, however, and suffers from a shortage of necessary expediters, managers, and capital. Thus far, at least, conventional public housing remains the dominant form of housing relief.

While public housing may target its beneficiaries, that advantage can also have toxic effects. Residents of public projects (other than those in single family units on scattered sites) are readily identifiable as people who are not very successful—if they were more successful, they would be compelled by regulations to vacate. An antidote might be to open public housing projects and make them attractive to non-needy persons who can pay higher rents than can the very poor, but there are experts who doubt that middle income families could be persuaded to cooperate. One such expert, Roger Starr, a New York housing and planning specialist, is skeptical that "higher-income white families are willing to pay higher rents in order to share an apartment house with lower-income

Negro families who are paying lower rents."[1] Even if the problem of social integration could be overcome, to make this kind of economic integration attractive to the middle class, more of the amenities would have to be built into public housing. Elevators, for example, would have to stop at every floor rather than at every third floor, a common current economy. Under these conditions, costs would escalate, subsidizing the poor would be more expensive, and the advantage of economy would disappear.

For many years, resolution of this dilemma was avoided by restricting admission to public housing to that segment of the economically unsuccessful population that was at least willing if not content to conform to the dominant mores. If the price of cheap, sanitary housing was the wearing of a scarlet letter, so be it. If public housing policy was an elevator stop every three floors, policy is policy. Being poor is taken less resignedly than it used to be, however; now it is more and more difficult to maintain public housing for the tranquil poor alone, if only because fewer of the poor are tranquil about their situation. With the product in scarce supply, it is increasingly difficult to avoid choices: should public housing cater to the upwardly mobile or to the multiple problem family, to the angry Negro ghetto dweller or to the peaceful aged? An antecedent policy problem is whether conventional public housing is worth preserving for anyone.

Evaluations

Success and failure in public programs are relative terms at best. If a universally agreed objective could be achieved at the minimum possible cost, a program presumably would be a success. There are no universally agreed objectives for most programs, however, and there are costs other than fiscal costs. Is social security a success because it benefits a substantial segment of the population and is popular with most Americans, or is social security a failure because its benefit levels will not sustain an elderly individual without other resources and because it continues to be tied to a singularly regressive tax? How much weight should be assigned popularity? Is a universally popular program always to be considered more successful than a controversial program? Applied to public

1. *The Living End* (Coward-McCann, Inc., 1966), p. 118.

housing, the question is no more easily answered. Is public housing a success because there is some growth in the number of units every year and because it provides a decent physical environment for two and a half million persons, or is it a failure because it has not provided for millions of others and because it has developed a negative image?

What tests are appropriate in evaluating public programs to provide a housing subsidy for the low income population? One seemingly reasonable line of response is likely to be couched in cost-benefit terms that are measurable. Do residents of public housing units show a lesser incidence of communicable disease, a lower divorce, separation, and desertion rate, a lower school dropout rate, a lower arrest rate, a higher nutritional level than does a comparable group of persons not living in public housing? To the extent that the answers are positive, and to the extent that the costs of achieving these desirable objectives cannot be lowered by alternative policies—for example, more public health facilities, community mental health clinics, stepped-up food stamp programs —to that extent could public housing be considered successful.

The test described above assumes a random selection of public housing tenants from among the low income population. The tenant group is not so chosen, however. For years, admission was denied the most troubled families, a policy still preferred by public housing professionals. Accordingly, one would expect the resulting near-normal group of tenants to be success stories. John P. Dean made this point two decades ago in commenting on the supposed rehabilitative character of public housing:

Compared with an equivalent number of dwellings in slum or blighted areas, public housing developments undoubtedly include fewer aged indigents, transients, single men and women, hobos, crackpots, criminals, panhandlers, prostitutes, alcoholics, bohemians, taxi-dancers, and other social misfits. Little wonder that indexes of social-welfare favor public housing.[2]

On the other hand, if it were the most troubled rather than the most nearly normal families that came to public housing in the first place, then not only would the control group be hard to find, but improvement or deterioration in the publicly housed group could not with any certainty be attributed to housing conditions in view of the complex nature of problems faced by these families.

2. "The Myths of Housing Reform," *American Sociological Review*, Vol. 14 (April 1949), p. 284.

Research that has been undertaken on the relationship between family life and housing environment is not conclusive as to the measurable benefits of improved housing. The most extensive study of the subject, by Daniel Wilner at Johns Hopkins, measured about a thousand families (five thousand persons) over a three-year period (1955–58).[3] During the life of the study, Wilner surveyed two samples of low income Negro families eleven times each to assess physical morbidity, social-psychological adjustment, and the performance of every child attending public school. The test group were families in a new public housing project who had originally lived in the slum. The control sample, matched to the test families on many characteristics, was the group that remained in the slum. Both high-rise and low-rise units were part of the public housing project to which the test group moved.

Wilner's conclusions were (1) that the incidence of morbidity (illness and disability) for persons under thirty-five years of age, and especially for children, in the project was lower than for those in the slum, but little different for persons over thirty-five, including the very old; (2) that a majority of the social adjustment tests—reactions to housing and space, relations with neighbors, personal and family relations, attitudes and behavior toward neighborhood and community, social self-concept and aspirations, psychological state—pointed to superiority in the public housing group, but that the differences between project and slum families did not always reach statistically acceptable levels of confidence; (3) that intelligence and achievement test scores of school children in test and control groups were not substantially different, but that test children were more likely to be promoted at a normal pace, perhaps because of more regular attendance made possible by fewer illnesses.

To judge from the Johns Hopkins work, the benefits of improved housing are not as clearly certain as we might like them to be. For all of the scientific uncertainty about the effects of improved housing on life adjustment, however, it is not likely that many policy makers or many ordinary citizens are prepared to defend the perpetuation of overcrowded or of substandard housing. If an overpowering case cannot be made for public housing by the reasonable tests Wilner posed, the results are encouraging enough to sustain support for government activity in the low income housing field. In addition, as a matter of public

3. Daniel M. Wilner and others, *The Housing Environment and Family Life* (Johns Hopkins Press, 1962).

conscience, there continues to be support for a public investment that somehow provides a low income family of, say, four persons with at least two bedrooms, heat, and hot and cold running water. The conventional public housing program is meant to accomplish exactly that objective—the production of decent low-rent housing units in numbers substantial enough to make a dent in the need of the low income population. But does it get the job done? No matter how exquisitely imaginative its design, any program that fails to produce enough goods to meet the needs of a big part of its clientele should merit reconsideration.

Tenant Judgments

Only about 10 percent of the poverty income population lives in public housing or benefits from rent supplements. Some of those in the other 90 percent, especially the aged poor, live with relatives as a matter of choice; others, who live in jurisdictions like San Diego, California, or Des Moines, Iowa, cannot opt for public housing because there is no program at all in those places; some low income people own their own homes, a happy circumstance that is usually not considered cause for striking them from the statistical ranks of the poor. But after all of these cases are considered, the residuals still are a consequential number.

A substantial number of the residuals simply are not interested in public housing because it is inconveniently located, because the possibility of integrated housing is distasteful, because any kind of public charity—even an indirect variety like this one—is abhorrent, or because the quality of life in public housing is badly regarded. There is evidence that eligible prospective tenants reject conventional public housing at a high rate. Peter Marris cites a Philadelphia Housing Association finding that during two years of relocation service there, almost 80 percent of families studied appeared to be eligible for public housing, but less than 15 percent actually moved to public units. Relocation cases accounted for only 4.2 percent of new tenancies in the period studied although families dislocated by urban renewal had first preference and public housing was available for them.[4] In San Francisco the findings were similar: it was estimated that a third of both Negro and white families living in the city's slums had refused public housing.[5]

4. "A Report on Urban Renewal in the United States," in Leonard Duhl (ed.), *The Urban Condition: People and Policy in the Metropolis* (Basic Books, 1963), p. 120.
   5. *Ibid.*, p. 121.

The overwhelming majority of five hundred families relocated from Boston's West End refused to consider the possibility of public housing, Chester Hartman has reported. Fifty-one percent of those citing negative factors mentioned population density; a third of the objections dealt with the supposedly undesirable qualities of the people living in housing projects or with the general atmosphere and environment; a quarter of the objections cited the institutional quality of public housing.[6] Comments of respondents in the Boston study thus suggest objections based on the fact that there are not only too many people in one place—half of Boston's 10,710 units were concentrated in five projects in 1967—but that there are so many of the wrong kind of people.

Nor is there an outburst of enthusiasm from those who do become tenants. For a complex of reasons, some psychological and some practical, its clients show little affection for public housing, a point that comes through clearly in a review of the personnel histories of a large number of housing managers in New York City. Most of the managers had been in public housing administration for at least fifteen years, many of them had worked in half a dozen different projects. One could hardly calculate the total number of public housing tenants with which this group had had contact—100,000 families would seem a conservative number. In a sample of twenty-five folders, crammed with the important and the trivial papers pertaining to the lifetime careers of these managers—the highest status line jobs in public housing—covering perhaps 250 to 300 man-years, there were just two unsolicited letters of commendation from tenants.

Apparently it is easier to find unsolicited complaints about public housing. Abner Silverman, assistant commissioner for management in the federal Housing Assistance Administration, reported some of those complaints found in a daily flow of "a seemingly endless stream of mail from Local Housing Authorities frequently complaining about PHA [Public Housing Administration] practice or policy, and from tenants or applicants usually complaining about Local Housing Authority practice and policy." Silverman detailed the "more frequent complaints."[7] They amount to invasion of privacy ("Why does the maintenance man have

6. "The Limitations of Public Housing," *Journal of the American Institute of Planners*, Vol. 29 (November 1963), p. 284.

7. "Low-Rent Housing Program in an Era of Social Change" (address at the annual meeting of the Carolinas Council of Housing and Redevelopment Officials, Asheville, N.C., Oct. 7, 1965; processed), p. 13.

the right to walk into our dwelling any time of day without advance notice?"); injustice ("Why must I pay for a broken window when I didn't break it?"); poor management ("Why is our apartment only painted every six years?"); bureaucratic rigidity ("Why must I lose a half-day's pay to see the Manager—why can't the office stay open one night a week just as the stores do?"); discourtesy ("Why doesn't your staff address me as *Mister?*").

A study of tenant attitudes done by Austin Hollingshead and L. H. Rogler, reported in Leonard Duhl's *The Urban Condition*, has not been widely replicated—which is probably just as well for the ego of public housing. The Hollingshead-Rogler study matched two groups of families in San Juan, Puerto Rico. Matched for age, socioeconomic status, marital union, and area of residence, all the families lived either in a slum or in public housing. The families in public housing were housed more adequately, paid less rent, were less crowded. Questioned about how they liked their environment, 65 percent of the men and women who lived in slum homes liked the slums; 85 percent of the men and 71 percent of the women disliked public housing. Questioned about the neighborhood as a place to raise children, 38 percent of slum dwelling husbands and 15 percent of the wives pronounced the slum a good place to raise children; only 7 percent of the public housing husbands and no public housing wife found the environment good for children.[8] The dilemma we face, Hollingshead and Rogler suggest, is that good housing by the standards of city planners, architects, and enlightened government officials results in social conditions people dislike.

Joseph Lyford's description of life in a segment of New York's West Side, *The Airtight Cage*, adds another complaint—insensitivity to the anxieties of applicants. Lyford writes of one of his subjects, a Puerto Rican family of six living in a combination kitchen–living room–bedroom with a six-by-ten cubicle in back: "Mrs. Acosta sent in two applications for public housing: No. 930245, dated November 4, 1957, and No. 1254784, November, 1961. No answer. In the six years she waited to hear, she never had a communication of any sort from the housing authority." Describing the plight of a Negro mother living in unbelievably bad housing, Lyford notes that she had received notice that her application for public housing would be "processed downtown." "To be

8. "Attitudes Toward Slums and Public Housing in Puerto Rico," in Duhl, *The Urban Condition*, pp. 228, 293.

processed downtown is the end of hope. Mrs. Leighton has never heard a thing about her application since April, 1961."[9]

The critically important message for public housing is that it is disliked by too many of its primary beneficiaries. Spokesmen for local poverty-action groups participating in the White House Conference "To Secure These Rights" in June 1966 charged repeatedly that the local public housing authorities were only a little less inhumane than private slumlords.[10] Whatever particular form the new public welfare takes, it is certain that it will scorn what Charles Silberman has termed "welfare colonialism." The social revolution of the sixties insures that the judgments of people to be served by welfare programs will be respected in considering the style of those programs, just as the judgment of the farmer has always been considered in formulating agricultural programs. Welfare programs disliked by their clients are not part of the wave of the future.

Nontenant Critics

Many architects, social critics, civil rights leaders, sociologists, housing economists, journalists, and liberal politicians were also dissatisfied with public housing by the mid-sixties. "Public housing had become, by the early 1960s," Lawrence Friedman and James Krier have written, "one of the least popular federal welfare programs, devoid of all capacity for major growth and subject to withering attack."[11] A committee of New York's architects solemnly reported in 1964 that that city's low income program "has seldom produced distinguished or even satisfactory architecture from human and environmental viewpoints."[12] Low income housing projects were written off by urban critic Jane Jacobs in her chronicle of The Death and Life of Great American Cities as "too dangerous, demoralizing and unstable within themselves," with the result that "they make it too hard in many cases to maintain tolerable

9. The Airtight Cage: A Study of New York's West Side (Harper & Row, 1966), pp. 42, 60.

10. George Schermer Associates and Kenneth C. Jones, Public Housing Is the Tenants: Rethinking Management's Responsibility and Role in Tenant and Community Relations (National Association of Housing and Redevelopment Officials, 1967), p. 5.

11. "A New Lease on Life: Section 23 Housing and the Poor," University of Pennsylvania Law Review, Vol. 116 (1968), p. 611.

12. Quoted in Richard J. Whalen, A City Destroying Itself (William Morrow & Co., 1965), p. 72.

civilization in their vicinities."[13] Speaking as national director of CORE, black leader Floyd McKissick told a Senate committee that there were problems with public housing from construction to rental:

White construction companies reap the profits of building federally funded public housing built in ghetto areas. . . . Regulations base eligibility on maximum income limits, keep out families receiving public assistance, or families without steady incomes and with personal problems, and pitch rents to construction costs. The result is that poor people and black people who have suffered the ravages of a punitive, prejudiced society either cannot afford or are declared ineligible for the so-called low-rent housing that is claimed as being built for them.[14]

Liberal journalists and liberal legislators have pounced on the deficiencies of public housing after years of service in active defense of the cause. Their complaint is that authorized units are not started, that public housing has lost its drive, that it suffers from what former Senator Paul Douglas describes as "middle age letdown," and Senator Warren Magnuson deplores as "mountains of red-tape and constant delays" and inability "to create bold and workable solutions."[15] Writing a few years ago of "The Long Trial of Public Housing," Elizabeth Drew typifies the attitude of informed journalists. She blames stodginess and administrative reticence in the public housing Washington bureaucracy for failure to change the lot of the poorly housed poor. "The P.H.A. [Public Housing Administration]," wrote Mrs. Drew, "cannot eliminate all the roadblocks that have contributed to its failures, but it would help if it were staffed with people less resigned to them."[16]

Academics write of the failure of public housing as a given. "Opponents of public subsidies for housing low-income groups view the federal program as a failure and its advocates recognize its basic shortcomings," concludes Paul Wendt, a University of California housing economist. Wendt acknowledges the significance of housing industry opposition but pins major blame on "the widespread criticism of the administration and leadership in the federal low-rent program," criticism that, in 1963 at least, he clearly felt was justified.[17] Roscoe Martin, a political scientist interested in federal-local relations, found public hous-

13. (Random House, 1961), p. 393.

14. *Federal Role in Urban Affairs*, Hearings before the Subcommittee on Executive Reorganization of the Senate Committee on Government Operations, 89 Cong. 2 sess. (1966), Pt. 11, p. 2290.

15. *Congressional Record*, daily ed., Sept. 20, 1967, p. S13325.

16. *Reporter*, Vol. 32 (June 17, 1965), p. 18.

17. *Housing Policy—The Search for Solutions* (University of California Press, 1963), p. 193.

ing to suffer by comparison with urban renewal: "The differences in spirit, attitude, and point of view between the public housing and the urban renewal agencies seem unmistakable, particularly to the local executives and commissioners who deal with both."[18] The conservative economist, Milton Friedman, finds public housing to be dominated by local special interest groups of property owners or central business district merchants. "Public housing served as a convenient means to accomplish their objective," says Friedman, "which required more destruction than construction . . . ."[19]

Lee Rainwater, an urban sociologist who has studied the St. Louis Pruitt-Igoe housing project, adds some judgments on public housing based on the Pruitt-Igoe and other studies. He has characterized the public housing community environment as intolerable. Rainwater would substitute for conventional public housing an equivalent cash grant or a program limited to scattered sites and small developments. Another well-known urban sociologist, Herbert Gans, told a Senate committee that public housing has been a failure—but added charitably "through no fault of its own."[20]

Some public housing professionals are worried about the program too. With national attention focused on urban problems early in 1967, the National Association of Housing and Redevelopment Officials (NAHRO) sponsored a housing policy forum to consider critical issues in low and moderate income housing. By the third day of that forum, NAHRO leaders were so seriously concerned about excessive critical self-analysis of public housing that they belatedly added an articulate spokesman for public housing to the program to preclude the press from reporting only negative judgments.

Of course, critical analysis of public housing is not new, but the origin of some of the criticism has changed. Many old supporters are infuriated by small production totals and are ready to abandon the concept, but some old opponents who found public housing wrong in principle in the early days of the program no longer seem so disturbed. This is true, for example, of the National Association of Home Builders (NAHB). In supporting the Johnson administration rent supplement proposal in 1965, an NAHB spokesman predicted that rent supplements and below-market-interest-rate programs could do the job that public

18. *The Cities and the Federal System* (Atherton Press, 1965), p. 142.
19. *Capitalism and Freedom* (University of Chicago Press, 1962), p. 179.
20. *Federal Role in Urban Affairs*, Hearings, Pt. 9, p. 2030; Pt. 11, p. 2387.

housing was once supposed to do—house the low income population unable to afford conventional housing. This competition from subsidized but privately owned housing could be expected to drive public housing out of the market. NAHB would not endorse systematic phasing out of the public housing program, however, any more than it would endorse increased authorizations for public housing starts. Although the Home Builders had opposed public housing for twenty years, what was once a fiery attack had become indifference.

It is not enough to assert administrative reticence (Drew), middle age letdown (Douglas), a lack of spirit (Martin), and an absence of leadership (Wendt) without defining their characteristics. No middle age letdown has overcome public housing if increases in the formation of local housing authorities is the measure or if some upturn in the number of new public housing units is the measure or if the introduction of new acquisition techniques is the measure. By these measures the program is alive and growing. But it is a success in the areas where the action is not. It is, as we shall see, a success in meeting the housing needs of many senior citizens with little money, an important enough objective in itself; it is successful in meeting the housing needs of an important part of the low income population in the smaller cities and towns of the country, again a desirable function; public housing, moreover, is successful in improving the physical environment of its tenants wherever it exists. Even in Pruitt-Igoe, Rainwater reported his interviewers found that the people "who live in the apartments are pleased with the apartments, at least these are better than the places they lived before." This confirmed an earlier Public Housing Administration survey of families moving out of public housing that indicated that the physical aspects of the housing was a relatively minor source of tenant dissatisfaction within the total program.[21]

But public housing is not a great success in the areas where the action is: in coping with problems of race and of economic inequality related to race. The action in America in the 1970s is not in the small towns, and the most critical welfare problem is not with the elderly. If public housing is to matter, it must become part of the mainstream efforts to improve the condition of the nonelderly, nonwhite poor. It is not certain that the program is at all suited to such a role. Public housing was

21. *Ibid.*, Pt. 9, 2029; U.S. Department of Housing and Urban Development, Housing Assistance Administration, "Public Housing Today—A Critical Evaluation" (February 1967; processed), p. 11, n. 2.

first assigned to do a particular kind of job for a particular needy population: to provide decent, safe, and sanitary low-cost rental housing for a decent, safe, and sanitary population. Unlike public assistance policy, public housing policy has never been extended or amended to suggest another kind of job—social and psychological rehabilitation—for a different population, nor have its leaders ever claimed competence in doing that other kind of job. Some of those leaders explicitly deny that public housing can or should deal with psychosocial problems. For this group, public housing is the housing equivalent of food stamps: for a lesser amount of money than would be required in the free market, public housing provides the needy client with a tangible benefit roughly adequate to meet his minimum need for that necessity of life.

Nonetheless, public housing is vulnerable from two directions. When it is conceived as a social service rather than a physical facility, the Gans-Kennedy-Rainwater-McKissick judgment is valid. When it is conceived as a physical facility rather than a social service, the Douglas-Wendt-Drew criticisms are especially telling because its production totals are so limited. In the absence of direction about program purpose, many of public housing's leaders remain confused about their role. Unhappily, there is nothing approaching a unanimity of feeling among public housers themselves regarding program goals and objectives.

Nonproduction

Unlike food stamps which were discontinued for a twenty-year period, public housing has never been entirely abandoned as a part of American public relief efforts, despite the evident reluctance with which Congress breathes new life into it from time to time. In the forties and fifties when public relief was less controversial and certainly less expensive than it is today, public housing was fighting successive losing battles against World War II's military priorities, against the Eightieth Congress's reluctance to back public enterprise where private enterprise existed, against still another round of military priorities generated by the Korean War, against a hostile House Appropriations Committee so effective in its antagonism to public housing that no veteran of the program fails to shudder when referring to the early fifties, and finally against President Eisenhower's continuing hope that a free enterprise substitute would present itself. In a lucid and influential article in *Architectural Forum,* Catherine Bauer wrote in 1957 that "public housing, after more than two decades, still drags along in a kind of limbo, continuously controversial, not dead but never more than half alive."[22] The description remains apt after more than three decades.

An intensive effort to increase public housing production mandated by the national administration in 1967 was overdue. It had been fifteen years since annual public housing starts exceeded 35,000 (Table 6).

Table 6. Nonfarm Housing Starts, by Ownership, 1949–69

In thousands

Year	Private ownership	Public ownership
1949	1,430	0.7
1950	1,908	31
1951	1,420	69
1952	1,445	56
1953	1,402	32
1954	1,532	16
1955	1,627	9
1956	1,325	5
1957	1,175	21
1958	1,314	22
1959	1,495	16
1960	1,230	29
1961	1,285	30
1962	1,439	22
1963	1,583	24
1964	1,502	26
1965	1,451	33
1966	1,142	32
1967	1,268	34
1968	1,484	44[a]
1969	1,446	63[a]

Source: *Annual Report of the Council of Economic Advisers*, January 1970, p. 224; *Report of the National Commission on Urban Problems*, December 1968, p. 130; *First Annual Report on National Housing Goals*, H. Doc. 91-63, 91 Cong. 1 sess. (1969), p. 19; *Second Annual Report on National Housing Goals*, H. Doc. 91-292, 91 Cong. 2 sess. (1970), p. 45.

a. Fiscal year, not calendar year.

Puny production had come to be a routine story evidenced by the striking contrast between the authorization in the National Housing Act of 1949 for 810,000 units over a six-year period and actual completion, from inception of the original program in 1937 through December 1966, of only 636,000 units. At the beginning of 1967, just 607,000 units were

22. "The Dreary Deadlock of Public Housing," *Architectural Forum*, Vol. 106 (May 1957), p. 140.

occupied, 186,000 of them by the elderly. By the most optimistic count there were more than 25 million individuals living alone or in family groups with poverty level incomes at the end of the sixties; but there were only 2.5 million public housing tenants—not all of whom had poverty level incomes—in occupied units. No one pretended that decent, safe, and sanitary private housing existed for the 23 million poor outside of public housing. To be sure, not all of these 23 million needed public housing, but some who very likely did were among the 4.3 million non-farm families with incomes under $3,000 occupying housing units classi-fied as substandard. Long waiting lists of eligibles were reported in city after city, adding to a nationwide total of over 400,000. In addition, the distribution was less than ideal, a not uncommon phenomenon when states and localities decide how much relief they will provide and to whom. In housing as in other welfare aids, the bounty is provided for only a small fraction of the needy, but the fraction is larger in New York than in California, larger in North Carolina than in Indiana, larger in Georgia than in Virginia, larger in New Jersey than in Michigan.

Why have more units not been produced to reduce the gap between the number of poorly housed poor and the number of available public housing dwellings? Production deficiencies are not readily attributed to one common affliction of welfare programs, economy in government expenditures. A strategic advantage of public housing is that its annual cost is small—and would still be relatively small if there were twice as many units as there are—but that once the deceptively small initial commitment is made, there is no way to turn back. The contract for federal subsidy covers debt service on the total capital cost of the project, including land, leaving only operating costs to be met from rental income. For a given number of units, however, the federal budget impact is small in any one year because only the amount of annual con-tribution required for those units in the particular year is included. The subsidy is stretched out, in most public housing, over forty years. On top of the annual contribution, an indirect federal subsidy is provided in the form of tax exemption on the income of local authority bonds issued to finance the projects. In the jumble of complaints about public housing that comes from its most conservative critics, expense does not occupy a prominent place because financing imposes no strain on the federal budget in any one year, imposes no burden ever on state or local govern-ments, and creates a highly desirable investment opportunity for private investors. It would be difficult to find another formula that would permit as much federal subsidy with so little impact on the annual federal budget. Unlike bridges, highways, post offices, and other long-lived federally financed capital projects, the costs of public housing are stretched out to cover the anticipated useful life of the building—and perhaps even more than the useful life. By 1967 there was a modernization cost backlog of $250 million for units not yet paid for in the first place.

The total federal obligation over the life of the bond is substantially greater, of course, than is indicated in any single year or even in the five-year cost projections that are part of internal federal budget planning. But it adds up slowly. Total expenditures by the Department of Housing and Urban Development (HUD) and its predecessor agencies for the public housing program over the thirty years ending June 30, 1966, were only $2.1 billion, a figure that includes administrative costs.

Understandably, there is a steady market for local housing authority bonds that are secured by a first pledge of annual contributions unconditionally payable by the federal Housing Assistance Administration to the local authority pursuant to an annual contributions contract. It is legally conceivable, but for practical purposes inconceivable, that Congress would fail to appropriate money to meet the costs of the contracts outstanding. "What will happen if we don't provide this supplemental?" Chairman Joe Evins of the Independent Offices and HUD Appropriations Subcommittee asked HUD's budget officer, John Frantz, in 1968 when the department needed supplemental funds to meet annual contributions contracts. The ensuing discussion, joined in by HUD Secretary Weaver and Representative Burt L. Talcott (Republican of Kansas), gave Evins an answer he probably did not expect:

FRANTZ: If you didn't provide any of this $30 million at some point there would be another supplemental which would be for $30 million, or some larger amount.

EVINS: The payments would be postponed.

FRANTZ: No, sir. The funds have to be appropriated because they really serve to pay, in effect, the amounts due to the bondholders on these bonds—and these bonds are guaranteed by the Federal Government.

WEAVER: We have no choice. Otherwise, the Federal Government could be in default on the contracts with the local authorities.

TALCOTT: This is a threat comparable to Ho Chi Minh.

WEAVER: Entirely different motivation and process.[23]

23. *Second Supplemental Appropriation Bill*, 1968, Hearings before Subcommittees of the House Committee on Appropriations, 90 Cong. 2 sess. (1968), p. 436.

Full faith and credit of the United States is pledged by the enabling legislation to the payment of all amounts agreed to be paid as security for the bonds. Both Moody's and Standard and Poor's rate housing authority bonds AAA. As an added fillip, in many jurisdictions the bonds carry state and local tax exemptions. In the late 1960s, investors could readily buy local housing authority bonds yielding 4⅜ percent with a fifteen-year protection against redemption. Thus it was possible for a person in the 50 percent tax bracket to invest in an AAA bond returning the taxable equivalent of 8¾ percent and still feel that he was putting his money into improving the conditions of life for the poor. No other welfare program can offer the affluent population comparable economic and psychic attractions.

Political Ambivalence

It is not, then, either impossible demands on the annual federal budget or investor reluctance that has restrained public housing production. The slow pace is attributable to other factors. One of those factors was the long period of reluctance at the federal level to give the program any assurance of continuity. Throughout a critical decade, public housing was treated as an expedient to be considered de novo every year or two. In the manner of the steel mills that bank their furnaces in anticipation of a strike and then lose production again as the furnaces are reheated, the low income program went through a long cycle of banking and reheating while proponents searched for a way of assuring continuous, uninterrupted growth and opponents searched for a way to phase it all out.

Given an important role in the ambitious postwar housing program belatedly enacted in 1949 as the National Housing Act (the so-called Wagner-Ellender-Taft Act), public housing promptly met a series of disasters that cast so much doubt on its continued existence, let alone growth and development, that the fifties can only be characterized as the program's lost decade. During those years a modest figure well below that fixed by the National Housing Act dominated annual new start authorizations; discouragement, even a sense of futility, took hold in the Public Housing Administration; interminable production delays fed upon themselves, making it appear that public housing could never work.

The circumstances under which the generous authorizations of the 1949 bill were enacted foreshadowed continuing strong opposition. In

1946 and again in 1948 the Senate easily passed a housing bill incorporating numerous recommendations of its special Committee on Postwar Economic Policy, including authorization for construction of relatively large numbers of public units. On both occasions an unfriendly Banking Committee chairman and an unfriendly Rules Committee majority blocked House action. But after the Democratic victory in 1948 resulted in both a change in control of the House Banking Committee and the institution of the twenty-one-day rule by which Rules Committee inaction could ultimately be overcome, a bill incorporating authorization for 1,050,000 units of public housing over a six-year period was reported to the House floor in 1949. Four separate votes—all close, three of them in Committee of the Whole—were taken on the public housing section: to reduce the number of units authorized to 810,000, the number in the Senate bill (adopted by voice vote); to delete the public housing section entirely (rejected by standing vote, 136-135); again to delete the public housing section completely (adopted by teller vote, 168-165) thereby eliminating the newly adopted 810,000 figure; and once more—the Committee of the Whole having resolved back into the House—to delete the public housing section (rejected by roll call, 209-204), thus restoring the original Banking Committee proposal of 1,050,000 units.[24] The net effect was House authorization for a higher number of units—the Banking Committee's 1,050,000—than the House actually desired, to judge from its initial adoption of the amendment to reduce the committee's figure to the smaller Senate approved figure. Psychologically the effect was a warning that support for any public housing program in the House was thin and uncertain, that after four years of debate and hearings on the future course of federal housing policy, public housing was sustained by only a handful of votes.

It may be that a vigorous program could have begun then in spite of the handicap posed by the substantial bloc of unfriendly congressmen. Other policies have moved ahead despite close votes. If a close vote is not a mandate for uncontrolled growth and development, neither is it a direction to shut up shop. Public housing did win, it was not stricken from the bill, and the final version of the National Housing Act of 1949 authorized 810,000 units over six years. In dollar amounts, authorization for public housing appropriations then totaled $336 million annually.

But it turned out to be a tease. The Public Housing Administration

24. *Congressional Record*, Vol. 95, Pt. 7, 81 Cong. 1 sess. (1949), pp. 8636, 8644, 8667.

had barely begun to face its job when the last friendly President with whom it would deal for a decade found it necessary to cut away at the new construction authority. President Truman's request of July 18, 1950, to the Housing and Home Finance Agency (HHFA) to reduce the construction of public housing units to 30,000 for the first six months of fiscal 1951 because of the Korean War emergency had the effect of braking the forward thrust achieved by the 1949 legislation.[25] The scaling down of the public housing provisions was the tipping-over point for the program. Although starts were permitted to pick up during the latter part of fiscal 1951, other troubles soon developed.

Subsequent to the Truman cutback, three successive appropriations acts undid what the 1949 act had set out to do in public housing. Where authorization for 810,000 units over six years could have meant an average of 135,000 units a year, the appropriations act for fiscal 1952 limited starts to 50,000 during that year; the act of 1953 limited starts to 35,000 for 1953 and prohibited the Public Housing Administration from entering into future contracts exceeding 35,000 units during any one fiscal year subsequent to 1953 without authorization from Congress. The appropriation for fiscal 1954 limited starts to 20,000 and prohibited any future construction contracts unless authorized by act of Congress. Prospects for a long-term career in public housing could not then be regarded as bright. Public housing bureaucrats referred to these as the "dark days."

Control over public housing so evidently assumed by the House Appropriations Committee in the early fifties is significant on two counts. In the first place, it amended the order of magnitude originally fixed by the combined forces of President Truman's liberal supporters in the Eighty-first Congress and Senator Robert Taft, a persistent public housing supporter. From an original plan for new public housing production equal to about 10 percent of total new residential starts each year, the limitations written into the appropriations measures scaled the percentage down to about 2.5 percent of total starts. Where the 1949 legislation made 135,000 public units per year the target, the revisions settled on 35,000 as a target. Ever since, the 35,000 figure has been the base line for annual or biennial negotiations between the Public Housing Administration, its parent organization (whether the old Housing and Home Finance Agency or the new Department of Housing and

Urban Development), the Bureau of the Budget, and the House and Senate banking committees. House Appropriations has since withdrawn from the numbers game as an active participant but the boundaries it first drew are still important. A measure of the persistence of the 35,000 figure is that even when the social-minded Eighty-ninth Congress authorized 240,000 units over four years beginning in 1965, only 140,000 —or 35,000 per year—were tagged as new construction, with the balance designated leased and rehabilitated housing units.

Second, House Appropriations set a tone that left the national public housing bureaucracy cowed. While Appropriations Committee members are regularly preoccupied with saving money rather than spending it, the savings effort is usually carried on in an impersonal fashion that may even leave the impression that the committee would like to be able to do better for the program.[26] When public housing was being emasculated in the 1952, 1953, and 1954 acts, however, no tone of regret softened the cutting process or veiled legislative judgments about either the value of the program or the competence of its administrators. It was in this period that Albert Thomas (Democrat of Texas), who was soon to start a twelve-year reign as chairman of the Independent Offices Appropriations Subcommittee, told the public housing administrator, "Everyone of you should be fired." The attitude was bipartisan. Norris Cotton of New Hampshire, then ranking Republican subcommittee member, characterized the public housing statute as "the most monstrous law ever passed by Congress—a law that is utterly impossible of decent administration, that insures the maximum of expenditure with the minimum of results."[27]

The program was further weakened by the defection of many southern Democratic supporters after the Supreme Court's ruling in 1954 that separate but equal is inherently unequal. If that principle controlled in public education, it was obviously valid in public housing. Shortly after *Brown v. Board of Education*, Senator Burnet Maybank of South Carolina led his southern colleagues out of the public housing camp with an effort to amend the 1954 Housing Act to delete all public housing.

While a special commission on housing policy appointed by President

26. On the House Appropriations Committee, generally, see Richard Fenno, *Power of the Purse: Appropriations Politics in Congress* (Little, Brown, 1966).

27. *Independent Offices Appropriations for 1954*, Hearings before the Subcommittee of the House Committee on Appropriations, 83 Cong. 1 sess. (1953), Pt. 3, pp. 1202, 1223.

Eisenhower had reluctantly concluded that public housing was a necessary program for the short run at least,[28] it was all that Republican leaders in Congress could do to get approval in the Housing Act of 1954 for 35,000 starts limited to use in 1955 by persons displaced by slum clearance or other public programs. The President had named as housing and home finance administrator Albert Cole, a former Kansas congressman whose opposition to the Wagner-Ellender-Taft bill had been so intense as to provoke Hubert Humphrey to complain that "it is like putting the fox in the chicken coop." The new administrator acknowledged his reservations about the program he controlled: "If I could believe that there is a fair and feasible way to terminate the present [public housing] program now, as to new construction, I would recommend it to the President and to [the Congress]."[29] But the probability of displacement of people by local government action financed by federal highway and other grants compelled continued administration support for what it described as a limited minimum program.

A delicate balance was maintained throughout the remainder of the Eisenhower years between an administration that made no effort to hide its antipathy to the public housing principle and program proponents who succeeded in keeping it alive with small annual authorizations. The administration kept seeking Cole's "fair and feasible way to terminate the program." He was still explaining in 1957 that there was no public housing section in the administration housing bill of that year because time to study the entire public housing situation was needed. As it developed, the Eisenhower period began and ended with studies of public housing. In between, it was nourished just enough to stay alive. Supporters were glad enough to have the 35,000 starts for 1957 and 1958 authorized by the 1956 Housing Act. They were disappointed when the best the liberal Congress elected in 1958 could do was to substitute incrementalism for standpatism: instead of the usual 35,000 figure, 37,000 contracts were permitted by the Housing Act of 1959.

There was good reason for disappointment because one of the areas in which the Democratic congressional election victory of 1958 was ex-

28. U.S. President's Advisory Committee on Government Housing Policies and Programs, *Recommendations on Government Housing Policies and Programs: A Report* (December 1953).

29. *Independent Offices Appropriations for 1955*, Hearings before the Subcommittee of the House Committee on Appropriations, 83 Cong. 2 sess. (1954), Pt. 3, p. 2042.

pected to make a difference was housing legislation. In 1959, Democrats had thirteen more Senators than in 1957–58, and forty-seven more members of the House than in the previous Congress. What some liberals then characterized as the "good majority" finally seemed to exist. Moreover, housing could not be avoided as a subject for legislation in 1959. The Federal Housing Administration had virtually exhausted its insurance authorizations, its home improvement and repair loan program was to expire during 1959, the college housing loan program had come close to the end of its loan authorizations, the Urban Renewal Administration had instituted a rationing procedure for capital grants reservations, and new contracts in public housing had last been authorized for fiscal 1958. Major housing legislation was inevitable. For public housers it appeared to be a propitious moment to achieve a breakthrough.

The good majority was not good enough to end the stalemate in public housing. When all of the battles over housing legislation ended—congressional-executive battles so intense that two bills were vetoed before a housing act was signed—authorization for only 37,000 additional units was provided. President Eisenhower and his budget and housing advisers began by denying the need for new authorizations, noting that over 100,000 units were in the pipeline—that is, already under annual contributions contracts, but not yet under construction. Public housing adherents emphasized that the Public Housing Administration held 57,000 applications that could not be moved to contract stage for want of authorization. Since they were talking about different things, both groups could be right. Authorizations could be exhausted but local inaction or second thoughts or processing delays in Washington could leave big gaps between authorization and construction figures. It was not unreasonable to insist that the gap be attended to. At the same time, an absence of new authorizations would result in a subsequent cutoff of construction. An effective program must deal with both authorization and construction.

The conflict was between those who insisted that cities holding reservations for public housing be compelled to move along before proposals be admitted from new authorities and those who argued for a less static interpretation of urban public housing needs. The latter position took into account that cities newly coming into the urban renewal, highway, and other public programs would be debarred from getting public housing contracts to meet their needs unless additional authorizations were legislated. The time from application through approval through preliminary loan through annual contributions contract to construction in public housing could run eighteen months to two years on an open site and four to five years on a slum clearance site. It was clear, therefore, from the arithmetic of the situation that failure to authorize new units would result, as Senator Homer Capehart—normally an Eisenhower supporter—put it, in "a hiatus, a void."

Nothing, however, shook the administration's view that the 100,000 units previously authorized but not yet constructed was the critical figure. "Recent experience," explained HHFA Administrator Norman Mason, "indicates an annual rate of public housing construction starts of approximately 20,000 units. At this rate, we have approximately a 5-years' supply of unused public housing authorizations under annual contributions contract."[30] The first veto message described the bill as "so excessive in the spending it proposes, and so defective in other respects, that it would do far more damage than good," and cited new authorizations as a case of excessive spending. "Even though we have over 100,000 previously authorized public housing units as yet unbuilt, the bill would authorize 190,000 more," Eisenhower complained.[31]

Having infuriated public housers by showing an apparent inability to recognize a difference between authorizations for new starts and contracts in the pipeline, Eisenhower now allowed his HHFA leaders to revert to the position from which he had approached public housing at the beginning of his administration in 1953: the need for a moratorium on action pending a study. "The administration felt," said Mason, "that with the program, with all the units that had been authorized being put in the pipeline so they could be built, and with the backlog existing in our cities—and this backlog exists in every one of our major cities today—that we could safely take 1 year's breather and try to find some better way to do this job."[32]

Ernest Fisher, then approaching retirement as professor of urban land economics at Columbia, was commissioned to try to find "some better way." By late 1959, however, with seven-eighths of the Eisenhower era over, Fisher did not have enough time both to develop and sell his innovative ideas in public housing to an administration that seemed to

30. *President's Message Disapproving S. 57*, Hearings before a Subcommittee of the Senate Committee on Banking and Currency, 86 Cong. 1 sess. (1959), pp. 124, 97.

31. *Ibid.*, p. 6.

32. *Ibid.*, p. 126.

find the whole concept distasteful. In a report that urged decentralization of authority and encouragement of experimentation everywhere, Fisher proposed acquisition and rehabilitation of existing dwellings for public housing use.[33] He recommended, too, development of "a balanced inventory of graded public housing facilities" that would spare the poor from being publicly pinpointed; the graded unit concept would permit over-income tenants—the public housing success stories—to pay part or all of an economic rent. Presumably, graded facilities would also make it possible to admit families with incomes too high for eligibility for traditional public housing. Leased housing was also part of Fisher's effort to break away from the stereotyped public housing high rise as a home for the poor. Virtually all of Fisher's recommendations became part of the program during the Kennedy-Johnson years. But all that Administrator Mason said about the report was perfunctory and polite: the analysis was "penetrating," the recommendations "thought-provoking." To be tagged "penetrating" and "thought-provoking" is to be consigned to oblivion.

While Fisher was developing his paper, Mason extended an invitation to selected public housing specialists outside the federal policy-making apparatus to offer opinions. In mid-October, over Mason's name, HHFA announced a "belief that we need to rethink the whole public housing question. We must take a fresh look at the housing problems of low-income families and search for new and better ways of dealing with them." For this purpose, he solicited opinions and ideas from seventy-eight experts in one or another phase of public housing. Their collective views favored the idea of good housing for all Americans but brought the Eisenhower people no closer to a solution of the dilemma they had been wrestling with for years: how to reconcile philosophical opposition to public action in a traditionally private area with an admitted need to increase the supply of low income housing. It was a dilemma that the Eisenhower administration never resolved and only infrequently acknowledged.

In any event, responses to the Mason inquiry were less divergent in viewpoint than in tone.[34] Virtually all respondents agreed on continued federal participation, on the disadvantages of high-rise projects, on the

33. "A Study of Housing Programs and Policies," prepared for U.S. Housing Administrator Norman P. Mason (January 1960; processed).

34. U.S. Housing and Home Finance Agency, *Views on Public Housing,* Symposium of Letters Written at Request of Norman P. Mason (March 1960).

importance of encouraging local experimentation in construction styles, and on the need to develop services helpful to socially maladjusted families. Unfortunately, instructive as any individual response might have been, all the responses did not automatically add up to a program. Even if they had, without endorsement from the administration there could be no changes. Therefore, Mason's decision simply to publish the letters without comment left public housing policy where it had been before the exercise began: tolerated, but not endorsed, by the political appointees responsible for its administration; lacking a long-range construction goal expressed as a percentage of total housing supply; unable to stimulate development of a professional training program; holding too many reservations for "no shows"—cities that reserved units but never went to construction—and having too little authority to make reservations for new applicants; and without policy guidance as to whether the program was to be limited to the well-adjusted poor or was meant to close its eyes to emotional and psychological problems.

The President's final budget message, that for fiscal 1961, took the same line Eisenhower had taken during the controversy over the omnibus housing bill of 1959: no new public housing authorizations were required at least until the gap between contracts entered into and construction starts was appreciably reduced. Although the Senate approved 25,000 new units, in accord with the President's original recommendation only a stopgap housing bill—without any new public housing authority—was ultimately enacted in 1960.

What to do about public housing policy also occupied the attention of some of the people in the private housing business as the 1960 election approached. Sensitive to the fact that its years of principled opposition to the public housing concept had contributed to a stalemate on the issue and thus indirectly to the absence of an alternative, the National Association of Home Builders commissioned an "independent study" by Joseph McMurray, formerly staff director of the Senate Banking Committee.

McMurray undertook to find "Ways and Means of Providing Housing for Families Unable to Afford Rentals or Mortgage Payments Necessary for Adequate Private Housing."[35] His report addressed itself more

---

35. McMurray's study, dated Dec. 30, 1960, is reproduced in *Housing Act of 1961*, Hearings before a Subcommittee on Housing of the Senate Committee on Banking and Currency, 87 Cong. 1 sess. (1961), pp. 509–44.

to intergovernmental relations than to an evaluation of policy alternatives. Essentially a proposal that the problem of low cost housing be referred to local governments for solution with federal money, McMurray's work passed no explicit judgment on the public housing program then in precarious existence. The McMurray plan depended on federal subsidies to local governing bodies—but not to home-owners, tenants, or sponsors—for use in a flexible fashion to be locally determined. McMurray urged a federal statute drawn broadly enough to allow approval of a wide variety of locally conceived programs so that each community could develop and administer that program or combination of programs that best met its own circumstances and the housing needs of its own people. To allow for a variety of programs, some of which might not involve construction subsidies, McMurray recommended fixing an average subsidy on a family-unit-per-year basis rather than in terms of numbers of construction units to be provided. Local governments could then make proposals for direct housing subsidies to families, or for payments to landlords, or for the acquisition of units of housing for low rent use.

McMurray's proposal was really a proposal for what Lyndon Johnson would later call creative federalism. Locally developed ideas for low rent housing programs would come up the tube and federal money would go down the tube in return. Eventually, low rent housing policy was to come to have some of the look of the McMurray plan. By 1967, traditional public housing had locally chosen variations: leasing, rehabilitation, turnkey, self-help. Rent supplements were developed to serve the same low income group eligible for public housing. But in 1960 the McMurray report's principal effect was only the softening of the Home Builders' earlier adamant stand against all public housing.

At the end of the Eisenhower administration, no easy way to terminate the need for public housing had yet been found, but the administration managed to run out the clock while considering the problem. Where the Wagner-Ellender-Taft Act of 1949 had contemplated 810,000 units in six years, congressional and presidential second thoughts reduced authorized totals to 322,000 units in the twelve years from 1949 to 1961, and only 270,000 of the authorized number were completed for occupancy. If there was no spirit of satisfaction and of anxiety to get on with the job among federal and local housing administrators, its absence was understandable. By every normal political sign, they and their program were really unwanted.

Public Housing as Social Improvement

When John Kennedy was elected, considerably fewer than half a million low rent public housing units had been completed for occupancy in the twenty-three-year history of American public housing. That situation did not change very dramatically over the ensuing nine years. Outright presidential antagonism to the conventional program was no longer heard, but the search for an alternative to public housing continued and new starts between 1961 and 1968 actually averaged less than did new starts between 1949 and 1952.

A new kind of impediment to production presented itself in the Democratic era: preoccupation with social improvement rather than with building public housing units. Little attention had been paid between 1953 and 1960 to improving the system for producing units because the administrators involved were not disposed to produce units. After 1961 the administration was sympathetic to public housing construction, but top Kennedy appointees got caught up in the social service side before attending to the question of how to get dwelling units built. National and local bureaucrats were not certain which direction was to be emphasized: more units or a better public housing environment. Having been frequently burned on the production question and sensing a New Frontier receptivity to social services, administrators pushed the latter. Finding a workable program of social services was more than the Public Housing Administration could accomplish; and from 1961 until 1967, when President Johnson ordered a production push, public housing was to do a poor job of social work and a poor job of production.

President Kennedy chose a local housing authority director interested in social services to run the national side of the program. Mrs. Marie McGuire, executive director of the San Antonio Housing Authority, came to the job of public housing administrator with twenty years' experience in operating public housing, culminating in a highly successful San Antonio project for the elderly, Victoria Plaza. Mrs. McGuire believed that "were it not for the continuous and strong trade opposition to public housing . . . necessary changes could have come about in an orderly fashion."[36] The necessary changes she envisaged at that time had

36. *Views on Public Housing*, p. 21.

to do with design, with financing, and with management. She was clear about the importance of social service aspects of public housing: intensive assistance for problem families; reduced concentration on disciplinary regulations; a manager–social worker for each fifty to one hundred units; established standards for employees, particularly directors.

Mrs. McGuire's deputy director, Francis X. Servaites, was plucked from the job of executive director of the National Capitol Housing Authority, to which he had just come from the executive vice-presidency of the National Housing Conference, the public housing lobby group. Before that, he had served ten years as director of housing for Puerto Rico and the Virgin Islands. The McGuire-Servaites combination, then, was a combination of experienced true-believers persuaded that the program had been administered unsympathetically. "I have no direct suggestion to make on how to resolve the public housing problems except to say that a great many of the problems have been created by the policies of the Administration and could be corrected by the same method that created them," Servaites had written Norman Mason not long before the 1960 election.[37]

Trying to put public housing back in business, the new Democratic leadership undertook to pick up where the program had been sidetracked almost ten years earlier. As if to say that now it was finally possible to get back on the track, the 1961 Housing Act authorized the balance of the $336 million in annual appropriations that had first been authorized by the 1949 Wagner-Ellender-Taft Act to finance whatever number of new units it would now finance. About 100,000 new units would have been possible under these arrangements. Leaders of the Public Housing Administration accepted the production objective, but they were more interested in services than in production and they were not skilled in administrative management techniques that might have simplified the cumbersome application-review-approval-contract-construction-occupancy process.

The new public housing administrator and the veteran bureaucrats in the agency who had endured, in their own view, ten years of martyrdom were both anxious to establish the program as a major mechanism for improving the life of the poor. But there were no good clues as to the kind of specific approach that the new President would endorse. The report of the preelection Kennedy Conference on Urban Affairs, endorsed

37. *Ibid.*, p. 114.

by the President, emphasized mortgage assistance for the home building industry and damned the Republican administration for nonproduction of public housing units. At the same time, the conference report recommended a "shift from large to small projects which blend into existing neighborhoods, as well as rehabilitation of existing substandard private units." Recognizing in a backhand fashion the existence of public housing tenants' social problems, it called for "a program of family counseling and technical assistance patterned after the successful experience of the Agricultural Extension Service."[38] This obviously left plenty of room for PHA to emphasize a program of new construction, of rehabilitation, or of social services.

With the apparent White House enthusiasm for rehabilitation of the poor through the provision of social services—the Ribicoff approach in the Department of Health, Education, and Welfare—as a cue, "concerted services" became the dominant theme in public housing and remained the dominant theme until the middle of the decade. Thus, without a clear signal from Congress or the White House, PHA put its limited energy into an emphasis on service and therapy for the public housing tenant rather than into an emphasis on techniques to speed up construction once authorizations for new starts were legislated. Moving ahead on the service front made it possible at least to appear to be in the mainstream of New Frontier activity. Unlike a construction emphasis, the services approach did not have to wait for a congressional directive, presidential blessing, or neutralizing of home builders' opposition. Public housing was now to team up with public welfare through a joint task force on health, education, and welfare services and housing. Conceived in informal conversations between Mrs. McGuire and Wilbur Cohen, then assistant secretary for legislation of HEW, during a series of White House–sponsored regional meetings on aging in the fall of 1961, the task force took life in March 1962. Its plan was to concentrate on five or six localities "in which there are local housing authorities anxious to extend services to their tenants and develop specific projects for each community, which grouping of projects might cover the whole gamut of HEW's services."[39] As the public housing people acknowledge,

---

38. The text of the report is in the *New York Times*, Oct. 20, 1960.

39. Elizabeth Wood, *Review and Evaluation of the Work of the Joint Task Force on Health, Education, and Welfare Services and Housing*, U.S. Department of Health, Education, and Welfare and U.S. Department of Housing and Urban Development (October 1966), p. 1.

the task force plan was an early but generally unrecognized precursor of the later neighborhood service centers concept.

In the process of helping problem families overcome their problems through concerted services, it was anticipated that a bonus would accrue to the account of local housing authorities in the form of an improved reputation for public housing projects and therefore an easier path to enlargement of the program. Ideally, concerted services would have resulted in minimizing public distaste for "bad" public housing projects because "bad" projects housing poorly adjusted people would be turned into good projects housing well adjusted people. Unhappily for this goal, concerted services made no real impact; only the professionals in HUD and in HEW were committed to its achievement. The local housing authorities had a limited interest and were not willing to yield autonomy in policy, regulations, and procedures where such yielding was necessary to make services possible. The tenant population was more concerned with income maintenance than with any kind of noneconomic service.

Four locally sponsored concerted services projects were developed during the four years of the task force's life. In all four cities involved— St. Louis; New Haven, Connecticut; Pittsburg, California; and Miami, Florida—there was extensive initial planning. For lack of money, Miami never came to the point of action; the others never moved very far. In a wistful terminal memorandum to the secretaries of HEW and HUD in October 1966, the task force cochairmen cited a few new and expanded services in the other three communities: a vocational rehabilitation unit was set up in each of the three; branch offices of the public welfare departments were located on the St. Louis and New Haven projects; a variety of educational programs for children, youth, and adults was provided on the three projects.

More significant probably is the list of obstacles that the task force could not resolve. In three of the four projects (New Haven was the exception) it could not translate official local commitments of assistance into tangible, lasting support. And it could not overcome such legislative constraints as inadequate levels of income maintenance and limitations on tenure in housing projects.[40] The concerted services project began

40. "Joint Task Force on Health, Education, and Welfare Services and Housing" (memorandum to the secretaries and other officials of HEW and HUD from I. Jack Fasteau of HEW and Abner Silverman of HUD, Oct. 31, 1966; processed), p. 3. See also Committee on Use of Program Resources of the Joint Task Force on Health, Education, and Welfare Services and Housing, *Services for Families Living*

with the hope that by bringing services to public housing tenants, their ability to achieve self-help and self-support would be enhanced. The project ended when, lacking high-level support, time, and money, the task force floundered and ultimately drowned in reports of locally established committees and agencies all anxious to "mount" concerted services projects and all lacking any clear definition of what was involved.

A task force that had no steam and no money, that owed its existence to a joint memorandum issued by an assistant secretary and a bureau chief, was no competition for a presidential task force, a special message, a declaration of "unconditional war," an agency based in the Executive Office of the President, and an opening appropriation of $1.2 billion. Sponsored by the Office of Economic Opportunity, community action programs, which emphasized income problems of tenants and did battle with local housing authorities, made concerted services—with its conventional ways—irrelevant. Who needed the cumbersome concerted services approach once they had seen community action? Community action felt no need for advice or help from public housing executives. "I have no contact with OEO," Mrs. McGuire said sadly to an interviewer at the end of 1966. Tenants were less interested in "coordinated, focused, onsite services" than they were in income assistance and in getting help to do battle with the welfare department and the local housing authority. Community action undertook the latter job while the task force just dumped traditional services from a big barrel and hoped for the best.

With the great concerted services push officially over, services continue to be haphazardly offered. "It is sort of happenstance," was Robert Weaver's characterization of community services in public housing.[41] If some local group, such as Boy Scouts, will take on an activity, it becomes part of the program. If another local group will take on another activity, it too will go in. But in most jurisdictions there is still no program for dealing with the social and emotional problems of tenants that is tailored to the particular population; instead, the population accepts or ignores community services that outside groups happen

in Public Housing, U.S. Department of Health, Education, and Welfare and U.S. Housing and Home Finance Agency (July 1963); Abner Silverman, "Techniques and Methods of Coordinating Public and Voluntary Services at the Neighborhood Level (Multi-Purpose Centers)" (paper prepared for delivery at the International Conference of Social Work, Washington, D.C., Sept. 9, 1966; processed).

41. Federal Role in Urban Affairs, p. 3684.

to find it convenient to offer. The HUD tendency is to count available services without regard to their value or use. Assurances to Congress that tenants "are given lots of services" gloss over the question of what kind of services.[42] There is good reason to doubt that many of the thousands of community service activities HUD lists with pride are relevant to the needs of public housing tenants.

Lyndon Johnson's last budget proposed a tiny $15 million appropriation for tenant services grants to local authorities. Services to be provided would have included counseling and referral activities related to education, job opportunities, housekeeping techniques, money management, and other programs to help tenants cope with day-to-day problems of urban life. HUD anticipated a big bang for only a few bucks, estimating that the $15 million would permit funding of local programs in 75 cities affecting 1.5 million people in 400,000 public housing units. President Nixon's 1970 budget revisions withdrew the item. According to the department's spokesman, "We want to obtain voluntary citizen participation [in tenant services] by local individuals and organizations."[43] A year later, voluntary citizen participation seemed less promising: HUD's 1971 budget requested $5 million for tenant services. Congress declined to make the appropriation. Ironically, the House Appropriations subcommittee suggested the use of local volunteers and civic groups.[44]

After more than thirty years, then, public housing administrators still cannot be sure whether they are supposed to be running a public social service or whether they are supposed to be running a public business with unusual financing arrangements but nevertheless an impersonal we-have-apartments-to-rent-to-people-who-can-afford-to-pay-for-them-and-whose-behavior-does-not-discourage-other-customers-from-coming kind of business. The ambivalence between a brick and mortar activity and a social welfare activity ends in castigation from supporters of each who feel, quite properly, that the program has not made sufficient progress in either area.

42. *Independent Offices and Department of Housing and Urban Development Appropriations for 1970*, Hearings before a Subcommittee of the House Committee on Appropriations, 91 Cong. 1 sess. (1969), Pt. 4, p. 272.

43. *Ibid.*

44. *Independent Offices and Department of Housing and Urban Development Appropriation Bill, 1971*, H. Rept. 91-1060, 91 Cong. 2 sess. (1970), p. 17. The item was reinserted in the Senate, but lost in conference.

5
Tenants and Landlords

Public housing production totals are low because presidents, congresses, and city councils have so willed. Public housing landlord-tenant relations are poor because the landlords are not equipped to deal with multi-problem, dependent families of the kind that are inexorably coming to dominate the tenant population.

Nothing worries program leaders more than the transformation of public housing into a kind of institution for the disadvantaged and the disabled. More and more tenants have come from outside the fully employed population to the point where half of all tenants now are also public assistance cases; meanwhile, the housing indigents—families not on public assistance who would be able to make their own way in other respects if only they could find reasonably priced housing—are less and less willing to accept conventional public housing. Housing officials are concerned about the erosion of a vision of economic and social integration before it ever became much more than a vision; about their own admitted inability to cope with the problems of a multiproblem tenant population that has few peer group leaders interested in a stable living environment; and about the resulting public relations consequences of a publicly supported program that often takes on the characteristics of an urban slum.

Both federal and local public housing administrators insist that one of the best aids to the rehabilitation of problem families is nonproblem neighbors who can serve as live examples of rehabilitation. The argument continues that selective admissions, selective evictions, and a basic policy change in present regulations requiring so-called over-income tenants to vacate are all necessary if the stability of many public housing projects is to be maintained and if the public image of public housing as a social program that has failed is to be reversed. This view that local administrative discretion in tenant selection, assignment, and retention should be maximized in order to promote a desirable kind of tenant mix is by no means universally accepted; to the contrary, administrative selectivity is under attack: both existing restrictions on the admission of so-called undesirables and the right of local authorities to evict undesirables are being challenged. Nor is there much indication that change in policies fixing maximum income limits for continued occupancy will soon take place. The dilemma is an old one: whether, when there is not enough relief to go around, to provide it to those most in need or to those who, by conventional standards, are most deserving.

The original plan for public housing assumed that it would cater to the most deserving, and would do so in racially segregated projects. Recent survey research found a continuing disposition to favor the well-adjusted poor over families likely to be troublesome: Chester Hartman and Gregg Carr report that nearly two out of five (38 percent) commissioners of local authorities feel that "families with severe social problems ought to be rejected for public housing altogether," and that one out of three directors of local authorities share that view. Another 24 percent of the commissioners and another 18 percent of the directors would accept families with severe social problems but segregate them in separate projects or separate parts of projects. Fewer than half (48 percent) of the commissioners agreed with the proposition that the authority's tenant assignment policies should seek to promote racial integration.[1] Both racial integration and social problems—unmarried mothers, deserted families, delinquent children, the chronically unemployed, illiterate or nearly illiterate family heads—are now in the mainstream of American concern, however, so that there is pressure on the local commissioners and directors to change their ways if not their minds.

Tenants and Tenant Selection

A Future for the Aged

A chance to have it both ways—to help some of the poorest people who are also among the best adjusted and hence most deserving—is

1. "Housing Authorities Reconsidered," *Journal of the American Institute of Planners*, Vol. 35 (January 1969), pp. 10 ff.; "Housing the Poor," *Transaction*, Vol. 7 (December 1969), pp. 49 ff.; and "Local Public Housing Administration: An Appraisal" (draft manuscript).

made possible by an emphasis on housing the elderly. The growth of that program has led to two separate worlds of public housing. One is the world pictured by Frances Carp in "A Future for the Aged," the story of San Antonio's Victoria Plaza, where elderly tenants are poor, mentally alert, reasonably healthy, clean and well groomed, and possessed of a general attitude that reflects a healthy acceptance of reduced income, a sense of humor, and an ability to contribute to community activity through hobbies and interest in group affairs.[2] Another is the world of St. Louis' Pruitt-Igoe Homes, described by its social biographer, Lee Rainwater, as a far less genteel world populated by nonelderly people who lack a healthy acceptance of reduced income and who develop a sense of frustration as they become aware of the impossibility of finding a self-sufficient and gratifying way of living. Where Mrs. Carp's elderly have an ability to contribute to community activity through hobbies, Rainwater's subjects have a different strength: the ability to tolerate and defend against degrading verbal and physical aggressions from others and not give up completely. Participation in group affairs is a notable feature of public housing life among the elderly in Victoria Plaza; Rainwater finds in his subjects an "inability to embark hopefully on any course of action that might make things better, and particularly action which involves cooperating and trusting attitudes towards others."[3] The duality of public housing suggested by this comparison has been given bureaucratic recognition: in the low rent project directory published by the Department of Housing and Urban Development (HUD), projects for the elderly have been grouped separately and listed on colored paper.

For a good many years America's principal welfare program, public assistance, has had a comparable kind of dual identity. In its old age assistance (OAA) aspect it is genteel, popular Victoria Plaza; in its aid to families with dependent children (AFDC) aspect it is Pruitt-Igoe, neither genteel nor popular. But public assistance and public housing now have different clientele balances. The aged are a declining percentage of the public assistance caseload as universal social insurance based on work history cuts slivers from the OAA rolls. The dependent children category grows both in absolute numbers and as a percentage

2. Frances M. Carp, A Future for the Aged: Victoria Plaza and Its Residents (University of Texas Press, 1966).

3. Lee Rainwater, "Crucible of Identity: The Negro Lower-Class Family," Daedalus, Vol. 95 (Winter 1966), p. 204.

of the total public assistance load. As this shift develops, public assistance's troubles grow.

Public housing follows a contrary distribution pattern. Well over a third of all public housing dwellings are occupied by the elderly, and the trend has been upward (Table 7). In recent years about half of all new

Table 7. Occupancy of Public Housing by Low Income Elderly, 1964–69

Date	Total occupied units	Units occupied by elderly	
		Number	Percent of total
December 31, 1964	557,014	148,185	27
December 31, 1965	581,190	174,081	30
December 31, 1966	608,697	197,611	33
December 31, 1967	638,437	226,365	36
December 31, 1968	707,467	261,728	38
June 30, 1969	735,382	276,272	38

Source: U.S. Department of Housing and Urban Development.

starts have been for the elderly.[4] In 1967, for example, 57 percent of the new and rehabilitated starts were for the elderly, down from 62 percent in 1966 but up from 48 percent in 1964. An additional federal bonus of up to $120 a year has been payable since 1961 on units for the elderly. Its effect is to encourage the growth of the elderly segment by minimizing the risk of an authority that builds for the elderly finding itself without receipts from rents to meet operating costs. No comparable federal bonus for very large or very poor families was provided until 1968.

It may be, as Chairman John Sparkman (Democrat of Alabama) of the Senate Banking Committee suggests, that "it is like starting from a zero base, the elderly housing started from a very low base and therefore, naturally, we are getting an overbalance in the first few years, which I think may not be at all permanent."[5] But not everyone is as sanguine as Senator Sparkman about the overbalance being temporary. For example, McClinton Nunn, late director of the Toledo Metropolitan Housing Authority, saw it differently even as long ago as 1963, when he noted that where public housing was originally thought of as a stepping stone

4. *Building the American City: Report of the National Commission on Urban Problems to the Congress and to the President of the United States*, H. Doc. 91-34, 91 Cong. 1 sess. (1969), p. 114.

5. *Housing Legislation of 1965*, Hearings before the Subcommittee on Housing of the Senate Committee on Banking and Currency, 89 Cong. 1 sess. (1965), p. 268.

for "fine people who were retarded only by a national depression . . . today we have turned our special attention to that of providing housing for the elderly, those individuals and families who are now in the eventide of life." Public housing now, said Nunn, is thought of "as a final relay station for independent living before the 'headstone' instead of as a 'stepping stone.' "[6] Paul Douglas, for years a most vigorous congressional proponent of public housing, concluded regretfully in 1965 that "public housing is now more and more becoming a program of housing for the elderly," a judgment affirmed three years later in the report of an urban problems commission he headed.[7]

Another escape route for the public housing program is through small town activity where the needy are less likely to be of the wrong color or to follow deviant behavior patterns. While formation of new authorities has been taking place in impressive numbers—in March 1961 there were 1,174 local authorities; by the end of June 1968 there were 2,185; for June 1970 the estimate is 2,738—most of that growth is in communities under 10,000 population with small programs. Five hundred eight local authorities entered the program from 1965 to early 1969; of these, 394 had programs of less than 200 units. Almost one-third of all local authorities have programs of less than 50 units. The National Commission on Urban Problems (Douglas Commission) found that nonrural localities under 2,500 that account for 0.6 percent of the nonrural population contained one-fourth as many units as localities over 1 million that account for 15 percent of the nonrural population.[8] An explanation of this phenomenon of disproportionate strength of public housing in the small towns was once made by Robert Weaver. It continues to be pertinent:

It is a problem of finding sites. It is a problem of the fact that in continental United States of America, the only place that you build public housing is in your central cities or in your small towns; you do not build in the suburbs. You have great difficulty in finding a site for public housing in the central city, except in well-established neighborhoods, as we know so well even in New York where we have difficulty.[9]

6. "Paper Prepared for Demonstration Institute on Management of Public Housing for the Elderly" (April 1–4, 1963; processed).

7. Housing Legislation of 1965, Hearings, p. 268; Building the American City, pp. 108–33.

8. Building the American City, p. 112.

9. Federal Role in Urban Affairs, Hearings before the Subcommittee on Executive Reorganization of the Senate Committee on Government Operations, 89 Cong. 2 sess. (1966), Pt. 1, p. 194.

The Racial Mix

Site selection is an impossible problem because there is a 100 percent chance that tenants will be poor and at least an even chance that tenants will be black, but vacant sites are most likely to be in outlying white neighborhoods where everybody is not poor. Nationally, only a little more than half of all public housing units are occupied by non-white families, with the percentage somewhat above the national average in the Chicago and Philadelphia areas, much below in the San Francisco area, and slightly below in the New York and Atlanta areas.[10] Everywhere, however, projects have traditionally been in white or black neighborhoods and have been white or black occupied or, especially in the South, buildings have been segregated within a project by site.

A racial mix in public housing tenancy is more likely to occur outside than inside a ghetto. But few nonghetto areas believe they will be upgraded by a public project, and fewer still contain land cheap enough for the public housing budget. In Washington, D.C., with twenty-two —exactly half—of the city's forty-four housing projects located in the Anacostia area in the far southeast quadrant of the city, the executive director of the National Capital Housing Authority (NCHA) explained his problem:

Everybody and his brother has been telling me I shouldn't concentrate public housing in Southeast or Southwest, but I don't know where else the housing can be put. Economically, we can't afford property west of Rock Creek Park. Not only can we not buy the land, but the rents west of the Park are too high for us to lease the land with what the Federal Government provides in subsidies.[11]

A few months later, NCHA did contract to purchase an existing luxury apartment building in the middle class, white, upper northwest part of the city and announced a plan to house elderly tenants there. Most tenants would be black. Not only did a Committee of Concerned Citizens organize to oppose the purchase through court action, but unsympathetic questions were raised by both the chairman and the ranking minority member of HUD's House appropriations subcommittee.[12]

10. *Building the American City*, p 114.
11. *Washington Post*, Sept. 27, 1967.
12. *Independent Offices and Department of Housing and Urban Development Appropriations for 1970*, Hearings before a Subcommittee of the House Committee on Appropriations, 91 Cong. 1 sess. (1969), Pt. 4, p. 51.

Although the department approved the purchase finally, the political atmosphere surrounding the transaction does not encourage further actions of the same sort.

To add to an existing project or to develop a new project in the neighborhood of existing projects is the more common path of least resistance, and sometimes it is the only path. In Chicago the housing authority habitually would drop efforts to build in wards whose aldermen objected to the proposal. As a result, a federal court concluded in 1969, only 2 of 41 building sites tentatively slated for white neighborhoods since 1955 had received City Council clearance. One of the 2 sites finally approved for 400 units was adjacent to a predominantly Negro area and was partially occupied by dilapidated Negro shacks. The other site provided for only 36 units. During the same period, 103 sites in predominantly Negro areas were tentatively selected, and 49 of them were finally approved.[13]

No proposal to build or to acquire public housing in a middle class neighborhood in any city is peacefully received. From Martin Meyerson and Edward Banfield's classic account of site selection in Chicago in the late 1940s, *Politics, Planning, and the Public Interest,* to Washington, D.C.'s problems in 1969, the record of opposition to public housing in white neighborhoods has a sameness about it. The varieties of ways in which opposition to a particular site can be reflected have been evident in recent years as New York City struggled to disperse its projects. With increasing pressure from Congress and from the White House on the federal agency to clear its pipeline, and with consequent pressure on the local authority to get its reservation into at least preconstruction stage, delay becomes one weapon of opposition. So, for example, when the New York City Planning Commission proposed projects in the Corona section of Queens, the president of that borough argued that a June hearing on the subject should be continued to the fall. While the city had to designate sites by a June 30 deadline or face loss of its reservation, the opposition claimed that it needed more time to study the proposals. The same plea for study time had been made at a hearing in May in connection with another Queens site. In both cases, however, the use of time as a strategic weapon was accompanied by more forthright demands for the status quo by elected officials from the districts involved:

13. *Gautreux, et al.* v. *Chicago Housing Authority, et al.,* 296 F. Supp. 907 (1969).

Do not change the area. Do not give us a project. We are happy and we want to stay that way.

It is neither unfair nor un-American for middle-income parents to aspire to have their children raised in a community where they come in contact with children of similar economic and cultural level.[14]

In order to make some progress in the city's public housing program, New York's Mayor John Lindsay found it necessary to overturn a long-standing "borough courtesy" policy by which the president of each of the city's five boroughs had been able to veto a public housing site in his borough. When Lindsay formulated his public housing policy for the city, it emphasized two basic guidelines: concentration of new construction on vacant land and underutilized areas in outlying parts of the city; "vest-pocket" projects in the already densely populated areas with heavy concentrations of existing projects. Since most vacant land was in white areas and since most of New York's public housing tenants were Negro or Puerto Rican, the result would be to integrate previously white neighborhoods. To eliminate the borough president's veto power under these conditions meant that there would be some chance of getting housing; to retain the veto meant that there would be none.

Long after school desegregation had become an announced public policy goal, public housing policy was largely indifferent to racial integration. Sites were selected in accordance with prevailing patterns of segregation, and projects were routinely all white or all Negro, with occasional token integration in the North and West. Even by HUD's generous definition of an integrated project—"white and more than one nonwhite, including at least one Negro family"—the pages of its low rent project directory were studded with segregated projects. Little Rock, Arkansas, for example, had 8 projects with 1,178 units in June 1966; 4 were all white, 4 all nonwhite. That was still the case in November 1968 when the Department of Justice filed suit against the Little Rock Housing Authority, accusing it of unlawfully segregating its tenants. HUD was apparently the last to know: the same day the suit was filed, HUD announced a model cities planning grant to Little Rock. Segregated public housing was not a pattern restricted to the South. At that same time, for example, to choose almost at random from the HUD directory, the 5 projects in Danville, located in east central Illinois, had 630 units: 241 in 3 all nonwhite projects, 389 in 2 all white units. All 50 units under management in Princeton, New Jersey, were nonwhite

14. *New York Times*, May 12, 1966; June 2, 1966.

occupied. In 1969 the Chicago Housing Authority operated 54 buildings with 30,848 units. Only 4 of the buildings were in white neighborhoods. While projects in black neighborhoods were 99 percent black occupied, buildings in white sections had Negro occupancy rates of 1 to 7 percent.[15] Chicago's largest project, the Robert R. Taylor Homes, had 4,413 units, all nonwhite occupied.

No militant position on public housing integration came from the federal public housing bureaucracy during either the Eisenhower or the Kennedy-Johnson years until the administration was publicly shamed in 1967. The issue never surfaced at all during the Eisenhower period, when administrative energies were directed to finding a way to terminate the program, not to integrate it. The three goals espoused by Marie McGuire, Kennedy's public housing commissioner—to change the image in design, in financing, and in management—did not include breaking the pattern of segregated housing. Mrs. McGuire was fond of describing with pride, Victoria Plaza, a 185-unit "future for the aged"; it was an all white future. "The Constitution does not require us to provide integrated housing," the general counsel of the federal public housing agency remarked to an interviewer shortly before the National Committee Against Discrimination in Housing (NCDH) charged publicly, in February 1967, that the Department of Housing and Urban Development had "taken no meaningful action to desegregate existing public housing projects."[16] The charge was part of a report that had been made privately to the White House ten months before it was made public. While there was never a response to the earlier, nonpublic submission, publication brought an instant response. Secretary of Housing and Urban Development Robert Weaver—a past president of NCDH—issued a long statement that really confirmed the fact that federal approval for ghetto public housing had not been withheld because "it is one of the tools to revitalize these areas." Weaver went on to assert, "I am committed to encourage public housing outside as well as within the ghetto. My objective is a balanced program which recognizes the great and pressing need for low-rent public housing throughout the community." The statement also included the first official HUD pronouncement on racial concentrations as a factor in site selection:

15. *Gautreux, et al.* v. *Chicago Housing Authority, et al.,* 296 F. Supp. 907 (1969).

16. National Committee Against Discrimination in Housing, *How the Federal Government Builds Ghettos* (February 1967), p. 7.

HUD considers a local program of public housing which provides sites only in areas of racial concentration as *prima facie* unacceptable. When such proposals are made, the Local Housing Agency will be asked to submit additional sites, so as to provide a more balanced program. If none are forthcoming, the LHA must make a conclusive showing that no other sites are available outside of areas of racial concentration.[17]

This was, as one department official put it, "a clear strengthening of our site selection policy." Three weeks after publication of the NCDH report, the low rent housing manual was amended to include the "*prima facie* unacceptable" finding for local public housing proposed only in ghetto areas. In the course of the following eighteen months, fifty-two local authorities were asked to submit a more balanced program, two authorities were asked to make a more conclusive showing that no acceptable sites were available outside the ghetto. In the main, however, the site selection policy came after segregated public housing was well entrenched. As Weaver said later, "It is fundamental, of course, that, of all the housing in this nation, public housing should never have been developed on the basis of white projects and Negro projects—but it did happen in many areas. . . ."[18] Southern congressmen obviously had been prematurely concerned in 1954 about the consequences for public housing of the Supreme Court's rejection of the separate but equal doctrine. Through the following thirteen years, a period covering over 450,000 starts, the controlling theory—if there was a theory—was that federal rejection of ghetto site units could only reduce the number of public housing starts; it was better, therefore, to accept local proposals for segregated housing than to insist on nondiscrimination by dispersing sites throughout the community.

If public housing projects could not be brought to white neighborhoods of the central cities because of land scarcity, high costs, and pressure on local governing bodies to refuse approval for such projects, what about bringing white tenants to projects in operation that might otherwise be all nonwhite? HUD began to develop this moving-Mohammed-to-the-mountain approach sometime after the NCDH bill of particulars went to the White House.

17. "Statement by Robert C. Weaver, Secretary, U.S. Department of Housing and Urban Development" (Feb. 8, 1967; processed), p. 6.
18. Message telephoned to 31st National Conference of National Association of Housing and Redevelopment Officials, Oct. 11, 1967, *Journal of Housing*, Vol. 24 (December 1967), p. 610, and *Congressional Record*, Vol. 113, Pt. 21, 90 Cong. 1 sess. (1967), p. 28713.

The result was a major modification of the existing rules that allowed prospective tenants to discriminate in selection of units. Heretofore, a free choice policy had been acceptable. Freedom of choice meant freedom of the local authority to discourage integration, meant that there could be a substantial number of vacancies in the projects occupied by one race even though many applicants of another race were on the waiting list, meant that in actual experience segregated patterns continued. A freedom of choice policy, in the rather belated judgment of HUD, really did not result in actual freedom of choice. The department made official what many people who had been involved in the freedom of choice policy already knew:

In such situations, for various reasons, such as the mores of the community, fear of reprisals, types of neighborhoods, inducement by local authority—whether by subtle suggestion, manipulation, persuasion, or otherwise—or other factors or combinations, such "freedom of choice" plans, in their operation, did not provide applicants with actual freedom of access to, or full availability of, housing in all projects and locations. The existence of a segregated pattern of occupancy was in itself a major obstacle to true freedom of choice, since few applicants have the courage to make a choice by which they would be the first to change the pattern. Even without inducement of local authority staff, the plans tended to perpetuate patterns of racial segregation and consequently separate treatment and other forms of discrimination prohibited in section 1.4(b) of the department regulations.[19]

Applicants for public housing, if the local authority was so disposed, could turn down any number of units offered while waiting for a vacancy in a preferred project. White applicants regularly declined assignments to Negro units and waited for an ultimate assignment to a white unit. No formal segregation policy was necessary to maintain white and nonwhite projects under that arrangement. Now it was proposed that a "rule of three" be substituted: local authorities were to be required to offer prospective new tenants accommodations on a first-come-first-served basis in projects having the highest vacancy rates. Refusal to accept three consecutive offers of accommodations in locations having the highest vacancy rates would, with certain exceptions like inaccessibility to a job or a child's day care center, drop an applicant to the bottom of the local authority's communitywide list of eligibles. Weaver referred to the rule of three in his response to NCDH, using the future tense—an appropriate choice. The effective date of the rule

19. Opinion of the general counsel of the Department of Housing and Urban Development, quoted in *Journal of Housing*, Vol. 24 (December 1967), p. 609.

of three regulation was delayed ten months and then was still being fought by the National Association of Housing and Redevelopment Officials (NAHRO). Even in the summer of 1969, a conference of regional housing officials heard the rule of three denounced as "this most hated policy" by a local director who urged that the issue be reopened with the Nixon administration now that "the ego of the former administrators is no longer at stake."[20]

Whatever its specific details, any imposed uniform tenant selection and assignment plan would antagonize local housing officials who would rather be realtors than social workers and have grown accustomed to calling their own shots. Much of the overt objection from NAHRO spokesmen to the rule of three is based on what they term "a uniform policy of uncertain effectiveness" promulgated without local participation. Rather than having the plan originate with the federal agency, local authorities believe that—like local school districts—they should be empowered to submit integration plans subject to HUD approval.

But the opposition is based on more than procedural grounds and on more than the uncertain effectiveness of the rule. The rule of three could ultimately result in the end to the hopes of many local public housing officials for a tidy program in which some tenants set good examples for others and whole projects full of poor people set good examples for poor people everywhere. Applying a kind of Gresham's Law to tenancy—bad tenants drive out good—local housing officials argue that as desirable prospective tenants come to the top of the waiting lists, most will decline units in locations with the highest vacancy rate because these tend to have an already high proportion of problem families. Similarly, it is claimed, white prospective tenants will decline assignments to Negro locations even at the risk of dropping to the bottom of a communitywide list. The predicted consequences, therefore, are high vacancy rates (and loss of local income) due to declinations, increased segregation as whites flee from public housing, and projects that are twentieth century asylums for misfits and social deviants.

To avoid this, subjectivity in admissions and assignments is considered necessary. A policy that precludes local officials from plucking names from its lists to fit the social and economic and racial integration plans

20. Remarks of Richard G. Jones, executive director of the San Antonio Housing Authority, at 29th Annual Southwest Regional Council of the National Association of Housing and Redevelopment Officials, June 1969; reprinted in *Congressional Record*, daily ed., July 17, 1969, p. E6049.

of the local authority could result in a tenant mix that would, as a New York City tenant selection official told an interviewer, "damage the image of public housing and limit local support for more projects." Then, according to this analysis, nobody would win. Available units would become populated by multiproblem families who could not be helped by the example of some success stories. Projects would deteriorate. With 100,000 wait-listed applicants in New York depending on either turnover or new construction, there would be neither.

Another way in which some local officials state their objections is that in the process of pushing racial integration, the federal administrative amendment to all annual contributions contracts unilaterally resolved the question of whether public housing is primarily a real estate or a relief program in favor of the latter. The most needy applicants will take an assignment under the rule of three; but the most desirable white tenants—usually the working poor who are the most reluctant to move in in the first place—will decline to be integrated with blacks or with problem families, as the case may be. Public housing's white clientele will be limited to the most miserable of public assistance cases for whom rehabilitation has no significance in anything but very long run terms. It will be some years before there is empirical evidence on which to judge the actual consequences of the rule of three regulation. The belief that its inevitable consequence is the triumph of relief over real estate may turn out to be correct, but that was not a premeditated consequence. In the summer of 1967, Secretary Weaver's and President Johnson's primary goal was to counter a valid charge of racial isolation in public housing.

The Rent Game

While considerable attention focuses on racial imbalance in projects, on problems of selecting sites, on the merits of a freedom of choice versus a tenant assignment policy, and on whether to debar or evict social deviants, money is also an important problem in public housing. Policies governing rent and income limits for admission and for continued occupancy continue to steer an ambivalent course between the relief and real estate options.

To get into public housing it is first necessary to have an income adequate to pay some rent, but not so large an income that it is possible to pay an economic rent. The real need of the local authority to collect rents automatically keeps public housing from becoming a kind of Salvation Army Mission for families and for the aged without resources. Public housing is not available to the poorest of the poor who have no means of meeting the minimum rent. Like food stamps, the housing bonus must be bought. Federal contributions through the annual contributions contract meet principal and interest payments on the building, but maintenance and operation—so-called residual costs—are met from rents. From this fact of public housing practice, Robert Weaver had deduced a valid economic rule:

If you have more than a given percentage in any project of families who cannot afford to pay rents that cover these operating expenses then this project is in financial straits and it cannot operate.

So there is a limit as to how many very poor people can be housed in public housing.[21]

Because it is a public program with a social conscience, public housing will not allow a low income family to pay a disproportionately large percentage of its income for housing. Accordingly, income must be high enough so that the minimum public housing rent does not constitute more than about one-fifth of that income. Weaver has made this point clear too:

Public housing assumes a responsibility for two things: First, the provision of decent housing; secondly, at rents people can afford. This means rents that do not take 30, 40, or 50 percent of the families' income but usually, on an average 20 percent. It does not solve a person's housing problem if you give him decent housing, and do not leave him enough money to feed his family adequately. . . .[22]

The responsibility of local authorities is to fix income limits for admission low enough to admit the poor but high enough to admit an adequate number of families whose rental payments of about 20 percent of income will meet the individual authority's costs of operation and maintenance. With rents tied to tenants' incomes, the higher the maximum income for admission, the more likely is the local authority to be able to meet its obligations. But since an avowed purpose of public housing is to serve the poor rather than to minimize the accounting problems of local housing authorities, that purpose itself serves as an implicit counterforce to any temptation to fix relatively high admission limits. That counterforce is strengthened by a statutory rental gap requirement,

21. *Housing and Community Development Legislation*, Hearings before the Subcommittee on Housing of the House Committee on Banking and Currency, 88 Cong. 2 sess. (1964), p. 99.
22. *Ibid.*, p. 100.

adopted in the 1949 Housing Act, designed to keep public housing out of the private housing market. Under its terms, an annual contributions contract may not be entered into unless the local authority can show that a gap of at least 20 percent has been left between its upper rental limits and the lowest rents at which private enterprise provides "a substantial supply of decent, safe, and sanitary housing toward meeting the need of an adequate volume thereof."[23]

Admission limits and rents are currently set at low enough levels everywhere to justify the conclusion that whatever deficiencies public housing may have as a social program, whatever deficiencies it may have in design and in the style of life it engenders, whatever its limits as a method of developing integrated housing, it is a program whose economic benefits are principally received by the poor. Moreover, the trend is toward serving progressively lower income families: in 1944 the median income of families in public housing was 54 percent of the national urban median; by 1967 it had declined to about one-third of the national median. The median income limit for admission of a four-person family was $4,100 in 1969, up from $3,100 ten years earlier. The lowest approved admission limit was $2,400. Admission limits of at least $3,450 obtained in about three-fourths of all localities with low rent projects; limits in only about one-third of all localities were as high as $3,950. Approximately one-fifth fixed limits at a point roughly coincident with the poverty level figure of $3,300.

Low income, however, is not a sure ticket of admission even for socially desirable families and even in those jurisdictions with very large programs. For example, Boston selects tenant families alternately from two ranges to which eligible applicants are assigned according to the rent to be charged them. A lower range extends from the minimum rent to just below the authority's break-even point; an upper range extends from the break-even point to the maximum rent. The alternate selection is designed to assure that tenants pay rents that average enough to meet operating expenses. Similarly, the former director of the Norfolk, Virginia, authority, recently HUD's assistant secretary for renewal and housing assistance, explained how he kept Norfolk in the black:

. . . Among the low income families there is a range. Let us assume you have $4,000 as a ceiling. You discriminate against the $3,000 to $4,000 if you do not take any of them just like you would discriminate against the

23. 42 U.S. Code Annotated #1415(7)(b)(ii). The rental gap requirement was eliminated in projects for the elderly in 1961.

$1,000 to $2,000 if you took none of them. Our plan is to take some of all. In the process we average out with the rent higher than we would average if we took all the $1,000 to $2,000 income families. We do not find this discriminatory. We feel in effect that you cannot take them all anyway. . . .[24]

Like Boston and Norfolk, most authorities, in order to insure income sufficient to meet operating costs, have established a rent range system that limits the percentage of tenants within various income ranges and fixes appropriate rents within the income groupings. The very lowest rent, paid by the lowest income group, may be available to perhaps 35 percent of the tenants, with $500 gradations resulting in a typical rent range control of the following sort:

Range	Income	Rent	Planned percentage of tenants
1	$2,500 or less	$46 or less	35
2	2,501–3,000	47–56	15
3	3,001–3,500	57–66	20
4	3,501–4,000	67–76	13
5	4,001–4,500	77–86	10
6	4,501–5,000	87–96	5
7	5,001 or over	97 or over	2

The graded rent system imposes constraints on how vacancies are filled. Departure of a single family from range 6, say, and its replacement by a family falling in range 2 could be absorbed in a large program but it is not a substitution pattern that could go on indefinitely without impairing the ability of the authority to meet its operating costs. The special federal payment of $120 per year per dwelling unit occupied by an elderly family has helped make possible a bulge in the bottom rent ranges for elderly tenants since the effect is to increase the operating funds available to the local authority by $10 monthly. Before Representative Leonor Sullivan successfully sponsored a comparable provision in 1968 for the very low income tenant, however, the latter was at a comparative disadvantage in the competition for public housing space. The planned percentage of range 7 tenants could always be exceeded without financial chaos for the authority; the maximum percentage of range 1 tenants could not be ignored if the authority was to remain solvent.

More than half of the country's eighty-two largest local authorities, operating nearly two-thirds of all the units in the program, now find themselves approaching a crisis point because rents do not or soon will

24. *Independent Offices . . . Appropriations for 1970*, Hearings, Pt. 4, pp. 59–60.

not meet operating costs. The situation is already serious in at least eight jurisdictions. In Washington, D.C., St. Louis, San Francisco, and New York, routine expense already equals or exceeds income; in Boston, Newark, New Haven, and Philadelphia, routine expense is between 95 and 99 percent of income. Barring an infusion of federal funds, the whole local rent structure will have to shift upward, thus freezing out a larger number of families at the lower end of the income (and rent) scale. New York, for example, anticipates that, using 1967 as a base year, its average rent will soon be rising at twice the rate the average net income of its tenants has increased.

Both HUD Secretary George Romney and Assistant Secretary Lawrence Cox came up with the same short-run answer: supplemental federal funds to bail out authorities in distress, an arrangement that out-rages Chairman Joe Evins of the HUD House appropriations subcom-mittee. Evins' outrage at the prospect of adding to the federal subsidy can be attributed in part to the absence of options. If an authority in trouble went bankrupt, HUD would become the receiver and the obliga-tion to meet operating costs would simply become a direct federal obli-gation. The long-run solution to the fiscal problem is to compel authori-ties favoring admission of the very lowest income families—Detroit is an example of this policy—to develop an income and rent range plan that is designed to yield enough money to meet operating costs. Of course, the practical aspects and the social costs of mandating such a change in policy—especially in Detroit—can be considerable:

The citizens and the governing body and everyone there feels that the best job in public housing is done only when you take the lowest of the low income. They have them established in occupancy. Many of them are on welfare. Half of their families are on welfare. What do we do? Do we arbitrarily take part of their food budget and clothing budget to apply to rent? Do we put them out and bring in these higher income families?[25]

One convenient way for HUD to ease the fiscal crisis slightly would be to push the social goals for public housing explicitly if quietly ap-proved in 1967 by Don Hummel, then assistant secretary for housing assistance. One of those goals reads:

Management policies of local housing authorities should be so designed that public housing projects house a broad cross-section of low-income house-

25. *Ibid.*, p. 62. For an analysis of beneficiary groups in publicly assisted rental housing, see George von Furstenberg and Howard R. Moskof, "Federally Assisted Rental Housing Programs: Which Income Groups Have They Served or Whom Can They be Expected to Serve?" *The Report of the President's Committee on Urban Housing*, Vol. 1, *Technical Studies* (1968), pp. 147–65.

holds, so as to avoid concentrations of the most economically and socially-deprived households.[26]

In order to accomplish this goal, there is broad agreement among the management specialists at the federal level that raising income ceilings for continued occupancy is critically important, that wider use should be made of present statutory authority to continue an over-income family in occupancy when it is unable to find suitable housing in the locality, and that rental policies and requirements for the examination of tenants' income should be adjusted to minimize the difference between public housing and normal real estate practice. Whatever the social advantages, if the present tiny percentage of over-income tenants were allowed to increase and the present continued occupancy ceilings were raised or eliminated, an economic consequence would be an increase in rent receipts for most authorities.

Retention of over-income tenants and elimination of maximum income limits in favor of economic rents for higher income tenants is the theme played again and again by proponents of the "take public housing out of the public relief category" philosophy. It is urged by Abner Silverman, patriarch of the federal bureaucracy, as the single most significant innovation that could occur in the program; by John Lange, executive director of NAHRO, as the one hope for achieving stability in public housing projects; by Elizabeth Wood, executive secretary of the Chicago Housing Authority from 1937 through 1954, who came to HUD in 1966 (at the age of sixty-seven) to develop the first official program of social goals in the history of public housing.

Without firm support from the secretary, prospects for achieving elimination of income limits for continued occupancy are not bright on two counts. First, as long as the demand for units exceeds the supply by large numbers, it is difficult to justify retaining families relatively better off at the expense of families relatively worse off. Proponents argue abstractly that a mix is desirable and that leadership is important; badly housed or overcrowded low income applicants are realities who can be seen. Nor is it certain that higher income tenants have any interest in staying in public housing. Leonard Duhl, who once served as consulting psychiatrist-in-residence for the secretary of housing and urban development, scoffs at the higher income leadership argument, claiming that leaders want out of public housing and feel neither desire nor obligation to make management's job easier by showing the way to other tenants.

26. Elizabeth Wood, "Social Goals for Low, Moderate Income Housing Management Defined," *Journal of Housing*, Vol. 24 (June 1967), p. 265.

And while Congress has been content to let income limits both for admission and for continued occupancy be locally determined, its committees are more likely to ask about income limits than they are to ask about the presence of leadership families.

Income limits for continued occupancy have been responsive to the inflationary pattern of recent years, but with a $2,800 median income most of the public housing population remains well below the limits. From 1961 to 1966 the median limit nationally for continued occupancy by an average-size family rose by 15 percent, from $4,000 to $4,600. Thus an income almost one and one-half times as much as the Social Security Administration's 1967 poverty line would not debar a family from remaining in public housing in half the programs. Indeed, outside the Fort Worth ($4,400) and Atlanta ($4,500) regions, the median limit was higher: in the New York region, $5,500; Philadelphia, $4,900; Chicago, $5,400; and San Francisco, $4,900. Only 1 percent of all the 1,885 localities with approved income limits at the beginning of 1967 denied continued occupancy to a 4-person family that achieved an income of $3,250, just adequate statistically to remove it from poverty; 22 percent of the localities had limits pegged as high as $5,250 and over. This was a steady increase from 1962, when under 10 percent of the total reported continued occupancy limits as high as $5,250, and over 1964 when the percentage had gone only to 16.

While more and more authorities are apparently willing to set limits high enough to keep tenants who are out of the technical poverty classification, there is little local use of the statutory authority that allows over-income families to remain in residence if they are unable to find decent, safe, and sanitary housing in which they can afford to live. A study of seven geographically representative authorities found fewer than 3 percent over-income families in 1968. About two-thirds of them were required to move. More than half of all local authorities recently had no over-income tenants at all.

If income improves, families voluntarily move out rather than wait for reexamination. This conclusion was reached by a careful study made at HUD in 1967. What is not known is whether families move out because they anticipate being asked to move or whether they move as soon as their incomes permit an alternative without considering the possibility of remaining on an over-income basis. There has not been an official study of reasons for moving since the midfifties although it would seem to be crucial to a program of social goals. Clearly enough, most mobile families do not find public housing so attractive that they hang on until the last possible moment or until income reexamination forces them out. The result is a tenant income distribution skewed toward the bottom end of the range—which probably is bad for the self-perception of tenants who cannot get out and surely is bad for the fiscal stability of local housing authorities.

Good Behavior

The social goal most favored by local authorities is conventional good behavior by tenants. Even after discarding a list of twenty-eight behavior standards it had previously applied to all applicants, the New York City authority, for example, continues to adhere to an imprecise and subjective admissions policy "designed to create in its developments an environment conducive to healthful living, family stability, sound family and community relations and proper upbringing of children."[27] While moralistic judgments are no longer supposed to control, "healthful," "sound," and "proper" are in the values of the beholder, and the chances are good that New York officials behold them in accord with many of the old twenty-eight standards, which included such things as stability in employment history, presence of a father in the home, freedom from drug addiction, and good housekeeping habits. One big breakthrough is that applicants—specifically including unwed mothers—are no longer declared ineligible solely on the basis of data furnished in a written application. Eligibility decisions now are based upon interviews and "such further inquiries as may be necessary."

A federal court in Arkansas has insisted that the Little Rock Housing Authority must avoid an arbitrary policy of exclusion on moral grounds. At the same time, the court recognized the authority's right to exclude for cause. Little Rock's Authority had denied admission to two Negro women, each a mother of three children born out of wedlock, on the basis of a regulation denying both admission and continued occupancy if a member of the family had one or more children born out of wedlock. Challenged as a violation of the due process and equal protection clauses of the Constitution, the regulation fell as the court ruled it arbitrary and capricious for a failure to make distinctions as to the number

27. "Statement of Ira S. Robbins, Vice-Chairman of the New York City Housing Authority, Before the New York State Joint Legislative Committee on Child Care Needs" (March 22, 1968; processed), p. 1.

of children involved, the circumstances of illegitimacy, or the possibility of reform. But perhaps more important, the court declined to order the admission of the women, sustaining the right of the local authority not to tolerate indecent conduct and to formulate reasonable procedures for admission and retention.[28]

Eviction is the traditional instrument through which local housing authorities have enforced their behavior standards, often with an indefensible disregard for due process. Tenants begin at a disadvantage because public housing leases are habitually drawn on a month-to-month basis. HUD's Local Housing Authority Management Handbook, in recommending this arrangement, noted that it "should permit any necessary evictions to be accomplished with a minimum of delay and expense upon the giving of a statutory Notice to Quit."[29] Until February 1967, HUD had never instructed local authorities that they must inform tenants why they were being evicted and hear their reply; most authorities made it clear that they preferred not to specify the reason for eviction. Thus, for example, the lease form in use in Minneapolis, judged a model of clarity, brevity, and size of print by NAHRO consultants, specifically provided: "This lease may also be terminated by the Management at any time by the giving of written notice not less than 30 days prior to termination. No reason need be stated for such termination." And even after HUD prohibited this kind of bill of attainder, the requirements that tenants be told why they were to be evicted and that their replies be heard could be described as involving nothing more than a "closet conference."[30]

Termination of housing relief through eviction is comparable to termination of public assistance cash benefits. Out of local concern that the social deviant not be permitted to mingle with those who are merely

28. *Thomas, et al.* v. *Housing Authority of the City of Little Rock, et al.*, 282 F. Supp. 575 (1967).

29. *Local Housing Authority Management Handbook*, Pt. IV, Sec. 1, #6(d)(1).

30. George Schermer Associates and Kenneth C. Jones, *Public Housing Is the Tenants: Rethinking Management's Responsibility and Role in Tenant and Community Relations* (National Association of Housing and Redevelopment Officials, 1967), pp. A59 ff. Note, "Public Landlords and Private Tenants: The Eviction of 'Undesirables' from Public Housing Projects," *Yale Law Journal*, Vol. 77 (April 1968), p. 994. Citing the Feb. 7, 1967 HUD circular, the State Court of Appeals of Tennessee held that the Nashville Housing Authority acted arbitrarily and capriciously in seeking to evict a black welfare recipient with five children without giving her an opportunity to answer charges of misconduct. *Nashville Housing Authority* v. *Taylor*, 422 S.W. 2d 668 (1969).

economically disadvantaged, however, evictions have tended to be even more arbitrary than cash relief terminations. One eviction issue in dispute involves unmarried motherhood. In Richmond, Virginia, for example, the authority handled evictions for illegitimacy as a routine matter for fifteen years. Its policy was to forgive any history of illegitimacy occurring before admission but to require tenants to sign a statement indicating their understanding that the lease would be terminated if any future instances occurred. In giving absolution for past sins, the Richmond Housing Authority expected its flock to remain virtuous in return for the act of charity involved in providing a dwelling unit. But when four unwed mothers and their ten children were ordered out of Richmond's Creighton Court, a 504-unit (all nonwhite) project, in November and December of 1966, a Negro city councilman arranged for intervention by the National Association for the Advancement of Colored People (NAACP). NAACP lawyers argued that the circumstances of a child's birth are irrelevant to the legislative purposes of public housing and that the evictions could not be tolerated in view of the shortage of low income housing in Richmond.

Frederick Fay, executive director of the Richmond Authority and the 1967 NAHRO president, insists that the eviction policy was reasonable. Fay's position is that in the judgment of the authority "growing children cannot be expected to become good citizens if they are required to live in an environment that condones a disregard for law or proper standards of behavior and conduct." Richmond's Law and Equity Court subsequently agreed with this self-evident truth and found it applicable to the particular case. There was no discussion of whether the ten children to be evicted could be expected to become good citizens. Speaking of "conditions of moral degeneracy," the court ruled that the authority could not allow such conditions to develop when the legislative purpose of public housing was to eradicate them. Subsequently, the case was removed to the federal courts. Pending a final resolution there, Richmond's illegitimacy policy remained in effect and new applicants signed an acknowledgment of their understanding of the policy. The authority stayed evictions but continued to record known illegitimate births.[31]

Sometimes, of course, even what is supposed to be a liberal authority policy may not be understood or followed down the line at the tenant contact level. Ira Robbins, vice chairman of the New York City author-

31. *Washington Post*, Jan. 8, 1967; letter from Frederick A. Fay, July 31, 1968.

ity, thought his authority took a compassionate view of unwed, teen-age, pregnant tenants. Testifying at a hearing on services to unmarried parents in central Harlem held by a New York State joint legislative committee on child care needs, Robbins denied that it was authority policy to evict teen-age unmarried girls because they were pregnant. The audience of Harlem residents promptly shouted specific instances of such evictions; one participant summed up by describing the classical bureaucratic problem: "Listen, darling," she told Vice Chairman Robbins, "it's become obvious that you don't know what your staff is doing."

While both the NAACP Legal Defense and Educational Fund, Inc. (known in civil rights circles as the "Inc. Fund") and the Roger Baldwin Foundation of the American Civil Liberties Union would like to provoke a clear-cut ruling on eviction and due process, the appropriate case has been elusive. And if the appropriate case were found, there would still be what one Baldwin Foundation attorney refers to as the "bubble problem"; because no two cases are exactly similar, success in one case of this sort often results only in the bubble popping up in another place in slightly different shape necessitating new and slow and expensive litigation. Since HUD's eviction circular was issued, there has been a series of conflicting lower court rulings in eviction cases. In Texas a federal court would not enjoin the local authority from evicting tenants alleged to be unable to control their children who were involved in fights, gambling, and the shooting of firearms in and near the public housing units.[32] But another federal court, in Louisiana, has permanently enjoined the Housing Authority of New Orleans from evictions without providing precisely the procedural safeguards sought in Texas.[33] The supreme court of Georgia has affirmed the power of the Atlanta authority to evict a tenant who violated her lease agreement by misrepresenting the paternity of her four children and subsequently failing to report the birth of a fifth child. Advance notice of the causes for eviction had been given and the tenant had had an opportunity to present a defense.[34]

On the other hand, the Illinois supreme court held that a public housing authority's failure to state a reason or cause for lease termination

32. *Harris* v. *San Antonio Housing Authority,* Civil Action No. SA69CA22 (W.D. Texas, filed April 30, 1969). Jurisdiction retained. See *Journal of Housing,* Vol. 26 (July 1969), p. 361.

33. *Ruffin* v. *Housing Authority of New Orleans,* 301 F. Supp. 251 (1969).

34. *Williams* v. *Housing Authority of the City of Atlanta,* 155 S.E. 2d 923 (1967).

does not justify a tenant's refusal to vacate after proper notice has been given. Ruling that continued occupancy is a privilege rather than a right, this court found that privilege to be subject only to the terms of the month-to-month lease, which carried no requirement that reasons for termination be stated.[35] The appellate division of the New York supreme court, however, concluded that an authority cannot arbitrarily deprive a tenant of his right to occupancy simply by exercising a contractual provision to terminate his month-to-month lease. Instead, due process would at least require giving a reason for termination as well as timely notice to vacate; where the reason is improper, the eviction will not be allowed.[36] Meanwhile, the superior court of Pennsylvania ruled that where constitutional rights have not been violated, a tenant has no right to continued occupancy in a public housing project where the lease provides for termination by either party. Moreover, the court denied that the tenant had any right to challenge the authority's reasons—in this case, poor housekeeping—for terminating the tenancy.[37]

The United States Supreme Court sidestepped a recent chance to rule on the eviction question in a case that carried free speech overtones. Mrs. Joyce Thorpe's lease in McDougald Terrace, a 247-unit, all non-white project in Durham, North Carolina, was terminated in August 1965 without stated cause. North Carolina courts sustained the authority's position that it did not have to give a reason for refusing to continue the month-to-month lease. The "Inc. Fund" contended that the eviction took place because Mrs. Thorpe had been elected president of an active tenants group. Coupling the silence of the Durham authority with the then (1967) new HUD circular telling local authorities to give tenants the reason for eviction and hear their reply, the Supreme Court set aside the North Carolina supreme court's approval of the eviction and returned the case for further proceedings in light of the circular.[38] The eviction bubble continues to pop up because, as Justice Douglas put it in a separate opinion, the two issues the Thorpe case presented were left unresolved, that is, whether a public housing tenant can be evicted for any reason or for no reason at all, and whether a public housing tenant can be evicted for the exercise of a right guaranteed by the First Amendment. To put it another way, can public housing

35. *Chicago Housing Authority v. Stewart*, 237 N.E. 2d 463 (1968).
36. *Vinson v. Greenburgh Housing Authority*, 288 N.Y.S. 2d 159 (1968).
37. *Lancaster Housing Authority v. Gardner*, 211 Pa. Super. 502 (1968).
38. *Thorpe v. Housing Authority of the City of Durham*, 393 U.S. 268 (1969).

tenants be held to different behavior standards than is the rest of society?

A recent note in the *Yale Law Journal* concerned itself with procedural safeguards for public housing tenants faced with eviction as undesirables. Acknowledging that the courts have generally considered the local authority an ordinary landlord, the note suggests a distinction between private and public landlords because "the former are dependent on their property for income while the latter's only legitimate interest in their property is in its usefulness as a tool of national and state housing policies."[39] Ideally, then, tenants could avail themselves of federal protection since federal district courts have original jurisdiction in civil action suits to redress deprivation of constitutional rights under color of state law. This assumes that there is a protected right not to have a benefit revoked once bestowed. But such a procedure is simply not feasible in most eviction cases; the alternative proposed by the note's author is a fair hearing administered by the housing authority. The hearing should meet four conditions: the tenant should be given prior notice of grounds for his eviction; he should be confronted with the evidence and witnesses against him and be permitted to challenge them; he should have the right to counsel or other advice; prosecution and adjudication should be separated. Fair hearings decisions would be subject to review in accordance with administrative review acts.

The fair hearing proposal is not an adequate substitute for a federal policy statement, either legislative or administrative, dealing with evictions. Certainly, further procedural safeguards should be built into the eviction process to preclude a local authority from acting as both accuser and judge of a tenant who cannot defend himself against notice to quit because he is not told why it has been issued or given a chance to protest its validity. HUD's 1967 circular provides some of these safeguards; a fair hearing provision would provide some more. But substantive questions remain a matter of local discretion. Any reason is adequate, so long as it is a reason. At a minimum, the protections of the First Amendment should be written into public housing so that the Housing Assistance Administration, which is supposed to be encouraging tenant organizations, does not find itself making annual contributions to local authorities that evict tenants who become overactive in such organizations.

39. "Public Landlords and Private Tenants," p. 996.

The particular problem of eviction for unmarried pregnancy could be dealt with by borrowing from the philosophy of the Department of Health, Education, and Welfare's Flemming Rule dealing with discontinuance of aid to dependent children in homes deemed unsuitable. The Flemming Rule, adopted administratively in 1961 and later written into the 1962 Public Welfare Amendments, provides that a state using a suitable home test could not deny assistance unless appropriate provisions were made otherwise to meet the needs of the child involved. A comparable principle is involved here: if a local authority finds that it cannot abide an unmarried mother as a tenant, let its right to evict be conditional upon a showing that some other decent, safe, and sanitary housing has been found for the child who is wholly unresponsible for his bastard status. Neither HUD's present requirement that the mother be told that she had sinned nor the broader fair hearing idea gets to the question of what happens to the evicted tenant and, in the case of eviction for illegitimacy, what happens to the child or children involved.

Landlords

Controversy over admissions, evictions, and tenant behavior standards would more likely be muted if public housing's three classes of landlords—the public housing officialdom in HUD, local housing authority commissioners, and local authority directors—were better able to cope with the complicated problems of race, broken homes, unsupervised children, and public dependency posed by an increasing number of tenants. Each class of landlords, however, and the quasi-professional organization that links them, the National Association of Housing and Redevelopment Officials (NAHRO), has troubles of its own that complicate adjusting to the changing character of the tenant population.

The Vanishing Bureau Chief

Federal agencies tend to do better when they have leaders rather than caretakers and when they are strategically located in the hierarchy. Public housing is weak on both counts. The 1966 organizational plan for the creation of the Department of Housing and Urban Development depressed the hierarchical position of what had been the Public Housing Administration. Where the commissioner of public housing had

had a direct path to the housing and home finance administrator, in the new department the former was transformed into a deputy assistant secretary for housing assistance who must compete with both a deputy assistant secretary for renewal and a director of urban neighborhood services for access to an assistant secretary through whom filter approaches to and directions from the secretary.

When the organization chart is filled in with real live people and relationships, the leadership and access problems of public housing are intensified, not relieved. Between 1966 and 1970 it was not possible for the top national public housing administrator systematically to concern himself with the significance for public housing of civil disorder, black power, urban migration, increasing numbers of multiproblem tenants, and increasing signs of tenant militancy because during those years, save for one period of eight months and another of eight weeks, the public housing program was directed only by acting chiefs, one clearly a caretaker, the other just as clearly lacking the confidence of HUD's secretary and under secretary. For the first year and a half of its life, the Housing Assistance Administration was headed by an acting deputy assistant secretary, Marie McGuire, the former public housing commissioner, whose skills and interests were weighted on the side of housing the elderly. HUD leaders quickly decided to dump her, but did not quickly find the right successor. To be designated as "acting" after having been commissioner for five years was as explicit a show of no confidence as it seems possible to make. Mrs. McGuire's prolonged acting appointment under these conditions left the program without an authoritative national spokesman during the precise period that the failures of public housing were being assigned a share of the blame for the crisis of the cities.[40]

The leadership problem was no sooner resolved when it became unstuck. Public housing bureaucrats had hoped for a new chief who knew the business and also knew his way in matters of race and politics. They got Thomas Fletcher, formerly city manager of San Diego, California. None of the three cities Fletcher managed had had a public housing program; none had a significant black population. As a city manager, he was a political eunuch lacking ties to power centers in either party. But Fletcher reasoned that the appointment of an urban generalist–public management specialist was meant to emphasize an interest in effective administration—getting applications processed and annual contributions

40. See, for example, *Report of the National Advisory Commission on Civil Disorders* (Kerner Commission), (March 1, 1968), p. 262.

contracts signed and, above all, producing public housing units in timely fashion. Fletcher took to this assignment and put some vigor in what had been a lackadaisical operation. "The purpose of public housing," he later explained, "is to build low rent dwellings, and I viewed my job as bearing responsibility for getting units built." Housing Assistance personnel now look back on his leadership as a high-water mark in what is more commonly a sluggish operation. It was a brief leadership, however; Fletcher had barely had time to move the reluctant Mrs. McGuire from her choice office space in the HAA Washington headquarters when, in September, he was named deputy commissioner (mayor) of the District of Columbia. Fletcher's two-year commitment to the public housing job was thus cut to eight weeks by President Johnson's decision that the reorganized District government needed a manager.

Fletcher's successor was another ex-city manager, Elder Gunter, former president of the International City Managers' Association; once manager of University City, Missouri, of Des Moines, Iowa, and of Pasadena, California; then a Ford Foundation program advisor in Lebanon until anti-American feeling in the Middle East persuaded Ford to close up shop in the area. A successful manager, Gunter had been out of the profession just long enough to avoid being tagged as an administrator who could function only as a city manager. By coincidence, not design, Gunter's municipal experience, like Fletcher's, had been restricted to cities without public housing programs so that the actual mechanics of the activity were new to him. He claimed no expertise in race problems and denied any political affiliation.[41] Gunter lasted eight months—just long enough to begin to understand the program. Unlike Fletcher's, Gunter's relationship with the assistant secretary for housing assistance was not a happy one. That fact, even more than the imminence of a change in national leadership, led to Gunter's resignation in the summer of 1968 to accept a job as city manager of Yonkers, New York.

In the summer of 1968, vacancies in policy-making jobs were being filled by caretakers. Again run by an acting chief, the caretaker administration in public housing was expected to remain only until the new President took over in January 1969. But despite HUD Secretary Romney's asserted interest in housing production, public housing still had

41. Gunter tells the story of HUD Secretary Robert Weaver's inquiry to him: "Are you a Democrat or a Republican?" To Gunter's "I am a professional city manager and have never indicated a partisan preference," Weaver replied, "Do you mind if I tell the President you are a Democrat?" Gunter did not mind.

"acting" leadership as late as December 1969. Four critical years thus managed to slip away without continuing leadership ever being found for public housing which, among all public relief activities of the federal government, most needed effective and imaginative leadership to over-come the legacy of the fifties when the leadership had plotted homicide on its own program.

Reorganization eliminated half the problem. In November 1969, Romney announced a major reorganization of the department designed to separate production from social and financial management. The pub-lic housing production function was shifted to the Federal Housing Administration, management and finance stayed with Renewal and Housing Assistance. This reorganization had the usual advantage: it will take a while to determine its effects.

Local Leadership

The tenure problem is quite the reverse at the local executive level. Prolonged tenures are too common for housing authority executives. In 1955 there were 1,002 local authorities; in 1965, a decade later, 431 of the 1,002 had had no change in chief executives. This translates into a minimum tenure of ten years as chief executive for 43 percent of local public housing directors. Since only a handful of them were first ap-pointed in 1955, the actual tenure of this 43 percent is undoubtedly several years longer. For example, the first director of the Cleveland Metropolitan Housing Authority, Ernest Bohn, retired in 1968 after thirty-five years in the job. Robert Wolfe's tenure as director of the New Haven Housing Authority exceeded two decades. John Schulz ran the Long Branch, New Jersey, program for twenty-seven years until he died in 1967. Charles Ross retired in 1968 after twenty-three years as director of the Seattle Housing Authority. Emmett Burke had been director of the Yonkers authority for seventeen years when he resigned to run for mayor. James D. Richardson's service as director in Vallejo, California, covers a quarter of a century. M. B. Satterfield was Atlanta's director for seventeen years. Frederick Fay has served twenty years in Richmond, Virginia.

Examples of long tenures both in the authority's top job and in the ranks can be multiplied endlessly in large jurisdictions and small. Ninety-seven percent of all executive directors have served in that position only for their present authority, and 89 percent have worked only for one authority throughout their careers in housing.[42] While it is becoming increasingly common for top public and private executives to move several times in their careers, it is the unusual housing authority executive who moves at all, and a second move is extraordinary.

To the extent that stability and tranquillity are prized, localism in public housing administration has some obvious advantages. When the executive is a native, the public housing program is more likely to be accepted than when the administrator is an unknown. One reason is that an understanding and an acceptance of local mores, history, and power alignments diminish the chances that the executive will propose unacceptable sites. Another is that when innovation is encouraged or mandated by change in the federal statute or federal regulations—the "rule of three" tenant assignment policy is an example—it is useful to have a trusted native handling it. Other new techniques with uncertain consequences are scattered site housing and the leasing of private dwellings for public housing. Either of these could effect profound changes in a city's housing patterns if pursued by an administrator who was more concerned with increasing his inventory than with local approval.

An apt contrast is with the city manager. Longevity in office is not unknown in that profession of course, but mobility is taken for granted. Budget reforms, personnel shake-ups, and sharp changes from traditional practices are a routine part of a manager's bag. If the changes are too much for the city fathers, they send him on his way, yet his brethren credit him with adherence to professional standards and recommend him to another city. Most managers anticipate moving eventually in any case, and their reputation in the profession and with the International City Management Association (ICMA) is a more important determinant of their future than is their local reputation.

With local housing executives, the tendency toward localism can discourage attention to systematic study of professional methods of trying to cope with problems of low income families and encourage conformity with local values and maintenance of existing techniques. It is a daring thing, for example, for a housing executive to encourage formation of tenant councils because tenant councils are not routinely accepted in the low income housing business. If the tenant council backfires and disrupts the local peace, the executive has no place to go; if it works, success will

42. Hartman and Carr, "Local Public Housing Administration: An Appraisal."

not carry with it opportunities for a better job. In short, there is no incentive system to make it worthwhile to innovate or to reach out for problem families. So, while public housing tenants are changing, the middle-aged well-educated white male executives who manage the programs are staying the same. Many of them started in public housing in their communities when nearly all tenants were well behaved and upwardly mobile. Some directors do understand and accept the newer population, but the conclusion of researchers who have recently surveyed directors' attitudes is that inherent disparities between tenants and directors are reflected in the high proportion of directors who express lack of respect for their tenants and an unwillingness to give them any significant voice in running their affairs.[43]

Aside from the fact that directors devote all or most of their time to the job in return for a salary, they are not notably different in characteristics or beliefs from their bosses, the local housing authority commissioners appointed by mayors or county executives. Over ten thousand commissioners are involved in making public housing policy at the local level. For the most part they are housing dilettantes, primarily business executives, bankers, ministers, attorneys, and—whatever their regular occupation—always "civic leaders." Except in New York City where there is a salary attached and the job is demanding of full time, a commissioner is less likely to be a housing specialist than he is to be a man of good will. To be a housing commissioner is considered an incidental rather than a major service activity. Since it is not an elective office, the commitment can be undertaken more casually than is usually the case with a school board member or a city councilman. The housing authority commissioner has limited responsibilities, concerns himself with only a fraction of the city population, and will have less direct contact with the public housing tenant than the councilman and school board member will have with their respective constituencies.

Based on responses to the only national survey of housing authority commissioners ever undertaken, Hartman and Carr picture the typical commissioner of the late 1960s as very different from the generality of public housing tenants: a white male, in the middle or upper-middle

---

43. *Ibid.* Charles Abrams pinpointed the personnel problem 25 years ago: "While real estate experience makes a good background for management of a housing project, many real estate men are deplorably lacking in understanding of social and governmental problems. Social workers, on the other hand, are likely to be deficient in business judgment." *The Future of Housing* (New York and London: Harper and Bros., 1946), p. 293.

income ranges, well educated, in either business or a profession, middle-aged or elderly.[44] Fewer than one commissioner in ten is a woman, only six in one hundred are nonwhite, almost three out of four have had at least some college education, only 11 percent have incomes low enough to fall within the public housing limits. It may not be reasonable to expect commissioners to mirror the socioeconomic composition of the public housing population, yet the present incongruity invites conflict between tenants and commissioners unable to identify with the problems of that majority of tenants who are low income, under-educated, black, and part of female-headed families—everything that the commissioners are not.

While class differences are not necessarily an automatic barrier, difficulty in identifying with tenants is evident in commissioners' answers to queries about their attitudes to tenants. Only half of all the commissioners, for example, expressed disagreement with the proposition that "most public housing tenants have no initiative." That doubt about tenant capacity for self-help is coupled with an overwhelming—69 percent—rejection of the proposition that "it is up to the government to make sure that everyone has the opportunity to obtain a secure job and a good standard of living." But the belief in laissez-faire does not extend to tenant life styles: 59 percent of the commissioners believe that "the authority needs stricter rules and regulations, and proper means of enforcing them, in order to promote acceptable behavior on the part of tenants." And the commissioners see the landlord's job as lawgiver rather than bargainer: only one commissioner in four agreed that "management ought to recognize and negotiate with tenant unions."[45]

What this suggests is that by reasonable tests involving personal characteristics, life styles, and attitudes, no representative-constituency relationship exists between local public landlords—either commissioners or directors—and public tenants. The commissioner landlords are not chosen to represent the tenants, but are chosen as representative of the successful business and professional leadership of the community. The director landlords are more dependent on and more closely tied to the community's political and business leaders than to the public housing tenants or to a public housing administration profession.

44. Hartman and Carr, "Housing Authorities Reconsidered," p. 12. But see Edward White, Jr., "Tenant Participation in Public Housing Management," *Journal of Housing*, Vol. 26 (August–September 1969), p. 416, and an accompanying report that tenants have been appointed commissioners in at least 10 cities.

45. Hartman and Carr, "Housing Authorities Reconsidered," p. 16.

A group of nonrevolutionary New York City public housing tenants have promulgated a Public Housing Tenants' Bill of Rights to accomplish "self determination." One plank provides that "immediate steps shall be taken by the Housing Authority to turn over to the tenants control of public housing." But all wisdom is neither in the tenants nor in those nontenants who now manage tenant affairs. Independent tenant councils—officially estimated by HUD to number over 1,200 at the same time that the department's social services chief privately numbered effective councils at about 25—can be encouraged to substitute for the arrangement in many cities where the landlord group provides one of its own as spokesman for the tenants. In the New Orleans authority, for example, the tenant relations department has been headed by a tenant relations adviser, "who acts as tenant representative on the Central Office staff . . ." and also supervises tenant selection, community relations, project services, and public relations. How it is possible or why it is necessary for a key management figure to act as tenant representative on the central staff rather than encouraging tenants to provide their own spokesman is a mystery to which the obvious answer is that the public housing paternalistic tradition has been stronger than has been the concept of participatory democracy.

Collective bargaining between commissioners and directors, on the one side, and tenant councils, on the other, can be made obligatory in such matters as behavior standards, evictions, repair charges, and staff attitudes. Local housing authority commissioners can be socially and economically heterogeneous. Directors can be educated about their clientele. The governance of public housing can be modernized before its administrative offices are occupied by tenants whose patience has run out.

National Association

Modernization has been a concern of the housing officials' association, but the group's capacity to accomplish it is uncertain. Personnel from the various public housing landlord levels—local management staff, executive officers, commissioners, and federal officials—and personnel from the renewal and redevelopment programs related to public housing are brought together through the National Association of Housing and Redevelopment Officials (NAHRO). NAHRO, an unpretentious association, also accords membership status to housing agencies themselves.

With both animate and inanimate members the organization has considerable trouble deciding whether to focus on being a pressure group, a quasi-professional association concerned with training, a housing policy research unit, or a public housing public relations agency that works to counteract horror stories about the program. To play it safe, NAHRO does all of these things from its nonpublic housing quarters in Washington's new Watergate complex.

Locals who look to their own community for rewards and recognition simply do not lend energetic support to a national organization that has neither immediate nor long-range practical benefits to bestow. While a national organization of housing officials exists, its mission is uncertain, its influence limited. To make the city manager comparison again: the city managers' association can lead its individual members because those members are professionally oriented. The public housing official is oriented to his local community and cannot as readily be led from outside.

Within the association, the dominant voices are those of the federal bureaucrats and the local authority directors. The muted voices are those of the commissioners and of the project managers. The latter, especially, take a small role in so-called professional activities, probably because no public housing management profession really exists. Even the directors, who take the program seriously and worry over it, as we have seen lack an important characteristic of a professional group—mobility.

While the organization in 1969 claimed a total of 6,942 individual members—principally local, state, and federal officials—only half that number are full, active members, and one-sixth are no more than subscribers to the *Journal of Housing*. Principal financial support comes from the 1,703 agency members.[46] As a pressure group, lacking money and political influence, it is not surprising that NAHRO is rarely consulted at the highest levels. Its own executive leaders acknowledge that after thirty-five years of existence, NAHRO is more likely to be given post hoc "courtesy consultation" on federal public housing policy than to be taken into consultation during the period of policy development.

NAHRO leaders attribute their exclusion, in the years from 1965 to 1969 anyway, to the association's steadfast support of public housing and cool attitude toward rent supplements. Another explanation is

46. Membership Report as of Jan. 31, 1969, *Journal of Housing,* Vol. 26 (February 1969), p. 90

offered by members of the federal public housing bureaucracy. They point out that before the efforts to upgrade the Housing and Home Finance Agency (HHFA) into a cabinet department and before the statutory fusing of the old Public Housing Administration into the department, PHA, as a semi-autonomous agency, could go wherever it chose for advice and consultation. Now, consultation is with departmental leaders. Public housing policy proposals move up and down the pipe between the public housing bureaucracy and the HUD assistant secretary and secretary levels. In other words, the federal establishment, it is said, has increased its own capability and organization for internal consideration of policy. New internal channels of communication make it less necessary to seek advice from interested nongovernmental groups. Accordingly, both NAHRO and the National Housing Conference, a nonprofit group that originally was titled National Public Housing Conference but has broadened out to a concern with low income housing policy generally and with urban renewal, are left outside.

Whatever the explanation—and it should be remembered that many administration policy proposals in the Johnson years at least were secrets carefully guarded from outside groups until they were unveiled as messages to Congress or in the President's Economic Report—the outcome leaves the nearest thing to public housing professional and educational groups excluded from policy development. The National Housing Conference has felt strongly enough about this to adopt resolutions at several of its annual conferences, beginning in 1964, deploring the absence of consultation. NAHRO did have a couple of giddy years close to the apparent policy makers after President Kennedy named Marie McGuire to be public housing commissioner and before the creation of HUD. As a NAHRO stalwart, she consulted. But Mrs. McGuire's freedom to consult ended even before she was replaced. A NAHRO testimonial dinner in her honor in February 1967, five months before her successor was appointed, at once expressed association appreciation for past involvement and marked recognition of the new arrangements, then already in effect, which made NAHRO an association more to disseminate information about policy than to participate in making policy.

The leaders of NAHRO subsequently became especially upset over HUD's tactics in attempting to achieve change in the historic patterns of segregation in public housing, more so than they had been over exclusion from decisions about requests for authorizations for new starts in the program. This is not to suggest any explicit unwillingness on

NAHRO's part to help achieve an end to segregation. Rather, it was a reflection of the fact that NAHRO is very much oriented to problems of management as well as a reflection of the distribution of strength within the organization's membership. Just under half of the total member agencies in the housing field come from the southeast and southwest regions. Among individual active members, well over a third are located in the South. In addition, numerous agency members in other regions— like the Chicago Housing Authority—had fostered a segregation policy as rigid as any in the South. If associational membership has a value to these groups, that value must lie less in a monthly magazine and more in protection against or at least warning of major upheavals in established tenant-assignment practices.

NAHRO has chosen at least two of its major issues unwisely, tending to favor the status quo. With public housing bogged down badly in 1965, the administration made a move for the rent supplement approach. Admittedly, the initial proposal was for supplements to benefit people just above the public housing level. Unlike Senate housing liberals such as Paul Douglas and William Proxmire, however, NAHRO wanted no part of rent supplements even with a changed eligibility level, thereby provoking complaints that the organization wished to monopolize the housing problem of the poor for itself. "They haven't liked the [rent supplement] proposal," Paul Douglas said, "because they want to keep the poor as their special province. 'Keep off the grass,' they say."[47] Douglas' barb suggests that NAHRO acted selfishly, but there is no evidence to support that conclusion. It is at least equally probable that the NAHRO opposition to rent supplements stemmed from doubt that supplements could be made to work.

Then only a few years later, NAHRO took its ill-advised stand against the HUD effort to reform tenant assignment policy in order to achieve integration. Even after handling the opposition clumsily and losing, NAHRO did not go on to more positive concerns but continued to pout for months. "Mounting dismay among NAHRO members," to use the association's own prose, "over the sudden release by the Department of Housing and Urban Development of new policies and procedures, without any prior consultation with local operators on the workability of these procedures,"[48] resulted in an appeal in June 1968 from NAHRO's president to the secretary of housing and urban development for a

47. *Housing Legislation of 1965*, Hearings, p. 525.
48. *Journal of Housing*, Vol. 25 (June 1968), p. 313.

means of improving federal-local relations. Secretary Weaver agreed to arrange for prepublication comment by NAHRO on important changes in rules and regulations. When HUD officials and NAHRO officials met a month thereafter, two of the three issues cited as having provoked the association during the previous year were the circular on site selection (which had been issued only after public prodding by the National Committee Against Discrimination in Housing) and the rule of three circular on tenant assignment procedures. And for neither of these did NAHRO have a practical alternative despite its extended complaints.

On the positive side, NAHRO has asserted an interest in the new environment in which housing authorities must operate. It commissioned a report from George Schermer "to enable local housing authorities to grasp the psychological climate of the present situation and make appropriate adjustments in their approaches, policies, documents and procedures." Detailing tenant-landlord issues in six cities—San Francisco; Washington, D.C.; Syracuse; Bloomington, Illinois; Atlanta; and San Antonio—Schermer perceptively showed problems with leases, rent schedules, service charges, evictions, and social services, and made proposals for change.[49] But NAHRO lacks sanctions over the locals who, whether or not they grasp the psychological climate, are slow to make the appropriate adjustments. The result is a widespread intellectual awareness of the need for change in tenant-landlord relationships, an incapacity on the part of many landlords to change the style most of them have pursued for decades, and a continuing failure of national leaders to provide for the training of a new kind of local landlord.

49. See n. 30, above.

6

Stamps for the Hungry

Food stamps and other food assistance programs, including surplus commodity distribution and free or reduced-price school lunches, are a complicated way of acknowledging that people on public assistance are not provided relief allowances that permit them to be fed adequately. The availability of these programs to nonrecipients of public assistance with comparably low incomes is tacit, official acknowledgment that public assistance fails to reach all of the people who cannot afford an adequate diet. If relief allowances were adequate, providing additional food would be wasteful. But allowances are not adequate, and indirect methods of supplementation have been made optional for the client. The indirect method now preferred by policy makers is food stamps, a federally financed program benefiting over eight million people—about two-thirds the number receiving public assistance money payments. Since stamps have become the country's major family food-assistance technique, it is important to ask how, by whom, and why a case is made for them rather than money.

The Mechanics of Food Stamps

The modern food stamp plan, enacted in 1964, gives locally certified low income families and individuals an option to buy food vouchers bearing a face value well in excess of their purchase price. Stamps are good in normal trade channels for almost all food items. The actual difference between cost to the recipient and the face value of stamps varies according to family size and income based on the proposition that the family's "normal" food expenditures should be diverted to the regular purchase of stamps. For administrative purposes, "normal" expenditures are determined by reference to a table of family size and income rather than by case-by-case investigation.

Until July 1967, when the effectiveness of the plan was questioned for the first time at high government levels, the minimum purchase price anywhere had been $2 per person per month for $12 in stamps. That minimum has now been reduced to 50 cents for $28 in stamps. At the other extreme, the cost to a single person with an income of $100 a month is $18 for $28 in coupons. The monthly coupon allotment to a four-person family is $106 at a cost ranging from $2 to $82 (Table 8).[1] Food stamps are the same price for public assistance recipients and non-recipients. The former are automatically eligible, the latter can be certified if the family monthly income by household size is not in excess of the standards established by the individual state food stamp plan approved by the United States Department of Agriculture (USDA). At the beginning of 1970 those standards of monthly income for a four-person family varied from South Carolina's $160 to New Jersey's $360.

Food stamps are like postage stamps in their limited utility value. A postage stamp will only buy delivery of a piece of mail by the U.S. Post Office Department; it will not buy a bar of soap or a government manual, or anything other than mail delivery. A food stamp can buy only food, and it can only buy food at a participating outlet. Physically, food stamps are coupons about the size of a dollar bill, issued in denominations of 50 cents and $2 and $5. Books valued at $20, $10, $3, or $2 are procured at banks, currency exchanges, or government food stamp centers—as the individual state determines—located as conveniently or inconveniently as the state and local units determine. Retail food outlets may now give real change for coupons: if change in an amount less than 50 cents is involved, the user gets cash or secures credit; change greater than 50 cents is made with stamps previously accepted by the retailer and not yet redeemed. Each book of stamps must be signed by the recipient. While he is not required to countersign individual coupons, his food stamp identification card must be exhibited to the retailer on demand. Coupons are redeemed through normal commercial banking procedures.

1. Until early 1970, separate schedules had been used for North and South, presumably reflecting lower food costs in Alabama, Arkansas, Kentucky, Louisiana, Mississippi, North Carolina, South Carolina, Tennessee, and Virginia. Secretary of Agriculture Hardin ordered both an end to the dual schedules and generally more liberal bonus payments on Dec. 18, 1969.

Even if they really are modified grocery purchase orders, food stamps are made to seem more like money than like the grocery purchase orders written by a town relief officer in the depression days. The Social Security Act of 1935 made cash relief a basic principle of federally aided categorical assistance programs. The Food Stamp Act of 1964 did not set that principle aside; it simply rewards recipients who volunteer to abandon the freedom of cash in favor of regular use of stamps good only for food.

Political interest in the program and federal funds for its support have increased markedly since 1967. In that fiscal year, stamps were a $115 million effort. By 1969, however, the annual federal food stamp supplement to the needy was $250 million; for 1970 the supplement was first fixed at $338 million, later escalated to $610 million when the fiscal year was more than one-third over. President Nixon budgeted $1.25 billion for food stamps in 1971. Each house of Congress has been even more generous separately. In 1969 the Senate passed legislation authorizing as much as $1.25 billion for fiscal 1970 and $2.5 billion for 1972, while in 1968 the House adopted a four-year extension of the food stamp bill with an unlimited spending authorization only to have that part lost in conference. After some shilly-shally the Nixon administration embraced stamp expansion as a complement to its proposal for welfare reform. So, despite persistent difficulty in securing participation in the stamp program, policy makers in the House, the Senate, and the executive branch push ahead, apparently believing that providing a relief supplement with stamps is in the best interests of the needy.

The supplement is not provided in cash because cash does not preclude the possibility of its being used for purposes other than food purchases. Food stamps protect the welfare client from spending for any other purpose money that his caseworker and the Department of Agriculture believe should be budgeted for food. Many clients, however, have declined to buy stamps. In some quarters this is considered irresponsible and leads to proposals for compulsory use in lieu of the voluntary system. The District of Columbia Department of Public Welfare, for example, after reporting that the department was not able to "educate" more than 35 percent of its clients to use the stamp program in three years of operation, suggested in June 1968 that consideration be given to making participation a condition of eligibility for welfare assistance. Similarly, a Kansas Committee on Nutrition and Human Needs found itself distressed by the low level of participation in food stamp counties

Table 8. Cost of Food Stamps, Based on Monthly Income, 1970
In dollars

Monthly net income	Cost of stamps							
	1 person, $28 value	2 persons, $56 value	3 persons, $84 value	4 persons, $106 value	5 persons, $126 value	6 persons, $144 value	7 persons, $162 value	8 persons, $180 value
0 to 19.99	0.50	1.00	1.50	2.00	2.50	3.00	3.00	3.00
20 to 29.99	1.00	1.00	1.50	2.00	2.50	3.00	3.00	3.00
30 to 39.99	4.00	4.00	4.00	4.00	5.00	5.00	5.00	5.00
40 to 49.99	6.00	7.00	7.00	7.00	8.00	8.00	8.00	9.00
50 to 59.99	8.00	10.00	10.00	10.00	11.00	11.00	12.00	12.00
60 to 69.99	10.00	12.00	13.00	13.00	14.00	14.00	15.00	16.00
70 to 79.99	12.00	15.00	16.00	16.00	17.00	18.00	18.00	19.00
80 to 89.99	14.00	18.00	19.00	19.00	20.00	21.00	22.00	22.00
90 to 99.99	16.00	21.00	21.00	22.00	23.00	24.00	25.00	26.00
100 to 109.99	18.00	23.00	24.00	25.00	26.00	27.00	28.00	29.00
110 to 109.99	...	26.00	27.00	28.00	29.00	31.00	32.00	33.00
120 to 129.99	...	29.00	30.00	31.00	33.00	34.00	35.00	36.00
130 to 139.99	...	31.00	33.00	34.00	36.00	37.00	38.00	40.00
140 to 149.99	...	34.00	36.00	37.00	39.00	40.00	42.00	44.00
150 to 169.99	...	36.00	40.00	42.00	44.00	46.00	48.00	50.00

Range							
170 to 189.99	...	46.00	48.00	50.00	52.00	54.00	56.00
190 to 209.99	...	52.00	54.00	56.00	58.00	60.00	62.00
210 to 229.99	...	58.00	60.00	62.00	64.00	66.00	68.00
230 to 249.99	...	64.00	66.00	68.00	70.00	72.00	74.00
250 to 269.99	...	66.00	72.00	74.00	76.00	78.00	80.00
270 to 289.99	...	...	72.00	80.00	82.00	84.00	86.00
290 to 309.99	...	...	76.00	84.00	88.00	90.00	92.00
310 to 329.99	...	...	80.00	84.00	88.00	96.00	98.00
330 to 359.99	...	...	80.00	88.00	92.00	100.00	102.00
360 to 389.99	...	...	82.00	92.00	96.00	104.00	106.00
390 to 419.99	...	...	...	96.00	100.00	108.00	110.00
420 to 449.99	...	...	...	98.00	104.00	112.00	114.00
450 to 479.99	...	...	...	...	108.00	116.00	118.00
480 to 509.99	...	...	...	...	112.00	120.00	122.00
510 to 539.99	...	...	...	...	...	124.00	126.00
540 to 569.99	...	...	...	...	...	126.00	130.00
570 to 599.99	...	...	...	...	...	...	134.00
600 to 629.99	...	...	...	...	...	...	138.00
630 to 659.99	...	...	...	...	...	...	140.00

Source: U.S. Department of Agriculture, press release 3837–69.

in Kansas—only 30 percent of welfare families there were using stamps in the summer of 1969. The suggested solution was that "the amount of stamps which families were eligible for be assigned and issued. . . ."[2]

Orville Freeman, during whose long tenure (1961–69) as secretary of agriculture a continuing food stamp program was enacted and fought over, once acknowledged that increased cash welfare grants would have the same effect as food stamps if recipients could be depended on to spend such cash for food—but he had no confidence that that would be the case. Professional welfare specialists in the House Agriculture Committee hearing room paled while Freeman told the committee that he was particularly doubtful of the ability of the "old folks" to manage money: "When they give them the money, they do not use it for food. They go out and play bingo with it." Food stamps make this impossible: "But the advantage of the food tieup is that they use what they have been spending on food, secure the stamps which then means an additional amount—which means that the money is going for food. It is not going for something else. This is very important, very important."[3] One may ask whether rent stamps, clothing stamps, eyeglass stamps, and haircut stamps would have comparable social values and whether independence for the aged is not also a value that is very important.

Caseworkers, local welfare departments, committees of sincere citizens, and a secretary of agriculture are not the only people who sometimes have the urge to instruct poor clients as to what they ought to do about food. The most liberal legislators have been known to have comparable urges. So, Senator Paul Douglas, a conscientious and conspicuous friend of welfare programs during his eighteen-year tenure in the Senate, seriously attempted to legislate against food stamp recipients spending their stamps in a fashion that seemed unsuitable to him. Disturbed to discover that, under the bill being considered in 1964, the index of prohibited items for purchase with food stamps did not include soft drinks, Douglas offered an amendment to add "carbonated beverages" to alcoholic beverages, tobacco, and imported products in the roster for which food

2. "Report of the Kansas Committee on Nutrition and Human Needs to Senator Robert Dole, September 13, 1969," *Congressional Record*, daily ed., Sept. 23, 1969, p. S11174.

3. *Extend the Food Stamp Act of 1964 and Amend the Child Nutrition Act of 1964*, Hearings before the House Committee on Agriculture, 90 Cong. 1 sess. (1967), p. 38.

stamps could not be used. Douglas's motion, based upon his expressed belief that since carbonated drinks were not nutritious they should not be available to persons with limited food budgets, came, paradoxically, on the heels of an eloquent speech in support of food stamps in which the senator pointed out that the great merit of the stamp plan was that participants "could go into grocery stores and be indistinguishable from other patrons of the stores; they were not singled out as a pariah class or a dependent class." As a Chicago alderman during the New Deal food stamp experiment, Douglas was impressed by the fact that recipients could have relief with dignity: "One could almost see the improvement in their self-respect. . . . It was almost as though cold water had been sprayed over an arid flower garden."[4] But he had reservations about extending the opportunity for self-respect to the point of permitting food stamp beneficiaries to decide for themselves whether they might occasionally spray Coca-Cola over an arid throat.

Some explanations of the stamp plan have suggested that stamps are just like money. Orville Freeman, for example, noted that in eligible grocery stores, "food stamp users can spend the stamps exactly as though they were spending cash."[5] Stamps are thus a kind of magic: the same amount of money produces a greater amount of food for the low income family than was the case without stamps; still the grocer loses nothing, nor does the farmer. Instead, both of them are presumably benefited by the increased purchasing power made available to the poor. Low income families themselves need only meet minimum purchase requirements and participate regularly in order to have the advantage of this "instant money" provided by food stamps.

Judged by its ability to get supplementary relief benefits to a large segment of the welfare population in an efficient and dignified manner, the stamp program has been a failure from the beginning. Despite persistent evidence of client nonparticipation, stamp sponsors have insisted that it is a success. Like many magic tricks, food stamp magic requires some volunteer assistants: in this case, low income families. There is, it develops, a shortage of volunteers. Some potential volunteers are too self-conscious, others simply do not have a quarter for the magician to turn

4. *Congressional Record*, Vol. 110, Pt. 12, 88 Cong. 2 sess. (1964), p. 15437.

5. *Hunger and Malnutrition in America*, Hearings before the Subcommittee on Employment, Manpower, and Poverty of the Senate Committee on Labor and Public Welfare, 90 Cong. 1 sess. (1967), p. 122.

into a dollar. Again like a magic show, however, the magician's enthusiasm and ability to keep the audience diverted obscure the low rate of audience participation.

Farm Relief to Poor Relief

Food stamps are expected to substitute for federal government donation of surplus commodities to needy people. The latter began on a large scale with passage of farm relief legislation in 1933. Even as the New Dealers were being castigated for killing off little pigs while one-third of a nation was ill fed, the edible portions of the hogs purchased in the price stabilization campaign were processed into salt pork and by-products. By December 1933 about 100 million pounds of salt pork had been distributed to the needy. In 1934, and again in 1936, drought relief programs involved the salvage and distribution of cattle, sheep, and goats for human consumption.

Continuous, permanent financing of programs to encourage domestic consumption of agricultural commodities was first provided in 1935 by legislation that appropriates annually to the secretary of agriculture an amount equal to 30 percent of the gross receipts derived from customs revenues. Enacted initially because its sponsor, Representative Marvin Jones (Democrat of Texas), believed that "the farmer had been paying the burdens of the tariff for a hundred years without any corresponding benefits,"[6] this provision (known as Section 32) was Jones's way of making restitution. Spending options available to the secretary under Section 32 are (1) to develop new uses for farm products in order to divert them from the normal channels of trade where they could not be consumed, and (2) to encourage their use through benefits, indemnities, donations, or by other means among persons in low income groups. In the early years, direct donation was the primary way in which low income groups were helped. Contributions to school lunches, low priced milk, and direct donations of food to needy families all preceded the present food stamp activity as techniques to encourage the use of farm products among poor people. While these programs are not mutually exclusive

6. Later senior judge of the U.S. Court of Claims, Jones recounted the story of the writing of Section 32 in a speech at the national observance of the 35th anniversary of the signing of the Agricultural Adjustment Act of 1933. The speech appears in *Congressional Record*, daily ed., May 21, 1968, p. E4477.

in theory, food stamps and direct distribution may not now legally coexist indefinitely. In its modern form the food stamp program is designed to supplant direct distribution in areas electing to make the switch.

Actual food stamp history dates to May 1939. The brainchild of Milo Perkins, a New Deal economist, food stamps were first tried in Rochester, New York, as a new approach to developing wider markets for agricultural commodities among needy people. Families of relief clients, WPA workers, and others certified by relief agencies could buy orange food stamps in an amount of at least $4 and not more than $6 per person per month. While these orange stamps sold at par and were redeemable for any product sold in participating stores, purchasers were given free blue stamps equal to half the value of the orange stamps. Blue stamps were redeemable in retail stores for any of a list of surplus foods. From the first, the food stamp plan required a commitment from its beneficiaries that they would maintain an average "normal" rate of expenditure for food independent of any bonus provided. Based on the Rochester experiment, the plan, in substantially the form used there, was put into effect, at its peak, in 1,741 counties and 88 cities, lasting until 1943. (Over twenty-five years later, Monroe County, New York—in which Rochester is located—toyed with the idea of a food stamp plan again. But the county's social services director said that it was too expensive and required too many administrators.)

Orange stamps and blue stamps were at least one color too many. If the merit of food stamps is the use of normal channels of distribution, abnormal arrangements cannot be imposed without confusion and evasion. Lewis Meriam found that the limited negotiability of blue stamps and the awkwardness involved in separating items payable in orange stamps from those payable in blue stamps invited both honest and premeditated errors.[7] Diversions and evasions were said to have reached an amount equal to at least 25 percent of the federal assistance. When these problems and the war boom combined to bring the orange and blue program to an end in 1943, it had few mourners. Nevertheless, the possibility of developing an improved system interested some congressmen from the end of the war until eventual enactment of stamp legislation in 1964.

A critical difference between the food stamp plan in its modern form

7. *Relief and Social Security* (Brookings Institution, 1946), pp. 340–43.

and the plan used between 1939 and 1943 is that the old style program restricted the use of bonus stamps to surplus food items while the modern version imposes no such limitation. Precisely this same difference obtains between the modern food stamp program and the still widely used system of direct distribution of surplus commodities to the needy. The latter makes available only government-owned commodities previously purchased under a price support program. Thus, when food programs were being argued during the 1960 election campaign, only five commodities were on the direct distribution list. In July 1967 there were still only fifteen commodities being distributed. The number was increased to twenty-one at the height of the Poor People's Campaign early in the summer of 1968, and then to twenty-two. As Table 9 shows, this does not mean that all jurisdictions actually accept and distribute all twenty-two commodities, although three-fourths of the 1,313 units participating at the beginning of 1969 did distribute at least seventeen of the twenty-two.

The shift from commodity distribution to stamps good for all domestically produced food items is a shift from giving away selected farm products for which price supports were already being provided to increasing the ability of the poor to buy food of their own choosing. A farmer-oriented program has thereby been transformed into a welfare-oriented program run by the Department of Agriculture, authorized through House and Senate agriculture committees, and funded through appropriations subcommittees on agriculture. While the department executes policy according to its fashion, which means a limited orientation to urban welfare problems, the congressional committees involved clearly resent including in the Department of Agriculture budget what some members explicitly term "an improper charge against the farmer."

The presumed purpose of the stamp program now is all mixed up between welfare and aid to the farmer and to the retail food industry. Not only does the House Agriculture Committee call it a welfare program; so does the enabling statute, "for the purposes of budget presentations."[8] But many welfare officials around the country do not see it that way. Winifred Thompson, director of the District of Columbia Department of Public Welfare, says it is "not 'welfare' in the sense that the term is usually used";[9] the director of the Cambria County (Pennsylvania) Board of Assistance, while delighted with food stamps, says his personal

8. *The Food Stamp Act of 1964*, as amended, Sec. 16(d). 7 U.S.C. 2025.

9. *Food Stamp Appropriations Authorization*, Hearing before a Subcommittee of the Senate Committee on Agriculture and Forestry, 90 Cong. 1 sess. (1967), p. 50.

Table 9. Number of Surplus Commodities Distributed by Counties, July 1969

State[a]	Number of counties distributing				
	20–22 commodities[b]	17–19 commodities[b]	14–16 commodities[b]	11–13 commodities[b]	8–10 commodities[b]
Alabama	23	23	...	...	...
Arizona	...	1	10	4	...
Arkansas	...	17	...	...	...
California	23	5	1	...	...
Connecticut	4	...	...	...	...
Delaware	...	...	3	...	...
Florida	41	11	1	...	...
Georgia	9	45	23	1	...
Idaho	2	7	3	...	...
Indiana	11	27	17	8	3
Iowa	...	9	...	...	...
Kansas	5	8	1	...	...
Kentucky	15	46	...	...	...
Louisiana	2	1	11	...	...
Maine	...	11	4	...	...
Maryland	...	...	1	...	...
Massachusetts	9	7	4	1	...
Michigan	...	40	...	...	...
Minnesota	8	9	1	2	...
Mississippi	36	3	...	...	...
Missouri	12	33	18	1	...
Montana	...	...	6	3	...
Nebraska	1	...	1	...	...
Nevada	...	10	1	1	...
New Hampshire	...	6	3	1	...
New Jersey	...	7	3	1	...
New Mexico	...	10	...	...	...
New York	...	3	34	10	1
North Carolina	51	8	...	...	...
North Dakota	1	5	4	...	1
Ohio	...	4	10	2	...
Oklahoma	50	22	1	...	...
Oregon	32	2	...	...	...
Pennsylvania	...	2	7	7	...
Rhode Island	...	15	1	...	...
South Dakota	27	4	1	...	...
Tennessee	...	13	1	...	...
Texas	35	92	3	...	...
Virginia	17	22	1	...	...
Wisconsin	34	12	1	...	...
Wyoming	...	...	2	...	...

Source: *Congressional Record*, daily ed., Sept. 15, 1969, p. H7917.
a. States not listed did not have surplus commodity program.
b. A commodity group is counted if any one item in the group was distributed.

opinion "is that this is an agricultural program and not a welfare program."[10] California's welfare director says, "The Food Stamp Program is not considered to be a welfare program."[11] A substantial part of the program's troubles may be traced to the confusion of objectives. It appears expedient to proponents to rationalize the program as a marriage of agriculture and welfare, but it is a marriage that really benefits welfare far more than it benefits agriculture. In a nation where the total outlay on food purchased by United States families for use in the home is now $105 billion annually, even $1.25 billion in food stamps represents only 1.2 percent. Food stamp expenditures are simply too inconsequential to be important either to the food retailer or to the farmer. The latter's share of the total $105 billion outlay is only a little better than one-third. As a net addition to the $8.1 billion budgeted for public assistance, however, $1.25 billion becomes a more impressive figure.

Whatever is said about stamps increasing demand for farm products, that is only incidental to what must be the program's primary justification: to increase the volume of food that can be purchased by low income people without limiting freedom of selection among foods. If the program aids in the disposal of surpluses, it is only because holders of food stamps happen to choose to use them for items in surplus. If the program stimulates use of unused agricultural capacity, it is only because holders of food stamps happen to seek out food items for which there is unused capacity to produce. Which segment of American agriculture benefits from the food stamp plan is a decision that rests in the choices of the persons who hold and spend food stamps. A program designed principally to aid the agricultural population would have to have both a good deal more money and some additional built-in assurances that the money will fall in the right places.

Present and projected food stamp levels do not do much for the farmer if increases in food consumption are made the test. To achieve an increase in total food consumption of only a little more than 4 percent, which is about half of what the Federal Reserve Bank of Chicago terms the estimated annual "surplus" of agricultural production, it would be necessary to subsidize the consumption of nearly one-third of the total population.[12] Subsidizing 15 percent of the population would

10. Letter from Edward R. Golob to Representative John Saylor, April 2, 1964; reprinted in *Congressional Record*, Vol. 110, Pt. 6, 88 Cong. 2 sess. (1964), p. 7142.

11. California State Department of Social Welfare, *California Food Stamp Program*; reprinted in *Congressional Record*, daily ed., June 8, 1967, p. H6912.

12. "Food Stamps for the Needy," *Business Conditions* (a review by the Federal Reserve Bank of Chicago, July 1965), p. 10.

make for an increase in total food consumption of less than 2 percent. If that tenth of the population with the lowest income were subsidized, food consumption would be increased a little more than 1 percent, a figure characterized by the Chicago Federal Reserve as "almost insignificant in terms of reducing the stock of surplus commodities." But food stamps and commodity distribution together served about 5 percent of the population in mid-1970. Thus stamps cannot be taken seriously as a solution to the problem of excess agricultural production or to the problem of how to utilize unused agricultural capacity.

Political Beneficiaries

The modern food stamp program owes its life to the Kennedy administration's anxiety to show itself to have a more effective approach to meeting human need than did the Eisenhower administration. The program's political history before 1961 made it ideally suited for adoption by an administration that deplored its predecessor's resistance to innovation and preoccupation with economy. "This program," accurately claims Representative Leonor Sullivan (Democrat of Missouri), the House sponsor, "was initiated, expanded, and developed almost entirely as a Democratic effort."[13] Eisenhower's position had been that direct distribution accomplished the job of getting government-owned food to the needy with a minimum of additional financial outlay and in a fashion that properly put some of the costs—warehousing and distribution—on state and local units. Democrats, led with great intensity and persistence by Mrs. Sullivan, pushed consistently for food stamps, pledged themselves to a food stamp program in the Democratic platforms of 1956 and 1960, and actually enacted, as a rider to the 1959 overseas agricultural aid bill, authority for the secretary of agriculture to establish a food stamp program limited, however, to surplus food and to a two-year period. There was no expectation that then Secretary Ezra Taft Benson would act, but the unused authorization did serve to underscore the Eisenhower administration's rigid opposition to food stamps. That same year Senator John F. Kennedy introduced one of the several separate food stamp bills proposed in the Senate.

When President Kennedy signed his first executive order on Inauguration Day 1961, it provided a signal that there was concern at the

13. *Congressional Record*, daily ed., April 2, 1969, p. E2575.

highest levels about the techniques being utilized to bring food to needy families. Liberalizing and expanding the system of direct distribution of surplus commodities in accordance with the recommendation of a Kennedy task force on depressed areas, the executive order was understood to be an emergency action rather than a decision in favor of direct distribution over food stamps. Even then, a Department of Agriculture group was at work on a food stamp program pursuant to another recommendation of the task force and to the commitment in the Democratic platform. On February 2, 1961, Kennedy announced that a pilot food stamp program was to be developed in six depressed areas, and by May pilot projects were operating in the first of what ultimately became eight test areas.

A little more than a year after Kennedy's inauguration, Agriculture was ready to report that food stamps looked pretty good to it. Studies of the diets of participating low income families in two of the pilot areas showed that from over one-third to almost one-half of the families had diets that supplied the family with 100 percent or more of the allowances for each of the eight nutrients recommended by the National Research Council. Among nonparticipating families of comparably low income, however, only 28 percent had good diets. In the Detroit project area, significantly more of the participating families had diets providing recommended allowances for four critical nutrients—calcium, ascorbic acid, thiamine, and vitamin A—than did nonparticipating families. With smaller differences between participants and nonparticipants, the stamp program was also effective in other test areas, notably rural Fayette County, Pennsylvania, in providing recommended allowances of these four nutrients. The department reported, further, that the dollar volume of food sales in a sample of retail stores in the eight pilot areas was increased by 8 percent between test periods before and after inauguration of food stamps. Finally, families made significant increases in food purchases and in the total value of food used after joining in the program.[14]

For all of their seemingly encouraging findings, the Department of Agriculture evaluation studies of the pilot projects had some peculiarities. These studies included data detailed to the tenth of a percent regarding such items as per person use of particular food items among

14. U.S. Department of Agriculture, Consumer and Marketing Service, Food Stamp Division, *The Food Stamp Program: An Initial Evaluation of the Pilot Projects* (April 1962; reprinted June 1966), p. 5.

participating families; value, to the penny, of per person use of food before and after initiation of a project; and total dollar volume of food stamp coupons redeemed by sample stores as a percentage of total dollar sales, by five sizes of store. But evaluation reports dealing with attitudes about the program were less exact, sometimes because the questions asked were not sufficiently complete. A case in point is the report that over 90 percent of the participating families expressed a preference for the food stamp program over direct distribution primarily because the former offered a wider variety of food, yet there is no report as to whether the participating low income families most of all would have preferred additional cash payments in an amount equal to or even somewhat below the value of bonus stamps.

Again, data were not offered showing the percentage of eligible families actually participating in the program. Nor were families' reasons for not participating analyzed in detail. Among the "frequently given reasons" were doubts about eligibility and a belief that the purchase requirements were too high.[15] The latter point has had a way of appearing and reappearing whenever participants or potential participants have commented on the program. It is a problem that probably stems from different conceptions of what is involved in "normal expenditures for food." For the Department of Agriculture it must mean the amount of money at various income levels and household sizes that "should" be spent on food; for participants it means the amount they really do or can spend on food out of an unrealistic relief allowance or small social security income. Moreover, to arrive at "normal" expenditures within income classes, Agriculture admittedly struck a balance between families spending more than the "normal" figure and families spending less. For the former group, stamps would be a bargain; but for the latter group, stamps would be a hardship and participation would be unlikely.

Conclusions reached in the evaluation studies about the value of food purchases made with food stamps were based on a self-fulfilling prophecy. Participating families, by definition, were families who agreed to sell some of their cash for stamps that could be used only for food. Moreover, the cash to be sold could not be less than the amount usually spent for food. Consequently, the net effect was to compare the food intake of a group of low income nonparticipants with approximately x dollars to spend on food with a group of participants of comparably low

15. *Ibid.*, p. 21.

income whose x dollars have been changed into $x + fs$ dollars of restricted use. The point is that once a family decided to participate, it was inevitable that its food purchases and the total value of food purchased would increase. There was absolutely no other use for the stamps. It was, perhaps, not quite as certain that the nutritional value of the foods purchased would increase, although simply increasing the volume of food would surely account for some of this. In short, what the department demonstrated was that people who have only a small amount of money and spend a fixed part of it on food will eat better if they can transform all or part of the money budgeted for food into stamps worth more food than the money will buy on the open market. Only gross thievery could have changed the result.

Thievery was one of the things to be worried about. Resale of stamps at a discount is one possibility. Use of stamps for nonfood items is another. Where principal difficulties with the food stamp operation in the New Deal period was the use of stamps for the purchase of ineligible items, this problem did not appear to be consequential in the pilot program. Whether this was because retailers are now more resistant to collusion or because participants are more willing to comply with the limitations of the programs may have been less important than that the pilot program was closely watched. It behooved participants and retailers to avoid violations. By the same token, the likelihood of detecting violations was greater than would normally be the case. When the department was able to report, therefore, that of more than 4,000 retail food stores accepting food stamps, investigations through six months of the pilot project led to the suspension of only 6 retailers, it felt it reasonable to conclude that widespread violations would not be a problem.[16] (That judgment seemed confirmed after passage of the 1964 act. For example, during the period from 1964 to March 1967, of well over 60,000 retail stores participating, only 79 were disqualified for major violations. Another 251 stores received an official warning for minor violations.)

16. *Ibid.*, p. 18. While the program has generally been free of scandal, see *Department of Agriculture Appropriations for 1969*, H. Rept. 1335, 90 Cong. 2 sess. (1968), p. 44, for comment on a special study by the House Appropriations Committee's Survey and Investigations staff disclosing a "number of instances of laxity in the administration of this program." The committee reserved $25 million in food stamp funds to the Bureau of the Budget for release when corrections had been made. The Department of Agriculture and the Senate Committee on Appropriations concurred. *Department of Agriculture and Related Agencies Appropriation Bill, 1969*, S. Rept. 1138, 90 Cong. 2 sess. (1968), p. 19.

Only minor problems were said to have turned up during the pilot projects, but the Agriculture Department people were cautious. The food stamp program, they concluded, did not appear practical for those areas of the country with a relatively small proportion of needy families or where the need for the program was temporary because state and local contributions of time, staff, and money could not be expected unless there were a significant number of families in continuing need of additional food assistance. While it was deemed practical for and acceptable to economically depressed areas, gradualism rather than precipitous expansion was urged. More pilot projects was the logical conclusion. That conclusion also made it unnecessary to seek congressional action—a happy state of affairs since there was no certainty that legislation could be passed. Legislative authority and money already available under Section 32 appeared adequate to meet these limited objectives.

By the spring of 1962, then, the Department of Agriculture was attesting to the administrative practicality of a food stamp program and to the program's apparent ability to improve the diets of low income people. Still, Agriculture was urging restraint, not because it had doubts about whether food stamps could work, but to be sure that they would work well when a nationwide program started. Accordingly, continuation of food stamps on an essentially pilot basis with moderate expansion through the middle of 1963 was proposed. In the intervening twelve to eighteen months, state and local governments could prepare for their responsibilities, staffing and operational arrangements could be made, available funds could be concentrated in areas of greatest need, and the department itself could gain some additional operating experience. Few programs go through so extended and presumably so careful a pretesting.

An incidental effect of the gradualism approach recommended by Agriculture was to keep food stamps within the Democratic family. The first twenty-six pilot projects were all placed in the districts of Democratic members of Congress. "The Democrats," wrote Charles Bartlett late in 1962, "maintain the Republican Party has never shown any previous support for the program and that there is no reason why Republican congressmen should share now in its experimental phase."[17] Secretary Freeman said it was nothing like that at all. He explained that the pilot projects were chosen to embody "the combination of factors where we wished to test the workability of the program under given

17. "Republicans Want in on Food Stamp Plan," *Chicago Sun-Times*, Aug. 30, 1962.

conditions." Despite his department's earlier argument that continued pilot projects made it possible to concentrate funds in areas of greatest need, Freeman now claimed that "need was not the sole criterion. As a matter of fact, it was not the overwhelming criterion. The prime criterion was the combination of circumstances that we wanted to test out how the program could be administered, so that some of the weaknesses that have been disclosed in the food stamp program earlier would be tested out and hopefully overcome."[18]

Within these vague criteria for choice of pilot areas—criteria that did not include political balance—operating personnel in Agriculture made selections. As long as political balance was not a criterion, a qualified Democratic district was always found to compete with a qualified Republican district. Leonor Sullivan felt that an additional criterion was in order: close and careful oversight of a food stamp project by a congressional supporter of the stamp principle. Her own district qualified by that test, but it was not until January 1963 that a project was initiated in St. Louis. John Saylor of Pennsylvania, who had stood alone among House Republicans in support of food stamps through the years of Republican administration opposition, was finally rewarded with a project beginning in March 1963.

Before a bill to authorize a nationwide program was proposed, stamps were further tested in a total of thirty-one separate areas under a variety of operating conditions. Whatever additional wisdom the Department of Agriculture acquired in this period, it did not find it necessary to make major changes in the character of the food stamp program that had been in effect in the original pilot areas. As a matter of fact, as late as June 1966, the Consumer and Marketing Service reported that research on and evaluation of the pilot program begun in 1961 would continue "to serve as a guide in implementing the Food Stamp Act of 1964 over the next several years in those areas of the Nation that need and request the program."[19]

While the White House can usually mandate its decisions on most of its own cabinet officers and on at least some of its bureau chiefs in executive departments, it cannot mandate them on the Congress and its committees. The pilot food stamp program that operated between 1961 and 1964 required no congressional action. Secretary Freeman could em-

18. *Food Stamp Plan,* Hearings before the House Committee on Agriculture, 88 Cong. 1 sess. (1963), p. 23.
19. *The Food Stamp Program: An Initial Evaluation,* p. 2.

brace food stamps as an important way of meeting surplus production problems and put the plan in effect using authority and funds under Section 32. It served the goals and purposes of the administration to improve the food intake of poor people in this manner, and it was the secretary's job, after all, to serve the goals and purposes of the administration. But when Congress was asked to go along with the arrangements for tagging this welfare program as agriculture and with the consequent arrangements for federal financing of the full costs, Republicans and southern Democrats were reluctant. As everyone connected with food stamps or wheat-cotton support knows, and as Randall B. Ripley has shown in detail, it took overt, almost crude logrolling between backers of wheat-cotton price supports and proponents of food stamps to get the 1964 food stamp legislation out of the Agriculture Committee and then passed on the floor of the House.[20] Since then, food stamp–price support logrolling has been taken for granted. Mrs. Sullivan told the House Agriculture Committee in 1968 that "an arrangement" would be necessary to get bills on both subjects before the House and through the House. The arrangement was made, and Mrs. Sullivan helped round up enough votes to pass the farm bill—the day after passage of legislation extending the stamp program.

Food stamps continue to have hard going in the House of Representatives. As a federally financed program, they have superficial appeal for every member with low income persons in his district. No group is supposed to be hurt by the establishment of a stamp plan: the needy poor are said to be better fed than under a system of direct distribution of surplus commodities; retail food merchants get increased trade; demand for farm products is increased. Still, unlike a new post office, not every congressman fights for a food stamp program for his district, even if it is almost free.

Two indigestible or offensive aspects of the plan provoke opposition: its partisan history, and the absence of a compulsory state or local contribution. So, some Republicans are predisposed against food stamps because they were invented by the New Deal, specifically rejected by the Eisenhower administration, then embraced noisily by the Kennedy administration; because Democrats in Congress were outspoken in attacks on Ezra Taft Benson, Eisenhower's secretary of agriculture, for his re-

20. "Legislative Bargaining and the Food Stamp Act, 1964," in Frederic N. Cleaveland and Associates, *Congress and Urban Problems* (Brookings Institution, 1969), especially pp. 300–05.

fusal to initiate food stamps; and because Mrs. Sullivan has gone out of her way to criticize both Benson and former Republican Assistant Secretary of Agriculture Don Paarlberg. Some other Republicans are predisposed against food stamps because a totally federally financed program transcends their view of proper federal-state relations. Southern Democrats have disliked the fact that stamps provide a welfare bonus according to a standard that is determined at the federal rather than at the state level. Farm bloc congressmen from both parties dislike assigning costs to agriculture. And while congressmen holding these views are not a majority of the House, they are more than a majority of the House Agriculture Committee. In both the committee and the whole House, moreover, these personal and party positions on how far government should go in the welfare field appear more likely to influence a member's vote than does the promise of a food stamp program in his district.

A case in point is cost sharing, the crucial issue in 1967. The committee found, to its distress, that states were looking on stamps as "an additional source of 'free' aid from the Federal Government."[21] Its proposed remedy was to require participating states to share in the costs as they did in public assistance. Administration spokesmen had solicited and received communications from governors and welfare department leaders in several states to the effect that adoption of a cost sharing amendment would have the practical result of killing food stamps within the particular state. Given a choice between paying 20 percent of stamp costs and reverting to direct distribution with its 100 percent federal financing, state leaders—Governor James Rhodes of Ohio was an example—predicted widespread reversion to direct distribution. Food stamp supporters equated opposition to cost sharing with support for maintaining the stamp program. "In my opinion—shared, I might say by the Administration—this would cripple and probably kill the program," said Mrs. Sullivan. She called a vote for cost sharing "a vote against the food stamp program in most of the forty-one states and the District of Columbia now participating."[22]

Nineteen of the thirty-five members of the House Agriculture Committee already had stamp projects in operation in their districts in 1967, yet one point on which proponents and opponents of food stamps are

21. *Food Stamp Program*, H. Rept. 189, 90 Cong. 1 sess. (1967), p. 7.
22. *Congressional Record*, daily ed., March 23, 1967, p. A1494; June 8, 1967, p. H6895.

agreed is that the extension of the program voted that year probably could not have been moved out of the committee at all without adoption of a cost-sharing amendment. One strong supporter of the program, a Democrat from an urban district where the plan was pending but not yet in operation, states flatly that inclusion of restrictive amendments, including cost sharing, was the price for getting the bill out of committee, "the only way [Chairman Poage] could get the bill out was with these crippling amendments." Thomas Kleppe of North Dakota, who cast one of the four Republican votes to bring the bill out, agrees it would have been impossible to obtain a favorable report without the cost-sharing feature and other limiting committee amendments. In his own case, when the House rejected the cost-sharing proposal, Kleppe abandoned support of the bill. Poage himself carefully skirts the question of whether limiting amendments were a quid pro quo for a favorable report. He takes the position that cost sharing and an authorization limited to one year are not restrictions but perfecting amendments written by a committee that "wants to try to keep a program going."[23]

Cost sharing was defeated on the House floor. Where the Agriculture Committee voted in favor of cost sharing by a three to one margin (24–8), the whole House rejected it 191–173. Where the committee membership thereupon opposed the bill on final passage by 17–15, the whole House adopted it by 230–128. Democrats supplied 49 of the 173 votes in favor of cost sharing, but 47 of the 49 were cast by southern Democrats; 27 of the 47 had projects in their districts. On the Republican side, 124 members voted for cost sharing; 73 of them had projects; 19 Republicans from food stamp districts voted against cost sharing. To state it differently, Republicans generally voted about 5 to 1 for cost sharing; Republicans from food stamp districts still voted better than 3.5 to 1 for cost sharing. Northern Democrats voted in the ratio of 66 to 1 against cost sharing. Southern Democrats favored cost sharing by about 3 to 2. While all but one of the southern Democratic opponents of cost sharing had projects in their districts, so did a substantial majority of the southern Democrats favoring cost sharing. Having a project may have tipped the scales for the program in a few cases, but national party position and individual attitude toward social welfare policies were the factors that determined most votes.

The same kind of situation was to develop in subsequent years. Chair-

23. *Ibid.*, p. H6892.

man Poage and most of his Agriculture Committee colleagues were outvoted by Mrs. Sullivan's urban coalition in 1968 on the question of an
unlimited food stamp authorization, and there appeared to be plenty of
House votes available in 1969 for an important liberalization of the program if it could reach the floor. Mrs. Sullivan's 1968 victory was washed
out in conference, however, when the senior Agriculture Committee
members who constituted House conferees abandoned the House position. A year later, after the Senate overruled its Agriculture Committee
by adopting Senator George McGovern's (Democrat of South Dakota)
proposals to provide free stamps for the poorest families and to triple
the 1970 authorization, Poage's committee avoided the possibility of
again losing on the floor by simply not reporting a general food stamp
bill. After four months' delay, the committee did call up a resolution increasing the food stamp spending authorization for 1970 to half the
amount in the McGovern amendment, $610 million compared to $1.25
billion. By this time, some Republican members of the committee had
been converted since President Nixon had proposed expansion and
liberalization of the program. Not until the summer of 1970, however,
did the Agriculture Committee report its version of general food stamp
legislation. And it first brought in and had passed a bill extending supports for wool, wheat, feed grains, and cotton for three years.

Food stamps are kept alive, then, by legislation reported from the
Agriculture Committee and subsequently liberalized by vote of the
House. But the oversight and evaluation function is not performed.
Whatever failings stamps may have as a welfare program are barred
from exposure by the Agriculture Committee, which is simply not much
concerned about those failings. Big city congressmen assigned to Agriculture as freshmen leave the committee as soon as a vacancy develops
elsewhere, leaving rural conservatives in control. With the barest of
majorities available—and then only to provide a base for vote trading—
for support of the program as presently formulated, only the most intrepid of welfare specialists would ask that committee to keep an eye on
the two nagging problems in food stamps qua welfare: that they demean
the user by making him different from other food shoppers, and that
their benefits are not available at all to people who are too poor to buy
stamps regularly. Elaborate pretests of the food stamp idea were structured to strengthen a belief that purchase of stamps on a regular schedule was a highly desirable feature of the plan. This was accomplished
by measuring food consumption among participants. A more important

inquiry—the extent of and reasons for nonparticipation—was not pursued. If it had been, the glowing reports would have been less glowing and it might not have been possible to pass a food stamp bill at all.

Nonparticipation

Poor people simply have not used food stamps, a good reason for reconsidering their value as a welfare supplement. A September 1969 Senate committee document reported:

Nationally only 21.6 percent of the poor people living in counties with food stamp programs participate in the program. Only in the State of Washington and the District of Columbia do food stamp programs reach over 40 percent of the poor. Seven states have programs that reach less than 15 percent of their poor. Only 116, or 10 percent, of all counties with food stamp programs reach 40 percent or more of their poor.[24]

All this was eight years after the Department of Agriculture started in the stamp business with its pilot programs. The participation gap for commodities is only a little less depressing, but stamps were sold as an important improvement over commodities in providing relief for the poor, not as a less effective substitute. Yet, among all counties switching from commodities to food stamps during 1961 to 1968, there was an average decline of 40 percent in persons participating.

Given the care supposedly lavished on pretesting and analyzing the results of pretests of the food stamp program, the problem of a high rate of consumer nonparticipation should have been worrying proponents early in the game. Instead, it was obscured for years, while program information and evaluation came only from the administrative agency— Agriculture, through its Consumer and Marketing Service—and from the agriculture committees of House and Senate.

The principal interest of both congressional committees but especially that on the House side, as we have seen, was in the use to be made of food stamp legislation as a trade-off with urban congressmen for farm price support bills. Complaining that stamps are really a welfare measure charged to agriculture, the committees neither sought out nor inquired about food stamp users but instead concentrated on limiting the

24. *Poverty, Malnutrition, and Federal Food Assistance Programs: A Statistical Summary*, prepared by the Senate Select Committee on Nutrition and Human Needs, 91 Cong. 1 sess. (1969), p. 29.

program even while using it for bargaining. The Department of Agriculture, for its part, found that it could run a small food stamp program without jeopardizing relations with the legislative committees or with agriculture appropriations subcommittees. Through the seven years beginning in 1961, the congressional and administrative groups struck a tolerable balance. Either not knowing better or not wishing to disturb that balance, they all gave assurances that everything was just right with food stamps. Thus, after three years of elaborately tested pilot projects and another three years under specific authorizing legislation, the department, in 1967, assured the administration's chosen sponsor, Representative Sullivan, that there were no defects in the basic legislation. All that was needed, it was said, was to substitute an unlimited authorization for the three-year authorization of finite sums in the Food Stamp Act of 1964.[25]

A couple of months after providing Mrs. Sullivan with these assurances, and after new authorizations had passed through House and Senate agriculture committees, the department conducted an emergency study of nonparticipation.[26] The study was provoked by the work of a Senate Labor and Public Welfare Subcommittee on Employment, Manpower, and Poverty which in two days of hearings documented the existence of a hunger problem. At this late date the question of whether food stamps might be given away free and the question of whether minimum purchase requirements established by Agriculture were realistic had their first airings. The department's belated study confirmed that there were indeed some people who could not afford to buy stamps and that there seemed to be an even larger number who apparently resisted using them.

Evidence of the futility of the food stamp approach as a relief device was in Agriculture's files before it was pushed to the emergency study in 1967, but the department itself neither faced the evidence and its implications nor cooperated with skeptical outsiders who sought out the data. The most important test to be applied to food stamps is not whether they provide nutritional benefits for those who do use them

25. Letter from Orville L. Freeman to Leonor K. Sullivan, Aug. 24, 1966, in Congressional Record, daily ed., March 14, 1967, p. A1278. Mrs. Sullivan reported to the House that she again obtained assurances in 1967 that "no changes other than in the language on appropriations would be necessary."

26. "U.S. Department of Agriculture, Participation in USDA Food Programs, Two Mississippi Delta Counties, May, 1967" (Preliminary Report, June 20, 1967, revised; processed).

but how much of the target group uses them at all. One way to answer the latter question is to compare the number of food stamp recipients in various project areas with the number of recipients of surplus commodities when that program had been operating. Not all of the poor used surplus commodities, but at least as many should use stamps for the latter to be judged successful. It seems not unreasonable to conclude that where the number of needy people is admittedly larger than the number using a relief program, an alternate relief program is not successful if it reaches even fewer people than the original.

When food stamps replaced surplus commodities, the consistent result was that fewer people were reached by the new program than by the old. At the end of fiscal 1967, before Agriculture was willing systematically to examine the statistics in its files, 634 counties had transferred from surplus commodities to food stamps. Prior to the transfer, 2.773 million persons were receiving commodities. Subsequent to transfer, 1.377 million persons in those counties participated in food stamps, a drop of more than 50 percent. Even allowing for the entry of an additional 390,000 food stamp users in counties that had not previously accepted commodities, food stamps served 1 million fewer persons than had commodities.

Officially, however, stamps were a success. "The usual pattern," the responsible deputy assistant secretary explained to an interviewer, "is a drop off in recipients immediately after the transition from commodities to stamps followed by a building back up thereafter." A close look at participation during June 1967 in a sample of seventy-five counties that had entered the stamp program before June 1966 makes it clear that no such building back was really taking place. In sixty-five of the seventy-five counties sampled, there were fewer stamp participants in June 1967 than commodity participants in the June preceding transition, a period of not less than two years and more often three. According to data in Agriculture Department files, Jefferson County (Birmingham), Alabama, had had 41,151 commodity participants in June 1964 preceding its March 1965 transition to stamps. By June 1967 Jefferson had "built back up" to 11,484 stamp participants. Denver, Colorado, dropped from 22,259 commodity clients in June 1964 to 12,436 stamp clients in June 1967. (Not until May 1969 did Denver's stamp total approach the 1964 level.) Washington, D.C., dropped from 23,772 persons on commodities in June 1965 to 18,784 persons on stamps in June 1967. Using the same dates, comparable figures for Wayne County, Michigan, were 73,598 on commodities and 50,530 on stamps.

Earlier hints that food stamp costs were cutting off an important segment of the potential market had not been explored by the department. A stamp supporter, Representative John Saylor, noted the cash problem as early as 1963 in analyzing the pilot project in one of the counties in his Pennsylvania district that suffered from the highest persistent unemployment rate in the country. Where some 40,000 persons had participated under the direct distribution plan in this distressed county, the number was reduced to less than 14,000 under food stamps. Since eligibility requirements remained the same, the drop-off could not be attributed to stiffer eligibility. After suggesting that with direct distribution "people just got in the habit of going down merely because it was surplus food being distributed," the congressman also reported that "some people, I feel certain, have not had the necessary cash to go and buy the food stamps."[27] By January 1967, food stamp participants in the county involved were down to 5,615. Either the direct distribution program had involved a really scandalous waste of food or food stamps were failing to reach the people they were intended to reach. If the latter, cost of stamps and regularity of purchase requirements would be possible explanations.

The idea that "people just got in the habit of going down" to surplus food distribution centers is hard to accept in view of a description of that whole experience:

Under the direct distribution plan, people, many poorly clothed and some perhaps ill, had to stand in long queues on specified days (rain or snow) and at specified hours (or miss out), with boxes, baskets or some other type of container to receive and lug home their surplus food items. . . . Common items were cornmeal, cheese, dried milk, rice, etc. They were given impractical large amounts of the same item because the distribution was made only once a month, and it was, I guess, intended to be a month's supply. I've heard of families getting 20 pounds and more of cheese and large amounts of cornmeal and dried milk, which many children didn't like and didn't drink. You can only use so much milk in cooking. The first month 20 pounds of cheese or cornmeal or rice was not bad. It was probably relished. The second month it was OK, but by the third month, and after, you could hardly look at it let alone eat it. So you gave it away or threw it away—a terrible waste. Then there was spoilage to contend with because many of the poor did not have adequate refrigeration to cope with large amounts of perishables.[28]

27. *Food Stamp Plan*, Hearings, p. 57.
28. *Ibid.*, pp. 54–55.

Mrs. Sullivan had found some peculiarities in the initial cash purchase requirements established in the St. Louis pilot project:

The fact is that the original purchase requirements were so high, in many cases, compared to the actual amount poor people in St. Louis were spending for food, that it was just impossible for many families which wanted to do so to participate. To give just one illustration, families on public assistance receiving $65 a month, and paying the minimum of $47 a month for rent in a public housing unit, were nevertheless being called upon to spend $20 a month for food stamps.[29]

Congressional intervention—Mrs. Sullivan nurtured and protected food stamps, watching over the program's development in St. Louis as well as over its operation nationally—and a lively and socially conscious St. Louis press persuaded welfare and agriculture officials that something was wrong with that particular scale. It was abandoned. Yet, for all of Mrs. Sullivan's influence and her personal interest and determination that stamps be made to work, the drop-off figures in St. Louis even after cost purchase adjustments were made are significant. When the program became effective there in January 1963, the total number of people moving from direct distribution to stamps fell from about 50,000 to about 7,500. Six years later, long after purchase price reforms had been effected and long after a reasonable building back period had elapsed, stamp participants totaled fewer than 25,000, a 50 percent cut from the number of beneficiaries of direct distribution. This figure may be less disquieting comparatively than the falloff in Saylor's district to 15 percent of the direct distribution total; a 50 percent drop-off, however, is still far too large to be satisfactorily explained by the assertion that people "just got the habit of going down" to collect food under direct distribution.

Nor is the drop-off satisfactorily explained away by acknowledging that direct distribution was imperfect. "I would venture to say that a great portion of that free food was wasted or traded for other things or sold for cash. . . . We know that in some areas, when they were getting the free food, they were selling some of it or most of it for whatever cash they could get," said Mrs. Sullivan in March 1967.[30] How imperfect can a program be? Did one family out of two on the St. Louis commodity rolls find it unnecessary or too much trouble to avail themselves of the simplicity of food stamps as a way of stretching the food dollar?

29. *Congressional Record*, daily ed., March 14, 1967, p. A1278.
30. *Extend the Food Stamp Act of 1964*, Hearings, p. 81.

That there were large numbers of people who might consider day after day use of stamps demeaning, or who might be uninformed about the stamps, or unable to handle their complexity, or too poor to buy them regularly was a hypothesis that does not seem to have been considered, validated, or denied.

Serious nonparticipation problems developed early in the state of Oregon and provoked complaints from the governor. Observation of simultaneous operation of food stamps and direct distribution there over a four-year period showed a sharp falling off in the number of recipients between 1963 and 1967 in Multnomah County (Portland), where the food stamp program was put into operation in 1963, but an increase in the number of recipients in all other counties of the state where direct distribution remained in effect over the whole period. In November 1962, the last full month of the direct distribution program, 25,025 persons (4.75 percent of the population) participated in Multnomah County; in November 1966, only 10,557 persons (1.9 percent of the population) participated in the county's food stamp program. (In May 1969 the total was up only to 11,639.) This was not the result of a new affluence for Oregonians. The pattern was quite different in the rest of the state where food stamps were not instituted. Thus, in November 1962, 30,978 persons benefited from direct distribution; in November 1966 the figure increased to 44,323. Where there had been a 60 percent falloff in the stamp county, there was almost a 50 percent increase in the remainder of the state where stamps were not involved. Hidden within these totals is a massive decline in the number of nonrecipients of public assistance taking advantage of food programs in Multnomah. In 1962 about half the recipients of surplus commodities in Multnomah and in the other counties as well were public assistance cases. By 1966 the proportion of nonrecipients of public assistance participating in all counties other than Multnomah had risen to over 55 percent. Under Multnomah's food stamp program, however, the proportion of nonrecipients had dropped to 16.4 percent of the reduced total number served.

Interpreting these statistics, Governor Tom McCall of Oregon and the Oregon Public Welfare Commission did not attribute the comparative rejection of stamps to either of the stock explanations: laxity in the administration of direct distribution or the supposed inability of persons to break themselves of the habit of picking up surplus foods. Rather, Governor McCall found the federal Department of Agriculture too rigid about costs and about the underside of the cost issue, regularity of purchase:

One of the basic reasons for these results is the restrictiveness of the Food Stamp Plan coupled with the lack of clear guidelines on the part of the U.S. Department of Agriculture. . . .

The primary area of restrictive rulings is in the amount of the individual's budget that must be spent in order to qualify for the stamp program. A second area is the requirement of regularity of purchase, which means, as now interpreted, that if the individual misses purchasing more than two times in six months, he must go through the complete recertification process. . . .[31]

Since food stamp purchases were declining while the demand for free commodities was increasing, McCall and his social welfare advisers concluded with some logic that there was something inherently wrong with the food stamp arrangements. In March 1967, with the four-year comparison of the Multnomah County–remainder-of-state statistics in hand, Oregon officials sought to amend the regularity-of-purchase requirements. The proposed change would have provided that failure to purchase for two consecutive periods without reasonable justification would result in ineligibility for a period of one month. Agriculture turned it down. Instead, an additional provision to terminate eligibility of households that established a pattern of irregular participation over a period of time was suggested by the department, and so was a three-month disqualification penalty for failure to purchase as agreed rather than the one month proposed by the state. Aside from the administrative complexities that these additions would involve, Agriculture's proposals create an inconsistency in objectives: on the one hand, regular participation is emphasized in order to improve nutrition and dietary levels; on the other hand, either a prolonged ineligibility period or outright termination for irregular participation precludes raising nutrition and dietary levels of low income families.

If minimum-purchase and regularity-of-purchase requirements were eased, Oregon's McCall was even willing to consider participation in the cost-sharing arrangement that so frightened many other states. The position of Oregon's Public Welfare Commission and its governor is that the individual low income household should be allowed to make its own decision as to when it is able to purchase stamps, that a rigid pur-

31. Letter from Tom McCall to Wayne Morse, April 24, 1967, in *Food Stamp Appropriations Authorization*, Hearing, p. 54.

chase schedule is untenable in a program designed to help the poor. If misguided federal policy is to the contrary, Oregon accepted such policy reluctantly and only as long as all costs are borne by the federal government. Multnomah was still Oregon's only food stamp county late in 1969. Thirty-four of the state's thirty-five other counties were dispensing the full complement of surplus commodities. The food stamp program, wrote Governor McCall, "is not doing the job it should do. . . . When the time comes that we believe the Food Stamp program will surpass the Abundant Food [surplus commodity] program in efficiency and service to needy people we will change over to the Food Stamp program."[32] That is a message McCall had been unsuccessful in getting across to the Department of Agriculture for years; gubernatorial resistance did not get through any more clearly than participant resistance.

Oblique Oversight by the Poverty Bloc

That food stamps may have been something less than the splendid little program so many federal administrators claimed it to be was brought to national attention in April 1967 when a Senate Labor and Public Welfare subcommittee saw and heard from hungry people in Mississippi. For the first time in food stamp history a congressional oversight function was exercised. As this oblique oversight by a committee that did not have jurisdiction over the program continued, the Department of Agriculture finally acknowledged nonparticipation was a problem.

"There are children in the Mississippi Delta," Senator Robert F. Kennedy later reported, "whose bellies are swollen with hunger, who exist on grits for breakfast, no lunch, and beans or rice for supper . . . their hunger makes them so lethargic that they could not learn even if they were in school."[33] Kennedy's participation in the activity of the subcommittee insured extensive press coverage of its travels to Mississippi. When they returned, Senators Joseph Clark and Kennedy waited on Secretary Freeman to express their dissatisfaction with the job being done by federal food programs. One result was to put Agriculture very much on the defensive: something, it seemed, was not right with food

32. Letter from Tom McCall to Leonard Farbstein, Aug. 14, 1969, in *Congressional Record*, daily ed., Sept. 15, 1969, p. H7922.
33. Address to the Day Care Council of New York, Symposium—The Child and the City, May 8, 1967.

stamps in Mississippi—although the department was even then telling three different congressional committees that the program was in great shape.

Of course it was not in great shape, and this should have been no news to Agriculture. What had happened in the Mississippi Delta was the same thing that had happened in Multnomah County, Oregon, in St. Louis, Missouri, and in other food stamp areas around the country. The transition from direct distribution of surplus foods to stamps had been accompanied by a sharp falling off in recipients. Agriculture brushed this aside with assurances that one of the superiorities of the stamp plan was that it alone concentrated on the really needy, that surplus commodity distribution attracted people who took the food only because it was free rather than because they needed it. Now there were glimmerings to suggest that that explanation used the right phrases but the wrong connectives: surplus commodity distribution apparently attracted people who took the food because it was free and because they needed it. Free food was eliminated by food stamps but need was still present.

Supporting evidence had been made available several months earlier. The food stamp program had few defenders and many critics at a February 1967 hearing conducted by the Mississippi Advisory Committee to the United States Commission on Civil Rights. A Civil Rights Commission staff member reported on the effect on participation of the change from commodities to stamps: "There is a trend of change in Mississippi from commodity distribution to food stamps, with a definite decrease in participation when a county changes from the Commodity Distribution Program to the Food Stamp Program."[34] In eight counties that had made the change, there was a total decrease in participation after one year of almost 36,000 recipients. For example, participation in Jones County dropped from 17,548 in March 1965 under commodity distribution to 4,658 in March 1966 under food stamps. In Lowndes County parallel figures were 3,717 and 2,443; in Harrison County, 9,597 and 2,602; in Coahoma County, 21,012 and 14,334. Signed statements were filed with the advisory committee by Mississippi residents attesting to their inability to buy food stamps because of lack of cash or their difficulties in being declared eligible. Also filed were copies of petitions from Sunflower County residents rejecting a switch to food stamps as

34. *Transcript of Proceedings, Meeting of Mississippi Advisory Committee* (Commission on Civil Rights), Jackson, Miss., Feb. 17, 1967, p. 330.

not meeting "the needs of poor people in this County who will be required to purchase stamps with money they do not have in order to obtain food that many of them need desperately."[35] For the most part, the people involved had benefited from the commodity distribution program.

Nor was the leadership of Agriculture entirely dependent on the good offices of the Civil Rights Commission for information about the adequacy of the stamp program. During the second week of March 1967, Neil Carter of the Consumer and Marketing Service took testimony in Tallahatchie County, Mississippi, about the gap between available cash and the costs of stamps. One month later, Howard Davis, deputy administrator of the Consumer Foods Program, and William Seabron, assistant to the secretary for civil rights, heard testimony and took affidavits comparable to those supplied the Civil Rights Commission. A national conference of welfare recipients meeting in Washington in February 1967 had criticized the Mississippi food stamp program (and the entire philosophy of food stamps), noting that welfare payments in Mississippi were too low to leave money for the purchase of stamps. Agriculture took all of this in stride.

The inquiring senators—officially the Subcommittee on Employment, Manpower, and Poverty whose members included two Kennedys, and a range of political opinion from that of liberal Joseph Clark on the one side to conservative George Murphy on the other side—were sufficiently moved by their Mississippi experience to take unusual action: all nine members (some of whom had not made the trip to Mississippi) signed a letter to President Johnson asking him to provide emergency food aid to families in the Mississippi Delta. Specifically, the recommendations included:

1. Making food stamps available free under the Food Stamp Act to people without cash income.

2. Lowering the food stamp cash purchase requirements for families with low cash incomes.

3. Investigating and undertaking to correct incidents where food stamp recipients had been required to pay more for stamps than required by law.

4. Distributing free surplus commodities through local private and public agencies.[36]

35. *Ibid.*, Exhibit T1, "Food Stamp Petitions from Sunflower County."
36. Press release, Senate Subcommittee on Employment, Manpower, and Poverty, April 30, 1967. The letter was delivered to the President on April 28, 1967.

The letter also noted that while acute hunger and malnutrition were observed only among Delta families in Mississippi, the subcommittee had been informed by Agriculture, by the Office of Economic Opportunity (OEO), and by the Civil Rights Commission that similar conditions existed in other states. Consequently, it was urged that whatever action was taken be addressed to these conditions wherever they exist. In the Delta alone, however, it was estimated that some 40,000 to 60,000 people would be either without or almost without cash income by the summer of 1967.

President Johnson passed over the opportunity to respond. Instead, perhaps because the White House believed it a good opportunity to give the OEO budget request a boost, perhaps because the OEO was supposed to be the coordinating agency in the war on poverty, perhaps because it was not known how else to handle this kind of public, direct petition from a group of United States senators, six of whom were Democrats, OEO was asked to respond to the communication. The answer was aggressive ("We hope they will inspect comparable conditions in other parts of the United States—conditions which more than substantiate OEO's fervent pleas last year and this year for adequate money to wage the war against poverty"); irrelevant ("Every state whose senator signed the appeal to the President has a crisis of poverty within it"); defensive ("As a result of the Administration's persistent effort over eighteen months, there is more antipoverty money, more food, more education, more jobs, more housing, more justice being brought to the citizens of Mississippi than to nearly any other state"); argumentative ("The current crisis which has so aroused the members of the Committee was first described eighteen months ago to the Congress and in numerous speeches across the country by officials of the Administration, who literally begged that the minimum requests submitted to the Congress to finance these programs be granted").[37]

More serious was the too ready acceptance by OEO of Agriculture's argument that it was not legally free to make drastic changes in food stamp costs and to distribute surplus commodities on an emergency

37. Press release, Office of Economic Opportunity, April 29, 1967. All of the background material was subsequently published in *Poverty: Hunger and Federal Food Programs, Background Information*, prepared for the Subcommittee on Employment, Manpower, and Poverty of the Senate Committee on Labor and Public Welfare, 90 Cong. 1 sess. (1967). See also Elizabeth B. Drew, "Going Hungry in America: Government's Failure," *Atlantic Monthly*, Vol. 222 (December 1968), pp. 53–61; Nick Kotz, *Let Them Eat Promises: The Politics of Hunger in America* (Prentice-Hall, 1969).

basis. "[The] Department of Agriculture states," said the OEO response without further comment on these questions, "that it is unlawful for that Agency to distribute food stamps without cost to recipients, as the Committee suggests. The Department of Agriculture also states it cannot, by definition, authorize emergency action, as the letter suggests, under the provisions of the Food Stamp Act." This insistence on the inviolability of a cash purchase requirement simply reiterated Freeman's statement two or three days earlier in the course of Senate Agriculture Committee hearings on extension of the food stamp program that the "law requires that the person should make a token, at least, contribution toward getting these stamps."[38]

The secretary of agriculture was on bad grounds on several counts. His own lawyer, it was soon to develop, did not read the law that way at all. Research into the legislative history of the food stamp program would have shown that the chairman of the House Agriculture Committee had not read the law that way either, and that the Agriculture Committee report on the bill itself noted a specific exception to the cash purchase requirement. Perhaps most difficult to understand was why the secretary did not seek an appropriate amendment if he was persuaded the law unwisely prohibited free distribution of food stamps.

There was now evidence that the cash purchase requirement created critical problems not only in Mississippi but in other places as well. One non-Mississippi case had been raised during House Agriculture Committee consideration of the stamp extension legislation by Representative B. F. Sisk whose California district included the Fresno area. Sisk was concerned about the inability of migratory workers to buy stamps during several months of the year when they were unemployed and literally without any cash income whatever.

I have three counties in my district which are basically rural counties in which we have a great deal of farm labor, and these people, you know, are out of work particularly in the rainy season. I recognize it as being a peculiar situation, particularly different from the cities or other urban areas. There are times when these people do not have one dime of income, because, at the present time, there is no unemployment insurance for farmworkers. They have no income, period. . . .

The problem is such as I hope can be worked out where we can have the plan but at the same time not deprive these people the right to eat during that period in which they do not have one dime with which to purchase stamps.[39]

38. *Food Stamp Appropriations Authorization*, Hearing, p. 30.
39. *Extend the Food Stamp Act of 1964*, Hearings, p. 93.

Sisk explained further that according to the information provided him by Agriculture, the counties in question could not receive surplus commodities together with the food stamp program. The department did not find the problem described by Sisk to be an "other disaster" in the sense of the use of that term in the Food Stamp Act of 1964 authorizing simultaneous operation of the two food aid programs "during emergency situations caused by a national or other disaster as determined by the Secretary."[40]

The situation, then, was that cash purchase requirements were keeping some of the poorest people in California as well as in Mississippi out of the program. Inquiry would have disclosed that the same held true in Alabama. When Freeman made a tour of that state a few months later, ostensibly to inspect rural development projects, he was greeted with complaints from poverty-ridden farmers about their inability to buy food stamps. The first point made at an unscheduled meeting with about three hundred Negro farmers and farm wives in Eutaw, a west central Alabama town, dealt with the cost of food stamps. "I was told it would cost me $62," the complainant said. "I don't have enough money to buy food stamps." The Washington bureau of the NAACP reported a large number of concerned inquiries and comments about the program. Clarence Mitchell, director of the bureau, concluded that "it is obvious" that the recipient drop-off in the shift from free foods to stamps would take place in all depressed areas:

The rigid regulations now enforced that make a family purchasing stamps devote a large percentage of its income to food stamps and also require the purchase of stamps on a regular basis often defeat the objective of feeding the hungry poor. Those most in need often have little or no cash on hand. What is available must often be budgeted to meet other necessities. Emergency situations often divert income so that regularity in the purchase of stamps becomes an impossibility. Thus, in many instances, the program becomes unrealistic as a method of assisting the needy.[41]

In April 1967 it must have been known in the Department of Agriculture that the food stamp plan was critically defective in reaching persons without some regular cash income; it was the judgment of the secretary, repeatedly stated, that the law required that some cash be paid for stamps; enabling legislation was at that very time being con-

40. *The Food Stamp Act of 1964*, Sec. 4(b).
41. *New York Times*, June 29, 1967; *Extend the Food Stamp Act of 1964*, Hearings, p. 114.

sidered by the Senate Agriculture Committee. Nevertheless, the department announced itself satisfied with the law and claimed that:

The food stamp program is a success;
It has more than lived up to our very high expectations of three years ago;
It has, in fact, been an exciting, imaginative, and effective venture;
It has charted a new course in the wise and prudent use of this country's abundance of food;
It has improved the diets and health of our low-income families.[42]

After insisting that the law required a cash contribution to stamps from even the poorest recipient, Freeman heard from two sources, early in May, that his curbstone opinion was no good. John C. Bagwell, then general counsel of the Department of Agriculture and thus the secretary's lawyer, wrote Freeman on May 4 that the act required payment by recipients of their normal expenditures for food, and that "it seems clear . . . that if a household has no income the [House] Committee intended that such fact would support a determination that such a household has no normal expenditures for food."[43] An opinion of the Senate poverty subcommittee counsel, transmitted to Freeman in a memorandum on May 9, was stated clearly: "As discussed above, the Secretary unquestionably has authority to: (1) Issue free food stamps to recipients without cash income, and (2) Distribute free federally owned food to families without cash income in food stamp program areas."[44] The only clouded question, in the judgment of this lawyer, was whether it was within the power of the secretary to do both at the same time. In view of the fact that the secretary had not been disposed to do either, that did not seem to be a pressing problem.

Then, in June, the Field Foundation released a report by a team of six medical doctors who had just returned from a May 27–30 field inquiry into the health of children in rural Mississippi. The group of prestigious physicians concluded that children whom they saw "are suffering from hunger and disease and directly or indirectly they are dying from them—which is exactly what 'starvation' means. . . . Their parents may be declared ineligible for commodities, ineligible for the food stamp

42. *Food Stamp Appropriations Authorization*, Hearing, p. 114.
43. General Counsel to the Secretary, "Provision of Section 4(b) of the Food Stamp Act of 1964 permitting direct distribution in food stamp areas during emergency situations—Provision of Section 7(b) of the Act providing for amounts to be charged for coupon allotments" (May 4, 1967), p. 4.
44. *Poverty: Hunger and Federal Food Programs*, p. 40.

program, even though they have literally nothing."[45] Some Department of Agriculture officials felt that they were being picked on. One complained to a caller early in June that "John Gardner and HEW are not castigated because ADC doesn't reach every needy child in every county; why pick on us?"

The truth of the matter was that the committee was not picking on Agriculture. Clark, the active other members of his subcommittee, and an unusually competent, specially assembled subcommittee staff were simply looking at food stamps and commodity distribution programs in a context quite different from that of the Department of Agriculture. The subcommittee people were seeking to effect no less than a major overhaul in the extent and character of federal response to the existence of hunger in America, a phenomenon that the war on poverty had not directly highlighted but one that was becoming increasingly evident. Hunger, the subcommittee staff and members felt, was not something dealt with through regular channels.

Agriculture, on the other hand, still viewed the issue in the context of the life and times of the Department of Agriculture. Freeman and his staff acknowledged that an argument could be made for the proposition that the food stamp program had been administered too conservatively. They coupled that admission, however, with reminders that the legislation had a difficult history in 1964 when it took that celebrated logrolling arrangement to pass the bill, and with further reminders that it continued to face an unfriendly House Agriculture Committee. Keeping the food stamp program alive was a high priority matter for those who had nursed it from the eight-county pilot stage in 1961 to the eight hundred-plus–county-and-city stage it had reached in 1967. If conservative administration was necessary to keep it alive, it would be administered conservatively.

From Agriculture's point of view, the timing of the whole controversy could not have been worse because the department budget for 1968 was making its way through the agriculture appropriations subcommittees. Secretary Freeman's frequently quoted observation, "I have two bosses: Lyndon Johnson and Jamie Whitten," now took on special significance. Whitten, chairman of the House appropriations subcommittee on the Department of Agriculture, represents the Mississippi Delta. According to Whitten, "[Freeman] and I have maintained

45. *Ibid.*, p. 60.

a relationship of mutual respect and can talk about mutual problems at any time." After they talked about this one, Whitten reported the conversation: "I pointed out to him that the law required him to sell food stamps, and set up a formula for charges; that I did not believe there was any such general situation in my State, but if, as the Senators claimed, there were families in such condition, the answer was welfare."[46]

To undertake emergency food aid for the Mississippi Delta's population over Whitten's denials that any such aid was either necessary or desirable was to invite troubles with the 1968 Agriculture appropriation—or so it appeared to some of the department's leaders who tried to dissuade Clark from pushing for fast action. From their point of view, the best hope for improvement in the way federal food programs worked in Mississippi was to wait for the budget to be cleared, then to take incremental action. The incremental changes being considered were those that had been recommended by Davis and Seabron, the department team, after their visit to Mississippi in April.

Freeman came to the July hearings of the Clark subcommittee formally to report adoption of the Davis-Seabron proposals. Purchase price requirements for food stamps in Mississippi had been lowered to 50 cents per person per month; Agriculture was negotiating with state and county officials to achieve guarantees that public funds would be provided persons who could not meet the 50 cent requirement. In addition, Freeman hoped to effect changes elsewhere by the end of the year. It was too late, of course, to do anything about the fact that of the $140 million appropriation for food stamps in fiscal 1967, $22.5 million was unspent when the year ended.

The purchase price reduction for Mississippi and a new outreach effort through the use of food stamp aides had been publicly announced two weeks before Freeman's appearance. (The House of Representatives passed the Agriculture appropriation bill a few days before the announcement.) Most of the Democratic members of the Senate subcommittee were disposed to accept these changes as an act of good

46. *Congressional Record*, daily ed., May 11, 1967, p. H5345. Representative Leonor Sullivan has said that "I would say flatly that the Appropriations Subcommittee for Agriculture has given far more support to the food stamp program—many times over—than the legislative committee which has responsibility for the Food Stamp Act. . . . It has generally not been difficult getting the full appropriation from the Subcommittee on Agricultural Appropriations headed by the gentleman from Mississippi." *Congressional Record*, daily ed., May 26, 1969, p. H4095.

faith and to believe that they would really represent improvements. In a sense, there was no choice but to adopt a believing attitude. Secretary Freeman was a member of the fraternity. Save perhaps for Interior Secretary Stewart Udall, no member of the Johnson cabinet was as close as Freeman to the New Frontier political history and philosophy to which most of the Democratic members of the subcommittee subscribed. This was not a case of attacking the efforts and judgments of Dean Rusk, an intellectual from the Rockefeller Foundation turned into secretary of state, or of Robert Weaver, a housing professional turned into secretary of housing and urban development. Freeman had come up the political route as a liberal governor of Minnesota. He had been chosen to nominate John F. Kennedy for the presidency at the 1960 Democratic convention. In a speech that characterized Kennedy as a "man free from the commitments and clichés of the past," Freeman set the stage for Kennedy's own references to a new generation of leaders. For whatever reason, Freeman had stumbled, perhaps, in dealing with the food stamp problem, but he was now back on the track and would be aware of watchful oversight by a concerned poverty subcommittee. Together, the subcommittee and the secretary would overcome the conservatism of the agriculture committees.

Things did not work out that way. *Hunger, U.S.A., A Report by the Citizens' Board of Inquiry into Hunger and Malnutrition in the United States* was released April 22, 1968, after nine months' preparation. The twenty-five-member board of inquiry had been organized in the summer of 1967, following the reports of hunger and malnutrition in Mississippi, by the Citizens' Crusade Against Poverty (CCAP), a Washington-based group closely associated with the United Auto Workers. Walter Reuther, chairman of the CCAP, called on the board to examine the extent of hunger and starvation in selected poverty areas, the extent of nutritional knowledge in the country, and the impact of public and private programs, and to make short and long term recommendations.

Medical and nutritional studies conducted by the board indicate, according to *Hunger, U.S.A.*, "a prevalence of chronic hunger and malnutrition hitherto unimagined."[47] Ten million Americans and probably more are affected, the report suggests. It lays a large share of the blame on the Department of Agriculture: "Federal efforts aimed at securing adequate nutrition for the needy have failed to reach a significant por-

47. *Hunger, U.S.A., A Report by the Citizens' Board of Inquiry into Hunger and Malnutrition in the United States* (New Community Press, 1968), p. 16.

tion of the poor and to help those it did reach in any substantial and satisfactory degree." *Hunger, U.S.A.* called on the President to declare a national emergency in the 256 counties it identified as "hunger counties" and to make every effort to see that the hungry in those counties were fed adequately. The report also proposed a free food stamp program in every locality, providing enough stamps for an adequate diet.

Then came *Their Daily Bread*, sponsored by five nonpolitical national women's organizations, all with some religious connection, undertaken to find out why "so few children participate in the National School Lunch Program [administered by Agriculture] or are denied the opportunity to participate, and why the School Lunch Program is failing to meet the needs of poor children."[48] According to *Their Daily Bread*, about 18 million of the 50 million children in public elementary and secondary schools participate in the school lunch program, but fewer than 2 million of the 18 million receive a free or reduced price lunch. About 4 million needy children do not. A universal, free school lunch program was recommended as a long run goal, and lunches costing only 20 cents for those who can afford them and costing nothing for those who cannot afford them were set forth as immediate objectives.

Agriculture was still on edge when on May 21, 1968, CBS television indicted the department in "Hunger in America." In his opening remarks, Charles Kuralt, the narrator, cited the Citizens' Board of Inquiry claim that serious hunger exists in many parts of the country. Focusing on hunger in four areas—San Antonio, Texas, Loudon County, Virginia, the Indian reservations of Arizona and New Mexico, and Alabama—the documentary concluded, however, as had *Hunger, U.S.A.*, that hunger was not limited to the places it had visited:

Ten million Americans don't know where their next meal is coming from. Sometimes it doesn't come at all.

More than one thousand counties in need of food programs have no program whatsoever. . . . There is also the failure of these programs themselves. Surplus commodities are free but do not contain the right foods. Food stamps are not free and too often, the people who need them most can't afford them.

The Department of Agriculture has emergency power to bring food to

48. *Their Daily Bread,* a study of the National School Lunch Program by the Committee on School Lunch Participation under the direction of Florence Robin (Atlanta: McNelley-Rudd Printing Service, n.d.), p. 3.

hungry people in any county in the United States. So far, it has been reluctant to exercise this power.[49]

Responses to the three hunger studies varied. *Their Daily Bread* was not disputed, the other two irritated both Poage and Freeman. Chairman Poage found the CBS program and *Hunger, U.S.A.* both "quite inaccurate and misleading." His committee issued its own *Hunger Study* and *Hunger Study Supplement* containing statements by officials from some of the 256 counties designated as "emergency hunger counties" by *Hunger, U.S.A.* The supplement admitted that some borderline hunger and starvation cases, "caused principally by ignorance and neglect," were occasionally uncovered. It emphasized, however, that public agencies were feeding the needy "whenever and wherever they are found."[50] Secretary Freeman characterized "Hunger in America" as "a biased, one-sided, dishonest presentation of a serious national problem."[51] Freeman asked Frank Stanton, president of CBS, for equal time to "refute the errors of fact, the misinterpretations and the misinformation that were dispersed through 'Hunger in America' and to assure the hungry of this nation that the USDA 'does' care. . . . "

There was no more peace for Freeman and his department. While even some liberal members of Congress were reluctant to embrace *Hunger, U.S.A.*'s findings unreservedly, they used them as a springboard to launch inquiries of their own into the hunger problem. The House Education and Labor Committee opened hearings on a bill to create a bipartisan hunger commission, and the Senate Subcommittee on Employment, Manpower, and Poverty returned to the wars with hearings to investigate the extent of hunger and malnutrition and to consider the creation of a select committee on nutrition and human needs. Then, in June, the Poor People were led into Washington by Ralph Abernathy "to say that hunger in America must be abolished, and we cannot compromise on that fact." Agriculture became the campaign's focal point.

49. A transcript of the documentary appears in *Congressional Record*, daily ed., May 29, 1968, p. S6637.

50. *Hunger Study*, House Committee on Agriculture, 90 Cong. 2 sess. (1968); *Hunger Study Supplement* (*Supplement to Hunger Study, June 11, 1968*), House Committee on Agriculture, 90 Cong. 2 sess. (1968), p. 4.

51. Letter from Orville Freeman to Carl Perkins, May 27, 1968; reprinted in *Hunger Study*, p. 74.

The Senate subsequently established a Select Committee on Nutrition and Human Needs which absorbed some members and staff of the poverty subcommittee and spent much of the following year further documenting the inadequacies of food relief programs. For Freeman, the cruelest blow in that activity may have been the testimony of his former under secretary, John Schnittker, that food relief programs should be shifted to the Department of Health, Education, and Welfare. "All of us," Schnittker said not very subtly, "tend to get proprietary and defensive about our own programs and our own methods of operation after a time. In my opinion, new people can best administer any new programs, or can handle existing programs in new ways to meet new and ambitious objectives." Then Schnittker went on to describe food stamps as "only one step short of giving people cash to spend on food," and as "in many cases a supplement to welfare payments."[52] So much for the supposed advantages of stamps over a cash relief supplement.

Political Staying Power

Whatever the administrative arrangements, food stamps, after a decade of failure through the sixties, still resist fading away in favor of cash relief. Instead, the stamp program is defended more fiercely than ever by its old friends who have lately been joined by some new ones. When the Nixon administration, uncommitted on the stamp issue, first agreed to issue free food stamps on a pilot basis, then tentatively decided on welfare reform without a stamp component, it ran into opposition on one or the other count from all the congressional actors. The agriculture committees continued to oppose free stamps. "Our idea was to help people to help themselves by multiplying their money," said Chairman Poage in explaining why he found free stamps untenable.[53] At the other end of the stamp spectrum, the congressional food stamp liberals —typified on the Senate side by George McGovern, who served as chairman of the Senate Select Committee, and on the House side by Leonor Sullivan—would not abide an end to food stamps. Mrs. Sullivan, more-

52. *Nutrition and Human Needs,* Hearings before the Senate Select Committee on Nutrition and Human Needs, 90 Cong. 2 sess. (1968) and 91 Cong. 1 sess. (1969), Pt. 6: *Food Assistance Reform* (1969), p. 2089.
53. *Congressional Quarterly Weekly Report,* July 18, 1969, p. 1277.

over, did not approve of free stamps any more than did Poage. Her position is instructive in understanding the political strength of stamps.

If food stamps, like dollar bills, are to have a face imprinted on them, no likeness would be more appropriate than that of the gentlewoman from Missouri. Beginning in 1954, her second year in the House of Representatives, continuing through 1964, when the Food Stamp Act was passed, until the present, Mrs. Sullivan has been a constant, determined, and tough proponent of the program. Never a member of the Agriculture Committee, which has jurisdiction over food relief programs, she has become the House's food stamp expert: she was invited to sponsor the Kennedy administration's food stamp bill, manages stamp legislation on the House floor, and in 1964 arranged the deals whereby urban, liberal support for wheat-cotton legislation was traded for rural, conservative support of food stamps. In 1968 Mrs. Sullivan rejected the Agriculture Committee's proposed one-year extension and $20 million increase in authorization as inadequate. Instead, she maneuvered a four-year, open ended authorization of the program through an incompetent administrative agency that was too confused to know where it stood, around the unsympathetic Agriculture Committee, and past the House of Representatives in what she accurately describes as "an historic and bitter battle." (The battle was perhaps even more bitter in retrospect because in conference the House managers—the chairman and ranking member of the Agriculture Committee—agreed to both an authorization ceiling and a thirty-month extension in lieu of four years.)

Because sympathetic leadership in food stamps does not come from either the Agriculture Committee or from the agriculture appropriations subcommittee, and because it takes a great deal of effort for a congressman who is not on either committee to acquire the specialized information necessary to speak and to lead authoritatively, Mrs. Sullivan's position in the House on food stamp matters is unique. It is indicative of how effective she has been in mobilizing support for a bigger stamp program that in 1968, faced with a 26–4 rejection from the Agriculture Committee, and faced with a department that was asking only for marginal improvements, Mrs. Sullivan acquired 129 cosponsors for her program, spoke baldly of the need to make "an arrangement" on farm support and food stamp bills in order to get both through the House, and got the secretary of agriculture to shift his position and support her alternative without even providing advance notice of his shift in position to the chairman of the Agriculture Committee. That, as the ranking Republican member of the committee put it, "almost knocked the chairman off his chair. He got rather irked about it, and he was not happy about it, so he proceeded to get the Committee on Agriculture to disregard the Sullivan bill and pass out the chairman's bill, which came out almost unanimously."[54] Mrs. Sullivan, in turn, "got rather irked," took on the committee on the House floor, and won 227–172, thus underscoring the conclusion reached by numerous congressmen that she is more responsible than any other member for the fact that there is a food stamp program.

Having labored for fifteen years on behalf of a very particular kind of program in which she believes deeply, Mrs. Sullivan does not look cheerfully on the possibility of food stamps being transformed into a relief program that lacks the distinctive feature of stamps: supplementing what people normally spend for food with an added amount of purchasing power to enable not only very low income families but also large families of modest income to enjoy an adequate diet. Many students of welfare problems applauded a decision by Freeman's Republican successor, Clifford Hardin, to institute a pilot free stamp program in two South Carolina counties. Mrs. Sullivan did not share their reaction. "I firmly believe the free stamp idea is a mistake," she said.[55]

Progress in food stamp programs, from Mrs. Sullivan's point of view, has come inch by inch and step by step—it has been "bitterly and agonizingly hard." She is worried about excessive liberality resulting in a legislative and popular backlash. Her reluctance to give stamps away grows out of a fear that without continuing to insist on at least a token investment of some cash by recipients the pressures would mount irresistibly for free stamps for persons of higher and higher income levels until the program was transformed into "a general free food program for all." And, then, she asks, "Why not free rent? Why not free shoes? Why not free clothing? Why not free bus transportation? Why not free handouts of every necessity?" Viewing with alarm the free stamp idea, which she feels "could undermine and destroy the whole food stamp concept," Mrs. Sullivan asks rhetorically, "And how long would middle class attitudes in this country stand for a system of free necessities to every family of low income without even a token payment to show it is trying to help itself at least a little?"[56]

54. *Congressional Record*, daily ed., July 31, 1968, p. H7897.
55. *Ibid.*, April 2, 1969, p. E2574.
56. *Ibid.*

The significance of Mrs. Sullivan's position is that while hers is the most effective voice in the House for food relief liberalization, it is a voice that speaks for a specialized approach to food relief—the stamp approach—and it is a voice raised on behalf of food relief specifically rather than on behalf of any other kind of income assistance. Mrs. Sullivan thinks the public responsibility goes further, at least in the food area, than simply giving poor people more money or even simply giving them more food stamps. With giving people an opportunity to buy a better diet, she argues, goes the necessity to help them spend their dollars or stamps "intelligently." Since HEW would apparently continue to turn people loose with money to make their own decision, the stamp program should not be shifted out of Agriculture which "has always had expertise" in the nutrition field. She speaks scornfully of the cash approach traditionally favored by HEW:

From everything I have been able to learn, the people at HEW have always felt and still feel that if you want to help poor people, you just give them more money, and let them spend it for whatever they think they want to spend it for. This is the policy on public assistance—if a family uses the welfare check foolishly, that is their business, according to HEW.[57]

There is a surprising rigidity in this attitude, surprising because legislators who adopt a liberal approach to relief programs rarely put a protective embrace around a single program. Congressmen brought up in the era of cash relief have not raised their voices against food stamps as a restriction on the freedom of choice of the recipient to spend his relief allocation as he decides. But Mrs. Sullivan has served fair warning that she will hold firm on stamps and that she is disposed to stick with Agriculture. With a friend like Mrs. Sullivan, who has demonstrated great skill in putting together a pro-food stamp legislative bloc, with the program still important to farm legislators for logrolling on price support, and with new support for food stamps coming from a group of southern Democratic senators who for whatever reasons—new convictions, old consciences, or a choice between stamps and the less desired but inevitable alternative of cash—acknowledge the existence of hunger in their states and urge relief in kind,[58] the stamp program has

57. Ibid., p. E2575.
58. Press release, Report by Senator Ernest F. Hollings (Democrat of South Carolina) before Senate Select Committee on Nutrition and Human Needs, Feb. 18, 1969; statement by Senator Herman Talmadge (Democrat of Georgia), accompanying introduction of S. 1864, Congressional Record, daily ed., April 18, 1969, pp. S3861–63.

come to have more political strength than it does success as a relief measure.

The truth about food stamps is that it is, to use Secretary Robert Finch's characterization, a demeaning program. Wisely laid to rest in 1943, stamps were unwisely resurrected in 1961. In an experimental period before the 1964 authorizing legislation, the wrong questions were asked. After 1964, the Department of Agriculture dedicated itself to documenting successes where there was no success. Not until oblique oversight was established by the Senate's poverty bloc in response to pleas from Mississippi civil rights workers did the program get proper evaluation. Then, Agriculture became defensive. Shifting administration to Health, Education, and Welfare would not overcome the program's inherent defects and its rejection by the poor.[59] It has now become evident that there is a political stake in the food stamp program that precludes its easy termination in favor of cash assistance once envisioned by some of President Nixon's welfare advisers. Food stamps may turn out to be harder to get rid of than they were to get.

59. An opportunity to express a choice between programs was given eligible families in New York's Nassau County (Long Island) in February 1970. Polled by the county, they voted nearly 8 to 1 (4,260–539) in favor of commodity distribution over food stamps. *New York Times*, Feb. 27, 1970.

7

Veterans' Relief: Separate and Unequal

Old age, disability, and survivor's pensions for wartime veterans who suffer no disability attributable to their period of service have been a source of exasperation to social planners, to federal budget specialists, to several presidents of the United States, and to one veterans' organization. At the same time, these so-called non-service-connected *pensions*—which should not be confused with *compensation* for service-incurred disability—have been warmly praised and supported by great congressional majorities and by the largest veterans' service organizations, including the competing giants, the American Legion (membership 2.4 million) and the Veterans of Foreign Wars (membership 1.35 million). To supporters the pension program is a variant of social insurance, wartime military service constituting the premium payment. To skeptics, veterans' pension is a dignified, but indefensible, separate public assistance program. There is now an uneasy truce between supporters and opponents of non-service-connected pensions based on agreement that pensions will be paid only to aged or disabled needy veterans and to veterans' needy survivors. The result is a program that pays $2.3 billion annually to over 2¾ million "needy" recipients, 1¾ million of whom are widows and children. And the boundaries of "need," the definition of disability, and the reciprocal relationship with social insurance are all fixed more advantageously for potential beneficiaries of this program than they are for the generality of poor Americans.

Under the present truce between proponents and opponents of pensions, there is room for cost of living adjustments and for periodic improvements in the definition of income to allow more veterans and their widows and children to qualify simultaneously for social security and pension payments. But the line is drawn this side of a general service pension that is only distantly related to need. At one extreme the American Veterans Committee, the liberal veterans' group organized after World War II, believes that the line should at least be held firm if not pulled back; at the other extreme, crossing the line and achieving a general service pension is the goal of the Veterans of World War I of the U.S.A., Inc. In earlier years the general service pension had an attraction, too, for both the American Legion and the Veterans of Foreign Wars. Now both have come to accept need as a condition for pension eligibility. But whether supporting a general service pension or a pension available only to needy veterans who cannot work, most service organizations emphasize the "honorable" character of veterans' pensions, thereby encouraging applications and keeping business brisk.

A different view of veterans' pensions is that they are a treasury grab organized by the service organizations and legitimized by congressmen who are fearful of antagonizing the 93.5 million veterans, members of their families, and surviving widows, minor children, and parents who were dependent on deceased veterans. Testifying once in opposition to pensions generally, and in particular to liberalization of existing pensions, a spokesman for the American Veterans Committee (the deviant veterans' organization that adopts the position that veterans are ordinary people) acknowledged that while his group would prefer to see the pension program abolished, it saw no prospect of such an abolition. An announced position in favor of repeal, explained the witness, "would be so far out that it would result in our being labeled crack pot, so we do not go quite so far. We live with what is in the law now."[1]

In the many decades when the country lacked any comprehensive policy either to protect individuals against financial need or to aid veterans in readjustment to civilian life, veterans' pension legislation—which can be traced back as far as 1832—could be thought of as half a loaf: a kind of social security for some veterans was better than no social security for anyone. The Social Security Act of 1935 and its subsequent extensions of coverage and liberalizations of benefits cut away at the half a loaf rationale. Now it looked more like a whole loaf for most people and a loaf and a half for the veteran. Similarly, in the "old war" era prior to World War II, before readjustment benefits were enacted to give the veteran a boost that would help him compete with the non-veteran, the pension program could be thought of as an equalization

1. *Pension Bills Providing Non-service Connected Pension Benefits for Veterans of All Wars,* Hearings before the Subcommittee on Compensation and Pensions of the House Committee on Veterans' Affairs, 88 Cong. 2 sess. (1964), p. 3924.

benefit for the veteran whose military service had left him behind in the competitive civilian world. Then the G.I. bill, with its unemployment compensation, education, housing loan, and business loan features, boosted the veteran abreast of the nonveteran and perhaps a little ahead.

By 1955 a presidential commission reported that in a survey it had made of the veteran population, more than half of the respondents believed that military service had not much effect, positive or negative, on employment and progress in civilian life. More than two-fifths reported that service had been either of some or of considerable benefit, while only about 6 percent considered military service to have been a handicap or disadvantage in civilian employment and progress. These findings helped to persuade the commission and its staff that the preferred status of veterans in the national social welfare benefits picture should be terminated—gently, leisurely perhaps, but terminated. "The provisions of the veterans' pension law should be adjusted to fit the pension benefits into a pattern consistent with benefits provided under OASI," said the commission.[2] Fifteen years and several improvements of the social security law later, however, the veterans' pension law benefits are still far from consistent with old age and survivors' insurance (OASI) benefits and public assistance benefits.

Veterans' pensions have demonstrated an impressive staying power as a welfare program that parallels old age assistance and aid to dependent children but takes on few of their oppressive characteristics. Given this separation of programs that can serve an overlapping clientele, persons in a position to make a choice are well advised to opt for a veterans' pension rather than for old age assistance or for aid to families with dependent children. The veterans' program usually pays better and comes easier. Unlike most public assistance beneficiaries, recipients of veterans' pensions are not conditioned to believe that they are a drag on society, are not subject to investigation to insure that their claim continues to be valid, are presumed to be telling the truth, are assisted in making a claim by a large network of volunteers and of agents of governmental units other than the unit paying the benefit, are not obliged to account for their spending behavior, may have significant amounts of income from other sources, are able to move freely without jeopardizing their benefits, and are not badgered to get off the rolls. Added to all this

2. *Veterans' Benefits in the United States*, A Report to the President by the President's Commission on Veterans' Pensions (April 1956), p. 375.

is an administrative agency instructed by law to be and naturally disposed to be sympathetic; a finely tuned congressional committee preoccupied with the problems of the veteran population but also sensitive to the importance of avoiding excesses; a financing system that depends exclusively on appropriations from federal general revenue without the need for any state participation whatever; and an appeals procedure that keeps disputes within the family, handles them informally, and strives to find an interpretation that will permit a favorable ruling.

No one knows how recipients rank these apparent advantages of the pension program. Case-by-case responses are likely to vary depending on individual circumstances. Undoubtedly there are some pensioners living perilously close to poverty who would trade the style of pensions for larger cash benefits even if accompanied by the restrictions of public assistance. But in the aggregate, common sense suggests a preference for the pension program and, in particular, for its "honorable" (read "nonwelfare") character. Maintaining the emphasis on pensions as an earned right rather than as charity is the special province of the veterans' associations, particularly the American Legion.

Service Organizations as Intercessors

It does not readily occur to many ordinary people in American life that they might qualify for payments from the public fisc. In many cases the potential beneficiary is not sufficiently in touch with public affairs to understand a grant or loan or benefit program. To overcome this, social security can use posters in places of employment, public service announcements on the airwaves and television, and notices in public places to reach its potential clientele and remind them to file for benefits in timely fashion. Social security is also helped by the earmarked tax and the withholding process, which automatically alert workers to the existence of the program. No crude relief program has all these built-in communications advantages. Some public housing authorities do distribute handbills and fliers. Food stamps, in some jurisdictions, will be featured in advertising space in buses and are publicized through posters in retail food outlets advertising the existence of the program. However, aid to dependent children is made known largely by word of mouth alone, and so is general assistance.

In other cases, applicants are awed or intimidated by officialdom, and in still other cases, suspicion of or prideful reluctance to accept a public

benefit explains nonparticipation. Illustrations of unawareness, intimidation, and pride as barriers to assistance have been provided in the
hearings of the United States Civil Rights Commission, in the reports
of outreach workers under the community action programs, and in the
stories uncovered by the Department of Agriculture as it attempted
belatedly to discover why food stamp nonparticipation rates were so
high. Even where these barriers are not present, not all relief offerings
are available in quantities sufficient to accommodate all technically
qualified applicants, a problem most pronounced in public housing
where there are long waiting lists. But the escalation in public assistance since 1965 underscores the conclusion that before the community
action program and welfare rights groups dug out potential welfare
clients, there must have been tens of thousands who could have been
on the rolls but were not. The very gap between the total number of
people known and acknowledged to be living at subpoverty-line incomes
and the total number of beneficiaries of public relief suggests imper-
fections in the system whereby government communicates with its
needy citizens; it also suggests the importance of intercessor groups to
locate, to explain to, and to represent people who cannot help themselves.

Within the universe of federally assisted relief programs, veterans'
pensions suffer least from the problem of nonparticipation attributable
to communications gap, to intimidation, or to reluctance to accept public relief. One reason is the existence and high competence of intercessor groups of veterans' associations. To dispel any image of pensions
as relief, these groups pay meticulous attention to rationalizing the pension program as delayed compensation, a rationalization developed most
thoroughly by the American Legion. Pensions, like all other veterans'
benefits in the Legion's view, are a delayed cost of conducting war. To
veterans who need them, pensions are made available out of gratitude,
in recognition of past services rendered. Pensions are a gratuity based on
appreciation, not solely on compassion or social necessity. During periods of national emergency there is an implicit understanding that a kind
of sinking fund is authorized to meet the subsequent needs of veterans
and of their widows and children who cannot provide for themselves.
It is the job of the Legion to keep that sinking fund solvent and to
perpetuate the idea that, as a delayed cost of war, the sinking fund is
entirely separate in concept from ordinary public relief, which lacks the
historic antecedent.

Legion pension theory—shared in the main by the Veterans of Foreign Wars and by the American Veterans of World War II and Korea (AMVETS)—can be characterized, then, as a belief in an invisible emergency account maintained in the federal treasury for every war veteran against which he may draw when necessary. Unlike a service bonus, the account will not be liquidated at any particular time. For many veterans there will never be a disbursement; after the death of the veteran and of his dependents, no claims against the account will be honored. If it is necessary to draw upon the account, no shame or stigma attaches, because military service in wartime constituted the premium payment in return for which the invisible emergency account was created. Payments are not made *for* non-service-connected disability and unemployability, but only to relieve or prevent need presumed to be due to such disability.

The pension as delayed compensation is a rationalization invented less to provide an excuse for the giver to give and more for the receiver to receive. It is not really necessary to insist on this rationalization in order to maintain the program in the Congress. Few legislators would be likely to turn aside an appeal for an out-and-out relief program for needy veterans. But in a society where relief cases are social failures, where "being on welfare" is a source of shame, the problem for those who wish to soften the needs of the very poor is to invent a moral equivalent of relief that will be acceptable to the needy old without depressing them emotionally and that will be acceptable to the needy young without causing them to resent the giver. Like social security, the beauty of veterans' pensions is in the appeal of the rationale to the beneficiary. Pension also has a way of explaining that rationale through tens of thousands of volunteer outreach workers deployed around the country who seek out possible beneficiaries, help them file applications, and process appeals if necessary. These outreach workers—service officers in the local posts of the veterans' associations—are key elements in overcoming for pensions all three causes of nonparticipation in ordinary public relief: ignorance, intimidation, and pride. By their very existence and by the anxiety of service officers from each association to outdo service officers from other associations, they uncover eligible cases and make them aware of eligibility for benefits. Backed up by a network of department (state) service officers who in turn are supported by a professional staff at the national level, post service officers cope with the barriers between the bureaucrat and the needy veteran. Finally, armed with the theory of pensions as delayed compensation, the service officer can sell those rugged individualists who view public welfare as indefensible.

The more effectively service organizations perform the intercessor role, the more they provide a justification for their continued existence between periods of postwar fraternal affection. Were there not some role to play between wars, it is hard to imagine that interest and membership could be sustained. This is not a problem only for veterans' groups. Whatever the field of activity, an organization needs some purpose and some activity on a continuing basis. Persons who undertake to do the work necessary to sustain the organization discover or invent reasons to perpetuate it that may never have been contemplated by the founders. As an organization ages, the intent of the founders is more and more an irrelevant consideration, for the current membership makes its own decisions about purposes and goals. Nor is there any immorality in changing the original purposes and goals. Occasionally an association will find itself on the verge of suicide because its mission unexpectedly has been fulfilled or has ceased to be consequential for most of its supporters. The often cited case is that of the National Foundation for Infantile Paralysis. When a polio vaccine was finally discovered, the foundation's sponsors shifted gears and transformed themselves into the National Foundation–March of Dimes—and concentrated on arthritis and rheumatism.

For those close to it on a day-to-day basis, loyalty to and respect for a voluntary association as an association may be no less intense than is devotion to the cause to which the association is dedicated. The happiest of all arrangements is to keep a voluntary association alive beyond the normal days of its years by developing a supplementary mission that is closely and logically related to the original mission. Fighting arthritis and rheumatism once polio had been conquered struck many people as more logical than dissolving an association and scattering its contacts and records. Similarly, benefits for the aging veteran and his survivors can be considered a logical extension of the fraternal feeling that first gives rise to an American Legion or to a Veterans of Foreign Wars.

Charters granted to, and the original declarations of purpose by, associations of veterans invariably emphasize the fraternal and patriotic purposes of the organization. The charter of the Veterans of Foreign Wars, for example, provides:

That the purpose of this corporation shall be fraternal, patriotic, historical and educational; to preserve and strengthen comradeship among its members; to assist worthy comrades; to perpetuate the memory and history of our dead, and to assist their widows and orphans; to maintain true allegiance to the Government of the United States of America and fidelity to its Constitution and laws; to foster true patriotism; to maintain and extend the institutions of American Freedom, and to preserve and defend the United States from all her enemies, whomsoever.[3]

Common military experience furnishes an appealing basis for association in a culture where people are predisposed to join clubs. Since an especially high value is placed by most people on wartime service in defense of one's country, it is doubly appealing to preserve the high status accruing to war veterans by joining a veterans' organization. Immediately after a war, the ranks of such veterans' groups swell. It is not only that the universe of eligible members is larger. Returning servicemen, still more at ease in a military than a civilian environment and still full of the comradeship made necessary by shared dangers, make the veterans' groups a sort of halfway house between military and civilian life. But as civilian status becomes the normal way of life, shared military experience alone seems less reasonable a basis for association. Membership growth then tends to fall away until, when advanced age brings a renewed interest in the lively activities of one's youth, older veterans join together to relive the exploits of ancient service days which may have been the high points of many of their lives. Thus, if common service and patriotic spirit were the only bases for continued existence of veterans' associations, their membership could be expected to expand, contract, and again expand, cyclically, over a long period of years.

There is one philosophy of veterans' affairs based on the proposition that nothing should set the veteran apart from the rest of the population once he is provided opportunities through a G.I. bill to overcome the loss of time in civilian life. To adopt such a position, as has the American Veterans Committee for example, means that the group forswears concrete benefit or privilege based on service. The American Veterans Committee has a small membership and little power.

To the contrary, some service organizations take as their theme the proposition that wartime service in the armed forces forever sets the veteran apart from the general population. The American Legion, the Disabled American Veterans (membership 230,000), the American

3. Veterans of Foreign Wars of the United States, *Guide for Service Officers* (1967), p. 1.

Veterans of World War II (membership 200,000), and the Veterans of Foreign Wars would be less powerful organizations if they were to confine themselves exclusively to comradeship and patriotism as raisons d'être. These four most successful veterans' organizations, with combined membership of more than 4 million, hew to the "forever different" line. Not only does this provide a reason for perpetuating comradeship and fraternity, it also provides a justification for participation in the political world as well as the purely social world. If the veteran is separable from the general population, then the question of how government allocates its values and resources between groups takes on particular interest; compared to other categories of persons, how is the veteran category doing in acquiring governmental benefits and services? The purpose of association becomes reward as well as fraternity. The most successful veterans' associations are those that have started with the bond of fraternity and shared experience, that insist that a war veteran should never lose a special, preferred status in society, and that maintain a set of goals that if not readily achievable are not so unrealistic as to discourage practical men from supporting the cause.

The philosophy of the most successful association—the American Legion—with respect to veterans and veterans' benefits holds that whatever may go into programs of assistance for needy nonveterans, "we simply insist that war veterans are deserving of special consideration through a separate system."[4] Separation is not sought for its own sake, but as a means to achieve special advantages. The goal is not a system that is separate but equal; it is a system that is quite frankly separate and unequal. American Legion standards for segregating beneficiaries of government subsidies are uncomplicated: a fundamental distinction is made between nonveteran and wartime veteran and a second distinction is made between the service-disabled veteran and the non-service-connected case. Foreign service, a requirement for membership in the Veterans of Foreign Wars, is not an acceptable test in the Legion's approach to veterans' benefits: "If the [veteran] is unemployable and in financial need," its Rehabilitation Commission director has said, "that is what he ought to be compensated for, not on the basis of whether he happened to have served in a foreign country during World War II."[5]

Legion spokesmen argue that the organization's position on veterans'

---

4. John J. Corcoran, "Veterans' Affairs from the Point of View of the American Legion," a statement of the American Legion's philosophy with respect to veterans and veterans' benefits (n.d.; processed), p. 6.

5. *Pension Bills . . . for Veterans of All Wars*, Hearings, p. 3722.

affairs does not differ materially from that of the general public, which is said to believe that wartime military duty is a public and patriotic service of the highest order and that a citizen who has performed such service is deserving of special consideration. To support the argument that this is a widely held belief, the Legion points to the long history of special veterans' benefits, "an integral part of the prevailing public policy of the people of this land since early colonial times."[6] At the same time the Legion acknowledges that the principle of special consideration is perceived most generally during and close to a time of national emergency but less generally as time passes. The American Legion, therefore, has assumed responsibility for sharpening public attention to the supposedly accepted principle of special consideration for the veteran. If there were no Legion to intercede, the argument goes, American policy makers might forget the agreed-upon obligation to the war veteran. The Legion keeps reminding them in hopes that all public officials will accept Senator Vance Hartke's formulation: "In short, pension payments represent an award given in return for performing 90 days of military service during a period of war."[7]

Pension Politics

"Reminders" by the American Legion and by its sister veterans' associations have produced a veterans' relief system that respects the dignity of its beneficiaries, combines explicit legislative payment standards with opportunities for administrative discretion in application, provides for liberal disregard of income that might otherwise reduce pension benefits, and maintains an "in the family" appeals procedure disposed to favor the veteran. These arrangements have been developed by and work smoothly because of a smooth relationship between the veterans' groups, the Veterans Administration (VA), and the House Committee on Veterans Affairs, the three focal points in veterans' politics. In two confrontations these three have so overrun presidential resistance and Budget Bureau opposition to special privileges for veterans that a confrontation over pensions is unlikely.

6. Corcoran, "Veterans' Affairs from the Point of View of the American Legion," p. 1.
7. *Congressional Record*, daily ed., July 2, 1969, p. S7514.

Aside from helping to discourage adoption of a service pension unrelated to need, no postwar president has been able to control the drive for a separate pension system providing special advantage to veterans without regard to service-incurred disability. Neither President Truman nor President Eisenhower supported pension liberalizations accomplished during their administrations. President Kennedy never came to grips with the issue. President Johnson, described by a high-ranking official in the Johnson executive office as "rather liking veterans," in hopes of saving some money allowed an oblique test to be made of the strength of the veterans' lobby; he found it to be strong. Thereafter guided by the "if you can't beat them, join them" principle, Johnson created a commission to submit recommendations on veterans' benefits "to assure that our tax dollars are being utilized most wisely and that our Government is meeting fully its responsibility to all those to whom we owe so much."[8] To make these judgments, he allowed the veterans administrator to appoint five past national commanders of as many veterans' associations (not including the American Veterans Committee), four directors of state veterans' affairs departments, a retired army colonel, and as chairman of the commission the twenty-three year veteran chairman of the American Legion's National Rehabilitation Commission, Robert McCurdy. Not surprisingly, the McCurdy Commission found the basic principle of a separate veterans' benefit system to be sound, found some additional ways in which the government could meets its responsibility, and gave assurances that tax dollars used on veterans' programs are used wisely.

The surrender to the veterans' lobby formalized by appointment of the McCurdy Commission came after a period of conflict between federal budget makers and veterans' groups that started five years after the end of World War II. At that time, President Truman set himself down on the side of those who believed that no special benefits should be provided veterans without service-connected problems. Noting that "before many years, nearly all the population may be veterans or the dependents of veterans," Truman's 1951 budget message proposed a policy of "clear recognition that many of the needs of our veterans and their dependents can be met best through the general programs serving the whole population . . . we should provide only for those special and

8. U.S. Veterans Advisory Commission, *Report of the U.S. Veterans Advisory Commission on the Veterans Benefits System,* transmitted March 18, 1968, p. ix.

unique needs which arise directly from military service."[9] Non-service-connected needs should be met through "general programs" of the government, presumably social security and public assistance.

That same year, Truman vetoed a so-called aid and attendance pension bill that had passed without opposition in either house. The measure established a $120 monthly pension rate for non-service-connected cases in which disability is so severe as to require the regular aid and attendance of another person. Approximately 24,000 eligible cases were expected to file under the aid and attendance provision, cases deemed by both House and Senate committees to be the most meritorious of the non-service-connected disability class. But if Congress was willing to separate out more meritorious non-service-connected cases from less meritorious cases, the President was not. Whereas Congress spoke only of the first-year cost ($16 million), Truman spoke only of the fifty-year cost. Moreover, he remained doubtful about separating income problems of any or all non-service-connected cases from income problems of nonveterans in general. The veto message claimed the bill "would aggravate an already existing disparity" in the treatment of pension cases of needy nonveterans and needy veterans with non-service-connected disabilities.[10] Disparity or not, the special aid and attendance cases appealed enough to both houses of Congress to result in the veto easily being overcome.

A year later, Truman had not changed his mind about non-service-connected pensions, but he shied away from another veto of a pension bill. It is doubtful that a veto could have been sustained since there was widespread agreement that both the modest cost of living and income limitation increases voted were overdue: pension payments were raised 5 percent in the basic rate, the first change since 1946; income limits, now raised by $400 for single veterans and by $200 for married veterans, had been unchanged since 1933. Truman was not disposed to quarrel with the argument that if there was to be a program, it should not unrealistically be tied to hopelessly outdated standards. He did not claim that a $3 monthly increase in the pension of a needy, disabled veteran was excessive. But he did again question the validity of the program, arguing that the non-service-connected gratuity should be tied to those paid other needy Americans. Simultaneous eligibility for social security and for a veteran's pension, the President said in a special message to

9. *Public Papers of the Presidents of the United States, 1951*, p. 99.
10. *Ibid.*, p. 444.

Congress, "is confusing, wasteful, and, to many people, hard to understand."[11]

The political situation was neither confusing nor hard to understand. It was then May 1952, with a national election to be held in November. The probability of General Eisenhower's nomination by the Republicans was strong; it would be a selection likely to appeal to many veterans. Already running scared, many congressional Democrats would have had no concern about bucking Truman who, two months earlier, had announced that he would not be a candidate for a new term. Truman could not block the 1952 increases, and it is not even clear that he felt they should be blocked. He could view them with concern as stumbling blocks to a rational integrated income maintenance system, as "bad legislation from the point of view of our long-run objectives." Faced with these conflicting pressures, the President chose a reasonable solution, that of approval "with great reluctance" emphasized by the special message.

More significant for the future development of the non-service-connected pension program than Truman's "great reluctance" was his suggestion to Congress "to authorize at this session a complete study of our veterans benefit programs and their relationships with our social insurance and other general welfare programs."[12] The idea of a study was much admired in the Bureau of the Budget and by some officials in the Veterans Administration. Their goal was to formulate an orderly plan that would be insurance against the possible consequences of a Budget Bureau nightmare that envisioned a demagogic chairman of the House Veterans Affairs Committee, a passive chairman of the Senate Finance Committee, and a timing situation comparable to that of May 1952, when a retiring president would be no match for a continuing veterans' lobby. It was not an impossibly unrealistic combination of circumstances. John Rankin of Mississippi had once been such a demagogic House committee chairman; Senate Finance had its hands full with internal revenue taxation and social security matters. Some defense against the veterans was a wise precaution.

Congress did not respond to Truman's proposal in 1952, but before the end of 1954 President Eisenhower saw the need for this kind of insurance. Despite opposition from both the Bureau of the Budget and the Veterans Administration, Congress—now Republican controlled—

11. *Public Papers of the Presidents of the United States, 1952–53*, p. 366.
12. *Ibid.*

enacted another 5 percent increase in pensions in the summer of 1954, just three months before the mid-term elections. When President Eisenhower signed the increase, he did so "grudgingly" according to a Legion spokesman, "reluctantly" according to his own statement. Echoing the Truman approach of 1952, Eisenhower, America's war hero turned statesman, indicated that social security and other federal welfare programs had probably made the veterans' pension program obsolete. And, like Truman, he asserted the desirability of a study committee.

Confrontation: The Bradley Commission

In January 1955, by executive order, Eisenhower created a President's Commission on Veterans' Pensions. Two months later the President wrote its chairman, General Omar N. Bradley, that it was incumbent on the commission systematically to assess the structure, scope, philosophy, and administration of veterans' benefits, "together with the relationships between these benefits and others which are provided our citizens without regard to their status as veterans. The objective of this effort should be to bring up to date and correlate these benefits and services so that veterans and their survivors will receive equitable treatment consistent with the orderly development of public policy in this important area."[13] This was a charge that almost seemed to preclude holding the line on veterans' pensions. The only ways to correlate veterans' benefits with those available to other citizens were either to bring benefits in nonveterans' programs up to the level of those available to veterans or to bring veterans' benefits down to the level of those available to nonveterans. Since the Bradley Commission had no authority to recommend changes in programs for nonveterans, it seemed free only to propose cutting away at veterans' benefits. Moreover, Bradley's prestige could provide congressmen with a justification for putting an end to special privilege except for service-connected cases.

But the White House fumbled its congressional relations by not clearing its plans with the appropriate committee chairman. A presidential commission with a charge that overlaps the jurisdiction of a congressional committee is a threat to the committee—the more prestigious the commission, the greater the threat. Olin Teague (Democrat

13. Letter from President Dwight Eisenhower to General Omar N. Bradley, March 5, 1955, in *Veterans' Benefits in the United States*, p. 25.

of Texas) became chairman of the House Veterans Affairs Committee the same month that the Bradley Commission was created, and Teague moved aggressively to prevent the locus of power over veterans' benefits policy from being located outside the House committee. Teague's antipathy to the commission idea was first reflected in a suggestion to the White House that the whole thing be reconsidered. Told that it was too late, Teague went before the House Rules Committee to ask that points of order not be waived in the consideration of VA appropriations for fiscal 1956 in order that he could make a point of order against legislation—that is, sanctioning the existence of the commission—on an appropriation bill. This was a serious enough possibility and a sophisticated enough use of the House rules to command attention. A meeting between Teague and Bradley was thereupon arranged at which Teague recalls telling Bradley that he "questioned whether or not a commission stacked with generals could take the proper perspective so far as veterans' benefits were concerned."[14] With his objections and concerns voiced at both the White House and the Capitol, and his determination to have a key role in benefits policy clearly established, the new chairman of the Veterans Affairs Committee then "reluctantly" agreed not to object further to the commission's existence. It was the last time a major piece of veterans' affairs policy was developed without consulting Teague.

It is easy enough to understand how the problem arose. Things were now different than they were when Truman had first suggested a special study. Teague felt that the history of his work on the Veterans Affairs Committee had been of a character to merit confidence from any fair student of veterans' pension legislation. He had opposed the chairman and ranking members in 1949 when they supported a "pension grab" and was on record in favor of a restrained pension program that included disability and unemployability as key features. At the same time, by virtue of his own distinguished military history as the most decorated veteran in Congress, Teague had a particular interest in and awareness of the special problems of the veteran. When the 1954 election results brought him to the chairmanship of the House committee, Teague could and did feel, reasonably enough, that he was the right man for the right job. But before he could do the job of setting the pension

14. *Findings and Recommendations of the President's Commission on Veterans' Pensions* (Bradley Commission), Hearings before the House Committee on Veterans' Affairs, 84 Cong. 2 sess. (1956), p. 3633.

program on a defensible path, an administration enamored of non-governmental, prestigious study groups had made its plans to take the ball out of Teague's hands. Ironically, this study group was first planned as a defense against the openhanded attitude of the previous Republican chairman, Mrs. Edith Nourse Rogers of Massachusetts.

To the leaders of the American Legion the Bradley Commission on one side and Teague on the other looked like a planned pincers movement, with entrapment of the veterans' pension program as the result. One classic response to a pincers is to sweep through the jaws before they close and pummel the enemy from his rear. A Legion bill, offered in January 1956, was such a response. The bill, which Teague neither sponsored nor supported, would have established a presumption of disability at age sixty-five and increased the basic pension payment to $90 a month (from $66) with a jump to $105 after ten years or at age sixty-five. To keep the pincers from closing, it was critical that the bill be acted upon before the Bradley Commission jaw of the trap could be strengthened by support from civic groups, chambers of commerce, newspapers, and others likely to be swayed by a multivolume collection of staff studies underpinning several hundred pages of rational conclusions subscribed to by seven eminent American leaders.

The Legion bill was in the Veterans Affairs Committee at the time that the Bradley Commission report itself was released in April 1956. The "national philosophy" suggested by the Bradley group to guide national policy was a philosophy that identified the non-service-disabled veteran as an ordinary citizen whose service as such should not entitle him to any special benefits. Not only would acceptance of the philosophy and recommendations of the report have destroyed the pending Legion-sponsored bill—a point that Teague took care to pin down specifically in subsequent hearings—but acceptance would have put the entire non-service-connected pension program in eventual jeopardy. The veterans' organizations, it will be remembered, argue that while military service may be an obligation of all citizens, in fact only certain citizens are called upon to discharge that obligation; veterans' benefits, therefore, are special and should be added to those benefits the veteran may obtain as a civilian alone.

Out of courtesy to Bradley—"I had about as much respect for him as for any man who lives," Teague says of Bradley[15]—and in hopes that

15. *Ibid.*

the report would help maximize rationality in policy making, Teague decided to schedule hearings on the report before letting the Legion pension bill come to a vote in committee. Fearful that the Bradley jaw would spring closed while the Legion spent itself fencing with the Teague jaw, National Commander J. Addington Wagner pulled all stops. In a press release he characterized the call for hearings on the report as unwise, unnecessary, and illogical. Calling on Legion posts all over the country "to flood" the committee with protests, Wagner told them that the Bradley report was being used as an "excuse" by the committee to postpone action and that the "stalling tactic threatens our entire effort."[16] Telephoning Teague, Wagner told him that Legion people all over the country were persuaded that Teague was the cause of delay on the bill. It was not the ideal strategy for wooing a forty-six-year-old new committee chairman from a safe district who could be in a position of power for two or three decades. Teague was annoyed, the more so because there had been committee sentiment against the Legion bill from the beginning.

The pressure campaign was a strategic mistake that seemed to polarize Teague and the Legion at a time when the veterans' groups needed Teague's help in countering the Bradley Commission. Some Legion leaders quickly regretted the confrontation with Teague. At best, the bill would come through the House to an uncertain Senate fate and, if it survived the Senate, to a reasonably certain Eisenhower veto. At worst, the House committee would coalesce behind its new chairman and that heretofore friendly group would be lost. Accordingly, Commander Wagner did not appear at the hearings. Instead, one of the Legion's past national commanders appeared to make peace with Teague and the committee and to declare war on the Bradley report:

The American Legion is of the opinion that the Bradley Commission's report is a "scare" document which is unfair, unworthy of the Commission that produced it, and in many material respects factually unsound. It should be promptly relegated to the obscurity which it deserves. Meanwhile this House Veterans Committee can continue with the important and progressive work which it understands so much better than the Bradley Commission and report out the pension and compensation legislation which it has been considering.[17]

Teague did allow a somewhat watered-down version of the Legion bill

16. *Ibid.*, p. 3634.
17. *Ibid.*, p. 3639.

to come to the House floor where it passed overwhelmingly. But whatever satisfaction the Legion took in seeing the chairman of the House Veterans Affairs Committee outvoted was overcome by frustration as Senator Harry Byrd, chairman of the Senate Finance Committee, insisted that his Finance Committee could not move on the bill at all because various administrative agencies had not responded to requests for information indispensable to the committee. With Congress anxious to adjourn for the national campaign, Byrd had no trouble adjusting the Finance Committee schedule so that the indispensable information did not come to the top of the pile before the end of the life of the Congress. The message for the Legion was clear. While Teague might be willing to let a bill he opposed come to a vote in his committee and while there was still enough political magic in a veterans' pension bill to insure lopsided House passage once it came out of committee, the Teague philosophy was admired in high places on the Senate side where a Finance Committee with multiple concerns could easily elevate or depress veterans' pensions on its list of priorities.

Arrangements between House Veterans Affairs and Senate Finance soon settled into an agreed pattern. All consequential veterans' benefits legislation would first be acted on in the House. Then the Finance Committee would move bills that Teague endorsed and drop the bills he opposed. "Mr. Teague is conservative and Senator Byrd was conservative," explained a principal Veterans Affairs Committee staff member who participated in the communications linkage between the two legislators. "The Senator depended on Mr. Teague to let him know which veterans bills he felt should be pushed, and to let him know which veterans bills should die. Through the years, we haven't lost many good ones in the Senate and they have not passed many bad ones that got through here."

Nor was there much change when Russell Long succeeded to the chairmanship of the Finance Committee. Although not the Byrd type of nonspender, Long was not particularly interested in veterans' legislation. The extensive jurisdictional range of Finance makes veterans' benefits a minor matter, and the chairman or any member who concerns himself with veterans steals attention from taxation and from social security. Even if a Finance Committee member were willing to steal such attention, control of the Labor and Public Welfare Committee over other segments of veterans' legislation would limit the return on the investment. Veterans' organizations found the problem of access in the Senate to be frustrating and became major proponents of a standing Senate committee on veterans' affairs. When they seemed on the verge of success in 1969, Long undercut the effort by creating a standing subcommittee on veterans' affairs, the first and only subcommittee of the Finance Committee since the Legislative Reorganization Act of 1946. The Reorganization Act of 1970 finally did create a standing Senate committee. But the locus of congressional power over veterans' benefits remains in Teague's House committee.

In the three-way power fight between the administration budget watchers, Teague, and the veterans' associations touched off by the Bradley report, Teague was the big winner. Having publicized the threat presumably posed by the Bradley report, the veterans' lobby insisted on credit for defense and preservation of the separate pension system. While the Legion and the VFW could claim that they held off the budget cutters, they could not claim that they were able to get their own program enacted. Teague won on all counts, however. He had opposed creation of the Bradley Commission; its program was not adopted. He had opposed the Legion pension bill, but did not autocratically deny it a hearing in committee or decline to bring it to the floor. Yet his influence clearly helped bottle it up in the Senate Finance Committee. Neither the budget watchers nor the veterans' associations could have things their way. Teague had wanted time to work out a restrained, separate program, and now he had it.

The budget watchers lost in this confrontation both because they had not enlisted Teague and because, in the last analysis, the Bradley Commission shied away from policy recommendations that were logical conclusions to its statement of philosophy. It declined to propose abandonment of the pension program and consequent dumping of qualified beneficiaries on the states' public assistance rolls. The commission's principal staff member acknowledged the contradiction without identifying it as such:

The Commission said that it could not see, after readjustment, how there was any real difference between a veteran and a nonveteran. In back of that lay thousands of pages of research about the conditions of military service and the amount of assistance that we today, particularly through the readjustment benefits bills, give veterans. Now, after all that is said and done, it did recommend continuation of a pension program for veterans.[18]

What the commission did was to fix some imprecise guidelines for

18. *Ibid.*, p. 3842.

policy makers to follow at some imprecise later time when social security coverage and benefits were both universal and adequate and when the residual public assistance load had accordingly fallen to the point where it was administered in a spirit of generosity and dignity. These happy circumstances were envisioned as within sight, so that "within the not too distant future, a separate veterans' pension program should no longer be necessary." The march of social insurance would in the normal course of events bring nearly everyone to the minimum subsistence level and, at that point, distinctions between nonveterans and non-service-connected cases could be thrown out in good conscience. Until then, however, supplements to inadequate social security payments and pensions without the stigma associated with public assistance should be available to veterans.

If the Bradley Commission's opponents could have known how wrong the commission was in its expectations as to the future course of public assistance, the opponents might have reacted more tranquilly to the commission's proposal. Any pensioner who volunteered to trade in his pension for public assistance the moment that the public assistance atmosphere took on the character predicted by the staff report to the commission would still be in no danger whatever of having to make the trade. Predicting a more ample standard of provision for the needs of beneficiaries, a change in the climate within which public assistance would be forthcoming, an end to the traditional attitudes of contempt for and the age-old stigma attached to public aid, a more understanding approach, and a time when public assistance would be considered no less "honorable" than veterans' pensions, a staff report (and the commission's conclusions based on it) missed the target.[19]

Had the Bradley Commission asserted in 1956 that a separate veterans' relief program was not tenable, that it should be abandoned as creating a most favored class of relief beneficiaries whose status could not be justified within the national philosophy espoused by the commission, the fight over acceptance of such a recommendation might have been a recurring one. Since the commission conditioned its action program in this area to a future state of affairs that never came about, however, the Bradley Commission proposals in respect to non-service-connected pensions have been irrelevant to the realities of policy.

19. *Veterans' Non-Service Connected Pensions*, Staff Report Number X of the President's Commission on Veterans' Pensions, printed for the use of the House Committee on Veterans' Affairs, 84 Cong. 2 sess. (1956), pp. 245 ff.

Renewed Confrontation:
Budget Bureau versus Veterans' Associations

It is more important to veterans' groups to maintain a separate benefit system than it is that that system be better than or even equal to
any welfare or health benefits or social services available to the nonveteran population. A separate benefit program suggests a clear connection between organizational strength and benefit improvement. Without a separate system the organized veterans' associations would become
just another group of active lobbyists, sharing attention with the AFL-
CIO, the United States Chamber of Commerce, the American Medical
Association, and the other critical interest groups in the welfare field.
Moreover, effort expended on behalf of social welfare programs available to the general population would be effort on behalf of great numbers of people who, as nonveterans, could not be expected to strengthen
the veterans' organizations to which they could not belong. Ultimately,
veterans themselves could reasonably come to doubt the value of the
American Legion and comparable groups as lobbyists. Nothing, therefore, is more threatening to the organized veterans than an apparent
challenge to the separate system. Such a challenge was clearly posed by
the Bureau of the Budget in 1955 through the Bradley Commission.
The challenge was renewed by the bureau in a different form in 1965.
Veterans' associations properly consider the latter confrontation an
important benchmark in their winning battle against budget rationalists.

When, on January 13, 1965, the Veterans Administration announced
a plan to save $23.5 million by closing thirty-two veterans' facilities—
eleven hospitals, four domiciliaries, and seventeen regional offices[20]—
the veterans' lobby reacted promptly, negatively, noisily, and effectively.
Although the VA announcement marked the first time since 1933 that
an administration had attempted a cutback in veterans' services, it
seemed to be a propitious moment for such a cutback. Public health
programs, social security, and social welfare in general had come a long

20. Details of the VA plan are set out in a letter from William Driver to Ralph
Yarborough, Jan. 13, 1965; reprinted in *Proposed Closing of Veterans' Hospitals*,
Hearings before the Subcommittee on Veterans' Affairs of the Senate Committee on
Labor and Public Welfare, 89 Cong. 1 sess. (1965), pp. 2–3. The discussion of the
closings controversy in the next several pages has been helped by a paper by Eric E.
Miller of Ohio University, "The 1965 Veterans Hospital Closing Controversy and Its
Relationship to the Future of National Veterans Programs" (1967).

way since 1933. Moreover, at the time the 1965 cutback was first announced, the Korean War had been over for twelve years, and the massive escalation in Vietnam had not begun. The veteran did not weigh heavily on the conscience of the country. Had a decision been made at the highest levels that the time had come to mount a major effort to fold veterans' programs more closely into general welfare programs?

Just after his election the previous November, President Johnson had tempted an already willing Bureau of the Budget to move in that direction. It was no secret that the irrationality of a separate veterans' program had been deplored in bureau circles even before the Bradley inquiry when Budget's Michael March, who served as commission technical director, became the specialist on the subject. After Johnson stated that "as a nation we cannot afford to waste a single dollar of our resources on outmoded programs," and had urged all administrators to "take a cold, hard look at your existing programs,"[21] the bureau found it natural to narrow in on some veterans' programs. Within the bureau it appeared that equity and economy merged in this case, but there was surely a larger dose of equity than of economy since only a little over $20 million could be saved by closing infrequently used veterans' facilities. In turn, Donald Johnson, Legion national commander, wrote his constituents accurately enough that "the axe raised by the VA on January 13 was made and sharpened in the U.S. Bureau of the Budget."[22] Phillip (Sam) Hughes, a career deputy director of the Budget Bureau, later formally confirmed the bureau role. Before a meeting of the Legion's National Rehabilitation Conference, Hughes acknowledged that "the Bureau of the Budget did press the Veterans Administration to close hospitals,"[23] and subsequently justified the closings as "necessary adjustments to meet the changing needs of our veterans." He also claimed, however, that it was "the Administration's intent to strengthen, not reduce, services to our veterans," and that "this is a question of how the government best gets its money's worth."[24]

21. "The Great Society," statement of the President at the Cabinet Meeting, Nov. 19, 1964, transmitted with "Memorandum for Agency Heads" by Kermit Gordon, director of the Bureau of the Budget, Nov. 23, 1964; reprinted in *Closing of Veterans' Administration Hospitals, Domiciliaries, and Regional Offices*, Hearings before the Subcommittee on Hospitals of the House Committee on Veterans' Affairs, 89 Cong. 1 sess. (1965), Vol. 1, pp. 667–68.

22. "The Slash in Veterans' Services," *American Legion*, Vol. 78 (March 1965), p. 2.

23. American Legion, *Proceedings, National Rehabilitation Conference* (1965), p. 200.

24. *Closing of Veterans' Administration Hospitals*, Hearings, pp. 629, 634.

The President, dubious at first about the politics of a clash with veterans, had not been easily persuaded. Before agreeing, Johnson insisted on an unpublicized independent review and appraisal by a White House aide in whom he had confidence, Ramsey Clark, later his attorney general. Clark spent several weeks learning the subject before recommending in favor of the Budget Bureau proposal on its merits. Among veterans' groups and congressional participants it is widely believed that the VA leadership warned the White House about the likely political reaction to closings, and because he was right, newly appointed Veterans Administrator William Driver gained an influence that he retained throughout the Johnson years. In turn, Driver used his influence to preserve the independent status of veterans' programs; like most dedicated administrators, he was not willing to be coordinated to the point of potential absorption, whether by social security, public assistance, or any other social welfare program of general availability.

Congressional reaction to the VA announcement was wild. No member, of course, can be calm when a federal installation in his district is eliminated. It is enough of a sign of limited influence to be unsuccessful in competition for initially locating an installation. But to what avail is it to send a man to Congress who cannot even retain a previously acquired facility? Nor was the situation helped by the administration's failure widely to consult with or to notify affected legislators long enough in advance so that any necessary cover stories could be invented. Instead, to use Senator Mike Mansfield's description, it was "notification by avalanche."[25] In tampering this way with veterans' facilities, the Budget Bureau hit too many congressmen, too suddenly, too close to home. Members from districts involved were predictably outraged; some other members whose districts were not affected by the pending plan believed there would be more plans that would affect them; still others found it expedient to build up credits with veterans and their families. There were few defenders of any of the closings; none of closing the medical facilities. If there was to be a renewed fight with the budget rationalists, the veterans' groups could not have been more pleased with the issue chosen.

Swinging into action, one group outdid another in trying to establish a basis for claiming later that it had led the holy war against those who sought to make the veteran an ordinary citizen and veterans' benefit programs the same as those for similarly situated ordinary citizens. The

25. *Proposed Closing of Veterans' Hospitals*, Hearings, p. 7.

American Legion policy statement on the announcement solemnly termed it "the fifth major crisis in the history of modern war veterans benefit programs," and foresaw far wider actions to come: "All of the Budget Bureau actions point to a future when the status of the war veteran and his dependents will be downgraded."[26] Legion Commander Johnson claimed "the real target of the January 13 order is not the facilities marked for closing. It is the special status and recognition historically accorded America's veterans."[27] He called for a "total mobilization of the efforts and resources of the American Legion to prevent this disastrous proposal from becoming a reality."[28] VFW National Commander John A. Jenkins saw the closings as "the most recent and vicious and wholly unwarranted attack on veterans in the never-ending effort of the social planners and Budget Bureau dreamers to dismember the Veterans Administration and eliminate all veterans benefits."[29] AMVETS Executive Director Don Spagnolo joined Johnson and Jenkins stating, "We are particularly concerned to see veterans programs in any aspect equated with social, welfare, or charity programs administered by any other agency than the Veterans Administration."[30]

Opportunities for a display of congressional rhetoric were probably irresistible once the bandwagon began rolling, but few members seemed disposed to try to resist. Mike Mansfield, the Senate majority leader whose Miles City, Montana, hospital was marked for closing, called the plan "milked economy," "the economy of reduced service," and "an outrage"—strong language for Mansfield—and termed the administration "heartless."[31] Ralph Yarborough, Democrat of Texas, protested that "the Bureau of the Budget is thwarting the wills, aims, and hopes of the American people."[32] To many, including some legislators who had been indifferent to poverty programs in general, the closings now seemed inconsistent with the war on poverty. Senator Richard Russell, Georgia Democrat, was in this group. "In my opinion," said Russell,

---

26. "American Legion Statement of Policy on Announcement of Closing of 31 Veterans Administration Facilities" (March 1, 1965; processed), p. 2.

27. "What's Behind the VA Closings," *American Legion*, Vol. 78 (April 1965), p. 2.

28. "Statement by Donald E. Johnson," *American Legion Rehabilitation Bulletin*, No. 1-65 (20-1), (Jan. 14, 1965).

29. *Congressional Record*, Vol. 111, Pt. 2, 89 Cong. 1 sess. (1965), p. 1815.

30. *Proposed Closing of Veterans' Hospitals*, Hearings, p. 576.

31. *Ibid.*, pp. 8, 35.

32. *Congressional Record*, Vol. 111, Pt. 1, 89 Cong. 1 sess. (1965), p. 782.

"these closures . . . will only add to the complexity of the problems which confront us . . . in dealing with distress, with poverty, and with those unable to help themselves."[33] From the Republican side, it was asked, "Is there to be nothing in the Great Society for veterans?"[34] And Senator Jacob Javits of New York turned alliterative to describe the plan as a "pennywise, pound-foolish, pennypinching policy."[35] All in all, even for congressmen who often find it necessary to attack policy makers with a vehemence they do not really feel at all, it was an impressive performance that could not be ignored by the administration.

When rhetoric gave way to legislative action, it was plain that there was real trouble. The Senate delayed action on Driver's pending nomination as veterans administrator. Less than one month after the first announcement, Congress adopted a rider to the farm money bill prohibiting the VA from using any funds to effectuate the closings before May 1, 1965. In the meantime, hearings before the subcommittee on veterans' affairs of the Senate Labor and Public Welfare Committee (which had jurisdiction over veterans' hospitals) and before the subcommittee on hospitals of the House Veterans Affairs Committee provided a continuing forum. Members of Congress waited in line to enter testimony protesting the closings, to voice concern for the convenience of the veteran, and to support his right to services. Senator George Aiken, Republican of Vermont, announced that, "a veteran . . . wants his services to be provided as near as possible, especially when matters pertaining to his happiness, his welfare, and even his life are involved, and he has earned these rights to which he is fully entitled."[36] Senator Milton Young, North Dakota Republican, found veterans the "most needy, most deserving people in the country."[37]

The Veterans Administration loyally argued that physical obsolescence, decreased patient load, staffing difficulties, geographical remoteness, and shifting veterans' population necessitated the closings. For the most part, legislators felt too badly stung to be interested in the nonpolitical merits of the case, but some members had acquired figures and reports from home and from the Legion and the VFW with which to contradict the justifications offered by the Veterans Administration. In

33. *Ibid.*, p. 779.
34. *Ibid.*, p. 966. The same question came from a Democrat; *ibid.*, p. 780.
35. *Ibid.*, p. 1768.
36. *Proposed Closing of Veterans' Hospitals*, Hearings, p. 54.
37. *Ibid.*, p. 59.

the case of Mike Mansfield's Miles City Hospital, a comptroller general's report was produced that stated: "Generally the statements printed by the Veterans Administration as the justifications or considerations for closing the VA hospital at Miles City are either untrue or only partially true."[38] Robert Kennedy concluded that in the case of the three New York hospitals marked for closing, the announced reasons—obsolete buildings, staffing difficulty, and ease of caring for patients at other hospitals—"were factually disproved. They just did not stand up. . . ."[39]

President Johnson stayed out of the controversy while congressmen and veterans' lobbyists carefully avoided involving him as a partisan in order that he could act to end it without loss of prestige. Once asked about the possibility of reassessment, Johnson said, "That decision has been made by the Veterans Administrator. That is a matter for him."[40] By April 3 it was no longer a case for the veterans administrator, it was time to stop the fighting and proceed onward with the Great Society. The President announced that "there is considerable evidence to believe that a further examination and study are necessary before a final decision is implemented. . . . It may be that some of these hospitals are not, in fact, outmoded, and that they can continue to serve veterans as effectively as our standards require."[41] What Johnson did not announce was that a substantial segment of the Congress, the veterans' associations, and the Senate majority leader had all made it clear that Johnson's initial doubts about the wisdom of battling the Legion and the VFW were well taken. His insistence on a careful review apparently had not extended to an assessment of the current strength of the veterans' lobby or to a matching of the particular facilities affected with the particular congressmen involved. The closings, which in January had been an honest effort at economy, by April 3 had become a danger to a workable rapport with Congress.

Concessions were made through the face-saving mechanism of what the President termed a committee of distinguished Americans. Formation of a study committee chaired by Circuit Judge Barrett Prettyman, and a presidential promise that "as soon as the Committee reports, I

38. *Closing of Veterans' Administration Hospitals*, Hearings, Vol. 2, p. 1768.
39. Letter to the Editor, *Washington Post*, Feb. 28, 1965.
40. *Proposed Closing of Veterans' Hospitals*, Hearings, p. 32.
41. "Statement by the President," April 3, 1965; reprinted in *Closing of Veterans' Administration Hospitals*, Hearings, Vol. 2, p. 2225.

will promptly act on its recommendations,"[42] meant that the fight was over. With four legislative members on the committee (Olin Teague, Ross Adair, Russell Long, and Milton Young) the congressional point of view was not lost. The climax came on June 8, 1965, when, acting on the committee's report, the President sent a "Dear Bill" letter to Driver, who had loyally taken the heat for a policy he had warned would generate heat. The letter directed the Veterans Administration to continue the operation of five of the hospitals, two of the domiciliaries, and eight of the regional offices.[43]

Veterans' associations won an important tangible victory as well as a symbolic victory with overtones beyond the immediate objectives. Starting with nothing, the protesters salvaged fifteen of thirty-two facilities. Admitting the loss of half the stakes, the VFW called it a great "moral victory," accurately noting that "the ground work has been laid so that in the future it seems unlikely that a precipitous action of the magnitude of the original closing order will occur again."[44] The Veterans Administration emerged as a second big winner. Willing to close facilities if it was directed to do so, the agency had also privately warned against the proposal. The intensity of the protest reaction made it obvious that the VA had been correct with its warning; but when it was all over, the VA was still able to close seventeen facilities. Administrator Driver came out with the admiration of the President, of the director of the Bureau of the Budget, and of the leaders of the veterans' lobby. The final winner was the House Veterans Affairs Committee where it is believed—with satisfaction—that the outcome obliges any President to consult that committee's leadership before proposing any policy changes in the veterans' area.

In January 1967 President Johnson himself answered any questions about the independent status of the veterans' programs when, in the first special message on veterans' affairs ever presented by a president to the Congress, Johnson proposed a legislative program "for additional steps to fulfill our obligations to those who have borne the cost of conflict in the cause of liberty."[45] Simultaneously establishing the McCurdy

---

42. *Ibid.*, p. 2226.

43. *Congressional Quarterly Almanac*, 1965, p. 398.

44. *VFW Legislative Newsletter*, Vol. 19 (June 1965), p. 1.

45. *America's Servicemen and Veterans*, Message from the President of the United States Relating to America's Servicemen and Veterans, H. Doc. 48, 90 Cong. 1 sess. (1967).

Commission, composed exclusively of spokesmen for special benefits for veterans, President Johnson thus marked the end of any attempts in his administration to integrate veterans' programs with nonveterans' social and public welfare programs. The next president gave an earlier signal. After William Driver found it too great a strain to wait for the Nixon administration to decide about his future, he resigned, and in the summer of 1969 President Nixon appointed as veterans administrator, Donald Johnson, the former Legion national commander who had worked so hard and had been so outspoken on behalf of preserving "the special status and recognition historically accorded America's veterans."

The veteran retains that historically accorded special status and it is unlikely, at least in the near future, that this status will again be challenged. Vietnam may explain short range interest in the veteran. In the long run, the lessons of the Bradley Commission and of the closings controversy are likely to slow any move to end a special program.

Pension Policy

The eventual legislative outcome of the Bradley Commission work on non-service-connected pensions was an agreed bill adopted in 1959. That bill, with incremental improvements made after the closings controversy confirmed the likelihood of separate veterans' benefit programs, became the basic legislation controlling present pension policy.

Political realism based on reactions to the Bradley report defined the area of common ground reluctantly shared by the veterans' organizations, the executive branch, and Representative Teague. All major participants in veterans' pension policy making having tried each other out, each of them now knew that no one position could be imposed on the others. Both the Legion and the VFW abandoned the idea of a general service pension. The Budget Bureau, in view of the Bradley recommendation that a separate pension program be continued, could not sustain a drive for integration of pensions with social insurance. Teague could continue to support orderly, restrained development of a separate system. The understanding, therefore, was that a separate pension program would be retained for the indefinite future; the program would concentrate on the needy veteran and his survivors; the idea of a general service pension unrelated to need would be laid to rest; growth of social security and its relationship to the pension program would get continuing attention; public assistance, however, did not have the social respectability long accorded pensions as an honorable means of substitute income and would not be considered an acceptable substitute for pensions. To accomplish all this, the 1959 agreed bill established three levels of pension payment related to income, allowed a claimant to exclude from income the total amount involved in recouping his own contribution to a public or private retirement plan, and "equalized" the widows and orphans of World War II and Korean War veterans with their World War I counterparts by permitting the former to draw survivors' pensions.

Need has become the sole practical test of pension eligibility for a veteran at age sixty-five, when disability is presumed. But a crucial question is how need is established either for the pension payable to a veteran himself or for the death pension that may be payable to his widow and children. Income limits in dollar amounts are the most obvious test. Such limits are fixed by statute, have been increased from time to time, and have recently been refined to provide finer gradations of pension payments for various income ranges (Tables 10, 11, and 12). For

Table 10. Single Veterans' and Widows' Monthly Pension Benefits, According to Annual Income, 1971

Annual income, in dollars	Monthly pension, in dollars	
	Single veteran	Widow alone
0–300	121	81
300–400	119	80
400–500	117	79
500–600	115	78
600–700	112	76
700–800	108	73
800–900	104	70
900–1,000	100	67
1,000–1,100	96	64
1,100–1,200	92	61
1,200–1,300	88	58
1,300–1,400	84	55
1,400–1,500	79	51
1,500–1,600	75	48
1,600–1,700	69	45
1,700–1,800	63	41
1,800–1,900	57	37
1,900–2,000	51	33
2,000–2,100	45	29
2,100–2,200	37	23
2,200–2,300	29	17

Source: Public Law 91-588.

Table 11. Monthly Pension Benefits of Veterans with Dependents, According to Annual Income, 1971

Annual income, in dollars	Monthly pension, in dollars, of veteran		
	With one dependent	With two dependents	With three or more dependents
0–500	132	137	142
500–600	130	135	140
600–700	128	133	138
700–800	126	131	136
800–900	124	129	134
900–1,000	122	127	132
1,000–1,100	119	119	119
1,100–1,200	116	116	116
1,200–1,300	113	113	113
1,300–1,400	110	110	110
1,400–1,500	107	107	107
1,500–1,600	104	104	104
1,600–1,700	101	101	101
1,700–1,800	99	99	99
1,800–1,900	96	96	96
1,900–2,000	93	93	93
2,000–2,100	90	90	90
2,100–2,200	87	87	87
2,200–2,300	84	84	84
2,300–2,400	81	81	81
2,400–2,500	78	78	78
2,500–2,600	75	75	75
2,600–2,700	72	72	72
2,700–2,800	69	69	69
2,800–2,900	66	66	66
2,900–3,000	62	62	62
3,000–3,100	58	58	58
3,100–3,200	54	54	54
3,200–3,300	50	50	50
3,300–3,400	42	42	42
3,400–3,500	34	34	34

Source: Public Law 91-588.

the professional in the pension business the issues over which to stand and fight are the application procedure, definitions of disability and income, exclusions from income, the range of discretion permitted the VA by a net worth test, and the maintenance of a system of appeals that keeps everything about veterans' affairs, including pensions, entirely within the control of friendly administrative agencies.

Table 12. Monthly Pension Benefits of Veterans' Widows and Children, According to Annual Income, 1971

Annual income, in dollars	Monthly pension, in dollars, of widow and child[a]
0–600	99
600–700	98
700–800	97
800–900	96
900–1,000	95
1,000–1,100	94
1,100–1,200	92
1,200–1,300	90
1,300–1,400	88
1,400–1,500	86
1,500–1,600	84
1,600–1,700	82
1,700–1,800	80
1,800–1,900	78
1,900–2,000	76
2,000–2,100	74
2,100–2,200	72
2,200–2,300	70
2,300–2,400	68
2,400–2,500	66
2,500–2,600	64
2,600–2,700	62
2,700–2,800	59
2,800–2,900	56
2,900–3,000	53
3,000–3,100	51
3,100–3,200	48
3,200–3,300	45
3,300–3,400	43
3,400–3,500	41

Source: Public Law 91-588.

a. The monthly rate is increased by $16 for each additional child. If there is no widow who can qualify, a pension of $40 per month is paid to the first child and $16 per month is paid to each additional child whose unearned income does not exceed $2,000 annually.

Eligibility

One important way in which pensions have been set apart from public assistance is in the application process. The practicality of establishing benefit eligibility by a declaration system that does not include field investigation was established in veterans' pensions long before the Department of Health, Education, and Welfare dared to push it in public assistance. While declaration has been routine in establishing a claim to social security benefits, the claimant is popularly presumed to be drawing on his own insurance account rather than on public general revenue. With such a presumption, whatever its technical validity, it is considered enough to take only routine steps to verify age before proceeding to pay a social security claimant what under the law is his and what, in the view of most Americans, has been earned. On the other hand, the elaborate public assistance eligibility investigation, in recent years the bane of welfare reformers, was long thought to be necessary to protect the program itself against ineligible cheats who could cause Congress to take repressive steps unless controlled. Persuaded of their unique ability to help the poor, social workers welcomed the eligibility investigation for more years than they should have on the theory that every investigation is a social service because it provides a point of contact between a client in need and a helping worker.

Should the VA be investigator, social worker, or just check writer? In pensions there is no "account" to which the claimant has made payments in the fashion of social security; pension benefits must be paid out of general revenue rather than out of a trust fund. A case might be made therefore for constraints comparable to those of public assistance, including field investigation of eligibility. But the importance of the pension theory developed by the veterans' associations is evident: an invisible account based on delayed compensation introduces a right to pension more comparable to the automatic right to social security than to the request for public assistance. And the system operates accordingly.

The veteran's application for pension or that of his widow or children for death pension can be completed through the mail with or without assistance from a service officer of the VA or of the veterans' associations. Any communication from or action by a claimant or his duly authorized representative, or some person acting as next friend, that clearly indicates an intent to apply for the specific benefit will be considered an informal claim. Although a formal application will be forwarded by the VA for subsequent completion, the claim itself is considered filed as of the date of receipt of the informal claim. This presumption of claim validity, which means in effect that any delay is at the expense of the government, protects the claimant against slow formal processes.

Income statements are accepted as filed because the word of the veteran, it is said, should not be doubted. (In general, benefit applications need not be sworn to but are acceptable on the claimant's own certification.) Since income is usually the only critical issue in the case of death pension payments to widows and children, eligibility and benefit payments to them are uncomplicated. As long as the annual income questionnaire is returned in timely fashion and does not show actual or expected income changes adequate to debar or reduce benefits, payment goes on indefinitely and without intrusion or other inquiry by the Veterans Administration.

Defining Disability and Income

Where the veteran himself is the pension claimant, disability as well as income is a test. The disability test is met if the VA finds him to be "permanently and totally disabled." But total disability does not really mean total. If, under the VA's disability rating schedule, a veteran's disabilities do not combine to a rating of 100 percent, employability and age become considerations. Where a veteran is deemed to be unemployable by reason of disability, the required rating drops so that under age 55 one disability rated at 60 percent, or one disability rated at 40 percent plus one or more disabilities combining to a rating of 70 percent will be defined as total disability and will produce a pension. So will a combined rating of 60 percent at age 55 to 60 or a combined rating of 50 percent at 60 to 65. At 65 a veteran is presumed by law to be 10 percent disabled which, at that age, constitutes total disability. Presumptive disability at 65 had been vigorously opposed before 1967 by the Budget Bureau, which envisioned untold thousands of old veterans filing pension claims once disability ceased to be required. Although the bureau, in 1964, compelled Veterans Administrator John Gleason to recant testimony in which he had approved presumptive disability, three years later—after President Johnson's special message on veterans—there was no objection to the presumptive disability provision.[46]

Income determines the amount of pension paid to claimants qualified under service and disability tests. The most sophisticated pension policy participants pay careful attention to income that is officially deemed to

46. *Pension Bills and Bills to Provide Additional Wartime Benefits for Veterans of the Vietnam Conflict,* Hearings before the Subcommittee on Compensation and Pensions of the House Committee on Veterans' Affairs, 90 Cong. 1 sess. (1967), p. 286.

be nonincome, a highly important element in the whole pension area. For example, in reporting income for pension purposes, a claimant will find it legally proper to exclude such items as the value of maintenance provided by a relative or friend, charitable donations, VA disability and death insurance payments, profit from sale of real or personal property other than in the course of a business, and a variety of others. "Income" also excludes either all earned income of a claimant's spouse or $1,200, whichever is greater. Thus a veteran is penalized not at all for having a working wife but will be penalized for having one with substantial unearned income.

Since nearly all pension applicants are also eligible for old age or survivor's benefits under social security, the extent to which social security payments are part of the income computation is crucial to the individual claimant's benefit amount. In addition, decisions about social security payments as income affect the long-run future of the entire pension program. Income limits for pension eligibility go up very slowly, much more slowly than social security benefit increases. Thus the strategy of pension proponents has been to work for increases in income limits while the strategy of opponents has been to yield first on increases in pension amounts but to hold as firm as possible on income limits. Both proponents and opponents recognize that constantly increasing benefits under a universal social security system will ultimately erode the number of cases eligible for pensions—if pension income limits do not rise as social security benefits rise. An alternative strategy for pension proponents is to define social security payments in whole or in part as nonincome for pension purposes. It is a reflection of the political standoff in this field that, under current law, 10 percent of social security income is excluded in calculating eligbility for pensions.

Having been educated by the veterans' groups to believe that pensions are a rightful benefit related to wartime service and having been educated by the prevailing social security mythology to believe that social security is a rightful insurance type benefit, few beneficiaries of both programs can readily understand and fewer still can readily accept a reduction in the combined benefit total resulting from extensively publicized social security benefit increases. Such increases, however, have pushed some recipients into a higher income bracket which, in turn, pushed them into a lower pension payment bracket. Avoiding that result by statutory change has been a complicated problem, partly because House Veterans Affairs cannot know what kind of protective bills to push until Ways and Means has completed its social security work.

Even then, the possibility of further changes in the social security benefit structure being effected in the Senate Finance Committee, or on the
Senate floor, or in conference, is always present. But once social security
improvements are enacted, legislation to preserve pension rates must be
moved promptly or the social security increases may result in actual
income reductions for needy veterans and their survivors, the most
politically appealing categories of relief clients. Prior to legislation enacted in 1968, the steep gradation in pension payments based on only
three income brackets meant that such annual income reductions could
total $400 or more too commonly for congressional comfort. A new,
more gently graded system of twenty-one pension brackets restricts the
probability of traumatic income reductions and preserves the principle
of pensions as an allowable supplement to social security for low income veterans. Continuing improvement in social security benefits without increases in income limits for pensions, however, could eventually
wipe out the pension program. This is a most closely watched area by
all participants: the Budget Bureau in hopes that social security will
drive out pensions; the veterans' associations in fear of the same result;
and Teague's Veterans Affairs Committee in order to steer its middle
course.

Deciding about Need

Some seemingly poor veterans own enough real and personal property to lead many reasonable people to doubt the equity of providing
them a public subsidy. Although an individual claimant for pension
may fall within the statutory income limits, let us suppose that income
were derived from investments with substantial market values. Should
liquidation be obligatory at some absolute cutoff point without regard
to the individual circumstances of the claimant? Should a widow with
dependent children who must be provided for over a long number of
years of schooling be obliged to liquidate marketable property before
being admitted to the pension rolls? What about pension for the aged
veteran who could reasonably be expected to live out his remaining
years on the proceeds of liquidation? Just where would reasonable men
draw a line between excessive net worth that should debar public aid
to veterans and net worth that should not debar such public aid? In
short, how much pauperization should be demanded of those who seek
this form of governmental charity?

The Veterans Administration's answer to these questions is consistently equivocal. Empowered by law to deny or terminate pensions for excessive net worth, it does so according to its own wisdom, saying to questioners only, "Trust us." It is known that the value of the veteran's home, its furnishings, his clothing and personal effects, and items of personal property incident to daily living are not considered in determining net worth. Real property and improvements other than the homestead, bank accounts, stocks, bonds, and securities are included in the test. Like maximum feasible participation and like affirmative action in fair employment practices, however, no qualifying or disqualifying figure is acknowledged to exist. Whatever an allowable net worth is, about 2,600 applicants in a typical year have too much. In addition, during one recent year, almost 800 previously approved pension cases were terminated for "excessive corpus of estate." Each case, say VA officials in their stock answer to the question of what constitutes excessive net worth, is judged on its own merits, considering the type of property involved, the age of the claimant, his life expectancy, and the number and health of dependents. That stock answer may be in accord with the statutory authority granted to the veterans administrator; it is not an answer that enables a potential claimant or those who advise him to know where they stand.

Shortly after the net worth test was authorized by the 1959 legislation, the VA instructed its field officers to forward memorandum opinions to Washington whenever a pension was disallowed because of excessive net worth. In addition, opinions were to be forwarded in any case where the value of the estate involved exceeded $10,000. While VA spokesmen insist that they had no intention of fixing a cutoff point by that directive—"We merely did this so we could get consistency of opinions and uniformity of application of the law"—the effect was to require a formal defense of approval of pensions where there was a net worth above $10,000, a formal defense of any disallowance for excessive net worth, but no defense of pension approvals where the net worth was under $10,000. Lacking any other benchmark whatever, shoptalk in the field therefore focused on $10,000 as the figure fixed upon in Washington as maximum permissible net worth. Although $10,000 became the rule of thumb almost accidentally, its continued acceptance despite VA central office denial that there is significance to the amount reflects the anxiety of some claims personnel for guidelines on which to base day-to-day advice about net worth.

Study and analysis of experience under the net worth test during its first two years showed the average value of claimants' estates to be about $13,000. The average net worth of claimants whose pensions were denied under the test was $18,735. Satisfied that the situation was well in hand, Washington then dropped the instructions for forwarding of memorandum opinions in net worth cases. These opinions continued to be required but were retained in the individual claim folder, thus establishing a decentralized administrative adjudication system not subject to central office review as a matter of routine.

No support is forthcoming from Veterans Administration leadership for proposals to establish a more precise net worth test either by legislation or by administrative action. Pointing out that the agency had been making "decisions of great judgment" for thirty-five years on such subjective questions as whether a disability can be said to be service connected when it did not manifest itself during the period of service, former Deputy Administrator A. W. Stratton, who served as director of veterans' benefits, would not back away from making judgments in the VA about excessive net worth. He acknowledged that the use of the $10,000 cutoff figure for forwarding memorandum opinions was a major mistake. "We should have called them all in and then this $10,000 fictional level never would have been brought up time and time again." But as for fixing any minimum or any maximum figure, "It is better the way it is. I would never endorse changing it."[47]

The VA continues to resist saying what constitutes excessive net worth in the pension area. From data that do seep through, however, the national average value of estates held by veterans whose pension claims were denied on the net worth test could be fixed at $22,400 in 1966, up $3,700 from the 1961 average. During one test month, a Utah claim was denied on a net worth below $11,000, an Alabama claim on a net worth of $15,000, a West Virginia claim where the net worth was under $16,000, at least one Missouri claim with a net worth under $14,000, and at least one New York City claim with a net worth below $15,000; but no claim with a net worth below $29,000 was denied in Tennessee, nor was any claim with a net worth below $25,000 denied in Louisiana.[48]

Variations around the country in the average values of estates where

47. American Legion, Proceedings, National Rehabilitation Conference (1966), p. 105.
48. Disposition of Claims by Regional Offices, House Committee on Veterans Affairs, 89 Cong. 2 sess. (1966), pp. 132–33.

claims were denied are substantial enough to allow the conclusion that there is no secret figure known only to the VA personnel. On the other hand, those variations are substantial enough to warrant doubts that the present administrative discretion is justifiable. Would the adjudications officers in the fourteen field offices where there were no denials for size of estate have denied the two Utah cases that were denied on an average value of $11,000? Would the thirteen Philadelphia cases denied (average value $16,230) have been denied in Nashville, where it took $29,000 to provoke a denial?

To say that no one knows is to state the problem. The absence of guidelines inevitably means that some potential claimants will be discouraged from filing out of fear of rejection; others will be brash and successful. Even American Legion service officers were talking about $10,000 as the "departing point" at the same time that the average denial point nationally was well in excess of $22,000. Such a gap between "departing point" and actual national practice is uncomfortably large. Other conditions for pension eligibility, moreover, are spelled out in precise enough terms. Income limits, for example, are not adjustable by administrative discretion in view of the age of the claimant, his life expectancy, or the health of his dependents. Besides, there is no special wisdom in the Veterans Administration adjudications officer that fits him to make the subjective judgment. While compulsory liquidation of assets might have a severe enough traumatic effect on some claimants to justify approval of relatively high net worth, this is not a proper decision to leave to an administrative official whose expertise does not extend to questions of trauma.

A graduated net worth scale could be developed incorporating the considerations the VA now includes in its stock answer to what constitutes excessive net worth. The scale might set net worth maximums based on combinations of age, dependents, degree of disability, and type of property. Claims falling within the permissible limits should be allowed. It is service neither to the needy veteran nor to the taxpayer for the Veterans Administration to say, in effect, that it either can't or won't divulge the details of its system but to take its word for the fact that the system is a good one.

Income limits, pension rates, and definitions of income are regularly subjects of proposed change in the veterans' associations' programs of pension improvement, but the net worth test is not. Discretionary authority for the VA to rule on net worth without statutory guidelines was a principle proposed in Legion staff papers prior to enactment of the 1959 so-called new pension law, and uncontrolled discretionary authority in ruling on net worth is still supported by the professional veterans. To the contrary, the net worth recommendation first made by the Bradley Commission—that the value of an estate be capitalized, its likely income figured according to a presumed interest rate, and the result considered to be income—would restrict administrative discretion. The different positions accurately reflect support and opposition for any arrangement in veterans' affairs that permits quiet, in-house negotiations between men of good will dedicated to maintaining a preferred status for all veterans. Decisions about whether public benefits will be distributed or withheld should not be made, however, in quiet, in-house negotiations.

Appeals

The appellate procedure in veterans' matters, including pensions, underscores the positive value to the veteran of having a separate welfare world. No ombudsman could turn that procedure into an operation more oriented toward the claimant than it already is. The expressed mission of the Board of Veterans' Appeals (BVA) is not only to decide appeals as promptly as possible, but also to decide with sympathetic understanding. The mission, moreover, is expressed not in neutral terms like "adjudicate" or "rule on" but in positive terms: "to grant all benefits to which veterans and their dependents and beneficiaries are entitled."[49] Reconsideration of a rejected claim comes easily, "on the flimsiest of pretexts," in the words of one VA official. For most purposes the BVA does not even require a contention that there is new evidence to be presented. Service organizations go back two and three times and frequently achieve a reversal.

The Board of Veterans' Appeals perceives of itself as an agency to approve claims wherever it can without clearly violating the statute, to humanize both the consideration and the disposition of claims, to counteract the impersonal aspects of the VA forms that are used to establish communication between claimant and agency. Publicly stated policies of the board establish a presumption in favor of the validity of a vet-

49. Cited by James Stancil, chairman, Board of Veterans' Appeals, in American Legion, *Proceedings, National Rehabilitation Conference* (1965), p. 214.

eran's claim. Pursuing an appeal is facilitated by board procedures that are highly informal, very unlike judicial proceedings. Rules of evidence are not followed. The claimant can submit anything he can procure in support of his claim. Everything is admitted. The board is free to accept and evaluate for itself anything that is produced. Persuasive hearsay and the uncertified document that might not stand formal judicial scrutiny are acceptable to the BVA.

Of the 40,000 appeals initiated annually, roughly one-sixth involve pension claims. Typically, almost half of all the cases initiated will never come to the BVA hearing stage: one in six will be allowed at the field level on reconsideration; one in four will be closed when the appellant fails to pursue his appeal in the time allowed; one in twenty will be formally withdrawn by the veteran or his representative. Of the remaining total certified to the board, 70 percent will finally be denied, a handful will be withdrawn, and the remainder will be almost evenly divided between allowed claims and cases remanded to the field for another look—which often results in an allowed claim. The high denial rate is less a sign of board toughmindedness than of its ready willingness to hear virtually hopeless cases.

Since 1957, principal responsibility for establishing practices and philosophies and attitudes of the Board of Veterans' Appeals has rested on James W. Stancil, a lawyer who is chairman of the twelve-section, fifty-member board. Stancil, a World War II Navy veteran of the South Pacific, presides over a group of lawyers and doctors, divided roughly two to one between the professions. His view of the board's function emphasizes a concern for direct human contact:

The Board exists today, as the arm of the Administrator, to bridge the gap between system and man, to insure the continued recognition of the essential dignity of the individual, to attempt, as best it may, to sense the distinction between the operation of similar circumstances on different personalities, to individualize the claim of the individual.[50]

Hearings procedures and the style of decisions are matters of internal rule in which Stancil takes particular pride. Because there are a consequential number of claims that are palpably without merit on their face—one example sometimes offered is that of the claimant with seventy days of service who seeks benefits restricted by law to veterans with at least ninety days of service—a guaranteed personal hearing in every case where it is requested does represent a level of personal atten-

50. *Ibid.*, p. 213.

tion that should not be underrated. The board has even come to the point of ruling that failure of any of its sections to accord a hearing that was requested prior to the decision constitutes a substantive defect in due process serious enough to merit vacating the decision and granting de novo consideration.

To facilitate personal appearances before the BVA without imposing heavy costs on the claimant, traveling sections appear in VA regional offices around the country. Most offices will be visited every eighteen months to two years. In a typical year, such traveling sections may conduct 400 to 450 hearings in visits to 30 to 35 field offices, listening to those controversial cases in which the most benefit is believed to be derived from the personal appearance of the claimant.

The board prefers that a claimant be represented by a veterans' organization, and in 80 percent of all appeals reaching the BVA, claimants are so represented. No special advantage or disadvantage is supposed to accrue to an unrepresented appellant, but the board's leadership acknowledges a "great debt" to service officers. "Our relations with you," Stancil told a group of them a few years ago, "have demonstrated a faculty unique to our system; that is, the absence of any feeling of adversary status."[51] Characterizing the relationship as that of "friends, not foes," he gave assurances that "even in our disagreements, I have the feeling we are partners in seeking out ways in which the facts and law in cases may be recognized as satisfying the requirements for granting what is asked."

A practical demonstration of this attitude of "partnership" is the board's present practice of inviting comment from the claimant's representative on all new evidence and opinion obtained by the BVA. This prefiling takes place prior to a final decision by the board. Decisions themselves are not precleared but are released to the accredited representative, the claimant, and, if there is one, an interested congressman, simultaneously.

For all of the sympathetic and understanding language, it remains impossible to tell just how the VA and the BVA are administering the benefits programs. If the veterans' associations find the administration too restrictive, they believe it disadvantageous to complain publicly; if the administration of the law is excessively liberal, veterans' groups will

---

51. *Ibid.*, p. 216. Stancil's views are set out in detail in "A Comparative Analysis of the British and American Appeals Systems and Procedure in the Adjudication of Claims for Veterans' Benefits" (April 15, 1965; processed).

certainly not complain. At least one member of the House Veterans Affairs Committee is convinced that there are more "wrong" decisions coming out of the Veterans Administration than are ever corrected. In expressing a strong conviction that there is need to break through bureaucratic rigidity in the VA, Representative John Saylor complains that the American veteran "is the only person in the world who has a claim against Uncle Sam that can't get to court." Citing cases in which he has intervened to compel reconsideration, if not reversal, the congressman compares the appeals arrangements in the Veterans Administration with arrangements originally established in administration of the income tax laws when no court existed. "Well," says Saylor in equating the need for a court of veterans' appeals with the need for a tax court, "the income tax boys got just like the boys in the Veterans Administration. They thought that they were supermen."[52]

But both the service organizations and the VA look on the possible introduction of adversary proceedings as a departure that would throw the VA and the service organizations into an undesirable kind of antagonistic relationship. The VA is in business to give money away and the service organizations are in business to make it easy for the VA to do so—everyone is on the same side of the table. On the other hand, a court of veterans' appeals presupposes appellants and appellees. The veteran, through his claims representative, would be appellant; the VA would be cast as appellee. Judicial proceedings would invite the keeping of a won and lost record. Victories in individual cases would be public, decisions would be published. Even if the winners were modest, frequent losers would smart and the result inevitably would be a deterioration of personal relationships between VA and service association personnel.

The American Legion simply does not relish playing Civil Liberties Union to the Veterans Administration's Federal Bureau of Investigation. The Legion frankly acknowledges that it finds the present appellate system advantageous. Subjective determination of benefit eligibility on the net worth test is only one specific area where this is deemed true. "In our experience," says John Corcoran, recently director of the Legion's National Rehabilitation Commission and now general counsel of the VA, "there have been a substantial number of cases in which we have disagreed with the interpretation of the VA and after a substantial

52. *Proceedings, National Rehabilitation Conference* (1965), p. 208. See also *Pension Bills for Veterans of the Vietnam Conflict*, Hearings, p. 296.

period of time been able to persuade the Administration to change its interpretation of the regulations. . . . In the past ten or twelve years regulation after regulation has been modified, explained, clarified, all toward liberalizing the situation." Comparing these results with the likely consequences of judicial review, the Legion sees a less happy outcome if an independent court ruling were involved. Even where they are persuaded that a VA ruling has improperly interpreted congressional intent, American Legion officials prefer to keep the dispute in the family and out of court.

Keeping everything about veterans' relief in the family is a key characteristic of veterans' relief policy, and it is one that all groups involved consider advantageous. The VA, attentive to the needs of congressmen who find that a large part of their "casework" deals with veterans' problems, maintains offices in the Capitol itself. The physical proximity facilitates access to the agency by members of House and Senate. Understandably, VA efficiency is rated higher by legislators than by many individual veterans who approach from outside the family circle of VA, BVA, Legion, and VFW. Access to data, including subjective decisions in individual cases, is limited to the family circle, with even the courts largely excluded from veterans' benefits questions. The family circle avoids publicity about its activities, thereby minimizing the likelihood of attention being focused on whether a separate and unequal relief system is not wasteful and unfair both as a matter of general principle and in particular cases.

The theory of an invisible insurance account developed by the veterans' service organizations is an elegant one. It has resulted in a system that is in many ways a model for public relief by including federal standards and federal payments; intercession by a nongovernmental group; a presumption of eligibility; simplicity in application and subsequent reporting; and an easy appeals procedure. By creating a most favored group among the poor, however, it also results in unequal protection.

8

Organizing Welfare Clients

Millions of welfare clients and other millions of potential welfare clients remain uninvolved in any organized movement to improve their circumstances, but the thousands who have become involved follow a vigorous and aggressive protest style reinforced by lawyers, caseworkers, church groups, and some congressmen. Although eclipsed for a short time by the Poor People's Campaign—"the last great dream of the Rev. Dr. Martin Luther King . . . to give conspicuous and detailed witness to the poverty and degradation that rob millions of Americans of their human dignity"[1]—the National Welfare Rights Organization (NWRO) and its local affiliates have since the summer of 1966 been the channel for most welfare protest activity. Independent but noncompeting protest groups, the Poor People's Campaign and NWRO have presented views that turned out to be legally correct and politically troublesome. Each group has sometime managed to have itself received by presidential assistants and cabinet secretaries; each group has produced detailed proposals relating to statutory and administrative action; each group is primarily black; and, if sometimes disruptive, each is nonviolent. Given present alternatives, political leaders welcome the chance to deal with disaffected black spokesmen who will talk and who do not urge violence on their followers. Still, the existence of these separate movements—the one of northern urban origin with a specific emphasis on cash relief and the other a descendent of the southern civil rights movement with a spiritual-like call for justice and righteousness—complicates the prob-

1. "Statements of Demands for Rights of the Poor Presented to Agencies of the U.S. Government by the Southern Christian Leadership Conference and Its Committee of 100, April 29–30, May 1, 1968" (issued by the SCLC-PPC Information Office, New York Avenue Presbyterian Church, Washington, D.C.; processed), p. 1.

lems of welfare reformers who would like to have unified support from client groups for a reform effort.

The Poor People's Campaign was a comparative failure and NWRO is a comparative success. One likely explanation lies in NWRO's preoccupation with a single, specific program—public relief—while the Poor People spread themselves from hunger in Mississippi to protecting the hunting and fishing rights of Indians in Oregon. Even in public relief, demands of the National Welfare Rights Organization boil down to core questions: improving access to financial aid and achieving more adequate support levels. NWRO shows little interest in such public assistance issues as the size of workers' caseloads, no interest in the psychosocial services that have been so heavily emphasized in recent years by many nonclient observers, and interest in the question of federal versus state financing only as source of funds affects benefit levels. NWRO is concerned with overcoming restrictive eligibility conditions —residence is an example—and in changing the character of the welfare intake procedure by adoption of an eligibility declaration in lieu of investigation. In short, little or no NWRO energy is dissipated in attempting to improve the quality of public assistance delivery compared to the energy, attention, and interest focused on eligibility for relief benefits and on how much money is being delivered. While the NWRO leadership is able to avoid diversions from this focus, leaders of the Poor People were unwilling or unable to focus on specifics in a legislative and administrative system that responds only to specifics and to priorities.

A second explanation has to do with respective coercive styles. When the Poor People did their worst, they camped by the Potomac near the Lincoln Memorial; it was only a temporary inconvenience for part of the Washington population, and it benefited the campers not at all. Ultimately, their Resurrection City closed just as its inhabitants faced being jailed, a denouement similar to that of Coxey's Army of the unemployed which marched on Washington in 1894 only to be arrested for walking on the Capitol lawns. When NWRO did its worst in New York City in 1968, organizing clients to demand special grants authorized under law but rarely paid, it was costly for the city and rewarding for recipients. Later, when NWRO undertook to pressure department stores to provide charge accounts for welfare clients, its tactics made things inconvenient for some uninvolved, middle class persons not touched by an encampment on park land. And it was all legal.

NWRO's activities are possible because urbanization of the aid to families with dependent children (AFDC) caseload facilitates the growth of local groups of organized recipients. NWRO welcomes whites, but most of its members are black. To state it bluntly, at a time when other disaffections have made riots a terrible actuality or a fearful possibility in every large city, the cause of welfare change has been advanced by the organization of relief clients and the fear—which is not diminished by the absence of evidence to sustain it—that those organized clients will spark violent disorder. The National Advisory Commission on Civil Disorders (Kerner Commission) was told that an unpublished Department of Health, Education, and Welfare (HEW) study in Cincinnati indicated that "only a very small number out of the total number of people arrested were welfare recipients."[2] Although the Kerner Commission did not find that assistance clients rioted, it did conclude that the "present system of public assistance contributes materially to the tensions and social disorganization that have led to civil disorders."[3]

If the welfare system's inadequacy contributed to the causes of disorder in the recent past, it can continue to so contribute. When NWRO affiliates demonstrate, local officials must recall that disorder in the cities has been tagged a possible consequence of failure to effect change. NWRO has been called the weakest lobby in Washington, and its own leaders do not yet claim great success with the Congress. "Lobbying is a transaction in power and influence," said Tim Sampson when he was NWRO's number two man. "If you don't have much power and influence, you don't lobby." If it lacks strength in the Capitol, however, NWRO does better in the cities where political and business leaders worry about disruption of local business, commercial, and school activity. "We're directing our guns on the local welfare agencies," NWRO's director acknowledged in the spring of 1969. "We have no clout on a national level yet and we couldn't put a program through Congress."[4] There is more to policy than a congressional enact-

2. *Official Transcript of Proceedings before the National Advisory Commission on Civil Disorders*, Washington, D.C., Nov. 3, 1967, p. 3563. The witness, Assistant Secretary of HEW Lisle C. Carter, Jr., claimed only "a general hunch" that welfare clients probably did not participate in disorders, but asserted, "I am saying we have no evidence that they were significant participants anyway." *Ibid.*, p. 3566.

3. *Report of the National Advisory Commission on Civil Disorders* (March 1, 1968), p. 252.

4. "George Wiley: Premier Welfare Organizer," *Communique* (American University, Department of Communication, March 4, 1969), p. 5.

ment; NWRO keeps the pressure on HEW and on local welfare agencies to do no less than follow existing law.

Organizing for Welfare Rights

Organization of public assistance clients into a National Welfare Rights Organization was an unanticipated consequence of the beginnings of the black power movement. George Wiley, a young black Ph.D. in chemistry, on the losing side in the 1966 struggle that divided the leadership of the Congress of Racial Equality (CORE), that same year concluded that he was beyond returning to the life of a research chemist, and also concluded that "the poor at the grass roots needed a new voice."[5] He invented and took on for himself the role of full-time field leader in organizing welfare recipients—particularly AFDC mothers—into a militant union of nonwage earners to improve benefits and conditions of assistance. Putting together a strategy for action, Wiley promptly began to implement it by setting up, in Washington, a Poverty/Rights Action Center (P/RAC). Its declared ultimate objective was a guaranteed income.

With a potential constituency that would be disaffected by a long time lag between planning and results, Wiley had to move to action quickly if he was to attract followers. His immediate action vehicle was a June march to the state capitol at Columbus, Ohio, being planned by a small group of Cleveland welfare recipients. Broadening the action, P/RAC picked the day the Cleveland group expected to arrive in Columbus, June 30, 1966, as a day for national demonstrations. Coordinated by P/RAC, demonstrations were held in at least sixteen cities from California to Massachusetts. In Columbus the 40 or so recipients who had marched from Cleveland were joined by about 2,000 other protesters in their march to the capitol; in New York City about 2,000 persons picketed City Hall.[6] Demands put forward in the various demonstrations included higher grant levels, an end to welfare investigations, more day care centers, and improvements in food distribution programs. The day's activities have been dramatically summarized in the "official history" of NWRO:

5. *Christian Science Monitor*, Aug. 23, 1968.
6. "A Brief History of the National Welfare Rights Organization," *NOW!* (official publication of the National Welfare Rights Organization, Washington, D.C.), Feb. 9, 1968, p. 2; Richard Cloward and Frances Piven, "Weapon of Poverty: Birth of a Movement," *Nation*, Vol. 204 (May 8, 1967), p. 582.

The Birth of the Movement

On June 30th, at 12:01 AM, recipients in Pittsburgh began the day with a vigil in front of the State Welfare Department. As the sun rose, demonstrations spread from Boston, Massachusetts to San Bernardino, California.

By the end of the day, over 6,000 recipients had participated. It was the first such nationwide demonstration of poor people in over 30 years. A new movement had been born—THE NATIONAL WELFARE RIGHTS MOVEMENT.[7]

Aside from success in one state with one category—the needy aged—achieved by the California Institute of Social Welfare, welfare-client organization has never before been accomplished.[8] Built-in problems involving leaders, followers, and strategy are formidable. One problem in organizing this constituency is that the most likely helpers are indigenous leaders among welfare recipients. Those who can be leaders, however, are also most likely to be the members of the group best able to overcome dependency and thus to drop off welfare. Another problem is that dependent persons instinctively fear that protest will cause them to be stricken from the rolls, just as trade union members used to fear being fired for union activity. Still another impediment is the dilemma of how to proceed if organized: to invite backlash by pursuing belligerent, militant techniques espoused by black power advocates who express contempt for the welfare idea ("I don't believe in welfare," Floyd McKissick once said; "the fact that we have a welfare system means that something is wrong and somebody's stealing from somebody else"), or to invite middle class support by pursuing incremental change using the safe, conventional techniques of such groups as the Urban League and the National Association for the Advancement of Colored People.

NWRO has been able to take advantage of the support for participation engendered by the poverty program. Activists who are also relief recipients are now more likely to be retained than to be stricken because public agencies cannot expect to avoid legal challenge to termination of benefits to an activist. The tactical dilemma of quiet negotiation versus belligerent militancy has been resolved by the choice of a strategy that limits itself to neither and borrows from both. As early as its first birth-

7. "A Brief History of the National Welfare Rights Movement" (prepared by Poverty/Rights Action Center, Washington, D.C., n.d.; processed), pp. 2 ff.

8. Gilbert Y. Steiner, *Social Insecurity: The Politics of Welfare* (Rand McNally, 1966), pp. 153 ff.; Frank Pinner, Paul Jacobs, and Philip Selznick, *Old Age and Political Behavior* (University of California Press, 1959).

day, June 30, 1967, NWRO mobilized protest marches in more than 50 cities across the country. Outside of New York—where more than 1,000 pickets, some of whom were striking welfare department caseworkers, marched around City Hall—no demonstration was very large, but there was organized protest where before there had been only resignation. By the winter of 1968, affiliates existed in 35 states involving nearly 200 local groups with a dues-paying membership reasonably claimed to be over 6,000 family heads representing about 25,000 current or recent welfare clients. In the summer of 1969 the claim was 35,000 clients in 46 states. At that point NWRO extended its membership eligibility to members of family groups with incomes below $5,500 annually, thus inviting the working poor to join with the welfare poor. It also sent two of its officers to the founding convention of the National Tenants Organization (NTO) with the expressed hope that NTO would be the first of many "sister" organizations.

Wiley's own subjective judgment is that NWRO is the most important development in the low income population group since Rosa Parks refused to move to the back of a Montgomery, Alabama, bus and sparked the civil rights revolution in America. Objectively, it can be noted that the welfare clients' organization has weathered its theoretical and practical problems to the point where its director is known, recognized, and consulted by the secretary of health, education, and welfare and resented at other high levels in that department; its chairman, an AFDC mother, sits with bureaucrats, scholars, and lobbyists in all-day conferences to plan welfare change; and its prize local affiliate has helped to make welfare New York City's most costly public service if not its most troublesome.

NWRO performs three critically important functions for its constituency that no social agency can successfully perform:

1. It provides mutual reinforcement for a depressed social and economic group whose members heretofore have waged lonely fights, if they fought at all, against policies and procedures of the public agency with which they dealt.

2. It provides for participant representation in policy discussion independent of social workers or any other surrogate spokesmen.

3. It provides an associational tie for AFDC clients than can be their equivalent of the League of Women Voters or Planned Parenthood. Some American women preoccupy themselves with the Boston Mt. Holyoke Alumnae Club; NWRO gives others a chance to be involved with Boston's Mothers for Adequate Welfare.

Maintaining communication between the local welfare groups in order to give publicity to the activists and the success stories and to provide encouragement for those locals who feel isolated and discouraged is a function to which NWRO pays careful attention. Poverty is depressing and discouraging; battling to change established public policy, difficult enough for middle class groups, may appear impossible from below. Partly to offer assurance that success is not an impossible dream, Wiley's office has supplied the NWRO local leadership with a regular flow of readable, pertinent literature including a bimonthly newsletter originally called *NOW!*, a title with symbolic appeal both to those who had been involved in the civil rights fight for "freedom now" and those who had been supporting a "guaranteed annual income now." From the first, the newsletter—retitled *The Welfare Fighter* after an upheaval in NWRO's publications section in 1969—has recounted the activities of various welfare rights groups across the country. Thus the maiden issue of October 31, 1966, in the form of a letter to welfare rights leaders and organizers from Wiley, reported activity by welfare rights groups in New York City, California, Connecticut, and Mississippi. Recipients were exhorted to continue their organizing efforts, to work for benefits due them, to learn welfare rules and regulations, to develop local manuals summarizing the rules and regulations.

To encourage a feeling of solidarity, the subjects and tone of newsletter articles are all designed both to keep local welfare rights leaders up to date on the doings of other welfare rights leaders and to furnish transferable ideas. For example, one early issue reported the Los Angeles group's success in getting medical cards processed faster; another reported a request from the Massachusetts group for special $10 grants at Thanksgiving, Christmas, Easter, and school opening. At first, local items were only a paragraph or two of material, provided by the locals. More recently, articles about the welfare rights groups have often been reprinted from local newspapers and pictures have been used extensively. Not only are ideas and techniques shared, but reprinting of press accounts shows that some attention has been paid to those ideas and techniques, that they are stirring things up. These articles together with the editorial commentary are probably the most complete available running account of the activities of welfare recipient groups across the country. It is no more possible to follow welfare issues adequately without first *NOW!* and then *The Welfare Fighter* than to follow show business adequately without *Variety*.

By December 1968, *NOW!* could publish a "Winter Action Campaign" issue urging members to join in demanding full heat and utilities allowances, full rent money, money for winter clothing, special Christmas grants, and credit in department stores. Most important, it could report welfare rights activity in November and December in twenty-one cities from Providence to Detroit and from Memphis to Oklahoma City. It could reprint editorial comment and news stories from national magazines (*Time, The Nation*) and from newspapers ranging from the *Christian Science Monitor* to the *Arizona Republic* to the *Washington Post* to the *Toledo Times*, all featuring stories about Wiley or about NWRO or one of its affiliates. These reprints carry an implicit message: no welfare activist has to feel alone. Previously isolated individuals or tiny groups completely dependent on a welfare system they could not control or even influence can now feel that they have a way to approach the centers of power. If successful, they can expect tangible benefits; if not successful, they have at least thrown in the challenge that hundreds of thousands of clients have surely wanted to throw in.

Organization has always been Wiley's great push, its importance constantly emphasized. For example, while a substantial part of the NWRO newsletter published after Martin Luther King's murder reviews Dr. King's brief meetings with Wiley and NWRO ladies, the newsletter's cover carried only a quotation from Joe Hill, one of organized labor's martyrs, "Don't Mourn Me—Organize." Wiley believes it essential to build up NWRO to provide a grass roots base for the drive against the welfare system. Tactics of disruption, sit-ins especially, are an NWRO weapon: delegates to the NWRO convention staged a brief sit-in, for example, at the Senate Finance Committee in August 1967 during the hearings on the Social Security Amendments, and HEW Secretary Finch's office was "liberated" in May 1970 by an NWRO sit-in. Confrontation that leads to disruption has come to be employed with increasing frequency by the national leadership. Among many local groups, who make their own decisions about tactics, small-scale disruption is not uncommon. Milwaukee welfare mothers, for example, seized the Wisconsin State Capitol in September 1969 to protest welfare budget cuts. While NWRO reported the seizure sympathetically, it did not claim leadership, assigning that role to Father James Groppi, the activist priest, and to the militant Brown Berets of the National Association for the Advancement of Colored People.[9]

9. *Welfare Fighter*, October 1969, p. 1.

Wiley wants a self-sufficient, dues-supported organization that will not depend on churches, unions, or the poverty program. He believes that the way to reach this goal is to make NWRO attractive to its potential constituency in much the same way that the International Ladies Garment Workers Union makes itself attractive to its potential constituency—by emphasizing a unique, shared experience, and by building in the trappings and techniques of middle class organizations that Americans are apt to join. Welfare clients, in other words, are attracted by an opportunity to do the things that other, more affluent persons do and simultaneously to reinforce each other in efforts to better their condition. So, welfare mothers in Louisville held a dance to raise money to send delegates to one NWRO convention. The conventions themselves include "workshops" on public relations and fund raising even as they might appear on a convention program of Boy Scout leaders. "Lobbying" of Congress is planned. Preconvention mailings contain information on transportation, housing, meals, and preregistration together with such inducements as a tentative program of scheduled activities including the business agenda as well as "hospitality" and "movies." The latter are in the tradition of trade association films—for example, "The Poor Pay More" and "The Child Development Group of Mississippi." Kate Emerson, secretary of the National Coordinating Committee—NWRO's policy unit between conventions, composed of the national officers and one representative from each state with affiliated local welfare rights organizations—in a follow-up report on one convention even wrote of a decision that meetings would be better run if parliamentary procedure were more closely followed. While permanent chairman Carl Albert might have said the same thing after the Democratic National Convention of 1968, it is not likely that any such idea would be expressed by any leader of the Poor People's Campaign.

NWRO's history and style thus lend support to the proposition that formal organizations have certain unfailing characteristics whether they are businessmen in Rotary clubs, undergraduates in fraternities, physicians in medical associations, or welfare mothers in NWRO. The latter now has a written constitution, an annual convention, a regular publication. It sells its own distinctive jewelry and its own notepaper—"a lovely mother/child sketch on fine ivory stock, with matching envelopes, available at 10 sheets for $2.00, 25 for $4.00." A slate of national officers is headed by Mrs. Johnnie Tillmon, an AFDC mother of six from the Watts area of Los Angeles, and includes three vice-chairmen; corresponding, recording, and financial secretaries; a treasurer; a sergeant-at-arms; and a national coordinating committee. NWRO encourages organization of "friends support groups." It also has a kind of wholly owned, "nonpolitical" affiliate, the National Self Help Corporation (NASHCO), which accepts contracts and grants from federal agencies.

NWRO members are required to contribute $1 when they join; $1 a month thereafter is recommended as monthly dues. The current annual budget of the national organization is around $300,000, most of it raised by contributions solicited from churches, unions, social worker groups, and foundations. The Women's Division of the Methodist Church in reporting a $25,000 gift to NWRO to assist "its humanizing efforts" found it "cause for wonder and gratitude that through the support of an organization such as NWRO so many of these [welfare] mothers are finding a new self-esteem, a way out of a personal sense of depression, helplessness and discouragement."[10] Small amounts of money are also raised from sale of the newsletter, informational pamphlets, and other material.

Leaders are involved in conferences and meetings to the point where they have been known to find themselves with conflicting conference dates. Mrs. Tillmon, the national chairman, was unable to make NWRO's 1968 national conference, held in Lake Forest, Illinois, because she was a delegate representing poor people to the International Conference of Social Welfare in Helsinki, Finland, meeting at the same time. In a "memorandum to all affiliated groups," which sounded bureaucratic enough to have come out of HEW itself, Mrs. Tillmon delegated authority and announced appointments to committees of the conference.

Bureaucratic sounding or not, a group that began without nationally prominent leaders, with virtually no funds, with only a handful of preexisting local welfare client groups seeking a national affiliation, and with a constituency unaccustomed to joining anything or demanding anything is now a group whose leaders are known and consulted in the world of welfare policy. It has formulated immediate goals, a significant number of which have been recognized as valid by the courts and by administrative agencies, and it is independent.

10. United Methodist Church Joint Commission on Education and Cultivation, Board of Missions, *Response*, Vol. 1 (November 1969), p. 25.

Independence is especially highly valued. In choosing to play down disruptive tactics, at least for the time being, and putting first emphasis on building up a dues-paying organization, Wiley reflects a belief that support from nonwelfare groups cannot be relied upon in a confrontation with authority. He continues to look to extensive organization of the welfare constituency itself rather than to using small numbers of clients prematurely as leverage to move presumably sympathetic nonwelfare groups, most of whom he distrusts. "If we learned anything from the civil rights movement," Wiley believes, "it is that it is a mistake to think the liberals and moderates would grant what we are entitled to once the Negro stood up and demanded his rights." Even the assassination of Martin Luther King has led "to no significant mobilization by white America to rally to the support of basic issues for which Dr. King lived and died."[11]

Distrustful of support from most traditional liberal and moderate circles, Wiley did work for recognition from Dr. King when the Southern Christian Leadership Conference (SCLC) leader was alive. Shortly after the welfare rights organization was established as the Poverty/Rights Action Center, Wiley wrote King urging him to establish contact with the new movement. Wiley also chided King for his stated intention to lead a drive for a guaranteed annual income without taking into account "emerging local movements of welfare recipient groups in cities across the country, nor of the strategies or organization that these groups have developed for the purpose of pressing for substantial reform in the area of income maintenance."[12] In the letter Wiley expressed the hope that King would meet soon with the National Coordinating Committee to discuss national strategy. But no contact was made for more than a year. When it did come, Wiley maximized the value of formal recognition from Dr. King by devoting the entire February 23, 1968, NWRO newsletter to a so-called spectacular Chicago meeting at which NWRO "drove a solid organizational bargain with Martin Luther King," who was said to have apologized for not having been involved in the fight against the "anti-welfare bill" (the Social Security Amendments of 1967) and for poor communications with NWRO.

11. *Washington Post*, April 12, 1968.
12. Letter from George Wiley to Martin Luther King, Jr., Oct. 15, 1966; reprinted in Poverty/Rights Action Center Letter to Welfare Rights Leaders and Organizers, Oct. 31, 1966.

After Dr. King's assassination two months later, Wiley continued to seek an active role for his group in the Poor People's Campaign. Mrs. King led a Mother's Day March for welfare rights the day before Resurrection City opened. Wiley led several marches on the offices and later the apartment of Wilbur Mills. When the first of these resulted in eighteen arrests outside the Longworth House Office Building, SCLC officials, unhappy with that outcome so early in the effort, shunted Wiley and NWRO to a peripheral role. Inevitably, as the Poor People's Campaign took shape, there was a clear divergence of primary emphasis between its goals and NWRO's goals. NWRO continued its focus on welfare policy and welfare rights. The Campaign, feeling its way as it went along, found it more important or more expedient to cover an enormous area. When it did deal with specifics, it emphasized hunger and food relief programs rather than welfare rights. From then on, the different emphases of NWRO and the Poor People's Campaign meant that the two important client groups could not present a united front in pursuing changes in public relief policy. The more effective voice now is Wiley's because he leads a more tightly organized group and because his group confines itself to one area rather than dissipating limited strength across an impossibly broad sweep of issues. It is also more effective because there is still one leader, the founder, about whose competence to lead there is no doubt.

Organizational independence, Wiley's leadership, and the monolithic emphasis on welfare change became critical issues for NWRO around the time of its 1969 convention, when members of a black caucus in the Washington staff claimed that they were being manipulated by white people. For Wiley, it was a case of déjà vu. He had left CORE when it was transformed in 1966 into a black separatist group. Now NWRO's publications director, John Lewis, and his staff were both impatient with the absence of black emphasis and resentful of the leadership role of whites who served as Wiley's aides, as NWRO's legal staff, as chief accountant, as summer student project director, and as coordinators of activities among NWRO's local affiliates. Lewis's black caucus made its appeal to the recipients claiming that "at national headquarters, professionals have a paternalistic, frequently racist attitude about recipients, consistently making policy decisions the recipients themselves should have made."[13]

13. John Lewis, "Black Voices," *Washington Afro-American*, Aug. 19, 1969.

Wiley met the problem in the style of a high powered middle class administrator. He captured a critical black, Hulbert James, who had been director of the highly effective New York City affiliate before joining the Washington staff as director of field operations a few months earlier. With James dissociated from the black caucus and installed in a newly created position of director of operations, the next move was to reorganize the publications department out of existence, thereby eliminating seventeen black caucus members, including Lewis. Offered a job in public relations, Lewis declined and chose instead to try to appeal to the recipients by carrying the fight to the NWRO convention.

But an organization's professional leaders who have attended to the primary interests of the membership, including an interest in orderly, club-like proceedings, are not easily overturned. Lewis and five colleagues, "recently fired because of our criticism of NWRO's dominance by whites and whites with black faces"[14] went to the Detroit convention to pass out leaflets detailing the administrative jobs held by whites. The dissidents advised recipients that the only way to achieve recipient control would be to replace the top nonrecipient leaders, including Wiley, with recipient leaders "who would then move to eliminate the severe problems caused by white professional manipulators."[15] Although Lewis later attributed his failure at Detroit to the leadership's control of NWRO's important committees, including the committees on nominations and on the constitution, it was hard to make the case against "whites with black faces" when some unquestioned black leaders like Congressman John Conyers of Detroit and the no longer mild Whitney Young of the Urban League praised NWRO's leaders and their style. Echoing Wiley's stress on organization, Young—who told the delegates, "You may be the salvation of America"—said, "What makes America tick is organization. It only respects power organized. Once you get together then America and America's power structure is forced to recognize you."[16] And Conyers said, "Faced with a conservative and regressive Federal government, it is even more urgent that the poor of America follow the leadership of the NWRO in organizing to achieve dignity and political power."[17]

14. *Ibid.*, Aug. 30, 1969.
15. *Ibid.*
16. *Welfare Fighter*, September 1969, p. 4.
17. *Ibid.*, p. 3.

Hulbert James finished it off with an attack on Lewis and an affirmation of NWRO's preoccupation with the goal of adequate income. "There are those who will move to destroy and they will come not only from outside but unfortunately as we are now experiencing, some will come from within. . . . Our program is very simple. Poverty is the absence of the means to support oneself. Therefore our program asks for a Guaranteed Adequate Income for all Americans."[18] Lewis's call for recipient power might be more effective, of course, if it were being made by a recipient rather than by another staff professional. So far, recipients in NWRO remain less interested in either recipient power in the organization or black power in society than in Hulbert James's "very simple" program: specifically, a guaranteed annual income of $5,500 for a family of four.

Thanks to the Department of Labor's anxiety to get trainees enrolled in its work incentive (WIN) program, NWRO now has public financial support for the work of some of its field officers. A financial windfall came to the welfare rights movement when the National Self Help Corporation won a $434,930 contract in December 1968 from the Department of Labor to explore ways of involving welfare clients in leadership roles in the work incentive program, a program NWRO had fought in Congress and had characterized as slave labor. NASHCO is under contract to provide recipients with information about the WIN program, to provide feedback to Labor about WIN program operations, to train welfare clients to function as representatives of WIN trainees in dealing with sponsor agencies, and to provide technical assistance to groups to develop program components to be operated by recipients. The contract, which anticipated establishment of regional NASHCO offices to match Labor Department regional offices with a kind of counterbureaucracy, is differently perceived by the parties involved. Wiley claims that his group is only disseminating accurate information about the program and informing recipients of their rights, that the opposition to WIN is undiminished. At the Department of Labor the contract provides seeming assurance that for a relatively small sum the prospects for recruiting WIN trainees are enhanced. Taking a cue, perhaps, from no less an authority than Wilbur Cohen, who has expressed doubt about the probable success of "Barnard and Vassar girls" in involving welfare mothers in family planning programs, NASHCO also went after

18. *Ibid.*, p. 6.

$300,000 from HEW to create an information network to inform clients of relief benefits and services, but HEW shied away.

While some government officials and some welfare rights local groups questioned the wisdom of the Labor contract, the advantages for both sides are apparent.[19] Community action programs using indigenous workers in outreach efforts have had important successes in reaching hitherto unreachable groups. If the government can buy the support and the outreach efforts of the organized welfare leadership elite for half a million dollars, it will be a great bargain. If Wiley can sustain his organization with a great bloc of federal money, he can live to fight another fight. Unless the contract were to compel him to produce a particular number of trainees—an impossible and probably illegal condition—or unless NWRO were to go into open rebellion, there is no reason why Wiley should have rejected the federal gold. Claims of the Philadelphia WRO chapter that the contract involved selling out to the Establishment have more emotional than rational appeal. Rationally, the contract is a reasonable bargain for both sides, with whatever advantage there may be on Wiley's side. The money means more to him than to Labor, and the high-level recognition of NWRO's importance facilitates organizing. "NWRO got this contract because of our power," said an NWRO report, "and we are using it to protect and benefit our members."

Ironically, NWRO has had as much trouble as has the Department of Labor with its involvement in the WIN program. By the end of fiscal 1969 both were running behind, Labor in the development of work and training slots (70,000 rather than the 100,000 projected) and NWRO in organizing its regional evaluation units. While NWRO had held six regional meetings to discuss the program with recipients, only two (Kansas City and New York) of eight planned area units were then operating. The first to be established, in Kansas City, Kansas, was run by Robert Agard, director of the Kansas City Welfare Rights Organization, with a budget of $38,500 for the last nine months of calendar 1969. Agard's view of the arrangement was that while NWRO had been critical of WIN, "we have never tried to destroy the program but to work for its improvement. This grant has given us a chance to accomplish something."[20]

19. For an example of congressional criticism, see *Congressional Record*, daily ed., Aug. 13, 1969, p. E7033; an account of criticism from the Philadelphia WRO chapter is in *New York Times*, May 29, 1969.

20. *Kansas City Times*, July 16, 1969.

Welfare Rights in Action in New York City

At an earlier time, taking the Department of Labor's money to help make the work incentive program work could easily have compromised NWRO's position with its members because it might have appeared that the organization could exist only as a company union. By early 1969, however, this was not a problem. NWRO had shown itself to be skillful and effective in pushing its cause in cities around the country. Wiley and his local leaders had built up an image militant enough that charges of selling out simply seemed absurd. A likelier explanation was that Wiley had outfoxed the federal bureaucracy. Moreover, bringing Hulbert James into the national office helped sustain that explanation because James had led a tough New York City welfare rights effort that indicated no disposition to avoid a confrontation. In fact, the New York group served as an example for welfare officials there and around the country of just how troublesome a welfare rights organization could be.

In any consideration of welfare reform, it is difficult to overestimate the budgetary or the political consequences nationally of New York City's welfare problem. What nearly everyone in Washington reads is not the Philadelphia *Bulletin* but the *New York Times*. What happens in that city affects the nation. "Politics is where the millions are," it has been said, "not the hundreds, not the thousands, but the millions." Welfare in New York City qualifies. Since January 1969 a million people have been on New York City's public assistance rolls, three-fourths of them on AFDC. Comprising one-tenth of the city's population, AFDC recipients represent a potential political bloc that may be larger than any other economically homogeneous group of people with a common interest in a public program. Because many clients are on and off the relief rolls in cycles, some additional number that is not less than 150,000 has been on public assistance recently and will probably again be on public assistance soon, thus adding to the total size of the city's current relief constituency.

While there is dispute between leaders of the city's Human Resources Administration (HRA) and their critics about the probable future growth pattern, the "highly tentative" estimate made by HRA is that 1.45 million persons constitute New York City's total welfare universe, and that 1.3 million could be expected to be on the rolls in 1970, with the remaining 150,000 too ignorant or too proud ever to apply. Professor Richard Cloward, however, sees an additional 600,000 persons in low income, employed-worker families as eligible for wage supplements under the nonfederally aided general assistance program. An acerbic, vocal labor critic of the city's "permissive" administration of welfare, Nicholas Kisburg, legislative director of the Teamster's Joint Council, views the welfare group as constituting a rapidly expanding universe, and, like Cloward, regards the HRA projection as too conservative.

What is certain is that the city proposed a welfare budget of $1.733 billion for public assistance costs in 1969–70, up from $412.3 million for fiscal 1963 and up from $1.34 billion in 1968–69. In 1969–70, $756.5 million was tagged for AFDC. Even after reductions in benefit amounts were mandated by the state legislature, welfare costs—the largest single city expenditure item—accounted for more than one-quarter of the total city budget, substantially exceeding the portion allotted to education (26.6 percent to 21.4).

It is also certain that there has been a pattern of growth in the city's relief rolls in recent years that can only be described as explosive. In December 1962, public assistance recipients in New York City totaled 365,000. By 1965 the total was up to 500,000; in mid-1968 it was 875,000—100,000 higher than had been forecast a year earlier. The recipient total reached 1 million coincident roughly with President Nixon's inauguration; this was almost six months before the 1 million mark had been projected. In response to a May 1968 request by five New York City congressmen, a federal review of public assistance in the city was agreed to by HEW in October. Possibly ineligible recipients, excessive payments, the rapidity of the rise in costs and numbers, and city welfare department efforts to move employable recipients to self-support were the major areas of federal study. Ineligible clients and both overpayments and underpayments were found. The precise percentages and significance of the findings were subjects of dispute between federal and city officials.[21] What was not disputed was the federal prediction of a further sharp rise in AFDC cases during the early 1970s attribu-

21. *Report of Findings of Special Review of Aid to Families with Dependent Children in New York City*, transmitted by the U.S. Department of Health, Education, and Welfare and the New York State Department of Social Services to the House Committee on Ways and Means, 91 Cong. 1 sess. (1969), esp. pp. 161–93. See also *Report by the Comptroller General of the United States on Monitoring of Special Review of Aid to Families with Dependent Children in New York City*, transmitted to House Committee on Ways and Means, 91 Cong. 1 sess. (1969), esp. pp. 17–43; for reactions of city officials, see *New York Times*, Sept. 25, 1969.

table to the continuing increase in the city's low income Negro and Puerto Rican population. Other, more subtle items that should have been on the federal study agenda, but were not, are caseworker receptivity to client demands and activities of the organized client group that pursued a strategy of pressure to the point of disruption and to the edge of violence.

The now firmly established New York Citywide Coordinating Committee of Welfare Groups has constantly challenged New York's welfare system since the welfare rights movement began. Hulbert James, its original leader, has explained, "The system is vulnerable and we have really not exploited that. A lot of things, way short of guns, can work." In testing the system's vulnerability in New York City, James first led an extremely successful campaign to secure special cash grants for clients, next fought a change the city instituted because of the campaign's success, then threatened an upset of some of New York's retail department store business as part of an NWRO program to force those stores to open charge accounts for welfare clients. Directing the activities of about a hundred neighborhood based groups, James did so well in New York that at the time he joined NWRO, the New York Coordinating Committee almost overshadowed the national organization.

Special grants

A case in point is the great drive in the spring of 1968 for payment of special grants. New York's own rules—the State Code, the City Public Assistance Handbook, and city administrative policies—for years provided for the issuance of special cash grants to meet minimum standard nonrecurring needs for such things as furniture, household equipment, and children's school graduation expenses. This provision was not called to the attention of clients, few of whom apparently were either aware of it or courageous enough to demand that it be honored.

In the spring of 1968 the welfare rights organization undertook a campaign to compel the city's welfare administration to make such grants routine rather than exceptional. Because a large element of discretion is involved in determining, for example, whether an existing piece of furniture is or is not still usable, or whether a graduation dress must be a new dress or can be a hand-me-down, sympathetic caseworkers could help to control total special grant costs. In addition, if the workers followed the American Legion service officer model and familiarized both themselves and their clients with potential benefits, grants could be expected to be higher than if awareness were solely a client responsibility. When the Citywide Coordinating Committee of Welfare Groups began its campaign, the environment was ideal. The committee undertook to alert clients to their special grants rights. In turn, large numbers of workers who were both sympathetic to the client cause and also involved in their own labor dispute with the city were willing to go through the elaborate paperwork necessary and to put in the extra hours required to keep the papers moving for the bulging number of applicants. The result was to throw the city's welfare program into a state of crisis and near chaos.

In April 1967, a year before the drive began, $3.08 million in grants had been made; in June, when half the city's caseworkers were on strike for part of the month, the figure was $3.17 million. The monthly average through all of 1967 was $3.85 million. In April 1968, when the client drive started, special grants totaled $8.07 million; in May they increased further to $11.57 million. By June, more than $13 million was paid out in special grants based on such allowances as $50 for a new crib for every child under three years old, $8 for a couch cover for each couch, $25 for a boy's winter coat, $3.90 for a drying rack. Payments exceeding $350 were not unusual, some were more than $1,000. As the city's costs and consternation grew, so did publicity about the campaign, which came to include sit-ins in welfare centers by recipients whose grant applications were backlogged. Success begat success and heretofore nonmilitant clients began to inquire about special grants.

Mayor Lindsay, Human Resources Administrator Mitchell Ginsberg, and Social Services Commissioner Jack Goldberg were in the kind of a bind known only to public administrators who can neither, as a practical matter, administer a policy according to law nor, as a matter of conscience, ignore the law. With no end to the legitimate escalation of special grants costs, city, state, and federal administrators agreed to a critically important shift in the theory under which New York's liberal welfare program had functioned. The special grants, which, in effect, were an open-end authorization to spend whatever total amount might be required to meet minimum standards, were abandoned at the end of August 1968 in favor of a so-called simplified payments system. Under the latter, special grants would be paid on a flat sum basis of $100 per year per recipient to cover the variety of needs that had been met by special grants. A fixed figure of $100 per client meant that the open-end authorization was now closed off. Money would not be made available according to special need; special need would have to accommodate itself to the $100 fixed annual grant.

The official explanation for the change of course denied that economy was its cause, instead emphasizing three positive virtues in the new flat grant arrangement: it would eliminate the need for clients to demean themselves by identifying their expected use of special grants; it would eliminate caseworker discretion; it would equalize special benefits between clients who pushed for them aggressively and clients who out of ignorance or cowardice did not. But only the campaign of the organized welfare rights groups apparently set the administrators involved to thinking about inequities between active and passive clients. In a classic pattern, an employer confronted by a growing labor union movement in his shop may announce a shopwide wage increase hoping to discourage the union's growth by making it no less advantageous to stay out of the union than to join. That employer is also likely to express concern about equity for his loyal, nonunion workers; forestalling probable higher demands by the union is not likely to be an acknowledged purpose. So it was with New York City and its organized relief clients who, like organized labor, had protective legislation on their side.

The "union" was not disposed to accept this act of beneficence, certainly not at the $100-per-year level. Demonstrations, mass rushes against police barricades, sit-ins, and acts of vandalism became commonplace protest devices. At least two-thirds of the city's thirty-eight welfare centers reported protest incidents two days after the flat grant plan was announced. The caseworkers' Social Service Employees' Union issued a statement supporting both the end of discretionary grants and the automatic extension of grants to passive clients, yet characterizing the $100 annual figure as "so inadequate that it will probably do as much harm as good."

When protests turned destructive at several welfare centers—property destruction, telephones torn from the walls, papers scattered—no staff member could be found to lodge a complaint. A July memorandum on protest behavior from Commissioner Goldberg had made entering a complaint optional with welfare staff and supervisors. Arrest complaints were mandatory for special officers assigned to the centers, but, when the flat grant protests erupted, the special officers were themselves engaged in a slow-down growing out of a dispute with the city over their role in the welfare department. After a week of disorder and the issuance of revised orders by Mayor Lindsay concerning arrests at welfare centers, two clients were arrested. Thirty-four social workers were also arrested for sitting on the sidewalk in front of the City Social Service Department to protest the flat grant system's inadequacies. Disorders subsided as the weather began to turn colder, but then James shifted to a winter campaign of harassment designed to yield charge accounts in department stores for relief clients and to shame middle class Christmas shoppers by making them aware of the welfare population.

Retail Credit

James's department store program had unmistakable marks of the style of Saul Alinsky, America's professional radical who, in the depression era, became the first specialist in the art of organizing poor people to irritate the more affluent.[22] That style is typified by an Alinsky plan developed in 1966 when the Council of Churches of Oakland, California, considered inviting him to organize their poor. Responding that Oakland's problem was that its power structure was unaware of the city's Negroes, he mused publicly about a "watermelon march" and a "Sunday walk" as a way of creating awareness. Several hundred Negroes dressed in coveralls would carry watermelons in a march from City Hall to the Oakland Tribune, published by William Knowland, the former Republican leader of the United States Senate. Other elegantly dressed Negroes would take a Sunday walk through the best white neighborhoods. The goal of this endeavor would be to move Negroes into places where, in Alinsky's words, the "white establishment has built its finest amenities," with the anticipated result that the "white people will move out and you've got their goodies."[23]

For Alinsky's watermelon march, Hulbert James substituted the idea of welfare group participation in Macy's Thanksgiving Day parade, suggesting the addition of a mule-drawn cart. He spoke of a widespread walk-in campaign for credit at New York's department stores during the Christmas shopping season. The latter was no idle threat in that a rela-

22. Saul Alinsky, Reveille for Radicals (University of Chicago Press, 1946); Charles Silberman, Crisis in Black and White (Random House, 1964), pp. 321–28; Stephen C. Rose, "Saul Alinsky and His Critics," Christianity and Crisis, Vol. 24 (July 20, 1964), pp. 143–52; Marion K. Sanders, "The Professional Radical: Conversations with Saul Alinsky," Harper's, Vol. 230 (June 1965), pp. 37–47, and "A Professional Radical Moves in on Rochester: Conversations with Saul Alinsky, Part II," Vol. 231 (July 1965), pp. 52–59.

23. "Alinsky and Oakland," New Republic, Vol. 154 (May 21, 1966), p. 8.

tively small number of determined women could clog the check-out counters of busy stores. A day or two before James's announcement, one hundred and fifty welfare mothers had actually brought hundreds of items to be checked out at the huge Korvette store in Brooklyn and demanded credit. Any systematic extension of such activity could discourage impatient middle class shoppers who demand rapid check-out service. On the other hand, efforts by retailers to enjoin or otherwise repress this kind of welfare protest could only result in undesirable publicity and the probable antipathy of most of the city's black residents along with that of substantial numbers of sympathetic whites.

Of course, James was not necessarily anticipating that immediate credit would actually be furnished welfare clients any more than Alinsky was necessarily anticipating that a watermelon march would instantly change society in Oakland. In both cases the goal was to show what a miltant group could do on its own behalf in its own area. There was a demonstration at the Macy parade, resulting in four arrests, but the Christmas shopping disruption program never really took hold. Like Alinsky's watermelon march, it was more effective to muse about it to the press, even to formulate a plan to make it operational, than to dissipate strength in real efforts to persuade welfare mothers to participate. For one thing, department store harassment has no direct link to a larger relief check. Protests at welfare centers, picketing City Hall, sitting in at congressional hearings could conceivably directly affect decision makers with control over definition and delivery of benefits. Irritating the middle class shopper and unnerving the managers of New York's department stores could not be directly related to achieving improvements in welfare benefits. Moreover, if goals of the "instant credit" effort were instantly accomplished, the achievement could be self-defeating. Unscreened low income clients using such credit might find themselves unable to meet their payments. That result in a large number of cases would furnish support to opponents of cash payments in relief and would also further disturb the clients themselves. Whether the Citywide Coordinating Committee leaders actually meant to implement the shopping disruption plan is uncertain; it is certain that it did not come to much. It did not come to much because there was no clear payoff for the rank and file of the client population, and even the militant segment of the rank and file organized in the welfare rights groups respond best to a rational link between strategy, tactics, and welfare benefits.

The potential of the shopping disruption idea was not lost on New York City's retail leaders, however, nor was the importance of specific, tangible benefits attributable to the coordinating committee lost on James. Quiet negotiations continued, and by the spring of 1969 James could announce a breakthrough: three of the city's retail giants— Gimbel's, Abraham and Straus, and Korvette's—agreed to extend credit to welfare clients. Ironically, many more New York clients participated in the demand for credit than have subsequently applied for credit. By May 1970, Korvette's had not followed through with a specific plan; Gimbel's, however, had a plan but not a single applicant, and Abraham and Straus had received and accepted only nine applications. Welfare rights leaders in New York City clearly thought it more important to win in principle than to participate in the details of arranging individual charge accounts. And without that participation, nothing happened.

Nonetheless, organization and intervention by the welfare rights organization did have an important symbolic payoff. What clients had not been able or did not know enough to get by themselves, and what the welfare bureaucracy had not pursued on clients' behalf, the New York City welfare rights group could say it accomplished for them. Like special grants, access to retail credit was achieved by diligent attention to, and application of, Saul Alinsky's rule that "the only way to upset the power structure is to goad them, confuse them, irritate them, and most of all, make them live by their own rules. If you make them live by their own rules, you'll destroy them."[24] The major breakthroughs in welfare rights in New York and nationally have come from observing this bit of vintage Alinsky philosophy.

A Sympathetic Bureaucracy

Another reason for the effectiveness of the New York Coordinating Committee is that it knows and takes advantage of the fact that New York's welfare administrators and Mayor John Lindsay are embarrassed by the welfare system as a matter of intellectual conviction even without client protest. The city's social services commissioner, Jack Goldberg, acknowledged in June 1968 that AFDC allowances failed to meet any reasonable test of real living costs. Mitchell Ginsberg, for four

24. Patrick Anderson, "Making Trouble Is Alinsky's Business," *New York Times Magazine*, Oct. 9, 1966, p. 28.

years Lindsay's human resources administrator, is one of the most eloquent critics in the country of a relief system he describes as "bankrupt." Ginsberg is the author of the Kerner Commission's characterization of the system as one designed to save money rather than people
but that winds up saving neither. Mayor Lindsay's confidence in Ginsberg's assessment is complete. When protest occurs, therefore, the city's
leaders sympathetically put up with a good deal of harassment and
inconvenience.

New York City's public relief program operates in an atmosphere of
caseworker militancy on social issues. On the issue of relief itself, the
caseworkers exacerbate an already volatile situation. They struck for
twenty-eight days in 1965 and struck again twice in 1967 not only over
their own salaries but also over so-called professional demands that the
union claimed were needed to improve the services of the city Welfare
Department. These demands included such proposals as a 25 percent
increase in client budgets, twice yearly automatic clothing grants, and
allowances for a telephone for every client family. During the first of the
1967 strikes, a brief three-day affair in January, vandalism—cutting telephone wires and scattering clients' case records and financial data cards
—occurred in half of the city's thirty-two welfare centers. Some union
people regarded the destruction as deliberate symbolism: those involved
in destruction of the files, it was said, were showing a desire to destroy
the bureaucratic trappings of the relief system. Then-Commissioner (of
Social Services) Ginsberg, who has had plenty of criticisms to make of
the system, viewed the vandalism as immature behavior. "I would have
expected them to be more grown up," he said, declining to identify
"them" explicitly. For their part, union spokesmen, without admitting
that strikers were responsible, called vandalism misguided since "that is
not the way to win a strike." Of course, this was no ordinary strike, because it involved issues of client benefits as well as issues of caseworker
salaries and benefits. Ultimately, impartial fact-finding recommendations on caseworker salaries were acceptable to both sides, but no agreement could be reached on the so-called professional issues in dispute.

The relief system itself and the unwillingness of a large fraction of
the union membership to tolerate the system without protest then resulted in the second stage of the 1967 dispute: a work stoppage by more
than half of the city's caseworkers over a period of six weeks. Following
the traditional script in labor disputes, the striking employees insisted
that the Welfare Department was unable to carry on its normal busi-

ness. The department, acknowledging that it could not provide its usual full range of services, claimed that basic services were continuing and all emergencies were being met. What is certain is that the system did not break down; checks went out. Some clients picketed with the strikers, some were indifferent to the dispute, some lost patience with the strikers, blaming them for long waits in welfare offices and for delays in getting checks.

During the six weeks of the strike, each of the three principal groups involved—the city, the union, and the coordinating committee of welfare groups—moved cautiously to avoid driving the other two into an alliance that would have made its own position untenable. If the organized clients had moved to full-scale support of the caseworkers, the city's argument that the professional issues were not properly subject to negotiation in a labor contract would have become irrelevant. The strike could then have been interpreted by the union to the public as a sympathy strike by caseworkers in support of demands that clients legitimately enough could make and that uncowed clients were actually making.

In their efforts at least to keep the caseworker and client groups apart and at best to bring the clients to the side of the city administration in deploring the strike, both Mitchell Ginsberg and Mayor Lindsay accused the union of "exploitation" of the clients in order to meet union objectives. It is not an easy argument to accept. The caseworker salary issue had already been resolved by acceptance by both parties of the mediator's recommendation. If the striking workers were exploiting the clients, it could not have been for the purpose of improving caseworkers' salaries. Lindsay defined the problem more accurately when he said "the dispute is over who is going to run the Welfare Department." The mayor knew that whoever ran the welfare program, it would have deficiencies. Admitting that much, however, he could not govern New York City and allow either workers or clients to run the program any more than he could allow the schoolteachers to run the school system when that became an issue. To avoid loss of control, Lindsay and Ginsberg concentrated on deterring a worker-client alliance.

The welfare rights organization faced its own dilemma. On the one hand, in parts of the welfare world, caseworkers are considered the natural enemies of clients. In addition, the welfare rights philosophy emphasizes maintaining independence of middle class, liberal sympathizers who are considered undependable in times of real crisis. On the other hand, it was clearly unthinkable that the welfare coordinating committee could condemn the announced goals of the caseworkers. The result was that client groups stayed uninvolved because they could not afford to tie themselves to either side. Part way through the strike Mrs. Beulah Sanders, chairman of the Citywide Coordinating Committee, issued a neutral statement on behalf of eighty local recipient groups calling for a speedy settlement by mediation, factfinding, or any other effective method.

The caseworkers, for their part, were not in the position of sanitation-men who could be indifferent to client inconvenience or client attitudes. Workers who claimed to empathize with their clients supposedly were striking to achieve professional goals that would benefit clients. If client organizations were driven to support of the city, the grounds for the strike would be undermined. Accordingly the union played a careful game, showing concern for client suffering and insisting that the blame for the strike belonged to an intransigent city that defended unconscionable policies and practices but failed to meet an obligation to help its welfare poor. "We have no stake in the status quo in the department, which has had few successes and many failures," said Judith Mage, then president of the Social Service Employees' Union.

Both sides ultimately agreed to continue in disagreement and to invite a mediator to consider whether the disputed issues could usefully be submitted to further mediation. One important effect of the six-week stoppage was to permit socially conscious young caseworkers in the New York City Welfare Department to purge themselves of guilt they felt for being parties to a demeaning and inadequate relief system. Another effect, however, was to show that about half of the city's more than six thousand public assistance workers would make a prolonged personal sacrifice to fight the system. Any organized client action might expect a sympathetic response from those workers. That knowledge, as we have seen, was put to use by Hulbert James in the drive for payment of special grants. Right or wrong, it is useful to have specific demands and a sympathetic bureaucracy.

Poor People's Campaign

Not all of the poor in the Poor People's Campaign of 1968—the most dramatic and the best publicized protest against economic inequality in America since the bonus march and the sit-down strikes of the depression era—were public relief clients, and not all of the demands of the Poor People's Campaign related directly to public relief. But the campaigners were all in the class who could have been public relief clients and many of their demands affected the lot of all public relief clients. The Poor People's Campaign swallowed up the problems of public relief together with a score of other issues and fused them into a seemingly inchoate but well understood indictment of the American social system as indifferent to the wretched. To be sure, some of the wretched needed help other than better welfare benefits. But had there been an adequate system of public relief in America in 1968, there would have been no five-week Poor People's encampment across from the Lincoln Memorial in Resurrection City.

Inchoate as its protest appeared, and while seeking welfare improvement writ large, the 1968 Poor People's Campaign also came to grips with plenty of details—too many. One major segment of the detailed demands did deal with HEW's techniques of delivering cash relief, but the inadequacy of food relief programs became a principal specific focus of the campaign, and the Department of Agriculture's food relief attitude and apparatus became a principal point of attack. On top of that, however, wide-ranging demands—fifty-seven pages of them—were also made on the Departments of Justice, Labor, Housing and Urban Development, State, and Interior, and on the Office of Economic Opportunity.[25] And it was indicative of the problems of the Poor People's Campaign that it could produce fifty-seven pages of demands— ranging from a call to HEW to give pregnant women priority in health programs to a call to the State Department to sever ties to Portugal— while its nominal leader, the Reverend Ralph Abernathy, could say, "When it comes to specific legislation, this is not our job. If the leaders of this country have enough sense to put a man on the moon, they have enough sense to put an end to poverty in this country."

The simultaneous vagueness and specificity of the campaign stemmed from the dilemma posed by Martin Luther King's assassination and the subsequent civil disorders around the country, including Washington. After King's death, there was talk in and out of Congress about the need to call off the Poor People's March to avoid further violence and

25. "Statements of Demands for Rights of the Poor . . . May 1, 1968." The statements were prepared by the Women's International League for Peace and Freedom and the Friends' Committee on National Legislation.

riots. No one in the Southern Christian Leadership Conference, the argument ran, could fill King's shoes and effectively control the demonstration. The quandary facing SCLC was apparent: if they did not come to Washington, they would both renege on Dr. King's plan and seemingly plead guilty to charges of disorganization and lack of leadership; if they came and the campaign got out of hand, they would suffer greater losses than any gains they might achieve. Yet it was also true that some of the power of the campaign lay in its potential for violence. After the decision to come to Washington was made, SCLC leaders, themselves of differing degrees of militancy, continued to be confronted with this same problem. If they let the campaign become too peaceful and predictable—making clear just what their goals were and when they would leave—they ran the risk of being taken lightly. If their tactics threatened real disruption and their goals remained too vague and unspecified, however, they ran the risk of losing much of the support and sympathy they did have.

As it worked out, the campaign became two headed. Perhaps the best description was that of a National Welfare Rights Organization worker who referred to the Poor People as "so untogether." Through Ralph Abernathy, the Poor People's Campaign embraced nonviolent demonstrations and relatively violent rhetoric which shunned specifics in favor of veiled threats and vaguely stated goals. Through a young, black civil rights lawyer—Marian Wright, formerly NAACP Legal Defense and Educational Fund representative in Jackson, Mississippi—it produced a great volume of less well publicized but specific demands on the federal administration. From mid-May when the poor began arriving in Washington until June 12 when Abernathy issued an eight-page list of campaign goals, SCLC officials spoke with many voices about why they were there. Most of those voices did better in decrying the injustices of the American system and describing the lengths to which the speakers would go to reform the system than they did in making clear just what would constitute such reforms. This face of the campaign suggested that it was its job to make visible the needs and problems of the poor, while it was the job of Congress and the nation generally to find ways of meeting those needs and problems.

In early speeches Reverend Abernathy spoke of the campaign as an attempt to arouse the conscience of the nation to the tragedy of America. Nonviolence would be pursued but violence was possible. "If Congress and the Nation do not respond to the Poor People's Campaign then the responsibility is on their shoulders."[26] The marchers might stay five years; in any event, "we are going to stay down here with or without a permit until we change Congress because Congress isn't going to change us."[27] And on Solidarity Day, just a few days before Resurrection City was to be shut down, Abernathy said that the poor would stay until "justice rolls out of the halls of Congress, and righteousness falls from the Administration."[28]

There was no shortage of rhetoric, of ambiguity, or of internal disputes. For all of that, another face of the Poor People's Campaign presented specific recurring themes that were the subjects of communication between federal officials at very high levels and campaign spokesmen. Jobs and an adequate income were often referred to. Demands were made for repeal of the AFDC freeze and compulsory work provisions of the 1967 Social Security Amendments as well as for improvements in the federal feeding programs. At one point, Abernathy said that hunger and the lack of jobs were the chief issues of the Poor People.[29] The following day he added housing to his list of top priority items. Later, Abernathy said the Poor People's protest would continue until Congress met the protest's immediate goals, which included distribution of more food to the needy, jobs, and a guaranteed income for unemployables.[30]

But the campaign could not continue and that was its real weakness. The coercive style adopted—an influx of people and their encampment at Resurrection City—could not be prolonged until the fight was won. Money, morale, peacekeeping, sanitation, and boredom all became problems for the Poor People, who could not disperse to their homes and reassemble a day or a week later. The phenomenon of the nonviolent march on Washington has its strength in providing inspiration for people to stay with a fight which is likely to be prolonged. It is not an effective way to achieve an immediate goal because the lawgivers resist appearing to give in under pressure. When the march technique is accompanied by civil disobedience, it can also serve as a threat: if there

26. *Washington Post*, May 23, 1968.
27. *Ibid.*, May 31, 1968.
28. *Ibid.*, June 20, 1968.
29. *Ibid.*, May 28, 1968.
30. Press release, "Statement of Rev. Ralph David Abernathy on Goals of Poor People's Campaign," June 11, 1968; "Top Priority Goals of Poor People's Campaign," June 17, 1968.

is no progress, there will be further disobedience and inconvenience. In this case, however, all the inconvenience was to the Poor People themselves, and soon the nonpoor lost interest.

The Poor People's Campaign never made the costs of official inaction very high. It gave signs of being satisfied to exchange letters with cabinet secretaries for an indefinite period.[31] It issued no ultimatums with dates attached, yet time was not on the side of the campaign. It did not escalate its tactics of disobedience, but adjusted them downwards. A far cry from early talk of a sit-in at the Bethesda (Maryland) Naval Hospital, the most extreme action actually taken was refusal to pay a cafeteria bill at the Department of Agriculture—and even that was softened when Dr. Abernathy returned twenty-four hours later and paid. And while Hosea Williams, one of the campaign's leaders, threatened one Sunday that "the picnic is over . . . I'm telling you that Monday we're going to start demonstrations that the folks on Capitol Hill won't be able to stand,"[32] when Monday came, there was nothing new. Three Mondays later, to everyone's relief, Resurrection City was shut down.

The so-called Phase Two of the campaign, in the spring of 1969, never came to anything. The Poor People's Campaign had no threats left to make, so public officials could take it as part of the routine. The Poor People's Campaign had no achievements to point to, so its own constituents found it hard to maintain interest. The field was left for George Wiley.

31. There are lengthy exchanges, for example, with the secretary of health, education, and welfare who wrote Rev. Abernathy on May 25 and June 18, 1968, and to whom Rev. Abernathy wrote on June 12, 1968; with the attorney general who wrote May 22 and June 18, 1968, and to whom Rev. Abernathy wrote June 13, 1968; with the secretary of agriculture who wrote May 23 and June 14, 1968, and to whom Rev. Abernathy wrote on June 12, 1968. Exchanges of letters also took place with the secretary of state, the secretary of labor, the secretary of the interior, and the director of the Office of Economic Opportunity. All of the federal officials' letters were conciliatory and very detailed, giving evidence of considerable staff work. Most of this activity was carried on for the Poor People's Campaign by Marian Wright, the former Mississippi NAACP counsel. Miss Wright has also been credited by Andrew Young, SCLC vice president, as an originator of the idea of bringing a nonviolent demonstration to the North. James R. McGraw, "Massive Change Through Nonviolent Demonstrations or Destruction Through Riots?" An Interview with Andrew J. Young, *Christianity and Crisis*, Vol. 27 (Jan. 22, 1968), pp. 324–30.

32. *Washington Post*, June 3, 1968.

Theory and Strategy

In the whole welfare policy world, Wiley and NWRO represent minimum feasible participation. With over two million adult recipients of AFDC and more than three-quarters of a million adult recipients of general assistance, Wiley's National Welfare Rights Organization has enrolled what can only be called a trace—between 1 and 2 percent of the total. But it is some client participation where before there was none. The organization's impact on the national level is small; Wiley acknowledges that it has no strength in Congress. Over NWRO's insistent protests, the welfare titles of the 1967 Social Security Amendments were passed. Administrative improvements in welfare application and appeals procedures were announced late in 1968, but those changes were in the mill—that is, Secretary of HEW Wilbur Cohen's mind— long before Wiley came on the scene. Even if NWRO's efforts and the Poor People's Campaign of 1968 highlighted the desirability of the procedural changes, it was the special freedom to effect reform that belongs to a lame duck department head that controlled their timing.

NWRO's practical accomplishments on the local level are more impressive because they have led to increasing pressure on Washington from concerned local leaders. Strategy and tactics pursued on the local level are drawn less from the expressed position of NWRO's original theoretician, Richard Cloward of the Columbia University School of Social Work, and Cloward's recent collaborator, Frances Fox Piven, and more from the sentiments of Saul Alinsky. As NWRO has developed, it appears to have found Cloward's views less relevant than they were at the beginning.

Cloward and Piven, who tend to have less patience than either Wiley or Alinsky, argue the best way for the poor to get something more from the government is to disrupt it. They do not think the poor are likely to improve their situation through the ballot box because they are a weak minority. Similarly, they are critical of public programs for failing to bring about significant changes in economic arrangements while serving to distract the poor from the basic issues and injustices confronting them. The poor, it is argued, should compel public action by creating crises:

When crisis occurs, many groups are aroused; they view disorder as a failure of governmental responsibility and demand measures (whether concessions or repression) to restore order. Crisis thus has a potential political force far greater than the number of citizens, organized or not, who participate in the disruptive action itself.[33]

Crisis strategy banks on the supposition that government will respond to welfare crises with concessions and not repression. The ultimate concession sought is a guaranteed annual income. Overloading of the welfare rolls with all the eligible poor not currently on them is the crisis prescribed. Based on an estimate that for each one of the nine million welfare recipients there is another person qualified to receive benefits who does not, it is a fair bet that if a substantial fraction of these qualified nonrecipients applied for assistance, fiscal and political crises would result—particularly in large cities. And the only way to alleviate such a crisis—a crisis "which would exacerbate strains among the Negro and white working-class and middle-class elements in the urban Democratic coalition"—would be for the federal government to replace the public welfare system with a more equitable and less tyrannical guaranteed annual income.[34]

The strategy would offer immediate economic benefits to poor people on and off welfare. It would avoid some of the tedious organizational work. "Mass influence in this case stems from the consumption of benefits and does not require that large groups of people be involved in regular organizational roles."[35] The poor will have to do little more than claim lawful benefits. They will be able to yield mass influence without mass participation. Moreover, the plan offers incentives that appeal to both poor whites and blacks and provides them with a common cause, which Cloward and Piven stress has not been true of civil rights objectives of integrated housing, schools, or jobs.[36] Wiley does adhere to the common cause notion as evidenced by his rejection of NWRO's black caucus, but he rejects bypassing the organizational activity. He is, it may be, less of a gambling man than is Cloward or he may believe that association has advantages for welfare clients even without forcing policy changes.

The unexpressed difference between Cloward and Piven, on the one

33. Richard Cloward and Frances Piven, "Rent Strike: Disrupting the Slum System," *New Republic*, Vol. 157 (Dec. 2, 1967), p. 13.

34. Eli E. Cohen, moderator, "Strategy of Crisis: A Dialogue," *American Child*, Vol. 48 (Summer 1966), p. 21.

35. Richard Cloward and Frances Piven, "The Weight of the Poor: A Strategy to End Poverty," *Nation*, Vol. 202 (May 2, 1966), p. 514.

36. *Ibid.*, pp. 513–14.

hand, and Wiley, on the other, is not over the assumption that glut-
ting the welfare rolls will result in federal intervention and a guaranteed
annual income. The real difficulty is that Cloward and Piven do not
explain how to get all the eligible poor people on the rolls. They say
their theory offers mass benefits without mass participation but they
leave unanswered the crucial question: how to find, motivate, and
sustain these people while they are getting onto the rolls. And here
George Wiley responds, "Organize." While he shares Cloward's interest in long-range reform, Wiley in action concentrates on helping
those already on the rolls to get the benefits legally assured, and, when
the benefits are denied, to seek fair hearings.

Saul Alinsky's major weakness as a radical has been said to be his
concern with specific and immediate activity in a small geographic
area.[37] But this is the very thing that makes an adaptation of the Alinsky method ideal for welfare clients' organizations. The adaptation involves a switch from shaking up everything in a small geographic area
to shaking up an entire community or city on a single issue—in this
case, welfare. New York City's welfare power structure was never more
goaded, confused, irritated, and made to live by its own rules than during the drive for payment of special grants authorized under law but
never systematically demanded before the client group was moved from
apathy to concerted action. Alinsky's strategy is also faulted for not
being radical enough—it offers no basic, critical analysis of American
society, advocates no large-scale institutional changes, and involves no
national program. Frank Riessman, for example, complains that Alinsky's tactics call for action without direction and protest without a
program and ultimately wind up being "non-therapeutic."[38] It is true
that Alinsky does not really try to change the system so much as he
tries to help the poor to master the system and to succeed within it.
Welfare clients are satisfied with this limited objective.

Alinsky's goals vary with his clientele. His efforts are local in scope,
not national. He is not doctrinaire and his tactics are improvised. He
relies heavily on the technique of embarrassment and he places emphasis on the poor in a city or neighborhood organizing themselves. Even
if unable to move more than a fraction of his potential clientele—in his
most successful organizing effort, the Woodlawn organization in Chi-

37. Frank Riessman, "The Myth of Saul Alinsky," *Dissent*, Vol. 14 (July–August
1967), pp. 469–78.
38. *Ibid.*

cago, Alinsky was able to involve only 2 or 3 percent of the people living there—Alinsky finds ways for them to act in their own self-interest. Organized welfare groups in American cities have only been able to involve a tiny fraction of the huge welfare population. But they have combined Alinsky's idea of action in their own self-interest with Wiley's stress on organizing.

New York's Citywide Coordinating Committee of Welfare Groups owes whatever success it has had to its adoption of the Alinsky emphasis on a "specific, immediate, and practical" program and of his injunction to make the power structure "live by their own rules." But it has not lost sight of Wiley's concern for maximizing the size of the organization so that it need not be dependent on outside groups, nor has it ignored the potential of the Cloward plan to glut the rolls with eligible clients and thus paralyze the whole relief system. The protest activity in New York, directed toward the achievement of higher cash benefit payments as its specific, immediate, and practical objective, uses welfare clients to inconvenience important parts of the community; plays upon the guilt felt by the city's enlightened political leaders as they are visibily confronted with visibly needy children; and frightens the city's middle class into believing that the welfare issue can endanger the peace of the city. As greater inconvenience and comparable guilt and fear take hold in more and more jurisdictions, welfare rights leaders see the prospects for reform enhanced by pressure on Washington from below.

9

The Substance and Strategy of Reform

There are no solutions to the problem of public relief in the sense that a new family assistance program or the findings of a select congressional committee or an administrative restructuring can result in a course of action that will eliminate dependency in five years or ten years. The crises in welfare, Daniel P. Moynihan wrote in 1967, came about partly because the social welfare professionals in effect decided to say nothing about those crises as they developed, to "cover up."[1] While the social welfare professionals have been cut out of the new income assistance policy action, the danger now is that reform-minded presidential advisers—as euphoric over the prospect of achieving relief for the working poor as the social welfare professionals were earlier over the prospect of achieving a social services approach—will also "cover up" and invite a subsequent crisis by saying nothing about the more than 80 percent of AFDC clients spread over forty-two states whose benefits under family assistance will be no greater than under aid to families with dependent children.

Family assistance will be an important breakthrough—more so, however, for the working poor than for the welfare poor, only a small fraction of whom can look to higher benefits. By substituting for AFDC and federalizing the idea of wage supplements, family assistance will improve benefits for the country's most undersupported welfare dependents and will provide benefits for millions of working poor people who have been ignored. Family assistance may also make welfare costs more palatable to white taxpayers than did AFDC. Where AFDC served a clientele almost evenly divided between black and white,

1. Daniel P. Moynihan, "The Crises in Welfare," in *Position Papers for the Governor's Conference on Public Welfare Commemorating the 100th Anniversary of the New York State Board of Social Welfare* (1967), p. 66.

family assistance will serve 38 percent black and 62 percent white families, thus shifting the racial distribution of relief beneficiaries in the direction of the black-white distribution of the population in general. But family assistance has no bearing at all on the money problems of about seven million AFDC clients.

Even when family assistance is operating, food relief, housing relief, veterans' relief, and state-administered adult assistance categories remain. All of the assistance programs continue to present public policy issues to be reviewed periodically in assessing the state of welfare. From the range of relief techniques and procedures pursued and proposed, what matters most? Prescription has been freely interlarded with explanation and description in preceding chapters and will not be repeated here. The problem now is to focus on first principles—equity, simplicity, and adequacy in public relief—and on how policies change.

Benefit Improvements

Inadequate relief benefits continue to be inadequate whether they are called family assistance or AFDC. Inequities in benefits are reduced but not overcome by family assistance. Only the working poor and clients in the adult public assistance categories—where new minimum benefits are fixed well above preexisting averages—turn out to be sure winners.

Family assistance was not designed to assure benefit increases for the great majority of AFDC recipients. It accepts preexisting state average benefit payments in AFDC as its goal in any state where those payments were at least $1,600 for a four-person family. But by no stretch is $1,600 an adequate support level for a family without other income. In most states, including all the major industrial states where four-person AFDC benefits were already between $1,600 and the poverty line, the effect is to provide financial relief to the state without an accompanying pass-through to the individual client. The latter will find that the family assistance check coming from the Treasurer of the United States is no larger than the one that came from the state public welfare department. Family assistance does reduce extreme differences in benefits among the states by establishing a nationwide floor of $1,600 for four-person families and by admitting to relief a whole new category of previously excluded working poor whose incomes fall below the level at which benefits are paid the nonworking poor. In these respects there will be more but far from complete equity in benefits; and it is still equity within inadequacy.

The effects of family assistance on benefits are easier to accept when only the very poorest states that have paid low benefits are compared with the richer states that have paid benefits approaching the poverty level. A case can be made, for example, that it is more important to raise a Mississippi family's income from $400 to $1,600 than it may be to raise a New Jersey family's income from $3,500 to $4,700. Mississippi, with its $2,057 personal income per capita—fiftieth among the states—and with 45 percent of its total population poor, could not make that improvement unaided. The state's financial benefit from the new plan will not be large, but the benefit to its poor will be.

It is a different story when Delaware is substituted for Mississippi. Delaware ranks eighth in per capita personal income with $3,888. New Jersey ranks seventh with a $3,907 per capita figure. The former's average per person per month AFDC benefit just before family assistance was proposed was $32.75; the latter's $59.60. Benefits for Delaware and New Jersey clients are virtually unchanged under family assistance and AFDC. The gross disparity between payments in the two states will remain although the states are in the same region and are of comparable wealth. The effect is that New Jersey's poor will continue to be sustained close to the poverty level, Delaware's far below the poverty level. Neither adequacy nor equity is advanced by a reform that does nothing to alter that preexisting disparity.

Nothing in the history of public assistance suggests that state supplementary payments under family assistance are likely to be increased quickly to a level that will provide all clients an adequate cash income. The Mississippis cannot afford such increases, the Delawares choose not to make them. A national floor under assistance benefits should be followed now by an equalization program that will bring benefits to the poverty line. An appropriate step in this direction would have been a provision attaching maintenance of state effort to family assistance. Such a provision could have required every state to maintain existing welfare expenditures if the new federal benefit floor plus existing state expenditures did not bring average benefits to the poverty line. This would have provided some fiscal relief for the states paying the highest benefits, without rewarding the Delawares, Indianas, and Nevadas. It would also have assured some benefit increase for every client below the poverty line.

Clearly, however, family assistance was designed as working-family assistance and as assistance to the states, laudable enough but inadequate objectives. One of the boasts of its proponents was that "under the Administration's proposed welfare reform program, all States receive fiscal relief." Another was that the condition of all of the working poor would be improved. The same could not be said of all welfare poor clients. A prompt order of business should be fiscal relief for the seven million dependent persons not helped by family assistance. Since the time seems gone for choosing that course over fiscal relief for states, there is no alternative to greater federalization of welfare benefits. At least holding the line on present state payments and selectively adding federal supplements, until the state and federal payments together reach the poverty line in every state, are appropriate next steps.

Veterans' Pensions

Relief is a public activity made necessary by the low income level of as much as an eighth of the population. No relief program can be expected to or is designed to equalize income within the whole population. An acceptable system should equalize income for relief clients in similar financial circumstances. Yet, under present conditions, veterans who suffered no service-connected disability retain a preferred relief status, drawing $2 billion annually of federal relief expenditure under especially advantageous eligibility conditions. Asserting that the veteran is forever different, the organized veterans' associations can be expected to urge maintenance of pension in addition to family assistance and improvements in old age assistance. A more equitable policy would be to divert veterans' pension funds into the main body of federal relief expenditures in order to improve basic income guarantees for all persons on the basis of need rather than to reward military service even when that service is unrelated to the cause of need.

There has been no defensible case for a preferred and separate relief program for the veteran with a non-service-connected disability and his dependents since enactment of the post-World War II G.I. bill and its subsequent extensions. Carried to its logical conclusion, the 1955 Bradley Commission report on the pension program would have led to an end to the separate relief arrangements for non-service-connected cases.

As the nation now moves toward concern for a more generally equitable relief system, the abolition of special privilege for veterans with non-service-connected disabilities is appropriate. It will not be easy to arrange. Ironically, veterans' pension is the relief program with the least rational justification but with the smoothest political path and with the most admirable administrative features. In the best of all arrangements, veterans' pensions would not be folded into public assistance; public assistance would be folded into veterans' pensions.

Relief in Kind

Neither of the relief-in-kind programs considered—food stamps and public housing—scores high on tests of simplicity, equity, and client acceptance. In each case, availability to the client of the federally subsidized relief benefit is dependent on state and local action, but no compensatory benefit is provided a poor client if his jurisdiction chooses not to participate or if, in the case of public housing, his jurisdiction participates but there simply is no room for him.

The point to understand about relief in kind is that it limits freedom of choice by people whose self-image is likely already to have been damaged by their economic depression. It imposes a constraint typical of the kind of constraint imposed on children. Instead of children, however, relief-in-kind beneficiaries are adults who are supposedly being encouraged to achieve self-support. The goal of self-support is not made more likely by reducing client independence.

Why in-kind relief programs are sustained despite their clear liabilities is not easily answered. There has not been much systematic attention paid to the cash versus in-kind issue since relief reformers thought it was resolved by the cash payment requirements written into the public assistance titles of the Social Security Act. Perhaps the best clue to the persistence of in-kind relief is provided in the report of a 1966 Task Force on Income Maintenance. Without endorsing or condemning in-kind programs, the task force, composed principally of economists, noted that payment of benefits in kind disarms one group of opponents of income maintenance—who believe the poor will spend any cash benefits unwisely—and hence may enable a higher level of support to be given to the poor.[2] We can get through more benefits for the

2. The "administratively confidential" task force report, dated Nov. 21, 1966, was not publicly released.

poor, this argument suggests, by using this shrewd political strategy than we can by simply sticking to proposals for increased cash relief. Economists will also recall, however, that for every benefit there is a cost, and the costs of the higher level of support that in-kind relief provides for some of the poor include administrative complexity and a style of payment that demeans the recipient and sharpens class distinctions.

Food Stamps

If the stamp program were allowed to die and the resources were switched to an increase in cash assistance, the same federal dollar expenditure would increase the freedom of choice of the poor. Substituting federal cash for stamps would eliminate inequities stemming from rejection of a stamp program by some states and localities. Cash would also eliminate the demeaning aspect of a relief program that needlessly makes its beneficiaries reveal their dependent status to grocery clerks and casual observers; that introduces a second, limited-use currency inconvenient for legitimate users to acquire; and that carries attendant dangers—virtually impossible to police—of illegal diversion and misuse. There is neither psychic nor material advantage to be derived from $106 worth of food stamps purchased with $66 from an AFDC check (or a family assistance check) over a $40 increase in that assistance check. To the contrary, millions of poor have found the stamps disadvantageous and, in spite of unquestioned need, have declined to buy them. Consumer rejection of stamps is shown by the sharp fall in the rate of participation when surplus commodity distribution is replaced by the stamp plan. Having to buy in-kind benefits in order to stretch already inadequate cash benefits may be the ultimate indignity.

Food stamps do help to meet need, but meeting need seems not to be their primary purpose. Instead, the program's primary purpose is to permit its sponsors to retain a specialized leadership role in a highly visible area and to provide assurance for agricultural subsidy interests that a bloc of urban, liberal votes will be available to sustain wheat and cotton price supports.

Public Housing

Conventional public housing cannot so easily be abandoned although it too marks its clients and is only selectively available. And there is still too much confusion of purpose in public housing between poor relief and housing stimulant. The program is sometimes said to provide a desirable decentralized system of relief. It is true that the administrative structure does provide an opportunity for local participation in policy making through the local housing authorities. It turns out, however, that the local housing authorities are less spokesmen for the poor than ambassadors from the more affluent segment of the community. Most improvements in the program have been mandated from Washington.

When housing bureaucrats say that the program never had its postwar reexamination, they overlook the limitations imposed by the appropriations acts of the early fifties and the accepted emphasis on housing for the elderly. The result was implicit acceptance of public housing as a way to get grandmother out of the house and to relocate some families displaced by public highway and other construction. If meeting need was primary, per unit cost limits that have the effect of encouraging construction of smaller rather than larger apartments would be entirely abandoned and larger incentives would be provided for construction of units for large families. Presently, the aged poor who receive regular social security benefit increases and who are likely to be the easiest of the poor to house are still disproportionately large beneficiaries of conventional public housing. Actually, no explicit attention has been paid to the purpose of new public housing for a long time. If it were examined in terms of its purpose, it would be found that public housing provides some relief for a small fraction of the poor, mostly under segregated conditions; that its managed beneficiaries are largely multiproblem families who have only weaknesses and no strengths to trade among themselves; and that the program is going broke in most big cities.

Fact and Fancy in Reform Strategy

Political procedures, techniques, and strategies—how to get it through—may occupy more of the attention of income assistance planners than is worthwhile. To say this is not to embrace the facile nonexplanation of political change implied by the line that guaranteed income (or equal employment opportunity or pollution control) is an "idea whose time has come." The time only "comes" when the combination of forces necessary to effect change is properly put together. And some things are relevant, others irrelevant to fashioning the right combination. This review of the making and the results of public-relief policy invites at least tentative conclusions about which strategies and procedures are worth worrying over and which seem not to matter.

Given limited intellectual and political resources, should they be spent in encouraging and strengthening an intercessor group independent of the executive bureau–congressional subcommittee axis? in trying to shift program jurisdiction from one department to another? from one congressional committee to another? in nurturing a congressional specialist even if he is not on the appropriate committee? in seeking to federalize a federal-state program? in trying to effect an authorization for a long or even indefinite number of years rather than for only a year or two? in stimulating presidential interest or interest among particular high-ranking executive officials? One note of caution: the discussion that follows bears on strategies and techniques to effect change in public relief policy only, and not changes in foreign aid, transportation, economic regulation, or any other area of public policy.

Intercessors

No relief system should be left to the exclusive interaction of legislative subcommittee, administrative agency, and individual client. Client interests are most likely to be advanced by an intercessor group that monitors relations between the system's professed beneficiaries and the public agencies legally responsible for relief policy and administration. Without an intercessor, it is an unequal relationship because the relief client has no effective recourse against inefficiency, malevolence, official ignorance, or stupidity, all of which have been known in this field. An active intercessor group will concern itself with eligibility conditions and enrollment procedures, with benefit levels, with methods of appeals, and with the validity of administrative reports on program operation. At the same time, an intercessor will serve as a field service agency bringing eligible persons through what might otherwise be a discouraging maze of administrative procedures.

Consider the contrast between veterans' pensions, on the one hand, and public housing, on the other. Not all of the success of the pension program is attributable to the intercessor activity of the American Legion, the Veterans of Foreign Wars, and the several other veterans' groups performing comparable functions. They are surely responsible, however, for sustaining the myth—so comforting to the veteran—that pensions are different from public relief and that the pension beneficiary should think of himself (and be thought of) as drawing on an invisible insurance account to which he has a claim as a matter of right. With this explanation it has become possible to assure potential clients that no shame need attach to their application. More, the pension intercessor group assists in the paper work, provides representation, and strives to find a way in which an application of uncertain merit can be strengthened. And to protect its constituency from a loss of pension benefits because of improvements in other income maintenance areas, the intercessor performs a coordination function, keeping a close eye on interprogram relationships.

Although all relief systems are ostensibly designed to serve the needy, some programs beckon clients, others block them, and still others are passively indifferent. The varieties of attitudes are not inherent in the programs but are closely related to the nature and style of the intercessor, which can be a union of clients, an ad hoc civic group, a fraternal association, or even another congressional committee. An effective triangular relationship requires only that the third point—the intercessor—be occupied by a group with some kind of stake—fiscal, fraternal, ethical, or political—in advancing the client cause. If veterans' pensions beckon, it is because the several competing veterans' associations both reach out for likely eligibles and simultaneously keep the pressure on the Veterans Administration to serve them. If there is an impasse, the associations have shown an impressive ability to mobilize congressional support behind their position. By way of contrast, during the first several years of the food relief efforts of the sixties, potential food stamp users in some counties were more blocked than beckoned: stamps were sold only in a few places that were both inaccessible and infrequently open. While local American Legion posts look for and approach potential pension claimants, a substantial falling off in food relief clients was accepted calmly by both Washington and local officials. But the latter situation changed when an intercessor with a stake in the program challenged it. In this case it was a select Senate committee with a political stake. The result, however, was an aggressive new outreach effort by the Department of Agriculture, a revised benefit structure, and a stated anxiety to make food relief universally available rather than dependent on local whim.

The food relief intercessor was not an organization of beneficiaries comparable to the National Welfare Rights Organization or even of persons sharing an experience category—for example, veterans—with beneficiaries. It was a group with no stake in finding success stories, and with a stake in being able to show a gap between expressed policy and actual performance. The food relief gap turned out to be so large that the intercessor, a select Senate committee, unfortunately found it irresistible to demand more and more shoring up of the program rather than to support elimination of relief in kind in favor of cash benefits. Were it not for this functional equivalent of the American Legion, however, the Department of Agriculture's old passive approach to problems of food relief might still be dominant.

Against these long-standing advantages for the pension claimant, and the recent developments in food relief, consider the quite different situation of the family or individual with an income too low to compete for standard housing. In the absence of effective housing intercessors, pressures at federal and local levels to sustain a high volume of public housing construction are absent, so the supply has fallen far behind demand. The applicant is without a friend at court: he is on his own in dealings with the local housing authority regarding eligibility, rents, conditions of tenancy. It may be possible for an eviction issue to attract support from neighborhood legal services or from the NAACP Legal Defense Fund, but, unlike the veterans' case, no such help can be assumed. Rather than the meeting of equals that the veterans' associations have assured between the VA and its clients, most public housing meetings are between ruler and supplicant.

A recent illustration of how valuable an intercessor could be in public housing is seen in a review of a ten-month-long rent strike in St. Louis in 1969. Pressed for income to meet maintenance costs that had escalated while vacancy rates were high at the city's troubled, huge Pruitt-Igoe Homes, the St. Louis housing authority announced an increased rent schedule. Thirty-five percent of St. Louis's public housing tenants struck. The loss of rental income to the authority reached three-fourths of a million dollars as the strike dragged on. The strike also meant, however, additional emotional distress for participating low income tenants, and a further deterioration in maintenance. Tenant leaders looked for an intercessor. They enlisted help from Harold Gibbons, the scholarly Teamsters' Union official who is a member of the NAACP national board. Gibbons organized St. Louis industrialists, financiers, lawyers, and poor people into the Civic Alliance for Housing. The alliance negotiated a settlement with city leaders that provided for the appointment of two tenants to the housing authority, fixed a rent maximum at 25 percent of tenant income—a provision written into federal law a few months thereafter by the Brooke amendment to the Housing Act of 1969—and created an elected Tenant Affairs Board with final jurisdiction over authority-tenant disputes and with power to represent tenants in housing authority policy matters. The new and struggling Washington-based National Tenants Organization, delighted with the St. Louis agreement, termed it a turning point in the struggle for tenant power in public housing. Turning point or no, the agreement represented a new balance of power in St. Louis public housing and showed that an intercessor group could make a difference in public housing as it does in veterans' pensions and as it has in food stamps and school lunches.

The ideal intercessor is motivated by self-interest, speaks with assurance and out of experience, is strong enough to get a respectful hearing, and has some sanction to employ if it is not satisfied. These are the characteristics of organized labor in serving as intercessor in the employer-employee relationship. The same characteristics could be found among the civil rights group who challenged white supremacy in the South. Although no group in public relief yet fits the description, it is the model envisaged by leaders of the National Welfare Rights Organization. Unlike the American Legion, NWRO is composed largely of beneficiaries. Thus, the organization not only depends on success for survival, but all of its members stand to benefit from successful intercession on behalf of clients. George Wiley, NWRO's director, preoccupies himself with organization in order to build enough strength to assure being heard. If it can build up its membership, NWRO will have an importance in nonveterans' relief approaching that of the Legion in veterans' relief. The fledgling National Tenants Organization, modeling itself on NWRO, in the long run could serve as an effective intercessor in public housing. On the other hand, the Civic Alliance is not likely to be a permanent intercessor in St. Louis's public housing because its interest is too remote.

"People usually follow their self-interest," President Nixon said in his welfare message to Congress. While their cause may not be righteous and virtuous for ever and ever, the self-interest of relief clients is in uniting to maximize their strength.

Departmental Jurisdiction

Frustration over the apparent inability or unwillingness of the responsible federal executive agency to adopt an aggressive posture in providing relief for the needy often leads to suggestions for administrative restructuring. But administrative restructuring alone is unlikely to accomplish the goals of its proponents.

In the typical scenario the potential "receiving" agency will be prim and proper in acknowledging that it really is the natural repository of the program, all the while taking care not to appear cannibalistic. The "sending" agency will let it be known that it has carried out congressional and presidential intent with limited resources and will deny that the job can be done better elsewhere. No shift of function from one to another cabinet-level department will be undertaken lightly because it can carry the implication that one cabinet officer is more competent than another. Administrators doing first-rate jobs do not have their responsibilities reduced.

Administrative reorganization stimulated by failure of an important program to develop effectively sometimes can be accomplished within the boundaries of a single department. Embarrassment can then be minimized by characterizing the change as an effort "to achieve greater efficiency, cohesiveness, and productivity by combining related functions." That language was chosen, for example, by HUD Secretary Romney in reorganizing public housing production into the presumably construction-wise Federal Housing Administration while leaving service and management with the Housing Assistance Administration. Since the top public housing job had been vacant for a year, no awkward personnel problems were involved. Reorganization of HUD, however, is unlikely to affect the lives of Chicago's public housing tenants or of those on the waiting list in New York. Nor does splitting the total public housing responsibility resolve the hard question of whether public housing is to be a public poorhouse or is to be a public facility to be charged for according to ability to pay.

A neutral kind of intradepartmental shift was proposed as part of family assistance. Responsibility for administering payment of relief benefits goes to the Social Security Administration from the Assistance Payments Administration, both HEW agencies. In this case, Social Security really was unenthusiastic about expanding its "insurance" empire to cover relief cases, but its reputation for competence in making millions of individual payments was needed to help nurture public and congressional confidence. Moreover, family assistance does have more of the characteristics of social than of public assistance. Not to lodge it in the Social Security Administration would suggest an unwarranted lack of confidence.

Interdepartmental shifts of existing programs are of a different character. Invariably, they do suggest a failure by the "sending" department, even when a frankly experimental program has been established with the understanding that it may be spun off or delegated. This was the situation, for example, with Head Start, the popular early childhood education program begun in the Office of Economic Opportunity and spun off later to HEW. It seems clear that there would have been less pressure for spin-off if OEO had not fallen into troubles on other scores. A high-riding poverty agency that was universally acclaimed would not have had to give up one of its prizes along with one of its problem children—the Job Corps—in order to stay alive. Head Start, a success in OEO, is the same program in HEW. The Job Corps, in trouble in OEO, was virtually laid to rest in the Labor Department.

A proposal made by divers groups since 1967, when food relief policy became a prominent national issue, is the transfer of low income food assistance activity from the Department of Agriculture to the Department of Health, Education, and Welfare. Safely out of office, John Schnittker, who served as under secretary of agriculture during the Johnson administration, endorsed this idea, and Wilbur Cohen did so too in his last days as secretary of HEW. The Governors' Conference and the 1969 White House Conference on Food and Nutrition adopted resolutions along the same lines. If only food relief could be handled by a department sympathetic to the poor, the argument seemed to be, the barriers to an enlightened policy would fall away. But HEW put up for years with public assistance's low benefits, man-in-the-house rules, midnight searches, and absence of standards for fair hearings. Many poverty fighters who had worked to create the Office of Economic Opportunity in order to overcome or at least bypass HEW found it hard to understand why HEW now should be considered a preferred instrument sympathetic to the poor.

Interdepartmental shifting of food relief responsibility became much less pressing a question as the Nixon administration adopted a more liberal food relief posture than its predecessor. The shift in attitude in

USDA was first indicated by Secretary Hardin's early decision to provide stamps free to "no income" residents of two South Carolina counties. Later, after the decision to change USDA's old ways in food relief was made, it was symbolized by an intradepartmental reorganization that split off food relief activity from the Consumer and Marketing Service to a new Food and Nutrition Service. One of the latter's early actions was an improved schedule of purchase payments, bonuses, and coupon allotments designed to encourage increased participation in the food stamp program. Such a new schedule did not require a program shift to HEW, nor did it necessarily require creation of a new service within USDA, but creating a new service made the message plain. The President had decided in favor of at least limited action in the food relief field. So informed, Agriculture showed that it could provide as much of that action as could HEW. With the new cost schedule announced and transmittal to Congress of the President's food stamp reform proposal that would allow even further reductions in charges for stamps—including free stamps for the poorest families—administrative location of the program stopped being a matter of much interest. When the food and nutrition administrator overrode the little old ladies from Dubuque in the American School Food Service Association and eliminated the old barrier to the use of private food service companies in the school lunch program, USDA began to look better and better as the home for federal food relief programs.[3] If there is to be a program of relief in kind, there is now little that HEW can do for it that USDA is not doing.

That USDA handled food relief badly during all the years of the Kennedy and Johnson administrations is beyond dispute. The secretary of agriculture was badly informed about program operations. After critical public reports from several intercessor groups, the secretary became defensive. Improvement was slow in coming until the administration changed. But it is not clear that HEW would have done better.

The moral is that when the policy instructions from the top were unmistakable, USDA could be as liberal as any other department. With policy instructions labeled family assistance in lieu of AFDC, HEW

3. The conclusion that "there is no justification" for continued exclusion of food service management companies is stated in a letter from Edward J. Hekman, administrator of the Food and Nutrition Service, to Dr. J. W. Edgar, Texas commissioner of education, Jan. 14, 1970; reprinted in *Congressional Record*, daily ed., Feb. 24, 1970, p. S2249.

can be expected to handle a negative income tax as well as the Internal Revenue Service might. Nor was increased public housing production impossible under the Housing Assistance Administration, as Thomas Fletcher showed in his brief administrative tenure in HAA. Welfare reformers would seem well advised to worry more about getting the right instructions issued from the top than about arranging for any interdepartmental shift of boxes with unchanged contents.

Committee Jurisdiction

More attention than is probably warranted is also directed to the question of bypassing or shifting jurisdiction away from one or another congressional committee presumably unsympathetic to welfare issues. In the early days of the Heineman Commission on Income Maintenance, for example, staff personnel were searching for a legislative approach to income assistance that would avoid the House Ways and Means Committee as a gateway. For proponents of income assistance it was fortunate that the search was unsuccessful because Ways and Means approved family assistance almost exactly as it was proposed. Again, in the case argued for shifting food relief administration from the Department of Agriculture to HEW, strategists suggest that the move would close out not only an executive bureau that is incompetent in welfare matters but also close out a hostile legislative committee and a hostile appropriations subcommittee. When there seemed to be some doubt about how the Senate Agriculture Committee would move on school lunch legislation in 1968, Senator Wayne Morse took the floor to assure Agriculture Committee members that he "would be the last one in the Senate to raise any issue about the jurisdiction, at this time"; in the same breath, Morse reported that he was advised that the language of the Reorganization Act "very clearly" gave school lunch jurisdiction to Labor and Public Welfare.[4] The message to the Agriculture Committee seemed unmistakable: produce an enlarged authorization for school lunches or face a subsequent challenge over the committee's right to consider the program. But the evidence is not strong that present committee jurisdiction has really been a stumbling block to welfare improvement, nor is it necessarily true that jurisdictional shifts would add strength. In each of the means test relief areas, on the

4. *Congressional Record*, Vol. 114, Pt. 15, 90 Cong. 2 sess. (1968), p. 20287.

twin counts of "likelihood to occur" and "relative importance," concern for rearranging congressional committee jurisdiction over programs is not well taken.

Consider Ways and Means control over the basic income assistance programs established by the Social Security Act and its public assistance plan. Ways and Means is, in the political science jargon, an integrated committee that thrashes out its disagreements internally and presents a solid posture to the House, leaving no room for prolonged floor fights. It asks for and gets a closed rule that forecloses floor amendments. The chairman is remarkably successful in bringing the committee's bills to passage. Ways and Means has given presidential welfare proposals timely hearings. Pursuant to Kennedy and Johnson suggestions in 1962 and 1967, it adopted an unemployed-parent component in AFDC, a work-training program, a day care emphasis, and provisions for disregarding some earned income of welfare clients years before they became cornerstones of President Nixon's welfare reform package. While the services approach to economic dependency adopted by Ways and Means in the Public Welfare Amendments of 1962 is a failure, no program was ever urged more zealously by welfare specialists. Admittedly, Ways and Means was solely responsible for the so-called freeze on federal sharing in absent-father AFDC cases enacted in 1967. When a case was made for delay in implementation and later for repeal of the freeze before it ever went into effect, the committee did not find it necessary to save face and stand firm. Ways and Means accepted repeal as the appropriate course of action in 1969.

Again, the presidential family assistance proposal, introduced in October 1969, had public hearings that same year, executive session consideration in January 1970, and mark-up sessions a month later. Committee members were often at least as well informed on the substantive issues as the administrative officials, and on some issues better informed. Representative Martha Griffiths, for example, clearly embarrassed Secretary Robert Finch in 1969 with a superior knowledge of the failure of day care programs and of the piddling amounts the department had been able to spend in that field because of state foot dragging.[5]

Ways and Means never took the initiative to restructure the recipient benefit structure, the most serious problem in public assistance. It may be that the House Education and Labor Committee, for example,

5. *Social Security and Welfare Proposals*, Hearings before the House Committee on Ways and Means, 91 Cong. 1 sess. (1970), Pt. 2, p. 368.

would have taken the initiative on the issue of benefit amounts, but inquiries there prior to the Nixon proposal revealed no special sensitivity to the problem of assuring the poor a guaranteed minimum adequate income. And let it also be noted that Ways and Means inaction did not represent rejection of presidential proposals. No president addressed himself to the question of improving benefit levels during almost the score of years preceding the Nixon welfare message.

If a rational case for a jurisdictional shift is to be made, it would be for shifting veterans' pensions from the House Veterans Affairs Committee to Ways and Means. The case would not have anything to do with the failure of Veterans Affairs to show an appropriate concern for its constituents. Rather, the overlapping character of the public assistance and pension programs suggests the logic of a single committee jurisdiction over both in order to facilitate coordinated benefit schedules and exemptions. Until the Reorganization Act of 1970 created a standing Committee on Veterans Affairs, this was the arrangement in effect on the Senate side where the Finance Committee had public assistance and veterans' benefits legislation, leaving Labor and Public Welfare control over other aspects of veterans' affairs.

In congressional committee jurisdiction, as in administrative structure, however, coordination has its practical limits. Practically every governmental activity has more than one face; which face should "logically" control committee jurisdiction can always be argued. For example, public housing is regarded as primarily a housing issue. It falls to the Banking and Currency committees, which have jurisdiction over housing policy because of the tie between banking and the financing of houses. But is public housing really more of a public relief issue that should logically be considered along with public assistance by the House Ways and Means and Senate Finance committees? One can readily enough imagine that if the latter theory controlled, housing specialists would argue the inseparability of programs to increase the housing stock and the desirability of bringing housing relief policy within the purview of the housing specialists. Because the banking committees now provide public housing with sympathetic consideration, there is no apparent interest in effecting a shift.

But, as we have seen, there has been plenty of criticism of the congressional forces in food relief, especially of the House Agriculture Committee. Proponents of shifting administration from USDA to HEW see cutting out the House Agriculture Committee as an incidental benefit. There could be a great letdown; the administrative change would not automatically mean a congressional change. For all its complaints, while the Agriculture Committee has already insisted on classifying stamps as a welfare program for budget purposes, it has shown no interest in shucking off the stamp program. It is clearly to the interest of the agricultural subsidy supporters who dominate the committee to retain food relief as a trade-off with urban liberals for farm price supports. In recent years House Agriculture's principal strategy in effecting the trade-off has been delay in reporting a stamp bill. The committee procrastinates in reporting food stamp authorizations, and the House's disposition to wait on one of its committees outweighs the House's disposition to liberalize food relief. Yet Agriculture lacks the votes to sustain a highly restrictive stamp program on a floor test, having been overturned on federal-state cost sharing and on recommendations for lesser authorization amounts and shorter authorization periods than those supported by the pro-stamp bloc.

The rules of the game now seem well understood: House Agriculture will tarry over stamp legislation, eventually will bring out a weak bill; the urban opposition will rewrite the bill on the floor. In return for reporting out stamp legislation, however, the committee will pick up enough urban support to maintain farm price support programs. This is not an arrangement the committee can afford to dispense with, and it is unlikely that a majority of the House would vote to lift jurisdiction over the Agriculture Committee's protests.

Relief programs of all kinds do get heard in committees of all kinds and do come to the floor of House and Senate. If public assistance (or family assistance) were to come to the House from a presumably more liberal committee, like Education and Labor, the measure would also face the risks attendant on any bill coming from a fragmented committee that reports its bills under an open rule rather than under a rule prohibiting floor amendments. The bill would likely be rewritten before the House ended its consideration, but it is not at all certain that the result would be a better or even more generous bill. In other programs, too, committee jurisdiction is best left undisturbed. House Veterans Affairs, for example, has kept under control what might have been a massive raid on the Treasury. As for relief in kind, no small group of willful men in Congress is solely responsible for its inadequacies and style, and no reshuffling of congressional procedures is a sure key to improvement.

Federalization versus Federalism

With depressing consistency the problem of squeezing money from state and local governments has weakened or washed out relief programs with federal-state sharing provisions. Equally important, an effective sanction for making federal standards stick has not been invented. Withholding federal grant funds as sanction is simply too dangerous a game because it is the relief client who ultimately stands to be deprived of support.

In the newer programs or the additions to old programs where state sharing is required—the unemployed-parent part of AFDC, work training, and day care are all examples—a majority of states have chosen not to participate, or to wait out the federal government until an ever-larger federal share of costs is provided. Work training had few state takers as a 3 to 1 federal-state shared program in the early sixties; it did better as a fully federally funded aspect of the Economic Opportunity Act. Then, growth in work training fell off again as states failed to provide 1 to 3 matching for day care costs necessary to make the work incentive language of the 1967 amendments effective. When the states were given "options" and were simply "encouraged" to develop work training programs, Representative Wilbur Mills complained, they did not do it. So his Ways and Means Committee mandated a work incentive program. That, too, depended on state funding of part of the costs of day care for work trainees, however, and the states did not choose to act. By 1970 a desperate federal government, heavily dependent on day care to sustain its family assistance proposals, was ready to up its day care share to 90 percent. Instead of a state having to provide $1 to get $3, now 33 cents would bring $3. The Ways and Means Committee went even beyond the administration by approving 100 percent federal funding of day care.

In food stamps, just the possibility of incorporating a sharing-of-cost requirement was enough to bring out threats from state officials that they would decline to participate in a shared-cost arrangement and would choose instead the surplus commodity distribution plan with its full federal funding. Even meeting food relief distribution costs was more than some localities would agree to. Where USDA has taken the initiative to insist on a food relief program, judicial rulings have led to literally full federalization in some counties of what is supposed to be a relief program optional with, and in some partial measure supported by, state or local government.

There is little support from state political leaders for a continued state fiscal role in any public relief program. Meeting three weeks after President Nixon proposed his family assistance plan with its state supplementation feature (and its retention of the federal-state arrangements in the adult categories), the National Governors' Conference addressed itself to welfare reform. The governors (49–1) were ready for a phased withdrawal of the states from the relief business. Their resolution called for:

1. Substitution, on a phased basis, of a federally financed system of welfare payments for the current federal-state program for the aged, blind, disabled, and dependent children, and including also the general assistance programs now financed by the states themselves. Eligibility and grants would be determined by the federal government; the system should include realistic income exemptions to provide incentives for persons to seek employment. Adequate day care for children of working mothers and an expanded federal job training program should also be assured.

2. Increase in the present levels for all payments under the Old Age and Survivors Disability Insurance Programs with a minimum payment of $100 per month.

3. Transfer of the present Old Age Assistance, Aid to the Permanently and Totally Disabled, and Aid to the Blind programs to the Social Security Program, with payments being made from federal general revenues to the Social Security Trust Fund to cover the increased cost.[6]

A clean break with the tradition of intergovernmental involvement in relief comes hard. The governors' proposal unnecessarily stipulated state administration under federal guidelines of a cash pay-out system where both eligibility and benefits would be determined by the federal government. But there can be little meaning to state administration when states would not be empowered to decide either the "who" or the "what" in "who gets what." In the construction of a superior public relief system, the full federalization model of veterans' pensions is both preferable and politically acceptable. Architects of change need not waste their energies on trying to blueprint a system consistent with some kind of new federalism that continues to involve the states in relief. Whatever the case for decentralization of other governmental activity, both experience and political sentiment support centralization of the welfare function.

6. Resolution on "Welfare Reform" adopted by the National Governors' Conference at their 61st Annual Meeting in Colorado Springs, Colo., Aug. 31–Sept. 3, 1969 (processed).

The Authorization Period

Congressional committees are increasingly reluctant to provide authorizations for program expenditures beyond two years. But executive agencies find it difficult to move their activities into high gear in so brief a time without assurance of continued support over a longer haul. In the relief field, public assistance and veterans' pensions have always run on indefinite authorizations, allowing payments to be made to the states and to eligible veterans, as the case may be, unless and until existing law is amended. On the other hand, one of the great food stamp disputes turned on whether that program should be authorized for a limited two-year or three-year period or should be extended indefinitely. Public housing lives, for purposes of program additions, on a series of finite authorizations that specify a particular number of new starts or federal dollars for annual contributions contracts over each of the ensuing two or three years. Although one authorization—that of the 1949 Housing Act—projected six years of activity, it was ineffective in providing program stability.

The case for an extended authorization in the cash programs is based on the reasonable enough presumption that there is no turning back from a decision to provide basic support to the indigent. Consequently, it would seem pointless to authorize money for only a limited period. The draft bill accompanying the Nixon family assistance proposal, in the style of public assistance, authorized appropriations "for each fiscal year a sum sufficient to carry out [payment of family assistance benefits]." The sluggishness of the Congress in recent years in attending to the future of expiring programs has raised a new argument in support of long-period or indefinite authorizations. If Congress went about its business with reasonable efficiency, it is argued, biennial authorizations might be tolerated, but delays in legislative decision making occur now to the point where uncertainty makes efficient planning and operations impossible.

The case against the indefinite or the very long authorization for a relief program is strong. There is no assurance that an indefinite or an extended authorization will guarantee program success. Unless the program structure provides for automatic reimbursement to states or automatic payments to individuals, an appropriations committee can effectively negate the extended authorization, as it did in emasculating the six-year plan for public housing in the fifties. The surplus commodity distribution program, ingeniously designed by a congressman who understood how unpredictable authorizations and appropriations can be, bypasses both the authorization stage and the appropriation stage by making an automatic annual appropriation for the indefinite future out of a constantly refilling pot of customs revenues. Yet, with no worries about continuity or funding, commodity distribution is not, in its poor relief aspect at least, a model program. It should have been under periodic scrutiny in the years before the hunger issue forced it into a corner of the spotlight.

Similarly, with an indefinite authorization, public assistance ran for more than a quarter of a century without fundamental reexamination although it, too, merited attention years earlier. Public assistance policy and purpose diverged to the point where a relief program originally tailored particularly for old people was thirty years later the cornerstone of policy dealing with paternal desertion and with the needs of children born out of wedlock.

No service to the poor is performed by any authorization that makes it possible to perpetuate an inadequate or otherwise unsatisfactory program beyond a tolerable period. This does not mean that everything must be up for grabs every year. Authorizations over a quadrennial period would have the advantage of compelling every administration at least once during every presidential term to review each of the public relief arrangements, would provide ample time for program planning within the agencies, would insure a public forum for those affected by the several programs, and would offer some hope that program and purpose would be kept in phase. Family assistance, for example, could be protected against the fate of AFDC—to live beyond its time—by limiting each authorization to four years.

Presidential Interest

Presidential participation is the putative key to more public policy activity than any president can actually effect. Nevertheless, presidents really do matter when it comes to public relief policy. Even making appropriate allowances for the limitations on presidential power and authority shown, for example, by President Johnson's inability to close some veterans' facilities in 1965, White House interest and activity must be considered the sine qua non for change in relief policy. Not all relief policy change in which a president is interested will be accomplished, but none will be accomplished without presidential interest. Without that expressed interest, the status quo continues; with it, the seemingly most hopeless of public relief causes has been transformed into a live issue.

Illustrations of presidential interest making a positive difference are family assistance, food stamps, and public housing, public relief's orphan. In the case of public housing, after the restraints made necessary by the Korean War and those imposed by the House Appropriations Committee in the early fifties, public housing evoked little interest at the presidential level. During the Eisenhower years the apparent preoccupation of the administration was with the search for a way to cut off public housing. No way was found, but neither was there a push to turn the program into one that would get housing built, or would relate closely to other relief programs, or do both. Most of whatever high-level interest there was in the sixties focused on rent supplements, which eventually may displace public housing—if sustained presidential-level interest turns to housing relief policy. Rent supplements did have a short run as part of the preferred Johnson program. Had it not been invented coincident with Vietnam escalation, inflation, tight money, and an inadequate supply of specialists in nonprofit housing, the supplement program would now be further developed. Significantly, however, the upturn in public housing production at the end of the decade is directly traceable to President Johnson's August 1967 request to the secretary of HUD to double the previous annual production total.

Food stamps and family assistance waited in the wings for years while a few congressional and outside proponents tried to stir up support. Congress actually authorized a permissive food stamp program that President Eisenhower's secretary of agriculture declined to effect. But when John F. Kennedy made food relief a presidential concern, the issue of inadequate commodity distribution, food stamps as an alternative, and the relations between the two programs became important. This renewed interest in food relief did not find its way up the policy ladder from bureaucracy to secretary to President. It started with an expressed presidential concern and was transmitted down the line. When food stamps were reintroduced on a pilot basis in 1961, the question that drove the Agriculture Department was how soon the President could be assured that his interest in food relief was being attended to with a successful program. Now food stamps are a big enough business that presidential interest is unavoidable as long as the program authorization is subject to periodic expiration. In fact, given the determination of its congressional devotees who could not secure adoption without presidential interest but who are successful in resisting termination, it will take intense presidential determination to kill off the stamp act in favor of cash relief.

In family assistance, presidential interest and attitude were everything. While improvement in public assistance had been despaired of, guaranteed annual income was supposedly the impossible dream of academic reformers. Politically sophisticated congressmen dismissed it as too unlikely to command their attention. The support of a few strategically placed presidential advisers changed that picture and generated a great debate within high places in the Nixon administration. Then, the President's decision to support the radicals over the incrementalists made guaranteed income—with the name family assistance—a realistic possibility. Whatever the background for the presidential decision, it was a decision that could have gone either way without surprising any of the protagonists. Had the decision favored the incrementalists, nothing more than continued tinkering with public relief could have been expected. Guaranteed income need not be explained as an idea whose time had come. Rather, it was an idea firmly supported by several public officials in a position to urge it on the President; once his support was achieved, skeptics became scarce. Once skeptics became scarce, policy change became possible.

The State of Welfare

Relief should provide enough of a benefit so that clients are not half housed, half clothed, or half fed. And since most public relief money is federal money, equal protection of the laws should strike down arbitrary and unreasonable differences in payments to similarly situated clients. Benefits should be provided according to a simple formula and with simple procedures likely to be understood by disadvantaged people. The American welfare systems are costly, yet they do not meet these objectives.

Although political leaders still dream of work instead of relief, the state of welfare is better now than it has been for several decades because simplicity, equity, adequacy, and dignity are stated at high levels as goals of welfare policy. They have at least overshadowed and perhaps displaced balancing federal-state power relations, minimizing federal costs, and limiting eligibility. The new policy goals are attributable to the emergence of energetic intercessor groups with a stake in relief improvement and to the sensitivity of high-placed presidential advisers who have drawn on practical ideas and conclusions of several academics. Continued improvement that will integrate the veterans' program into that available to the general population, eliminate food stamps in favor of cash, provide an in-lieu cash benefit to persons who qualify for but cannot secure public housing, and bring cash assistance benefits everywhere to a livable minimum in a framework of honorable dependency should be the welfare objectives of the seventies.

Index